DATE DUE

Budgeting and Debt Management

PERSONAL FINANCE SERIES

First Edition

Budgeting and Debt Management

Advice from Finance Industry Experts about Personal and Family Finances, Banking, Handling Money, Building and Using Credit, Borrowing, Debt, and Recovery from Financial Difficulty, Along with a Glossary and Directories of Resources for Additional Help and Information

◆

Edited by Karen Bellenir

P.O. Box 31-1640 • Detroit, MI 48231-1640

Bibliographic Note

Because this page cannot legibly accommodate all the copyright notices, the Bibliographic Note portion of the Preface constitutes an extension of the copyright notice.

Edited by Karen Bellenir

Personal Finance Series

Karen Bellenir, *Managing Editor*
Elizabeth Collins, *Research and Permissions Coordinator*
Cherry Stockdale, *Permissions Assistant*
EdIndex, Services for Publishers, *Indexers*

* * *

Omnigraphics, Inc.

Matthew P. Barbour, *Senior Vice President*
Kay Gill, *Vice President—Directories*
Kevin Hayes, *Operations Manager*
David P. Bianco, *Marketing Director*

* * *

Peter E. Ruffner, *Publisher*
Frederick G. Ruffner, Jr., *Chairman*
Copyright © 2007 Omnigraphics, Inc.
ISBN 978-0-7808-0986-4

Library of Congress Cataloging-in-Publication Data

Budgeting and debt management : advice from finance industry experts about personal and family finances, banking, handling money, building and using credit, borrowing, debt, and recovery from financial difficulty, along with a glossary and directories of resources for additional help and information / edited by Karen Bellenir.
    p. cm. -- (Personal finance series)
  Summary: "Provides basic consumer finance information about managing money, credit, and debt, and avoiding fraud and risk. Includes index, glossary, and related resources"--Provided by publisher.
  Includes bibliographical references and index.
  ISBN 978-0-7808-0986-4 (hardcover : alk. paper) 1. Finance, Personal. 2. Consumer credit. I. Bellenir, Karen.
  HG179.B7977 2007
  332.024--dc22
                                                                    2007018896

Table of Contents

Part III: Building and Using Credit

Part IV: Borrowing Money

Part V: When Debt Is a Problem

Part VI: Additional Help and Information

Preface

About This Book

According to information from the Federal Reserve Board, total household debt grew at an annual rate of 10 percent during the first few years of the twenty-first century. Today, average household debt exceeds the average family's disposable income for the year by more than 8%, and total consumer debt is more than $2 trillion. Families find themselves in debt for a wide variety of reasons—student loans, medical costs, unemployment, excessive credit card spending, or simply being unable to keep up with the rising costs of food, transportation, and shelter. Maintaining or regaining financial health is a process that starts with understanding financial conditions, developing a budget, learning how to use financial tools and services, and planning for the future.

Budgeting and Debt Management helps people avoid common, costly money-handling mistakes, including spending too much, paying too much interest, carrying too many (or too few) credit cards, paying too little on credit card balances, going too deeply in debt, and saving too little. The book's sections focus on helping people understand their financial situations and budget accordingly, deal effectively with banks and other financial institutions, build and maintain credit, borrow money, and deal with problematic debt. The book concludes with a glossary and directories of resources for additional help and information.

How to Use This Book

This book is divided into parts, chapters, and chapter sections. Parts focus on broad areas of interest. Chapters are devoted to single topics within a part, and sections within a chapter provide details about specific concerns within a topic.

Part I: Assessing Your Financial Situation describes the process of organizing financial information and developing a plan for budgeting, spending, and saving. It offers tips for keeping track of fixed and variable expenses, making dollars stretch, and being prepared for emergencies.

Part II: Banking and Bank Services explains the different types of accounts and services commonly offered by banks, thrift institutions, and credit unions, and it includes tips about using internet services and automated teller machines (ATMs). It provides details about different types of checking accounts, explains how new laws have changed the ways checks can be processed, and offers suggestions for avoiding unexpected fees. A chapter about payment cards explains the differences between the use of debit and credit cards, and the part concludes with practical information about protecting yourself from card-related fraud.

Part III: Building and Using Credit discusses the importance of establishing and maintaining a good credit history. It explains the processes by which credit reporting companies obtain information and how they use and disseminate it. Individual chapters cover such topics as how to obtain a copy of your credit report, how to dispute errors, and how to repair your credit. A special chapter on credit and consumer rights explains the federal laws that govern credit-related issues.

Part IV: Borrowing Money begins with an overview of using indebtedness as a financial tool. It explains loan contracts and interest rates, and it offers cautions regarding the risks and responsibilities involved in cosigning a loan for someone else. Individual chapters address specific concerns related to the most common types of debt, including credit card debt, student loans, vehicle financing, and mortgages. A special chapter focuses on high-cost loans and predatory loan practices, including refund anticipation loans and payday loans.

Part V: When Debt Is a Problem addresses readers who are experiencing financial difficulty due to debt. It outlines the steps that can be taken to regain financial health, including self-help options and seeking assistance from professionals. It offers facts about debt collection, foreclosure, and repossession, and it explains the processes involved in filing for bankruptcy.

Part VI: Additional Help and Information offers a glossary of debt-related terms, facts about how to file a complaint against a bank, and directories of resources for help with budgeting and personal finance issues.

Bibliographic Note

This volume contains documents and excerpts from publications issued by the following U.S. government agencies: Board of Governors of the Federal Reserve System; Consumer Literacy Consortium; Federal Citizen Information Center; Federal Deposit Insurance Corporation (FDIC); Federal Reserve Financial Services; Federal Trade Commission (FTC); U.S. Department of Education; and the U.S. General Services Administration.

In addition, this volume contains copyrighted documents from the following organizations: Center for Personal Financial Education; Consolidated Credit Counseling Services, Inc.; Consumer Action; Consumer Federation of America Foundation; Experian; Fair Isaac Corporation; Federal Reserve Bank of Chicago; Federal Reserve Bank of Philadelphia; Federal Reserve Bank of San Francisco; Iowa State University Extension Service; National Association of Securities Dealers; National Consumer Law Center; National Consumers League; North Carolina Bar Association; U.S. Citizens for Fair Credit Card Terms; University of Idaho Extension; and the University of Minnesota Extension Service/Regents of the University of Minnesota.

Full citation information is provided on the first page of each chapter or section. Every effort has been made to secure all necessary rights to reprint the copyrighted material. If any omissions have been made, please contact Omnigraphics to make corrections for future editions.

Acknowledgements

In addition to the organizations, agencies, and individuals who have contributed to this book special thanks go to editorial assistants Nicole Salerno and Elizabeth Bellenir, research and permissions coordinator Liz Collins, and permissions assistant Cherry Stockdale.

About the Personal Finance Series

In testimony before the Committee on Banking, Housing, and Urban Affairs, Ben Bernanke, Chairman of the Federal Reserve Board, noted that there seems to be "a significant correlation between the level of financial knowledge and good financial management practices." According to a study he cited, individuals who were familiar with financial concepts and products were more likely to balance their checkbooks every month, budget for savings, and hold investment accounts.

Despite the value of having such financial knowledge, many people do not know how to obtain it. According to a report on financial literacy prepared for the National Conference of State Legislatures, several surveys have demonstrated that many Americans simply do not know how to accomplish basic financial tasks, including balancing their checkbooks, reading contracts, spending money wisely, managing debt, saving for the future, and coping with the money-related problems that accompany losing a job, financing a college education, dealing with a serious illness or injury, or adjusting to other major life events.

Omnigraphics' *Personal Finance Series* addresses these types of concerns and focuses on helping people interact with financial information in a way that helps them meet individual challenges. It covers a wide variety of financial topics focusing on economic decision-making and fiscal responsibility. It helps people understand basic principles about money management, and it describes practical applications of key concepts, including suggestions for making household budgets, instituting spending plans, managing debt, saving and investing, and securing long-term financial well being.

If there is a topic you would like to see addressed in the *Personal Finance Series,* please write to:

Editor
Personal Finance Series
Omnigraphics, Inc.
P.O. Box 31-1640
Detroit, MI 48231
E-mail: editorial@omnigraphics.com

Part One

Assessing Your Financial Situation

Chapter 1

How to Organize Your Financial Life

Organize your personal and financial papers: Ever been late paying a bill because you misplaced it? How easy would it be if you or a family member needed to quickly find crucial information about your savings, investments, credit cards, insurance or your other personal finances? Chances are you could stand to benefit from organizing your financial records. Here are some ways to get started:

- Maintain a central filing system at home for your bank, brokerage, tax, insurance and other financial records. Also designate one place for gathering your bills. For important papers you want to have easy access to but also want to protect against theft and fire—your passport or Social Security card, for example—consider a relatively inexpensive but durable home safe.

- Pay ongoing attention to your bank and credit card accounts. Keep your checkbook up to date. Record all transactions, including automated teller machine (ATM) withdrawals (along with any fees or service charges), debit card use, and other deductions that do not involve writing a check. Regularly balance your account to avoid bounced checks, which can be costly.

From "You Can Simplify Your Life," *FDIC Consumer News*, Federal Deposit and Insurance Corporation (FDIC), Winter 2004/2005. Additional details regarding record retention is from "Your Bank Records: What to Keep, What to Toss... and When," *FDIC Consumer News*, FDIC, Fall 2002.

And, review your bank statement as soon as possible after it arrives or monitor your account online or through telephone banking. "You want to make sure the charges to your account are accurate so you can quickly dispute any errors or unauthorized transactions," said Janet Kincaid, Federal Deposit Insurance Corporation (FDIC) Senior Consumer Affairs Officer.

- Consider renting a safe deposit box at your bank for certain papers or items that could be difficult or impossible to replace. Examples include old family records (such as birth certificates), bonds, and originals of important contracts. Some experts also recommend a safe deposit box for keeping copies of important account information or documents in case they are lost or damaged at home. What not to put in your safe deposit box? Anything you might need in an emergency—such as your passport or medical-care directives—in case your bank is closed when you need them. When it comes to your will, ask your attorney about the best place to leave the original (copies aren't valid). In some states or situations, says FDIC attorney Joe DiNuzzo, "it may be advisable to have your attorney or another trusted person hold your original will in case, after your death, your safe deposit box isn't easily accessible to the executor of your estate."

- For the benefit of your heirs, either dispose of information about closed bank accounts (after you no longer need the documents for tax or other purposes) or clearly mark the accounts as closed. This could save you and your heirs countless hours trying to resolve mysteries involving an old bank account or a life insurance policy discovered around your house.

"Take a little time now to develop or improve your recordkeeping system, and encourage your family members to do the same," added Kincaid. "The time you spend organizing your records now will be well worth the time and effort that could be saved in the future."

Get rid of the papers you're sure you don't need: Many people hold onto bills, bank statements, receipts, canceled checks and other documents far longer than necessary simply because they worry about some day needing them to prove a payment or another transaction. The FDIC can't tell you when it's safe to throw away certain financial documents—that's for you to decide, perhaps after consulting with your accountant or attorney. But the FDIC offers the following general guidance that many people can follow.

- **Canceled checks:** Those with no long-term significance for tax or other purposes probably can be destroyed after about a year. But canceled checks that support your tax returns, such as charitable contributions or tax payments, probably should be held for at least seven years—long enough to cover the six-year tax assessment period that starts when you file your tax return for the year the check was written. And, keep indefinitely (for other tax reasons) any canceled checks and related receipts or documents for a home purchase or sale, renovations or other improvements to a property you own, and non-deductible contributions to an Individual Retirement Account.

- **Deposit, ATM, credit card and debit card receipts:** Save them until the transaction appears on your statement and you've verified that the information is accurate.

- **Credit card and bank account statements:** Save those with no tax or other long-term significance for about a year, but save the rest for up to seven years. If you get a detailed annual statement, keep that and discard the corresponding monthly statements. Be sure to mark closed deposit accounts as such, so your heirs don't waste time wondering what happened to the money.

- **Credit card contracts and other loan agreements:** Keep for as long as the account is active, in case you have a dispute with your lender over the terms of your contract.

- **Documentation of your purchase or sale of stocks, bonds and other investments:** Retain these while you own the investment and then seven years after that.

- **Sensitive numbers:** Finally, before tossing away any document that contains a Social Security number, bank account number, or other personal information (especially financial information), shred it to avoid becoming a victim of identity theft.

Consider consolidating accounts: Think about how many different financial institutions you use and how many accounts you have. You may be able to simplify your finances, reduce mail and paperwork, and even get better deals by concentrating your business with fewer institutions. "Many banks will offer special services, discounts or more attractive interest rates if you maintain multiple accounts or keep a larger balance," added Kincaid. "The bottom line is that it just may not be worth running all over town to different banks for different services unless their offers are significantly better than what one bank would offer."

Also look at how many credit cards and department store cards you carry. You may be better off using just two or three cards for your purchases. This makes it easier to keep track of your purchases and payments. Many card companies will even send a statement at the end of the year that breaks out your spending into different budget categories, such as entertainment or clothing.

Use direct deposit: Ask to have your pay, pension or Social Security benefits automatically deposited into your account at a financial institution. The service is free and easy to set up. Deposits are made quickly—checks don't sit around your house waiting to be delivered to the bank. You avoid filling out deposit slips, preparing envelopes and waiting in teller lines. And, direct deposit is safe and reliable, while paper checks can be lost, misplaced or stolen.

Be aware that it can take weeks to have a direct deposit arrangement up and running. This is important to remember, especially if you already get paid via direct deposit and you decide to change banks. "To avoid delays, be sure to keep your old account open until all your direct deposits are going into your new account," cautioned Kathryn Weatherby, an Examination Specialist for the FDIC.

Put some savings on autopilot: Arrange with your bank, employer or benefits agency (such as the Social Security Administration) to automatically transfer a certain amount each month to a bank account or mutual fund, to purchase a U.S. Savings Bond, or for another investment. This approach helps you stick to a savings plan because the investments are made like clockwork, and the results can be impressive.

Consider using a credit card or debit card at the checkout counter instead of writing checks: Both offer speed and convenience over carrying a checkbook and writing checks. "Many consumers also like to use their debit card to obtain cash over and above their purchases," said Weatherby. "This saves you a trip to the bank or ATM to get extra cash, but make sure you understand your bank may charge a fee for that withdrawal." Check with your bank to find out if it charges a fee for this service and how much.

Unsure about how debit cards work? A debit card looks like a credit card and often has a MasterCard or Visa logo; however, the funds come directly out of the bank account you designate. Remember that some banks charge fees for using debit cards, especially when getting cash back at the checkout counter or with other transactions that may require you to key in a PIN (personal identification number) instead of signing your name.

Take advantage of ATMs: Automated teller machines offer quick, convenient ways to get cash, even when you're in a foreign country. But you also may be able to go to one of your bank's ATMs and make a deposit or loan payment, transfer funds between accounts, or inquire about your account balance.

Remember, though, that withdrawing cash from an ATM that doesn't belong to your bank or that's not part of its multi-bank ATM "network" can cost you anywhere from $1 to $4 per transaction. Some banks also charge for balance inquiries. You can keep a lid on ATM fees by using your own bank's ATMs whenever possible because practically all banks offer accounts with free ATM transactions to their own customers.

Automate recurring bills: Arrange for an automatic withdrawal from your checking account to cover a recurring expense—for example, a mortgage loan, utility bill, a health club membership or an insurance payment—at no charge to you. This takes the hassle out of making scheduled payments and helps avoid late charges or service interruptions.

Another option is to arrange with companies to automatically charge a monthly bill to your credit card, for you to pay back later along with other expenses.

Try banking by phone: Many banks allow you to use a touch-tone phone to manage your accounts any time, anywhere, free of charge. Just follow the voice-prompts to check account balances, verify recent transactions, transfer money between accounts and receive information on such topics as branch locations or current interest rates. First contact your bank to find out what's offered and what's involved in getting started.

While consumers today can transfer money by telephone only between linked accounts at the same bank, many observers say the phones of the future could make our lives even simpler as portable payment devices.

"As cell phones become more prevalent and more powerful, consumers will be doing a lot more with them than just making calls, taking pictures and playing computer games," according to Donald Saxinger, another FDIC Examination Specialist. For example, he said, "Mobile phones may soon be used as 'electronic wallets' that are able to transfer money directly to other people, to merchants or to vending machines."

Explore banking and bill paying over the internet: Online banking lets you review deposits and withdrawals, keep track of your balance, and transfer funds between linked accounts 24 hours a day, seven days a week. Most banks also allow you to pay bills quickly and easily online by keying in a few details and clicking "OK." Online bill paying often is either free of charge or for a fee that is usually less than what you'd spend on postage.

In addition, "the ability to monitor your account any time, without having to wait for a monthly statement in the mail, enables you to quickly report a billing error or even identity theft," said Michael Jackson, an Associate Director of the FDIC's Division of Supervision and Consumer Protection. "And the sooner you spot a problem, the easier it should be to fix.

"You can even use the internet to fill out a loan application from home, when and where it's convenient for you. "Most consumers like to finalize a loan in person, at the bank, with a pen and a handshake," said Weatherby. "But it's a big plus being able to take care of the bulk of the preliminary work at your leisure and at home, where you already have the income and expense records you may need, and where you can send encrypted information securely over the internet to your bank."

Use the internet to comparison shop for financial services: The internet also lets you research products and services among hundreds of financial institutions any time of day without ever leaving home. "And the more information available to the public, the more competition there is, and that can mean better prices for consumers," said Saxinger.

Remember, though, that not all websites and e-mail advertisements are from reputable companies, and some may be the clever work of crooks attempting to obtain personal information they can use to commit fraud. See the box on the right for some reminders about how to protect against scams.

Final Thoughts

The FDIC hopes this information has provided some new ideas you can use to simplify your financial life. If you're not sure what's best for you, speak with a bank representative or a trusted advisor.

Also consider starting small, maybe with one or two new ways of doing things that are easy and not too intimidating at first.

Chapter 2

Developing a Personal Financial Plan

The key to successful money management is developing and following a personal financial plan. Research has shown that people with a financial plan tend to save more money, feel better about their progress, and make more appropriate decisions—no matter what their income. Moreover, a written financial plan is far more effective than a mental one. Seeing your plan in writing helps to remind you about what actions are necessary to reach your goals and it helps you to check your progress more easily than relying on memory alone.

A successful financial plan can be developed in six steps:

1. Set goals

2. Prepare a net worth statement

3. Gather past income and expense records

4. Complete the spending and saving planner

5. Keep records of spending and saving

6. Evaluate Step

Spending and Saving Planner

Step 1: Set Goals

First take time to set goals and decide as a family what you hope to accomplish financially. Knowing what is important to you and your family is a critical first step in a successful personal financial plan. Use the Setting Goals worksheet (see Figure 2.1) to decide which financial goals are most important to the family and how much will be needed each month to accomplish these goals.

A well-defined financial goal is:

- specific: what you want to achieve.

- measurable: how much money you will need.

- tied to a time frame: when you want to achieve the goal

- reasonable: it can be achieved with the time and money available

The following is an example of a well-defined financial goal: "I want to buy a house that costs around $150,000 in 2010." This goal is specific, measurable, and tied to a time frame. It is reasonable when you are willing and able to include the goal in your everyday spending priorities.

Prioritize goals in terms of their importance to you and your family. Goals will differ in the length of time needed to achieve them. It may not be possible to start working on all goals in the same year. However, long-term goals need a place in the financial plan over time. Both short- and long-term financial goals will require regular savings.

The first short-term goal for every family should be an emergency cash reserve. In addition to the regular savings that are needed to achieve your specific goals, most families also need a "rainy day" fund for the unexpected financial emergencies that happen without warning. The emergency cash reserve should equal three to six months of your monthly expenses, if your job is secure. If your job is not secure, a 12-month cash reserve may be a safer cushion. No matter how much you choose to set aside for emergencies, your cash reserve should be easily available, safe, and only used for emergencies. One way to build your cash reserve is to have a regular amount of savings automatically deducted from your paycheck and deposited into a savings account.

Step 2: Prepare a Net Worth Statement

The next step in your financial plan is to look at your present situation by preparing the Net Worth Statement (also referred to as a Balance

Sheet, see the worksheet in Figure 2.2). A net worth statement adds up all your assets, the things you own, and subtracts from that your liabilities, all the debts you owe. Yearly net worth statements allow you to track your financial progress over time.

Worksheet 1: Setting Goals					
Priority	Goal	Total Cost	Target Date	Number of Months to Goal	Amount to Save Each Month
	Emergency Cash Reserve				
Totals					

Figure 2.1. Setting Goals

Instructions for Worksheet 1

- *Each family member who participates in the family's financial decisions should write down, on a separate sheet of paper, without any discussion, his or her own financial needs, wants, desires and goals. Then put a dollar cost next to each item.*

- *Share the lists with other family members and discuss the goals you have in common and those that previously were unknown to others.*

- *Combine the lists and agree on a single set of goals the family can work towards. Write the agreed-upon list of family goals above.*

- *List a priority for each goal. Decide which is the family's 1st priority goal, which is 2nd, 3rd, etc.*

- *Enter a date to be accomplished for each goal under Target Date.*

- *If saving for a goal will not begin during the next 12 months, do not fill in the Number of Months to Goal or Amount to Save Each Month on this form.*

Worksheet 2: Net Worth Statement

Date prepared: _____

ASSETS (what you own)	CURRENT CASH VALUE	LIABILITIES (what you owe)	CURRENT BALANCE
Checking Accounts		Home Mortgages	
Savings Accounts		Other Mortgages	
Brokerage Accounts		Automobile Loans	
Money Market Accounts/Funds		Credit Card Balances	
Certificates of Deposit		Installment Accounts	
IRA Accounts		Contracts/Money Borrowed	
Keogh Accounts		Income Taxes	
Other Retirement Accounts		Other:	
Pension/Profit Sharing		Other:	
Life Insurance - cash value		TOTAL LIABILITIES	$
Annuities			
Bonds - government		TOTAL ASSETS	$
Bonds - corporate		minus TOTAL LIABILITIES	$
Mutual Funds		Equals	$
Stocks		NET WORTH	
Other Securities			
Receivables - $$ owed to you			
Home			
Automobiles			
Other Personal Property:			
Household Furnishings			
Jewelry			
Other:			
Other:			
TOTAL ASSETS	$		

Step 3: Gather Past Income and Expense Records

To determine how your money has been spent in the past, use the Past Income and Expenses worksheet (Figure 2.3). To get an accurate picture of your past spending, sort through your checkbook registers, receipts, credit card bills, online statements, and whatever other financial records you may have.

Many people are amazed to see how much of their money is spent on take-out lunches, morning coffees, and other expenses that can add up over time. Decide whether these "extras" are really worth the trade-off. Are these everyday "extras" worth giving up money for current expenses and future goals? The reality is that your everyday spending decisions have a greater impact on your long-term financial well-being than of all of your investment decisions combined.

12

Figure 2.2. *Net Worth Statement*

Instructions for Worksheet 2

Assets

- *Gather financial all financial documents including checking and savings account statements, stock and bond information, and retirement account information.*

- *Determine the current value of your home, vehicles and other personal property.*

- *Add the amounts to determine what you own.*

Liabilities

- *Gather your most recent statements of the debts you owe (examples: mortgage, car loan).*

- *Enter the current balance on the worksheet.*

- *Add the amounts to determine what you owe.*

Net Worth

- *Subtract your Liabilities from your Assets to determine your Net Worth.*

Using Your Net Worth

- *If this is the first time you have determined your net worth, consider it as a baseline figure. It can be used to measure changes in your net worth next year and in the future.*

- *Strive to increase your net worth each year.*

Step 4: Complete the Spending and Saving Planner

Worksheets 4 and 4 (see Figures 2.4 and 2.5) will help you decide how you want to divide your money over the next 12 months. Before you fill in the worksheets, consider two things:

- the goals you've set for the future; and

- how you've spent your money in the past.

Will you be able to meet your future goals if you continue to spend as you have in the past? Use the worksheets to guide your everyday spending decisions. If you are looking for ways to control everyday spending, begin with your credit cards. Only use credit cards when you have enough money to pay the bill in full at the end of the month.

By reducing your credit card balances, you'll immediately start saving 12%, 18%, 20% or whatever your interest rate may be. Every dollar you spend for interest on credit payments has two effects:

- it increases the cost of current spending by adding interest to the purchase; and

- it reduces the amount you can spend and save tomorrow.

Worksheet 3: Past Income and Expenses

	Dollar amount	MVP (Monthly, Variable, Periodic)	Check months when periodic income and expenses occur											
	$		J	F	M	A	M	J	J	A	S	O	N	D
TAKE-HOME INCOME														
Salary 1			□	□	□	□	□	□	□	□	□	□	□	□
Salary 2			□	□	□	□	□	□	□	□	□	□	□	□
Bonus			□	□	□	□	□	□	□	□	□	□	□	□
Interest			□	□	□	□	□	□	□	□	□	□	□	□
Dividends			□	□	□	□	□	□	□	□	□	□	□	□
Child Support / Alimony			□	□	□	□	□	□	□	□	□	□	□	□
Rental Income			□	□	□	□	□	□	□	□	□	□	□	□
Gifts			□	□	□	□	□	□	□	□	□	□	□	□
Other			□	□	□	□	□	□	□	□	□	□	□	□
EXPENSES AND SAVINGS														
Saving / Investing Goal			□	□	□	□	□	□	□	□	□	□	□	□
Saving / Investing Goal			□	□	□	□	□	□	□	□	□	□	□	□
Rent / Mortgage			□	□	□	□	□	□	□	□	□	□	□	□
Property Tax			□	□	□	□	□	□	□	□	□	□	□	□
Homeowners / Renters Insurance			□	□	□	□	□	□	□	□	□	□	□	□
Appliances / Electronics			□	□	□	□	□	□	□	□	□	□	□	□
Home Maintenance			□	□	□	□	□	□	□	□	□	□	□	□
Water			□	□	□	□	□	□	□	□	□	□	□	□
Sewer			□	□	□	□	□	□	□	□	□	□	□	□
Garbage			□	□	□	□	□	□	□	□	□	□	□	□
Gas / Oil for Heating			□	□	□	□	□	□	□	□	□	□	□	□
Electric			□	□	□	□	□	□	□	□	□	□	□	□
Telephone			□	□	□	□	□	□	□	□	□	□	□	□
Car Payment			□	□	□	□	□	□	□	□	□	□	□	□
Car Insurance			□	□	□	□	□	□	□	□	□	□	□	□
Gasoline			□	□	□	□	□	□	□	□	□	□	□	□
Car Repairs / Maintenance			□	□	□	□	□	□	□	□	□	□	□	□
Clothing			□	□	□	□	□	□	□	□	□	□	□	□
Groceries / Household Supplies			□	□	□	□	□	□	□	□	□	□	□	□
Doctor / Dentist			□	□	□	□	□	□	□	□	□	□	□	□
Prescriptions			□	□	□	□	□	□	□	□	□	□	□	□
Health Insurance			□	□	□	□	□	□	□	□	□	□	□	□
Life / Disability Insurance			□	□	□	□	□	□	□	□	□	□	□	□
Childcare			□	□	□	□	□	□	□	□	□	□	□	□
Tuition / School Expenses			□	□	□	□	□	□	□	□	□	□	□	□
Child Support / Alimony			□	□	□	□	□	□	□	□	□	□	□	□
Personal Allowance			□	□	□	□	□	□	□	□	□	□	□	□
Entertainment			□	□	□	□	□	□	□	□	□	□	□	□
Eating Out / Vending			□	□	□	□	□	□	□	□	□	□	□	□
Cigarettes / Alcohol			□	□	□	□	□	□	□	□	□	□	□	□
Newspapers / Magazines			□	□	□	□	□	□	□	□	□	□	□	□
Hobbies / Clubs / Sports			□	□	□	□	□	□	□	□	□	□	□	□
Gifts			□	□	□	□	□	□	□	□	□	□	□	□
Donations			□	□	□	□	□	□	□	□	□	□	□	□
Work Expenses			□	□	□	□	□	□	□	□	□	□	□	□
Cable / Satellite			□	□	□	□	□	□	□	□	□	□	□	□
Internet Connection(s)			□	□	□	□	□	□	□	□	□	□	□	□
Cell Phone(s)			□	□	□	□	□	□	□	□	□	□	□	□
Student Loan			□	□	□	□	□	□	□	□	□	□	□	□
Debt 1			□	□	□	□	□	□	□	□	□	□	□	□
Debt 2			□	□	□	□	□	□	□	□	□	□	□	□
Other			□	□	□	□	□	□	□	□	□	□	□	□

If you think you may have too much debt, check your debt payments to take-home income ratio. Add together all of your debt payments for the year, excluding mortgage payments and credit card charges that are repaid in full each month, and divide by your annual take-home income (income after taxes, benefits and dues are subtracted).

$$\frac{\text{All non-mortgage debt payments for 12 months}}{\text{Take-home income for same 12 months}} = \begin{array}{c} \text{Debt Payments to} \\ \text{Take-Home Income} \\ \text{Ratio} \end{array}$$

Figure 2.3. *Past Income and Expenses*

Instructions for Worksheet 3

- *Gather information about how your money was spent last year by collecting pay stubs, checkbook registers, receipts, credit card bills, online statements, and any other financial records you may have. This will help you get the most accurate information. If you do not have complete financial records for the past year, use your best estimates to fill in the blanks.*

- *Some expenses occur monthly, some on a regular basis during the year (periodic), and others at unpredictable times (variable). Knowing when expenses occur will help prepare a picture of your cash flow over the next 12 months. You will be able to predict which months you will have more income than expenses and which months there will be less income than expenses.*

- *For income and expenses that are the same every month, enter an 'M' (Monthly) in the MVP box. For weekly or biweekly expenses estimate the amount spent during one month. For example: Rent or mortgage payments are usually the same each month; write M in the MVP box.*

- *For income and expenses that occur every month but aren't the same each month, place a 'V' (Variable) in the MVP box. To calculate the amount for a variable expense, average last year's monthly dollar amounts. For example: A phone bill varies each month; enter a 'V' in the MVP box and the monthly average in the Dollar Amount Box.*

- *For income and expenses that occur occasionally, enter a 'P' (Periodic) in the MVP box and check the months when it occurs. The Dollar Amounts box may have either a fixed amount or an average for periodic expenses that occur more than once during the year. For example: If insurance payments are made twice a year, enter a 'P' in the MVP box. If the payments vary, enter an average payment in the Dollar Amount box. Then, check the months when payments are due.*

- *Decide if the amounts on each line of the worksheet are the same as the amounts you plan to spend next year. Fill in the appropriate amount each month in the Planned column of the worksheet show in in Figure 2.5.*

For example:

All debt payments for 12 months = $10,200
Take-home income for same 12 months = $34,000
Debt Payments to Take-Home Income Ratio = 0.3

$$\frac{\$10,200}{\$34,000} = 0.3$$

Worksheet 4: Income							
Write Months here >							
	Planned	Actual	Difference	Planned	Actual	Difference	
Salary 1							
Salary 2							
Bonus							
Interest							
Dividends							
Child Support/Alimony							
Rental Income							
Gifts							
Other							
B: Total Income	$	$	$	$	$	$	

Figure 2.4. *Income*

Instructions for Worksheet 4

- *Make 6 copies of this worksheet so that you'll have spaces to forecast income for the next 12 months.*

- *Use Worksheet 4 to fill in all sources of income you expect during the next 12 months.*

- *List take-home pay rather than gross pay. If you are paid every week or every two weeks, figure out which months will have higher income.*

- *Try to project in which months periodic income will occur; enter the dollar amounts in those months.*

- *If you want to list expenses and savings that are deducted directly from gross pay, add the amount of each deduction back into your take-home pay and list it as an expense.*

- *As the year progresses, use this worksheet to record the actual income you receive and compare it to your plan.*

- *Round all figures to the nearest dollar.*

Research has shown that when a family's debt payments to take-home income ratio is above 0.2, that is, their total debt payments are greater than 20 percent of their take-home income, financial problems are more likely to occur. Reducing the amount of debt, increasing income, or both will lower the debt payments to take-home income ratio.

Another way to stretch your dollars is to comparison shop for all big ticket items and services. It may take more time to shop for the best deals, but when you convert the money you've saved into dollars per hour, you'll find that you're being paid very well for your effort.

Step 5: Keep Records of Spending and Saving

The fifth step involves keeping records of your spending and saving. For each spending and saving line listed on Worksheet 5: Savings and Expenses (Figure 2.5), there is an "Actual" column to track your spending and saving. Fill in the "Actual" column on a weekly basis. Remembering the items that were purchased and their prices can be difficult after more than week.

Step 6: Evaluate

The last step in a successful financial plan is to periodically evaluate and revise your plan (see worksheets 6 and 7 in Figures 2.6 and 2.7). Compare your planned spending and saving to the amount you actually spent and saved. This step will allow you to measure your progress toward your goals. If you find that, you are not reaching your goals or that family members are dissatisfied with the way money is spent or saved, you will need to decide:

- Are my/our goals still important?
- Is everyone in the family committed to the same goals?
- Are my/our financial goals too ambitious?

If the goals are still important to you, then you may consider:

- Are the planned amounts reasonable?
- Was spending out of control in one or more areas?

If you need to make some revisions to your plan, you are in the majority. No financial plan is set in stone. In fact, your plan should change as your needs change and as you make progress toward your goals. Another way to evaluate your progress is to compare annual net worth statements. Check your statements for the following:

- how assets have increased or decreased

Worksheet 5: Savings and Expenses

Write Months here >	Planned	Actual	Difference	Planned	Actual	Difference
Saving / Investing Goal 1						
Saving / Investing Goal 2						
Rent / Mortgage						
Property Tax						
Homeowners /Renter's Insurance						
Appliances / Electronics						
Home Maintenance						
Water						
Sewer						
Garbage						
Gas / Oil for Heating						
Electric						
Telephone						
Car Payment						
Car Insurance						
Gasoline						
Car Repairs / Maintenance						
Clothing						
Groceries / Household Supplies						
Doctor / Dentist						
Prescriptions						
Health Insurance						
Life / Disability Insurance						
Childcare						
Tuition / School Expenses						
Child Support / Alimony						
Personal Allowance						
Entertainment						
Eating Out / Vending						
Cigarettes / Alcohol						
Newspapers / Magazines						
Hobbies / Clubs / Sports						
Gifts						
Donations						
Work Expenses						
Cable / Satellite						
Internet Connection(s)						
Cell Phone(s)						
Student Loan						
Debt 1						
Debt 2						
Other						
C: Total Savings & Expenses	$	$	$	$	$	$

- how assets have moved from one category to another (for example, from a money market account to equity in your home)
- whether debts are growing faster than assets
- how debts have increased or decreased

Figure 2.5. *Savings and Expenses*

Instructions for Worksheet 5

- *Make 6 copies of Worksheet 5 so that you will have spaces for 12 months to plan savings and expenses.*

- *Fill in the names of the months across the top of the worksheets.*

- *Use last year's expenses, found on Worksheet 3, as a guide for planning this year's expenses.*

- *Adjust expenses that you think may increase or decrease during this year. Try to anticipate the actual month when purchases will occur.*

- *Cross out categories that do not apply and add new category names if you need additional lines.*

- *Purchases that you are planning to make by credit card should be entered by category name. For example, clothing to be purchased on a credit card should be listed as Clothing.*

- *For each goal listed on Worksheet 1, write the monthly amount you plan to save in the Planned box.*

- *Do not include goals that you do not plan to save for in the next 12 months.*

Worksheet 6: Summary Of Planned Income, Savings And Expenses						
Write Months here >						
A. Net Carried Forward						
B. Total Income from Worksheet 4						
C. Total Savings & Expenses from Worksheet 5						
D. Monthly Net (Line A + Line B – Line C)						

Figure 2.6. Summary of Planned Income, Savings, and Expenses (Worksheet 6 will give you a picture of how you want your cash to flow during the next 12 months. Some months may be negative. You may want to revise the plan by shifting spending to another month so that spending will not be greater than income.)

Instructions for Worksheet 6

*   Make two copies of this worksheet.

*   Take your total planned income and savings and expenses for each month from the previous worksheets and place these totals above in the corresponding months.

*   Place the balance at the beginning of the first month from your checkbook under Net in the first month.

*   Beginning in the first month of the plan, subtract the amount on Line C from the amount on Lines A and B. The difference goes on Line D, Monthly Net.

*   The Net figure is carried to the top line under the second month. Be sure the + or – sign goes with the amount. Add the second month's Total Income (Line B) to the top line, or, if the Net is negative, subtract the Net from Line B.

*   Then, subtract the second month total for Line C to calculate the Net amount.

*   This Net figure will be carried to the top line under the third month.

*   Proceed through the entire year calculating the monthly Net figure and carrying it forward to the next month.

Summary

Writing a basic financial plan is not difficult, however it will take time and effort on your part. Following the financial plan is the biggest challenge for most people. The pay-off for meeting this challenge will be increased family financial security and satisfaction.

Once you have mastered a basic personal financial plan, decisions will also need to be made about:

- risk management
- tax planning
- investing
- saving for college
- retirement planning
- estate planning
- dealing with later life issues

Worksheet 7: Summary Of Actual Income, Savings And Expenses							
Write Months here >							
A. Net Carried Forward							
B. Total Income from Worksheet 4							
C. Total Savings & Expenses from Worksheet 5							
D. Monthly Net (Line A + Line B – Line C)							

Figure 2.7. Summary of Actual Income, Savings, and Expenses

The real value in completing the worksheets in this Spending and Saving Planner is using them as a guide to achieve your goals. The amounts in the Actual columns will help you compare your plan with your actual spending in each category. If you find over several months that you are not spending approximately what you planned to spend, you may want to first examine your goals. Are these goals still important? Is everyone in the family committed to the same goals? If the goals are still accurate, then you may want to look at the amount of money planned for the categories where spending doesn't match the plan and decide if these categories need to be increased or decreased.

Chapter 3

How to Avoid Common Money Mistakes

Everybody makes mistakes with their money. The important thing is to keep them to a minimum. And one of the best ways to accomplish that is to learn from the mistakes of others. Here is our list of the top mistakes people make with their money, and what you can do to avoid these mistakes in the first place.

Buying items you don't need, and paying extra for them in interest: Every time you have an urge to do a little "impulse buying" and you use your credit card but you don't pay in full by the due date, you could be paying interest on that purchase for months or years to come. Spending money for something you really don't need can be a big waste of your money. But you can make the matter worse, a lot worse, by putting the purchase on a credit card and paying monthly interest charges.

Research major purchases and comparison shop before you buy. Ask yourself if you really need the item. Even better, wait a day or two, or just a few hours, to think things over rather than making a quick and costly decision you may come to regret.

There are good reasons to pay for major purchases with a credit card, such as extra protections if you have problems with the items. But if you charge a purchase with a credit card instead of paying by cash, check or debit card (which automatically deducts the money from

---

"If at First You Don't Succeed: Common Mistakes Young Adults Make with Money and How to Avoid Them," *FDIC Consumer News*, Federal Deposit Insurance Corporation (FDIC), Spring 2005.

your bank account), be smart about how you repay. For example, take advantage of offers of "zero-percent interest" on credit card purchases for a certain number of months (but understand when and how interest charges could begin).

Pay the entire balance on your credit card, or as much as you can, to avoid or minimize interest charges, which can add up significantly. "If you pay only the minimum amount due on your credit card, you may end up paying more in interest charges than what the item cost you to begin with," said Janet Kincaid, Federal Deposit Insurance Corporation (FDIC) Senior Consumer Affairs Officer.

Example: If you pay only the minimum payment due on a $1,000 computer, let's say it's about $20 a month, your total cost at an annual percentage rate of more than 18 percent can be close to $3,000, and it will take you nearly 19 years to pay it off.

Getting too deeply in debt: Being able to borrow allows us to buy clothes or computers, take a vacation or purchase a home or a car. But taking on too much debt can be a problem, and each year millions of adults of all ages find themselves struggling to pay their loans, credit cards and other bills.

Learn to be a good money manager by following the basic strategies outlined in this chapter. Also recognize the warning signs of a serious debt problem. These may include borrowing money to make payments on loans you already have, deliberately paying bills late, and putting off doctor visits or other important activities because you think you don't have enough money.

If you believe you're experiencing debt overload, take corrective measures. For example, try to pay off your highest interest-rate loans (usually your credit cards) as soon as possible, even if you have higher balances on other loans. For new purchases, instead of using your credit card, try paying with cash, a check or a debit card.

"There are also reliable credit counselors you can turn to for help at little or no cost," added Rita Wiles Ross, an FDIC attorney. "Unfortunately, you also need to be aware that there are scams masquerading as 'credit repair clinics' and other companies, such as 'debt consolidators,' that may charge big fees for unfulfilled promises or services you can perform on your own."

Paying bills late or otherwise tarnishing your reputation: Companies called credit bureaus prepare credit reports for use by lenders, employers, insurance companies, landlords and others who need to know someone's financial reliability, based largely on each person's track record paying bills and debts. Credit bureaus, lenders and other companies also produce "credit scores" that attempt to summarize and evaluate a person's credit record using a point system.

While one or two late payments on your loans or other regular commitments (such as rent or phone bills) over a long period may not seriously damage your credit record, making a habit of it will count against you. Over time you could be charged a higher interest rate on your credit card or a loan that you really want and need. You could be turned down for a job or an apartment. It could cost you extra when you apply for auto insurance. Your credit record will also be damaged by a bankruptcy filing or a court order to pay money as a result of a lawsuit.

So, pay your monthly bills on time. Also, periodically review your credit reports from the nation's three major credit bureaus—Equifax, Experian, and TransUnion—to make sure their information accurately reflects the accounts you have and your payment history, especially if you intend to apply for credit for something important in the near future.

Having too many credit cards: Two to four cards (including any from department stores, oil companies and other retailers) is the right number for most adults. Why not more cards?

The more credit cards you carry, the more inclined you may be to use them for costly impulse buying. In addition, each card you own—even the ones you don't use—represents money that you could borrow up to the card's spending limit. If you apply for new credit you will be seen as someone who, in theory, could get much deeper in debt and you may only qualify for a smaller or costlier loan.

Also be aware that card companies aggressively market their products on college campuses, at concerts, ball games or other events often attended by young adults. Their offers may seem tempting and even harmless—perhaps a free T-shirt or Frisbee, or 10 percent off your first purchase if you just fill out an application for a new card—but you've got to consider the possible consequences we've just described. "Don't sign up for a credit card just to get a great-looking T-shirt," Kincaid added. "You may be better off buying that shirt at the store for $14.95 and saving yourself the potential costs and troubles from that extra card."

Not watching your expenses: It's very easy to overspend in some areas and take away from other priorities, including your long-term savings. Our suggestion is to try any system—ranging from a computer-based budget program to hand-written notes—that will help you keep track of your spending each month and enable you to set and stick to limits you consider appropriate. "A budget doesn't have to be complicated, intimidating or painful—just something that works for you in getting a handle on your spending," said Kincaid.

Not saving for your future: We know it can be tough to scrape together enough money to pay for a place to live, a car, and other expenses each month. But experts say it's also important for young people to save money for their long-term goals, too, including perhaps buying a home, owning a business, or saving for your retirement (even though it may be 40 or 50 years away).

Start by "paying yourself first." That means even before you pay your bills each month you should put money into savings for your future. Often the simplest way is to arrange with your bank or employer to automatically transfer a certain amount each month to a savings account or to purchase a U.S. Savings Bond or an investment, such as a mutual fund that buys stocks and bonds.

Even if you start with just $25 or $50 a month you'll be significantly closer to your goal. "The important thing is to start saving as early as you can—even saving for your retirement when that seems light-years away—so you can benefit from the effect of compound interest," said Donna Gambrell, a Deputy Director of the FDIC's Division of Supervision and Consumer Protection. Compound interest refers to when an investment earns interest, and later that combined amount earns more interest, and on and on until a much larger sum of money is the result after many years.

Banking institutions pay interest on savings accounts that they offer. However, bank deposits aren't the only way to make your money grow. "Investments, which include stocks, bonds and mutual funds, can be attractive alternatives to bank deposits because they often provide a higher rate of return over long periods, but remember that there is the potential for a temporary or permanent loss in value," said James Williams, an FDIC Consumer Affairs Specialist. "Young people especially should do their research and consider getting professional advice before putting money into investments."

Paying too much in fees: Whenever possible, use your own financial institution's automated teller machines or the ATMs owned by financial institutions that don't charge fees to non-customers. You can pay $1 to $4 in fees if you get cash from an ATM that isn't owned by your financial institution or isn't part of an ATM "network" that your bank belongs to.

Try not to "bounce" checks—that is, writing checks for more money than you have in your account, which can trigger fees from your financial institution (about $15 to $30 for each check) and from merchants. The best precaution is to keep your checkbook up to date and closely monitor your balance, which is easier to do with online and telephone banking. Remember to record your debit card transactions from ATMs and merchants so that you will be sure to have enough money in your account when those withdrawals are processed by you bank.

Financial institutions also offer "overdraft protection" services that can help you avoid the embarrassment and inconvenience of having a check returned to a merchant. But be careful before signing up because these programs come with their own costs. Whenever possible, use your own financial institution's automated teller machines or the ATMs owned by institutions that don't charge fees to non-customers.

Pay off your credit card balance each month, if possible, so you can avoid or minimize interest charges. Also send in your payment on time to avoid additional fees. If you don't expect to pay your credit card bill in full most months, consider using a card with a low interest rate and a generous "grace period" (the number of days before the card company starts charging you interest on new purchases).

Not taking responsibility for your finances: Do a little comparison shopping to find accounts that match your needs at the right cost. Be sure to review your bills and bank statements as soon as possible after they arrive or monitor your accounts periodically online or by telephone. You want to make sure there are no errors, unauthorized charges or indications that a thief is using your identity to commit fraud.

Keep copies of any contracts or other documents that describe your bank accounts, so you can refer to them in a dispute. Also remember that the quickest way to fix a problem usually is to work directly with your bank or other service provider.

"Many young people don't take the time to check their receipts or make the necessary phone calls or write letters to correct a problem," one banker told *FDIC Consumer News*. "Resolving these issues can be time consuming and exhausting but doing so can add up to hundreds of dollars."

Final Thoughts

Even if you are fortunate enough to have parents or other loved ones you can turn to for help or advice as you start handling money on your own, it's really up to you to take charge of your finances. Doing so can be intimidating for anyone. It's easy to become overwhelmed or frustrated, and everyone makes mistakes. The important thing is to take action.

Start small if you need to. Stretch to pay an extra $50 a month on your credit card bill or other debts. Find two or three ways to cut your spending. Put an extra $50 a month into a savings account. Even little changes can add up to big savings over time.

Also remember that being financially independent doesn't mean you're entirely on your own. There are always government agencies, including the FDIC and the other organizations listed that can help with your questions or problems.

Chapter 4

How to Budget and Save

As a consumer, you face many choices on how to manage your money. Knowing how to manage money can help you make smart choices. Your money will work harder for you. You'll be more likely to avoid traps that can undermine your ability to attain your financial goals. You'll be in a better position to pay off debt and build savings.

Being smart about money can help you buy a house, finance higher education, or start a retirement fund. A money management game plan can help you get started and stay with it until you achieve the goals you set for yourself.

A Game Plan for Learning about Money Management

A few simple steps can make a big difference in making your money work harder for you.

- Establish goals. Where do you want to be?
- Create a budget. Determine your current situation. Where are you today?
- Save your way to a more secure future.
- Conserve—spend sensibly; pay wisely.
- Act—implement your plan/assess/adjust.
- Select a financial institution.

Reprinted from "How to Budget and Save," an online financial education publication of the Federal Reserve Bank of Chicago, http://www.chicagofed.org, 2006.

Create a budget. Determine your current situation. Where are you today?

Now that you've figured out your financial goals, you are ready to create a budget that will help you attain them. Start by writing down your expenses.

Monthly fixed expenses: Start with monthly fixed expenses such as regular savings, housing, groceries, utilities, and car payments. Put these continuing obligations under the heading: Fixed.

Use checking account statements, credit card statements, receipts, and other records to help you complete this estimate. Be realistic—it's better to estimate high than low.

Remember that savings is considered an expense even though you keep the money. You work hard. You deserve to keep some of what you earn every month. Savings is the key to meeting your financial goals.

Make estimates for all money spent—regardless of how you pay: cash, check, credit card, debit card, automatic checking account withdrawals, or savings through work plans such as 401K or 403B plans.

Monthly variable expenses: Once you have noted all your fixed expenses, write down your expenses that vary each month such as clothing, vacations, gifts, and personal spending money. Put these expenses under the heading: Variable. You might have these expenses every month, but the amount you spend could change.

Get a handle on variable expenses by writing down every expense for a month—even small purchases. Use a small note book or other informal method to track your spending. This is very important because it's the best way to understand your current spending behavior. Get receipts for all purchases—especially those you make with cash. Record and categorize each transaction. You may be surprised at how much you spend in certain categories.

Use a notebook to write down every purchase you make for one month. This is the best way to understand your current spending behavior.

List your monthly income: Now that you have figured out your expenses, write down your monthly income after all taxes and deductions. Write this under the heading: Monthly Income. Make sure this figure reflects the total take-home pay for your household after all taxes and deductions.

Now compare expenses to income: One of the advantages of doing a comparison of expenses to income is that it provides a quick reality check. If you are spending more than you're bringing home every month in income, you have a deficit. If you're spending less than you're bringing home, you have a surplus. In either case, it's time to step back and consider some options.

If you have a deficit—spending more than you're bringing home, ask yourself:

- Can I spend less in some of my variable expenses?

- How much interest am I paying with credit card and other loans?

- Where did my money go? (Consider writing down everything you spend for a month.)

Current Monthly Expenses

Fixed	
Savings	$
Rent/Mortgage	$
Gas (Cooking/Heating)	$
Electric	$
Water/Sewer/Trash	$
Home Upkeep/Repairs	$
Home Insurance	$
Life Insurance	$
Disability Insurance	$
Auto Insurance	$
Telephone	$
Groceries	$
Car Loans	$
Car Stickers/License	$
Bus, Train, Cabs	$
Laundry/Dry Cleaning	$
Haircuts/Hair Care Cosmetics	$
Newspapers/Publications	$
Other	$
Other	$
Other	$
Other	$
Total Fixed Expenses:	$

Variable	
Credit Card Bills	$
Other Loans	$
Clothing/Shoes	$
Gasoline	$
Parking/Tolls	$
Car Maintenance	$
Postage	$
Restaurants	$
Entertainment	$
Charity	$
Gifts	$
Vacation	$
Tobacco/Beverages	$
Medical/Dental/Prescriptions	$
Eye Glasses/Contacts	$
Home Cleaning Supplies	$
Personal	$
Other	$
Other	$
Other	$
Other	$
Total Variable Expenses:	$
	$
Total Expenses:	$

Monthly Income

Wages/Salary	$
(after taxes & deductions)	$
Part-time Work	$
Child Support/Alimony	$
Other	$
Other	$
Other	$
Other	$
Total Net Income:	$

Financial Summary

Total Net Income	$
Minus Total Expenses	$
Surplus or Deficit:*	$

*If you are spending less than you are bringing home, you have a surplus; otherwise, you have a deficit.

Your monthly surplus or deficit:	$

Figure 4.4. Monthly Expenses

If you have a surplus—spending less than you're bringing home, ask yourself:

- Am I saving enough to meet my goals?
- Are my spending estimates accurate?
- Have I included all my fixed and variable expenses?

Save your way to a more secure future.

An estimated seventy-five percent of families will experience a major financial setback in any given ten-year period. It's smart to be prepared for financial thunderstorms.

Save early, save often: A consistent, long-term saving program can help you achieve your goals. It also can help you build a financial safety net. Experts recommend that you save from three to six months worth of living expenses for emergencies.

Savings grow beyond what you contribute because of compound interest. Over time, the value of compound interest works to every saver's advantage. For example, if you save $75 a month for five years and earn five-percent interest, the $4,500 you contributed would grow to $5,122 because of the compounding interest.

It's easy to figure out how long it will take you to double the money you save. It's called the Rule of 72. You take the interest you're earning on your money and divide that number into 72. The result is roughly the number of years it will take your principal to double. For example, if you're earning 5 percent on your money, you divide 72 by 5 and you get 14.4. Your principal will double in 14.4 years without further contributions.

Keep in mind, however, that inflation reduces the return on your money. For example, five percent-interest, adjusted for three-percent inflation, only nets a two-percent real return.

What you don't see, you don't spend: Saving means giving up something now, so you will have more in the future. It's not easy deferring or eliminating purchasing things you want today.

It helps to pay yourself first. Take a portion of savings from every paycheck before you pay any bills. Use your company's payroll deduction plan if available. Arrange for a fixed amount to be taken out so that you never see it. What you don't see, you don't spend. You also can direct automatic checking account withdrawals into a savings account or money market.

33

Join the company's retirement-savings plan (such as a 401K or 403B). Your contribution avoids current taxes and accumulates tax deferred. Also, companies sometimes match some of your contributions. For example, for every dollar you contribute, the company could contribute 25 cents. That would be a 25-percent return on your money.

Other saving tips:

- When you get a raise, save all or most of it.

- Pay off your credit card balances and save the money you're no longer spending on interest.

- Shift credit card balances to a card with a lower interest rate and use the savings to pay off the balance.

- Keep your car a year or two longer. Do routine maintenance and make regular repairs. Save the money you would have spent on a new car.

- Stop smoking.

- Take $5 from your wallet everyday and put it in a safe place. That will add up to $1,825 in a year.

- Shop with a list and stick to it.

- Don't buy any new clothes until you've paid off your current wardrobe.

- Eat more meals at home.

- Look for inexpensive entertainment: zoos, museums, parks, walks, biking, library books, concerts, movies, and picnics.

- Shop for less expensive insurance.

- Save any tax refund.

- Drop subscriptions to publications you don't read.

- Postpone purchases or consider fewer features on the items you plan to purchase.

The less you spend, the more you can save. And the longer you can consistently save, the faster your savings will grow.

Conserve—spend sensibly; pay wisely.

Experts recommend paying with cash whenever possible. This helps you spend less than you otherwise would have spent if you had charged the purchase. You'll also avoid credit card interest charges and check-cashing fees.

Applying for a credit card: When you choose to apply for a credit card, shop carefully. There is a wide range of annual fees, interest rates, grace periods for which you do not pay interest, late fee charges, cash advance charges, and other fees. Watch out for "teaser" rates that offer low rates initially but increase dramatically soon after.

To get a card with a low interest rate, you'll first need to pay down your current debt. Second, let a year go by without applying for any new cards or loans, or accepting a higher credit limit on your current cards. Third, cancel cards you're not currently using. As a rule, limit yourself to two credit cards. Fourth, get a copy of your credit report and check it for accuracy.

The three major credit bureaus you can contact are:

- Equifax Information Service Center
  P.O. Box 740241
  Atlanta, GA 30374
  (800) 685-1111

- Experian Consumer Assistance
  P.O. Box 2104
  Allen, TX 75013
  (800) 682-7654

- Trans Union Corp. Consumer Disclosure Center
  P.O. 2000
  Chester, PA 19022
  (800) 916-8800

Credit cards: Visa, MasterCard, and Discover are revolving-credit cards. You can charge up to a certain limit and carry most of the balance forward from month to month. Be careful about only paying the minimum amount due. This is a very expensive form of credit because of interest charges. The best rule is to charge only what you can afford to pay off in full every month. Then actually pay the entire balance when you get the bill.

When you are paying down credit card debt, start with the card with the highest interest rate. Pay your bills as quickly as possible.

Charge cards: Some cards require that you pay the balance every month. They provide the convenience of not using cash and the discipline of requiring that you pay what you owe every thirty days.

Charge cards also provide the additional benefit of not charging interest, although you may pay an annual fee and other transaction fees.

Debit cards: A debit card looks like a credit card, but it works like the electronic equivalent of a check. You use it when you want to pay cash instead of using credit. When you pay with a debit card, your checking account will be debited for the amount of the purchase.

ATM cards (automated teller machine) are debit cards. They automatically withdraw money from your account.

Some consumers prefer to use debit cards rather than credit cards because debit cards don't incur interest charges.

Paying off debt versus saving: If you have credit card or other debt, it usually makes sense to pay off this debt first before contributing to savings. The interest rate you'll get on savings is likely to be far less than the amount of credit interest you're paying.

Checklist

1. Establish goals (where you want to be).	Goals	☐
2. Determine your current situation (where you are today).	Budget	☐
3. Save your way to a more secure future.	Save	☐
4. Spend sensibly; pay wisely.	Conserve	☐
5. Implement your plan/assess/adjust.	Act	☐

Figure 4.5. Checklist

Act—implement your plan/assess/adjust.

Once you have set goals, estimated your fixed and variable expenses, and identified monthly savings targets, it's time to put your plan to work.

Give it some time. Then see how you're doing. Were you able to meet your savings goals? If so, stick with it. If not, look at your variable expenses for opportunity areas to cut back spending and increase savings.

Evaluate your plan every three months and make adjustments as needed. If you're not saving enough to meet your monthly goals, you may need to spend less.

Saving is the key to successful financial plans. Use payroll deductions or automatic transfers to checking, savings, or money market accounts. It's easier to save if you never see the money.

Use budget plans for paying utilities if they're available. Use cash for purchases rather than charging if you can.

Enter each check you write in a check register. Balance the account every month. If you use a debit card, enter those amounts in your check register.

Select a financial institution.

Creating a safety net is easier if you work with a good financial institution such as a credit union, a bank, or a thrift.

Interview employees at several locations. Look for people who are willing and able to answer your questions. Be ready to talk about the services and the advice you need. For example, if it's important to you to conduct transactions face-to-face rather than by Automatic Teller Machines (ATM), ask if the financial institution charges for the services of a person at the counter. If you prefer to use ATMs, make sure they're readily accessible and don't charge transaction fees.

Once you select a financial institution, consider opening a checking account if you don't have one. A checking account can save you fees you may now be paying for cashing your paycheck and paying your bills.

Start now and stick with it. You'll find that being smart about money is well worth it.

Chapter 5

Developing a Spending Plan

A spending plan is a tool to manage your money. Making a spending plan involves setting long- and short-term goals, analyzing what income you have available to meet those goals, developing a plan, and putting the plan into action.

Identify Goals

Financial security starts with solvency, or the ability to pay monthly bills. The next step is building savings and access to credit to pay

Figure 5.1. *Steps to financial security.*

From "Money Mechanics: Spending Plans," PM 1454a, December 2004, © 2004 Iowa State University Extension; reprinted with permission.

unexpected bills. Buying insurance, buying a home, and developing investments come next. The last step is an estate plan (Figure 5.1).

Each step may include short- and long-term goals. A spending plan is the key to achieving those goals. List your goals on a form similar to Figure 5.3. Assign a dollar amount to each goal and a date the money will be needed. Then decide how much money you'd need to set aside each year and each month to reach that goal.

Spending Plans Worksheet

I. Fixed Expenses	January		February		March		April		May		June	
	Planned	Actual	Planned	Actual	Planned	Actual	Planned	Actual	Planned	Actual	Planned	Actual
Insurance												
Life												
Car												
Health												
Property												
Other												
Taxes												
Licenses												
Rent or mortgage												
Utilities												
Credit commitments												
Savings												
Emergency												
Vacation												
Education												
Other												
Total fixed expenses												

What's left for other expenses? $ _____ − _____ =

Expected annual take-home income   Minus   Planned fixed expenses for year

II. Flexible Expenses	January		February		March		April		May		June	
	Planned	Actual	Planned	Actual	Planned	Actual	Planned	Actual	Planned	Actual	Planned	Actual
Food												
Clothing												
Personal care												
Recreation												
Contributions												
Transportation												
Medical care												
Household operation												
Home furnishings, equipment												
Education												
Gifts												
Other												
Total flexible expenses												

Total flexible expenses (12 months) $ _____

Do the total flexible expenses
balance the remaining income above?

Figure 5.2. Spending Plans Worksheet

Evaluate Available Income

After you've listed your goals, evaluate your family's available income. Add all income sources including take-home pay, interest, dividends, and bonuses. If your income varies, underestimate income and overestimate expenses. Don't rely on expected bonuses or overtime pay. Neither may happen.

Directions: Use this worksheet to plan expenses and to record the actual amounts spent each month.

July		August		September		October		November		December		Total 12 Months	
Planned	Actual	Planned	Actual	Planned	Actual	Planned	Actual	Planned	Actual	Planned	Actual	Planned	Actual

$ _____
Remaining income
(to be allocated among the flexible expenses)

July		August		September		October		November		December		Total 12 Months	
Planned	Actual	Planned	Actual	Planned	Actual	Planned	Actual	Planned	Actual	Planned	Actual	Planned	Actual

41

Begin Planning

Use a Spending Plans Worksheet like the one shown in Figure 5.2 to identify your fixed expenses—those you promise to pay on specific dates and in specific amounts such as rent, utilities, and installment loans. Include savings goals as fixed expenses. A good way to do this is to have savings automatically withdrawn from your checking account each month. Add all fixed expenses and subtract the total from your expected income.

Next, identify flexible expenses such as food, clothing, and personal care. Since you aren't committed to specific payments for these expenses, you have more control over them. To arrive at dollar amounts for each flexible expense, consider what you've spent in the past, as well as changes you wish to make in your spending patterns.

Goal	Total Cost	Date Needed	Amount to Set Aside Each Year	Amount to Set Aside per Month
Pay car insurance	$600 per year	July 15	$600	$50
Buy new living room furniture	$3,000	3 years from now	$1,000	$84
Total	$	xxxx	$	$

Figure 5.3. *Plan how much money you'll need to set aside for meeting long- and short-term goals.*

Now compare how much you expect to spend on flexible expenses with the money you'll have left after paying fixed expenses. If some trimming is needed, ask yourself and your family what flexible expenses can be cut back or completely cut out. If total expenses still exceed income, look for ways to cut fixed expenses or to increase your family income.

Talk about Money

You may find that some long-term goals are unrealistic in light of current demands on your income. You might change the timeline or the amount you will spend. For example, you could save for new furniture for four years rather than three, saving $63 per month. Or, you might decide to shop furniture sales and spend $2,000 rather than $3,000. Rework your spending plan until it fits your needs. Changes in your family's needs and in current prices may require you to review and adjust the plan.

Chapter 6

Tips for Tracking Expenses and Getting More for Your Money

Tracking Income and Expenses

Tracking Your Spending

Where does your money come from? How much money do you have every month? Have you ever had $10 in your pocket and not known where it all went? It is important that you know where your money goes. Understanding how much income you have and where your money goes every month will help you take control of your finances. Some people get paid monthly so that's the time frame that will be the focus of this chapter.

Tracking expenses is useful for anyone who wants to develop a spending plan to help control expenses. While a spending plan lists what a person expects to spend, a list of actual expenses shows where the money really goes. It may point out areas where the plan is not working. Tracking expenses helps you make a realistic spending plan. It reduces stress to have an accurate picture of where your money goes.

This chapter begins with information excerpted from "Dollar Decisions: Tracking Income and Expenses," by Marsha Lockard and Marilyn Bischoff, University of Idaho Extension. © 2003 University of Idaho. Reprinted with permission. Additional text under the heading "66 Ways to Save Money" is from the Consumer Literacy Consortium, revised January 2005.

Five Tracking Methods

There are several ways to keep track of spending. Here are five that work for some families. Choose one. Keep a record of where every penny goes for a set period of time. Tracking your expenses for seven days will help you get an idea of where your money goes each week. To get a more accurate picture, track expenses for a month. This will help you establish the cost of all monthly expenses such as food and utilities. The Expense Tracker Worksheet (show in Figure 6.1) will help you track spending each week.

Receipt method: This is an easy and convenient way to track your spending. Get a receipt every time you pay for a product or service.

• Label all receipts with expense categories, such as food, transportation, or clothing.

Expense Tracker

Day	What did I spend my money on today?
Sunday	
Monday	
Tuesday	
Wednesday	
Thursday	
Friday	
Saturday	

Figure 6.1. Expense Tracker Worksheet

- Place receipts in a box or drawer. Use one envelope or divider for each category. Bills such as utilities and insurance should also be placed in the box after they are paid.

- If you use credit or debit cards, be sure to file those receipts also.

- If you don't get a receipt, make one, label it, and file it in the proper category.

At the end of each week sort the receipts. Write down how much money you spent in each category. Keep receipts for proof of purchase and taxes.

Envelope system: The envelope system works well if you like to pay for things with cash. It requires little paperwork.

- Make an envelope for each expense category (rent, utilities, food, etc.). Label the envelope with the category, amount, and date due.

- When you cash your paycheck or receive other income, divide cash into envelopes for each expense category.

- Inside each labeled envelope, put the amount of money you plan to spend in that category each month. You don't have to record how much you spend. Just replace the cash with receipts.

- Pay bills right away, so you won't get late charges or be tempted to spend money for something else.

- To pay bills by mail, use money orders (not cash), available at banks, grocery stores, and post offices. Money order fees vary, so shop around.

Keep envelopes in a safe place, preferably locked. Try not to shift money from one envelope to another. If there is money left in an envelope at the end of the month, you'll know you've done well. Save leftover funds for future emergencies in a savings account or safe place.

Calendar or notebook method: Some families use a calendar or notebook to track income and bills.

- List income on the date it is received.

- Write in bills and expenses on dates they are due.

- As bills are paid, mark off each one.

Establish goals. Where do you want to be?

Without goals, it's difficult to accomplish anything. When you think about your future and what you want to achieve, it's helpful to establish a timeframe.

- **Short-term:** Such as paying off credit card debt, saving for a vacation, or buying new clothes
- **Intermediate:** Such as saving to buy a car
- **Long-term:** Such as saving for education or for retirement

Estimate the cost of each goal and the date you want to achieve it. Then figure out how much you need to save each month. Try to set realistic goals and saving requirements.

Short-term Goals	Cost	Completion Date	Saving Needed per Month
Example: Vacation*	$1,200	12 months	$100
*For example, if your goal is to save for a vacation that will cost $1,200, you need to save $100 for 12 months. (Please note that these examples do not include the interest that would accrue over time.)			

Figure 4.1. Short-Term Goals (for example, paying off credit card debt, saving for a vacation, or buying new clothes)

Intermediate-term Goals	Cost	Completion Date	Saving Needed per Month
Example: Car*	$18,000	36 months	$500
*For example, if your goal is to buy a car that costs $18,000 in three years, you need to save $500 for 36 months.			

Figure 4.2. Intermediate Goals (for example, saving to buy a car)

Long-term Goals	Cost	Completion Date	Saving Needed per Month
Example: Educational Fund*	$36,000	60 months	$600
*For example, if your goal is to save for an education costing $36,000 you need to save $600 a month for 60 months.			

Figure 4.3. Long-Term Goals (for example, saving for education or retirement)

A calendar with large spaces to write on works best. The calendar may also be used to plan for larger irregular expenses. Examples are insurance payments, school supplies, or holiday gifts. The notebook can also be used to store bills so they are easy to find. Use Tracking Tools Worksheet (shown in Figure 6.2) as an example for how to set up the notebook method.

Checkbook method: This works best if you use checks or debit cards for most bills and purchases. In this system, you track your expenses in a checkbook register. By recording each check or debit card transaction, you keep an accurate record of what you've spent.

- Your checkbook register will include the date, check number, name of the person or business, and amount.

- For each entry, you'll also make a note of the spending category.

Tracking Tools

Month_____

Income	Expenses/Bills	Pay or Due Date	Amount	Paid
Paycheck		May 2	$800.00	
	Rent	May 6	$400.00	√

Figure 6.2. Tracking Tools

At the end of the month, you can track what you've spent by totaling expenses for each category. Then compare them with your spending plan.

In addition to valuable information about your spending, checks also provide proof of payment. Many checking accounts also pay interest on account balances. However, beware of possible bank charges that add to your costs. Examples are fees for low balances, numbers of checks written, or automated teller machine (ATM) card or debit card fees.

Computer system: Tracking your expenses on a computer is an easy way to identify spending in different categories. It also supplies you with accurate records for tax-time. You can buy personal finance software or develop your own categories on a spreadsheet.

Using a computer to manage your finances is relatively easy.

- You can quickly update your spending information.

- If you enter transactions often you will stay on top of your financial picture for the month.

- Besides helping you track your spending, programs such as Intuit Quicken or Microsoft Money can print checks, balance your checking account, and provide graphs to help you analyze your finances.

Tracking Time

Choose the record-keeping system that works best for you or your family. In most households, it works best when one family member is responsible for tracking the household spending. Schedule a regular time for record keeping and bill paying because getting behind can make it a challenge to catch up.

After you have determined your income and expense totals from tracking, it is then time to develop a realistic spending and saving plan.

Resources

Federal Deposit Insurance Corporation. (2001). *Money Matters.* FDIC Money Smart—Financial Education Curriculum.

Chan, K., Fitzsimmons, V., Hardy, R., Kimmel, M., Stiles, S., and Taylor, S. (2001). *All My Money.* Urbana-Champaign, IL: University of Illinois Extension.

Goetting, Marsha A., and Ward, Judith G. (2002). *Using a Check Register to Track Your Expenses.* Bozeman. Montana State University Extension. MT198703.

Swanson, Patricia. (2002). *Tracking Your Spending.* Ames: Iowa State University Extension. PM 1918.

—Marsha Lockard is a University of Idaho extension educator in Owyhee County. Marilyn Bischoff is a UI family economics specialist at UI Boise Center.

66 Ways to Save Money

For most kinds of purchases, you can get valuable advice and comparisons on the internet. Ask a librarian or friends which internet sites they think are helpful, or you can use a search engine like Google or Yahoo. Be aware that information you find is often biased. At many websites, the only products or sellers listed are ones that pay to advertise. Before buying anything on the internet, check several websites and make sure you deal with reputable dealers.

Airline Fares

1. Compare low-cost carriers with major carriers that fly to your destination. Remember, the best fares may not be out of the airport closest to you.

2. You may save by including a Saturday evening stay-over or by purchasing the ticket at least 14 days in advance. Ask which days of the week and times of the day have the lowest fare.

3. Even if you are using a travel agent, check airline and internet travel sites, and look for special deals. If you call, always ask for the lowest fare to your destination.

Car Rental

4. Since car rental rates can vary greatly, compare total price (including taxes and surcharge) and take advantage of any special offers and membership discounts.

5. Rental car companies offer various insurance and waiver options. Check with your automobile insurance agent and credit card company in advance to avoid duplicating any coverage you may already have.

New Cars

6. You can save thousands of dollars over the lifetime of a car by selecting a model that combines a low purchase price with low depreciation, financing, insurance, gasoline, maintenance, and repair costs. Ask your local librarian for new car guides that contain this information.

7. Having selected a model and options you are interested in, you can save hundreds of dollars by comparison shopping. Get price quotes from several dealers (over the phone or internet) and let each know you are contacting the others.

8. Remember there is no "cooling off" period on new car sales. Once you have signed a contract, you are obligated to buy the car.

Used Cars

9. Before buying any used car compare the seller's asking price with the average retail price in a "bluebook" or other guide to car prices which can be found at many libraries, banks, and credit unions. Have a mechanic you trust check the car, especially if the car is sold "as is."

10. Consider purchasing a used car from an individual you know and trust. They are more likely than other sellers to charge a lower price and point out any problems with the car.

Auto Leasing

11. Don't decide to lease a car just because the payments are lower than on a traditional auto loan. The leasing payments are lower because you don't actually own the car.

12. Leasing a car is very complicated. When shopping, consider the price of the car (known as the capitalized cost), your trade-in allowance, any down payment, monthly payments, various fees (excess mileage, excess "wear and tear," end-of-lease), and the cost of buying the car at the end of the lease.

Gasoline

13. You can save hundreds of dollars a year by comparing prices at different stations, pumping gas yourself, and using the lowest-octane called for in your owner's manual.

14. You can save up to $100 a year on gas by keeping your engine tuned and your tires inflated to their proper pressure.

Car Repairs

15. Consumers lose billions of dollars each year on unneeded or poorly done car repairs. The most important step that you can take to save money on these repairs is to find a skilled, honest mechanic. Before you need repairs, look for a mechanic who is certified and well established, has done good work for some-one you know, and communicates well about repair options and costs.

Auto Insurance

16. You can save several hundred dollars a year by purchasing auto insurance from a licensed, low-price insurer. Call your state insurance department for a publication showing typical prices charged by different companies. Then call at least four of the lowest-priced, licensed insurers to learn what they would charge you for the same coverage.

17. Talk to your agent or insurer about raising your deductibles on collision and comprehensive coverage to at least $500 or, if you have an old car, dropping this coverage altogether. This can save you hundreds of dollars on insurance premiums.

18. Make certain that your new policy is in effect before dropping your old one.

Homeowner/Renter Insurance

19. You can save several hundred dollars a year on homeowner insurance and up to $50 a year on renter insurance by purchas-ing insurance from a low-price, licensed insurer. Ask your state insurance department for a publication showing typical prices charged by different licensed companies. Then call at least four of the lowest priced insurers to learn what they would charge you. If such a publication is not available, it is even more im-portant to call at least four insurers for price quotes.

20. Make certain you purchase enough coverage to replace the house and its contents. "Replacement" on the house means rebuilding to its current condition.

21.   Make certain your new policy is in effect before dropping your old one.

Life Insurance

22.   If you want insurance protection only, and not a savings and investment product, buy a term life insurance policy.

23.   If you want to buy a whole life, universal life, or other cash value policy, plan to hold it for at least 15 years. Canceling these policies after only a few years can more than double your life insurance costs.

24   Check the National Association of Insurance Commissioners website (www.naic.org/cis) or your local library for information on the financial soundness of insurance companies.

Checking Accounts and Debit Cards

25.   You can save more than $100 a year in fees by selecting a free checking account or one with no minimum balance requirement. Request a complete list of fees that are charged on these accounts, including ATM and debit card fees.

26.   See if you can get free or lower cost checking through direct deposit or agreeing to ATM only use. Be aware of charges for using an ATM not associated with your financial institution.

Savings Products

27.   Before opening a savings account, find out whether the account is insured by the federal government (Federal Deposit Insurance Corporation [FDIC] for banks or National Credit Union Administration [NCUA] for credit unions). Financial institutions offer a number of products, such as mutual funds and annuities, which are not insured.

28.   Once you select a type of savings account, use the telephone, newspaper, and internet to compare rates and fees offered by different financial institutions, including those outside your city. These rates can vary a lot and, over time, can significantly affect interest earnings.

29.   To earn the highest return on savings (annual percentage yield) with little or no risk, consider certificates of deposit (CDs) or U.S. Savings Bonds (Series I or EE).

Credit Cards

30. To avoid late payment fees and possible interest rate increases on your credit cards, make sure you send in your payment a week to ten days before the statement due date. Late payments on one card can increase fees and interest rates on other cards.

31. You can avoid interest charges, which may be considerable, by paying off your entire bill each month. If you are unable to pay off a large balance, pay as much as you can. Try to shift the remaining balance to a credit card with a lower annual percentage rate (APR). You can find listings of credit card plans, rates, and terms on the internet, in personal finance magazines, and in newspapers.

32. Be aware that credit cards with rebates, cash back, travel awards, or other perks may carry higher rates or fees.

Auto Loans

33. To save as much as several thousand dollars in finance charges, pay for the car in cash or make a large down payment. Always get the shortest term loan possible as this will lower your interest rate.

34. Make certain to get a rate quote (or preapproved loan) from your bank or credit union before seeking dealer financing. You can save as much as $1,000 in finance charges by shopping for the cheapest loan.

35. Make certain to consider the dollar difference between low-rate financing and a lower sale price. Remember that getting zero or low-rate financing from a dealer may prevent you from getting the rebate.

First Mortgage Loans

36. Although your monthly payment may be higher, you can save tens of thousands of dollars in interest charges by shopping for the shortest term mortgage you can afford. For each $100,000 you borrow at a 7% annual percentage rate (APR), for example, you will pay over $75,000 less in interest on a 15-year fixed rate mortgage than you would on a 30-year fixed rate mortgage.

37.   You can save thousands of dollars in interest charges by shop-
       ping for the lowest-rate mortgage with the fewest points. On a
       15-year $100,000 fixed-rate mortgage, just lowering the APR
       from 7% to 6.5% can save you more than $5,000 in interest
       charges over the life of the loan, and paying two points in-
       stead of three would save you an additional $1,000.

38.   Check the internet or your local newspaper for mortgage rate
       surveys, then call several lenders for information about their
       rates (APRs), points, and fees. If you choose a mortgage bro-
       ker, make certain to compare their offers with those of direct
       lenders.

39.   Be aware that the interest rate on most adjustable rate mort-
       gages (ARMs) can vary a great deal over the lifetime of the
       loan. An increase of several percentage points might raise
       payments by hundreds of dollars a month, so ask the lender
       what the highest possible monthly payment might be.

Mortgage Refinancing

40.   Consider refinancing your mortgage if you can get a rate that
       is lower than your existing mortgage rate and plan to keep the
       new mortgage for at least several years. Calculate precisely how
       much your new mortgage (including points, fees and closing
       costs) will cost and whether, in the long run, it will cost less
       than your current mortgage.

Home Equity Loans

41.   Be cautious in taking out home equity loans. The loans re-
       duce or may even eliminate the equity that you have built up
       in your home. (Equity is the cash you would have if you sold
       your house and paid off your mortgage loans.) If you are un-
       able to make payments on home equity loans, you could lose
       your home.

42.   Compare home equity loans offered by at least four reputable
       lending institutions. Consider the interest rate on the loan and
       the annual percentage rate (APR), which includes other costs,
       such as origination fees, discount points, mortgage insurance,
       and other fees. Ask if the rate changes, and if so, how it is cal-
       culated and how frequently, as this will affect the amount of
       your monthly payments.

Home Purchase

43. You can often negotiate a lower sale price by employing a buyer broker who works for you, not the seller. If the buyer broker or the broker's firm also lists properties, there may be a conflict of interest, so ask them to tell you if they are showing you a property that they have listed.

44. Do not purchase any house until it has been examined by a home inspector that you selected.

Renting a Place to Live

45. Do not limit your rental housing search to classified ads or referrals from friends and acquaintances. Select buildings where you would like to live and contact their building manager or owner to see if anything is available.

46. Remember that signing a lease probably obligates you to make all monthly payments for the term of the agreement.

Home Improvement

47. Home repairs often cost thousands of dollars and are the subject of frequent complaints. Select from among several well established, licensed contractors who have submitted written, fixed-price bids for the work.

48. Do not sign any contract that requires full payment before satisfactory completion of the work.

Major Appliances

49. Consult *Consumer Reports*, available in most public libraries, for information about specific appliance brands and models and how to evaluate them, including energy use. There are often great price and quality differences. Look for the yellow Energy Guide label on products, and especially for products that have earned the government's ENERGY STAR, which can save up to 50% in energy use.

50. Once you've selected a specific brand and model, check the internet or yellow pages to learn what stores carry the brand. Call at least four of these stores to compare prices and ask if that's the lowest price they can offer you. This comparison shopping can save you as much as $100 or more.

Heating and Cooling

51.   A home energy audit can identify ways to save up to hundreds of dollars a year on home heating (and air conditioning). Ask your electric or gas utility if they audit homes for free or for a reasonable charge. If they do not, ask them to refer you to a qualified professional.

52.   Enrolling in load management programs and off-hour rate programs offered by your electric utility may save you up to $100 a year in electricity costs. Call your electric utility for information about these cost-saving programs.

Telephone Service

53.   Once a year, review your phone bills for the previous three months to see what local, local toll, long distance, and international calls you normally make. Call several phone companies which provide service in your area (including wireless and cable), to find the cheapest calling plan that meets your needs. Consider a bundled package that offers local, local toll and long distance, and possibly other services, if you heavily use all the services in the bundle.

54.   Check your phone bill to see if you have optional calling features or additional services, such as inside wire maintenance, that you don't need. Each option you drop could save you $40 or more each year.

55.   If you make very few toll or long distance calls, avoid calling plans with monthly fees or minimums. Or consider disconnecting the service altogether and use dial around services such as 10-10 numbers or prepaid phone cards for your calls. When shopping for dial around service, look for fees, call minimum, and per minute rates. Treat prepaid cards as cash and find out if there is an expiration date.

56.   If you use a cell phone, make sure your calling plan matches the pattern of calls you typically make. Understand peak calling periods, area coverage, roaming, and termination charges. Contracts offered by most carriers will provide you with a trial period of 14 days or more. Use that time to make sure the service provides coverage in all the places you will be using the phone (home, work etc.). Prepaid wireless plans tend to have higher per minute rates and fees but may be a better option if you use the phone only occasionally.

57. Before making calls when away from home, compare per minute rates and surcharges for cell phones, prepaid phone cards, and calling card plans to find how to save the most money.

58. Dial your long distance calls directly. Using an operator to place the call can cost you up to $10 extra. To save money on information calls, look the number up on the internet, or in the directory.

Food Purchased at Markets

59. You can save hundreds of dollars a year by shopping at lower-priced food stores. Convenience stores often charge the highest price.

60. You will spend less on food if you shop with a list, take advantage of sales, and purchase basic ingredients, rather than pre-packaged components or ready-made items.

61. You can save hundreds of dollars a year by comparing price-per-ounce or other unit prices on shelf labels. Stock up on those items with low per-unit costs.

Prescription Drugs

62. Since brand name drugs are usually much more expensive than their generic equivalents, ask your physician and pharmacist if a less expensive generic or an over the counter alternative is available.

63. Since pharmacies may charge widely different prices for the same medicine, call several. When taking a drug for a long time, also consider calling mail-order pharmacies, which often charge lower prices.

Funeral Arrangements

64. Plan ahead, making your wishes known about your funeral, memorial, or burial arrangements in writing to save your family or estate unnecessary expense.

65. For information about the least costly options, which may save you several thousand dollars, contact a local Funeral Consumer Alliance or memorial society, which are usually listed in the Yellow Pages under funeral services.

66. Before selecting a funeral home, call several and ask for prices of specific goods and services, or visit them to obtain an itemized price list. You are entitled to this information by law.

Chapter 7

Natural and Man-Made Disasters: Are You Prepared Financially?

While Hurricane Katrina was the dominant disaster story in the U.S. in 2005, other calamities such as floods, fires, earthquakes, tornadoes, hurricanes, or similar events occur frequently, forcing people to evacuate their homes. Minor disasters also damage or destroy property or personal belongings. Just ask anyone whose has had a water pipe burst at home, turning their storage or living space into a wading pool. Natural or man-made disasters strike without warning and can happen to anyone. They can also seriously impair victims' ability to conduct essential financial transactions.

Certainly, your first concerns in an emergency should be your safety and basic needs such as shelter, food, and water. But you also should be ready to deal with financial challenges, such as how to pay for supplies or temporary housing, if necessary.

If you had only a few moments to evacuate your home—and were away for several days or even weeks—would you have access to cash, banking services, and the personal identification you need to conduct your day-to-day financial life? Here are some tips from the Federal Deposit Insurance Corporation (FDIC), based in part on their recent experience staffing a 24-hour call center to respond to banking-related questions from victims of Hurricanes Katrina and Rita.

"Fires, Floods and Other Misfortunes: Are You Prepared Financially?" *FDIC Consumer News*, Federal Deposit Insurance Corporation, Winter 2005/2006.

What to Have Ready

Consider keeping the following documents, bank products, and other items in a secure place and readily available in an emergency. (Guidance on how and where to keep originals and copies of selected items will be addressed later in this section.)

Forms of identification: These primarily include driver's licenses (or state ID cards for non-drivers), insurance cards, Social Security cards, passports, and birth certificates. These documents will be crucial if you or your family should need to rebuild lost records or otherwise prove to a government agency, a bank or other business that you are who you claim to be. It's best to have the originals, but it's also important to have photocopies of these documents in case originals are misplaced or destroyed. Never keep the originals with the copies.

Your checkbook with enough blank checks and deposit slips to last about a month: Your need for checks will vary depending on how long you may be displaced or how often you write checks. Even if you rarely or never write checks, at least consider having a copy of a check or your checking account number handy. In an emergency, you can authorize an important payment by providing the recipient (for example, an insurance company) your checking account number over the phone.

Automated teller machine cards, debit cards, and credit cards: These cards give you access to cash and the ability to make payments on outstanding bills. Most ATM and debit cards require the use of personal identification numbers (PINs), so make sure you know those numbers. Don't write your PINs on or near your cards in case they are lost or stolen. Also, don't assume that merchants and ATMs in areas affected by a disaster will be immediately functioning as usual—that's why it's smart to have other options available for getting cash and making payments.

Cash: The amount you should have available will depend on several factors, including the number of people in your family and your ability to use ATM, debit, and credit cards to get more cash or make purchases. But remember that cash in your house or wallet and not in your bank account can easily be lost or stolen.

Phone numbers for your financial services providers: These would include local and toll-free numbers for your bank, credit card companies, brokerage firms (for stocks, bonds or mutual fund investments), and insurance companies. You may need to defer a payment, replace lost cards or documents, open new accounts, or otherwise request assistance. If you have people you regularly deal with, have their phone numbers on your list, too. Working with someone who knows you can speed things up and provide you with some additional peace of mind.

Important account numbers: These would include bank and brokerage account numbers, credit card numbers, and homeowner's, or renter's insurance policy numbers. It is suggested by the FDIC that you copy the front and back of your credit cards and keep them in a safe place because often times, if you have a copy of your credit card and a valid ID, you can make a purchase without having your actual card. Plus, the photocopies can help you keep track of your account numbers and company phone numbers.

The key to your safe deposit box: You can't get into your safe deposit box at the bank without your key, no matter how many forms of identification you have. Also, while many banks issue two keys when a box is rented, simply giving someone else a key doesn't allow that person access to a box in an emergency. He or she also must be designated in the bank's records as a joint renter or be appointed a "deputy" or "agent" who has access to your box. Contact your bank about the proper arrangements.

What to Keep Where

After you've gathered your most important financial items and documents, protect them as well as you can, while also ensuring you have access to them in an emergency. Here are some reasonable strategies:

Make backup copies of important documents: You'll want duplicates for yourself, but also consider giving copies to loved ones or at least let them know where to find your records in an emergency. You can make copies the old-fashioned way. But a more efficient option is to scan them onto disks, which can hold significant amounts of images and are easy to store or send to others.

Also, because a disaster can cover a wide area, it's often best to store backups some distance from your home or even in another state.

Determine what to keep at home and what to store in a safe deposit box at your bank: A safe deposit box is best for protecting

63

certain papers that could be difficult or impossible to replace but not anything you might need to access quickly. Examples of what should be put into a safe deposit box include a birth certificate and originals of important contracts. Your passport and medical-care directives are better left safely at home, preferably in a durable, fireproof safe, because you might need these on short notice. Consult your attorney before putting an original will in a safe deposit box. That's because a few states do not permit immediate access to a safe deposit box after a person dies, so there may be complications accessing a will in a box.

Seal the most important original documents in airtight and waterproof plastic bags or containers to prevent water damage: Be aware that safe deposit boxes are water resistant but not waterproof.

Prepare one or more emergency evacuation bags: Most of what you're likely to pack inside will be related to personal safety— first aid kits, prescription medications to last several days, flashlights, and so on. But your emergency kit also is the place to keep some essential financial items and documents, such as cash, checks, copies of your credit cards and identification cards, a key to your safe deposit box, and contact information for your financial services providers. Also periodically review the contents of the bag to make sure the contents are up to date. It won't do you any good if the checks are for a closed account.

Make sure each evacuation bag is waterproof and easy to carry, and that it's kept in a secure place at home. Remember that you are putting very valuable items into a bag that's intended to be easy for you to carry away in a disaster, not for a thief to carry away in a robbery.

What Else to Consider

Sign up for direct deposit: Having your paycheck and other payments transmitted directly into your account will give you better access to those funds by check or ATM because you won't have to deliver the deposit to the bank or rely on mail service, which could be delayed. Note that there could be delays in the processing of direct deposits in a disaster situation but the problem is usually fixed within a reasonable time frame.

Arrange for automatic bill payments from your bank account: This service enables you to make scheduled payments—such as for your phone bill, insurance premiums, and loan payments—and avoid late charges or service interruptions. Automatic bill payment greatly reduces your need to write or mail checks and you don't have to worry about essential bills being paid in an emergency.

Consider signing up for internet banking services: This also makes it possible to conduct your banking business without writing checks.

Review your insurance coverage: Make sure you have enough insurance to cover the cost to replace or repair your home, car, and other valuable property.

This warning about the financial side of disaster preparedness is to inform and motivate you, not to scare you. It is important for you to "expect the unexpected." Also, be aware that you don't have to go through this process alone. There are numerous organizations and government agencies on the local, state, and national level that can be tremendous sources of help and information as you plan your strategy and if you should ever need them in an emergency.

Chapter 8

How to Weather a Financial Storm

Even in a booming economy, millions of Americans face financial problems that can start with the loss of a job, a death or illness in the family, a divorce or separation, or an inability to control spending and borrowing. But when the economy slows down, many more people may have concerns about their financial well-being.

"Mounting job losses combined with high consumer debt levels are stressing the financial capacity of many households," Federal Deposit Insurance Corporation (FDIC) financial analysts Robert Burns and Lisa Ryu said in a report issued in early December 2001. Also, stock market losses and reduced yields on CDs (certificates of deposit) and bonds are part of the problem, especially for senior citizens who rely on this income for living expenses. And, if you live paycheck-to-paycheck, it's hard to build a rainy-day fund to weather a financial setback.

What can you do to protect yourself and your family if you're having financial troubles...or if you simply want to be better prepared financially? *FDIC Consumer News* offers the following tips and information, much of which can be good advice for anyone at any time.

Review your priorities and spending: Start with a look at your monthly expenses. Remember that your family's welfare comes first, so make sure to continue the payments on your home, utility bills, and insurance. Also make sure you have enough insurance to protect your

---

"Weathering a Financial Storm," *FDIC Consumer News*, Federal Deposit Insurance Corporation, Winter 2001/2002.

family—disability insurance to replace lost income during a serious illness, life insurance in case a wage earner dies, and health insurance to cover big medical bills. Next look at where you can consider cutting back. Possibilities include: restaurant meals, entertainment (including expensive ball games and "premium" TV channels), and costly internet and phone services you really don't need or use. You can decide to give up some expenses temporarily, and you may find you really didn't need them anyway.

Be smart about borrowing money: Interest payments on credit cards, home mortgages, and other loans are an expense, so think about what you can do to keep these and other borrowing costs down. Among the strategies to consider:

- Pay off your highest-rate loans (usually your credit card or department store charge card) with funds from your lowest-yielding savings and investments. If you have several credit cards, target the one with the highest interest rate, pay it off, and then move to the card with the next highest rate. As you pay off card balances, consider keeping just one or two cards (the ones with the best combination of rates, fees and features to suit your needs).

- "Try to pay all or as much as possible of your credit card bill each month, so you can avoid high interest charges," says Jane Schuchardt, the national program leader for consumer financial education at the U.S. Department of Agriculture's Cooperative Extension Service. "But if all you can manage is to send in the minimum payment, make this a priority."

- Be sure to get your credit card and other loan payments in by the due date to avoid late charges and black marks on your record. If your payments become more than 30 days past due, your lender may report this delinquency to credit bureaus. This information can remain in your credit file for seven years and make it more difficult or more costly to obtain credit.

- If you're having serious debt problems, think twice before using your credit card for new purchases. Instead, consider paying with cash, a check or a debit card (which deducts funds automatically from your bank account). And remember that when you use your credit card to get a cash advance from an ATM, that's considered a loan, and you will incur interest charges immediately, and maybe even transaction fees.

- Review interest rates and terms of existing loans to see if you can do better. For example, find out if your credit cards offer a "full" grace period (25 days or more of interest-free purchases) or if you are being charged interest immediately on new purchases. Ask your credit card issuer about a reduced interest rate, a more favorable grace period, or other features that can cut your costs. If you're not satisfied with the answer, shop for a better deal. Refinancing your home mortgage at a significantly lower interest rate also can greatly reduce your monthly payments, but you've got to shop around and consider the impact of loan origination fees and other costs. Many people also don't think about refinancing an auto loan or a student loan, but those can be other places to cut monthly payments.

- As the ads say, if you have equity (ownership) in your home you can get a home equity loan to pay off credit card debt, consolidate several existing high-rate loans into one new loan with a lower rate, or raise cash in an emergency. Your interest payments on home equity loans also may be tax-deductible. But because your home is the collateral backing the loan, if you can't make the monthly payments, you could lose your house. Shop for the best deal and know all the costs before you agree to anything. Here's another tip: with a home equity line of credit, which enables you to borrow up to the credit limit whenever you want, you'll get the best interest rate and loan terms if you apply when your finances are in good shape, not if you're out of work or having debt problems.

- A reverse mortgage is another type of home equity loan for people age 62 or older, and it, too, comes with certain risks and rewards. With a reverse mortgage, a lender will pay you money (which is why it's called a reverse mortgage) in a lump sum, monthly advances, through a line of credit, or a combination of those options. The money can be used for any purpose, and the principal and interest typically become due when you move, sell your house or die, or at the end of a specified loan term. But remember, the loan eventually must be repaid, so you will be reducing your equity in the home's value, perhaps substantially, after you add in the interest costs. The fees and interest charges can be high, so shop around. Because your home is valuable to you and your heirs, consult with your family as well as an attorney or another trusted advisor before agreeing to a reverse mortgage. "Understanding your rights and responsibilities is the best way to minimize the risk of borrowing against your home," says Susan Boenau of the FDIC's consumer affairs division in Washington.

- Obtain a copy of your credit report about once a year and make sure it accurately reflects your credit history. That way you can provide missing details or fix inaccurate information before you apply for your next loan. A copy of your credit report is available free in some states or for a small fee in others. Call any of the three nationwide credit bureaus at these toll-free numbers: Equifax at 800-685-1111, Experian at 888-397-3742, and TransUnion at 800-888-4213. Many experts suggest that you request copies from all three companies because content may vary significantly.

In an important development, Congress in November 2003 passed a law that helps ensure the accuracy of your credit information and monitor your credit files for signs of identity theft. The law enables you to obtain a free copy of your credit report once a year from each of the three major credit bureaus. You have the right to learn your credit scores, which are designed to help predict how likely you are to repay a loan or make payments on time. Merchants also must notify you if they plan to report negative information about you to a credit bureau.

Commit to a savings program: If you follow our previous suggestions for reducing outlays, you should have more money available to build an emergency savings fund in your bank or brokerage account that you can tap if you lose your job or have major, unforeseen expenses. It may take time, but many experts say you should try to build a rainy-day fund equal to three to six months of living expenses, to get you through a difficult period without having to take out a loan or borrow from your retirement savings. If necessary, temporarily cut back on your savings for long-term goals (such as retirement) until you've built up your short-term emergency savings.

How can you build an emergency savings fund if you're struggling to make ends meet? Consider a simple, tried-and-true system often called "pay yourself first." Each month, before you pay your bills, write out a check to be deposited into a savings account, even if it's for as little as $20 or $30. Or, arrange with your bank to automatically transfer each month a certain amount from your checking account to a savings account.

Know when and where to ask for help: If you think you've got a serious debt problem, it's in your best interest to address it immediately. You may be able to solve your problems on your own by doing some research at your local library or on the internet. But many people may need to turn to others for assistance. A knowledgeable friend or relative may be able to suggest solutions for your problems or direct you elsewhere. Your employer may have an arrangement with financial counselors as part of your employee benefits. Or, you can go to a credit counseling service that, at little or no cost, can help you get out of debt. It's easy to find a service—many are listed in the Yellow Pages or on the internet. The important thing is to find a reputable outfit that charges reasonable fees. Be aware that there are questionable operators or even credit repair scams, as described later in this chapter. Perhaps your attorney, accountant or some other trusted professional can refer you to a reliable credit counselor.

The FDIC can't recommend or endorse individual credit counseling services. However it is strongly advised to ask questions before signing any agreement. Among the questions to ask: What does your service involve? What are the fees? What are the qualifications of the credit counselors? Why will I be better off if I use your service? How much input will I have in working out the details of any program to improve my financial situation? Any reputable credit counselor should be willing to answer these and any other questions.

Suppose your debt problems are so serious that you'll have trouble making payments on your credit cards or other loans. Then, it's generally recommended that you (or maybe your credit counselor or another representative) contact your lenders to explain why you're having problems—especially any circumstances beyond your control—and ask about getting some flexibility. For example, a lender may agree, permanently or temporarily, to reduce your interest rate, monthly payments, or other changes, especially if you've had a good record in the past. Why would a lender renegotiate a loan, even if it may mean not getting back all that you owe? "A lender would rather get something rather than nothing, and not have to go through the cost of paying a debt collector," says Janet Kincaid, a Senior Consumer Affairs Officer in the FDIC's Kansas City office. "But for the most part, banks and other lenders want to work with you and see you succeed financially. They want you to be a good customer for a long, long time."

The time to go to your lender and ask for a renegotiation of your loans is before your credit cards are canceled, your loans are turned over to a collection agency, your credit record is severely damaged, or you face the prospect of bankruptcy. But be aware that there are potential risks in asking your lender for a break. "Many credit card agreements enable the lender to raise your interest rate or even close your account if the lender has reason to believe you may not be able to pay the debt," says Joni Creamean, a Senior Consumer Affairs Specialist with the FDIC in Kansas City. "Some lenders automatically close your credit card account or won't authorize new charges if they're notified that you've enrolled in a credit counseling program." Because of these and other potential pitfalls, Creamean says, your best bet may be to explore your options and, if you choose credit counseling, make sure to use a reputable organization you believe will best represent you in negotiations with your lenders.

Beware of scams: Unfortunately, con artists are always around, but they can be especially dangerous during uncertain times. Why? Because people who are worried about jobs, investments, or retirement savings are more likely to be taken in by attractive-sounding financial offers that, in reality, are frauds. Sadly, elderly people often are the intended victims, in part because they have special concerns about running out of money for necessities. Among the financial frauds that tend to flourish during tough economic times:

- Bogus offers of "easy credit" and "guaranteed loans" for people with credit problems. Swindlers will collect money up-front in exchange for nothing at all, for credit cards or loans that have big strings attached, or for basic services you could do on your own.

- Promises to erase a bad credit history for a fee. Don't fall for this scam. Under the Fair Credit Reporting Act, accurate information about your accounts can stay on your credit report for up to seven years, and a bankruptcy can be reported for ten years. "A bad credit history can only be repaired by steady and consistent on-time payments," says FDIC fraud investigator Gene Seitz. "Nobody can legally 'erase' bad credit overnight."

- Guarantees of easy money from investments or business opportunities typically are based on false or exaggerated claims. Much or all of the money you're asked to send will likely be lost. In general, be careful with any unsolicited offer. While legitimate companies do use "cold calls" to reach new customers, be very skeptical if the offer is for a "tremendous" deal from an unfamiliar company, and never provide your Social Security, checking account, or credit card number in response to an unsolicited call or letter.

Six Warning Signs of a Financial Problem

- More than 20 percent of your monthly net income is going to pay back credit cards and other loans (excluding a mortgage).

- You're borrowing money to make payments on loans you already have.

- You're frequently at, near or over the limit on your credit cards.

- You're only paying the minimum required on your credit card bill.

- You're paying bills late or putting off visits to the doctor because you don't think you have enough money.

- You're working overtime or a second job just to cover food, housing, and other living expenses.

Government Agencies That Can Help

The FDIC (http://www.fdic.gov) and other federal regulators of depository institutions offer publications, internet sites, staff, and other resources that can answer questions about saving and borrowing money and your rights as a consumer.

The Federal Trade Commission works to prevent fraudulent or deceptive business practices and provides consumer information about buying and borrowing. To file a complaint or to get free information, call toll-free 877-FTC-HELP, 877-382-4357, or fill out a form on the FTC's website.

The Federal Consumer Information Center in Pueblo, Colorado, offers a wide assortment of consumer publications, including the popular "Consumer Action Handbooks" Call toll-free at 888-8-PUEBLO, which is 888-878-3256 or go to http://www.pueblo.gsa.gov. Check out FirstGov for Consumers (http://www.consumer.gov), another U.S. government website offering online consumer information form federal agencies, including the FDIC. Another resource is the Cooperative Extension Service, a partnership between the U.S. Department of Agriculture and state and county governments that teaches personal finance skills through publications, websites and workshops. Contact the Cooperative Extension Service in the county government listings in your phone book phone book or go to the Cooperative Extension Service website (http://www.csrees.usda.gov/Extension/index.html).

Your state government also may offer assistance and information to people having financial or legal problems. Contact your state's

Attorney General's office of consumer protection office as listed in your phone book or other directories, or visit your state's official website.

Final Thoughts

You've known all along that it's smart to control your spending, to save money for a rainy day, and to be on guard against financial scams. But knowing and doing are two different things. Also, remember that you don't have to cope with financial problems and dilemmas alone— there are resources in the government, in the private sector, and even in your circle of family and friends, that you can turn to for help. "It isn't enough to be aware that financial emergencies can happen," says the FDIC's Kincaid. "You've got to be proactive, too."

Chapter 9

Your Financial Information and Privacy Concerns

You've probably been receiving privacy notices from banks and other financial companies. These notices explain the following types of information:

- What personal financial information the company collects.

- Whether the company intends to share your personal financial information with other companies.

- What you can do, if the company intends to share your personal financial information, to limit some of that sharing.

- How the company protects your personal financial information.

Companies involved in financial activities, such as those listed below, must send their customers privacy notices:

- Banks, savings and loans, and credit unions

- Insurance companies

- Securities and commodities brokerage firms

- Retailers that directly issue their own credit cards (such as department stores or gas stations)

- Mortgage brokers

"Privacy Choices for Your Personal Financial Information," Federal Trade Commission (FTC), February 2002.

- Automobile dealerships that extend or arrange financing or leasing

- Check cashers and payday lenders

- Financial advisors and credit counseling services

- Sellers of money orders or travelers checks

Financial companies share information for many reasons: to offer you more services, to introduce new products, and to profit from the information they have about you. If you like to know about other products and services, you may want your financial company to share your personal financial information; in this case, you don't need to respond to the privacy notice. If you prefer to limit the promotions you receive or do not want marketers and others to have your personal financial information, you must take some important steps.

First, it is important to read these privacy notices. They explain how the company handles and shares your personal financial information. Keep in mind that not all privacy notices are the same. This chapter tells you about the other steps you can take to help protect the privacy of your personal financial information.

What Can You Stop—and What Can't You Stop?

Federal privacy laws give you the right to stop (opt out of) some sharing of your personal financial information. These laws balance your right to privacy with financial companies' need to provide information for normal business purposes. You have the right to opt out of some information sharing with companies that are:

- Part of the same corporate group as your financial company (or affiliates).

- Not part of the same corporate group as your financial company (or non-affiliates).

But you cannot opt out and completely stop the flow of all your personal financial information. The law permits your financial companies to share certain information about you without giving you the right to opt out. Among other things, your financial company can provide information to non-affiliates:

- Information about you to firms that help promote and market the company's own products or products offered under a joint agreement between two financial companies.

76

- Records of your transactions—such as your loan payments, credit card or debit card purchases, and checking and savings account statements—to firms that provide data processing and mailing services for your company.

- Information about you in response to a court order.

- Your payment history on loans and credit cards to credit bureaus.

What Opting Out Means

If you opt out, you limit the extent to which the company can provide your personal financial information to non-affiliates. If you do not opt out within a "reasonable period of time"—generally about 30 days after the company mails the notice—then the company is free to share certain personal financial information. If you didn't opt out the first time you received a privacy notice from a financial company, it's not too late. You can always change your mind and opt out of certain information sharing. Contact your financial company and ask for instructions on how to opt out. Remember, however, that any personal financial information that was shared before you opted out cannot be retrieved.

Your Right to Opt Out

A privacy notice contains information about the company's data collection and information sharing policies. If a financial company does not plan to share your information except as permitted by law, the notice will tell you this; in this case, you don't have a right to opt out.

- **Non-affiliates:** If you have the right to opt out (that is, if the company plans to share your information), the privacy notice will include instructions on how to opt out of sharing some information. Unless you opt out, your financial company can provide your personal financial information (for example, information on the kinds of stores you shop at, how much you borrow, your account balances, or the dollar value of your assets) to non-affiliates for marketing and other purposes.

- **Affiliates:** The privacy notice may also give you the right to opt out of certain information sharing with affiliates. For example, if a company intends to provide an affiliate with personal information from your credit report or loan application, you will usually first be given a chance to opt out. Companies, however, can share information about you with affiliates when the

77

information is based solely on your transactions with that company (transaction information includes whether you pay your bills on time, the type of accounts you have with the company, and so forth). Read your notices carefully to see if this type of opt out applies.

Credit bureaus may also sell information about you to lenders and insurers who use the information to decide whether to send you unsolicited offers of credit or insurance. This is known as prescreening. You can opt out of receiving these prescreened offers by calling 888-567-8688.

If you want to opt out of information sharing, you must follow the directions provided by your financial company. For example, you may have to call a toll-free number or fill out a form and return the form to the company.

In some cases, your financial company may give you the choice to opt out of different types of sharing. For example, you could opt out of certain categories of information the company provides to other companies but allow the company to share other kinds of information.

Privacy Notices You May Receive

- **Initial privacy notice:** You will usually receive a privacy notice when you open an account or become a customer of a financial company. If you open an account over the phone, however, and you agree, the company may send you a notice at a later time.

- **Annual privacy notices:** Each financial company you have an ongoing relationship with—for example, the bank where you have a checking account, your credit card company, or a company that services your loan—must give you a notice of its privacy policy annually.

- **Notice of changes in privacy policies:** If a company changes its privacy policy, it will either send you a revised privacy notice or tell you about the changes in the company's next annual notice.

A privacy notice may be included as an insert with your monthly statement or bill, or it may be sent to you in a separate mailing. If you agree to electronic delivery from an on-line financial company, the notice may be sent to you by e-mail or it may be made available to you on the company's website.

If you have more than one account with the same company, the company may send you only one privacy notice for all of your accounts or it may send you separate notices for each of your accounts.

If you have a joint account with another person (for example, a joint checking account or a mortgage loan), the financial company may send a notice to one of you or to each person listed on the account. If the company provides an opportunity to opt out, it must let one of the account holders opt out for all joint account holders.

What to Do When You Receive Your Notices

1. Read all privacy notices.

2. Get answers to your questions from your financial company.

3. If applicable, decide whether you want to opt out.

4. If you want to opt out, follow the instructions in the notice— and, if necessary, shop around for a financial institution with the privacy policy you want.

More Information about the Laws Affecting Your Personal Financial Privacy

Two federal laws cover different aspects of how companies can share your financial information, as described in this chapter: the Fair Credit Reporting Act and the Gramm-Leach-Bliley Act.

The Fair Credit Reporting Act protects the privacy of certain information distributed by consumer reporting agencies (CRAs). Most CRAs are credit bureaus that gather and provide information about you, such as if you pay your bills on time or have filed for bankruptcy, to creditors and other businesses. Under the law, credit bureaus and other CRAs can release your information only to those third parties that have certified that they have a purpose permitted by the law to obtain your consumer report, such as to evaluate your application for credit, insurance, or employment, or to rent you an apartment.

When a financial company obtains your credit report from a credit bureau, it may want to share that information with an affiliate, meaning a company that owns your financial company, that your financial company owns, or that is part of the same parent organization or corporate family. Under the Fair Credit Reporting Act, however, if the financial company plans to share certain information—for example, from your credit report or your credit application—with its affiliates, it will usually first notify you and give you an opportunity to opt out.

79

This notice is likely to be included in the privacy notice you receive from the financial company under the Gramm-Leach-Bliley Act.

The Gramm-Leach-Bliley Act requires financial companies to tell you about their policies regarding the privacy of your personal financial information. With some exceptions, the law limits the ability of financial companies to share your personal financial information with certain non-affiliates. A non-affiliate is a company that is unrelated to your financial company, and may include:

- **Service providers:** Companies hired by your financial company to perform a specific service, such as printing your checks

- **Joint marketers:** Companies that have an agreement with your financial company to offer you other financial products or services

- **Other third-party non-affiliate:** Which could include companies that may want access to your financial company's mailing list to tell you about other products and services

Under the Gramm-Leach-Bliley Act, your financial company can provide your personal financial information to non-affiliated service providers including joint marketers. But before it shares your information with other third-party non-affiliates (outside of these exceptions), your financial company must tell you about its information sharing practices and give you the opportunity to opt out.

Chapter 10

Identity Theft:
Take Steps to Protect Yourself

In the course of a busy day, you may write a check at the grocery store, charge tickets to a ball game, rent a car, mail your tax returns, change service providers for your cell phone, or apply for a credit card. Chances are you don't give these everyday transactions a second thought. But an identity thief does.

Identity theft is a serious crime. People whose identities have been stolen can spend months or years and thousands of dollars cleaning up the mess the thieves have made of a good name and credit record. In the meantime, victims of identity theft may lose job opportunities, be refused loans for education, housing, or cars, and even get arrested for crimes they didn't commit. Humiliation, anger, and frustration are among the feelings victims experience as they navigate the process of rescuing their identity.

Working with other government agencies and organizations, the Federal Trade Commission (FTC) has produced this information to help you remedy the effects of an identity theft. It describes what steps to take, your legal rights, how to handle specific problems you may encounter on the way to clearing your name, and what to watch for in the future.

How Identity Theft Occurs

Despite your best efforts to manage the flow of your personal information or to keep it to yourself, skilled identity thieves may use a

Excerpted from "Take Charge: Fighting Back against Identify Theft," Federal Trade Commission, February 2005.

variety of methods to gain access to your data. Here's how identity thieves get your personal information:

- They get information from businesses or other institutions by:
  - stealing records or information while they're on the job
  - bribing an employee who has access to these records
  - hacking these records
  - conning information out of employees
- They may steal your mail, including bank and credit card statements, credit card offers, new checks, and tax information.
- They may rummage through your trash, the trash of businesses, or public trash dumps in a practice known as "dumpster diving."
- They may get your credit reports by abusing their employer's authorized access to them, or by posing as a landlord, employer, or someone else who may have a legal right to access your report.
- They may steal your credit or debit card numbers by capturing the information in a data storage device in a practice known as "skimming." They may swipe your card for an actual purchase, or attach the device to an ATM machine where you may enter or swipe your card.
- They may steal your wallet or purse.
- They may complete a "change of address form" to divert your mail to another location.
- They may steal personal information they find in your home.
- They may steal personal information from you through e-mail or phone by posing as legitimate companies and claiming that you have a problem with your account. This practice is known as "phishing" online, or pretexting by phone.

If Your Personal Information Has Been Lost or Stolen

If you've lost personal information or identification, or if it has been stolen from you, taking certain steps quickly can minimize the potential for identity theft.

- **Financial accounts:** Close accounts, like credit cards and bank accounts, immediately. When you open new accounts, place passwords on them. Avoid using your mother's maiden name, your birth date, the last four digits of your Social Security number (SSN) or your phone number, or a series of consecutive numbers.

- **Social Security number:** Call the toll-free fraud number of any of the three nationwide consumer reporting companies and place an initial fraud alert on your credit reports. An alert can help stop someone from opening new credit accounts in your name.

- **Driver's license/other government-issued identification:** Contact the agency that issued the license or other identification document. Follow its procedures to cancel the document and to get a replacement. Ask the agency to flag your file so that no one else can get a license or any other identification document from them in your name.

Once you've taken these precautions, watch for signs that your information is being misused.

If your information has been misused, file a report about the theft with the police, and file a complaint with the Federal Trade Commission, as well. If another crime was committed for example, if your purse or wallet was stolen or your house or car was broken into report it to the police immediately.

Identity Theft Victims: Immediate Steps

If you are a victim of identity theft, take the following four steps as soon as possible, and keep a record with the details of your conversations and copies of all correspondence.

1. Place a fraud alert on your credit reports, and review your credit reports.

Fraud alerts can help prevent an identity thief from opening any more accounts in your name. Contact the toll-free fraud number of any of the three consumer reporting companies below to place a fraud alert on your credit report. You only need to contact one of the three companies to place an alert. The company you call is required to contact the other two, which will place an alert on their versions of your report, too.

- Equifax: 800-525-6285; www.equifax.com; P.O. Box 740241, Atlanta, GA 30374- 0241

- Experian: 888-EXPERIAN (397-3742); http://www.experian.com; P.O. Box 9532, Allen, TX 75013

- TransUnion: 800-680-7289; http://www.transunion.com; Fraud Victim Assistance Division, P.O. Box 6790, Fullerton, CA 92834-6790

Once you place the fraud alert in your file, you're entitled to order free copies of your credit reports, and, if you ask, only the last four digits of your SSN will appear on your credit reports. Once you get your credit reports, review them carefully. Look for inquiries from companies you haven't contacted, accounts you didn't open, and debts on your accounts that you can't explain. Check that information, like your SSN, address(es), name or initials, and employers are correct. If you find fraudulent or inaccurate information, get it removed. Continue to check your credit reports periodically, especially for the first year after you discover the identity theft, to make sure no new fraudulent activity has occurred.

There are two types of fraud alerts: an initial alert, and an extended alert.

An initial alert stays on your credit report for at least 90 days. You may ask that an initial fraud alert be placed on your credit report if you suspect you have been, or are about to be, a victim of identity theft. An initial alert is appropriate if your wallet has been stolen or if you've been taken in by a "phishing" scam. When you place an initial fraud alert on your credit report, you're entitled to one free credit report from each of the three nationwide consumer reporting companies.

An extended alert stays on your credit report for seven years. You can have an extended alert placed on your credit report if you've been a victim of identity theft and you provide the consumer reporting company with an "identity theft report." When you place an extended alert on your credit report, you're entitled to two free credit reports within twelve months from each of the three nationwide consumer reporting companies. In addition, the consumer reporting companies will remove your name from marketing lists for pre-screened credit offers for five years unless you ask them to put your name back on the list before then.

To place either of these alerts on your credit report, or to have them removed, you will be required to provide appropriate proof of your identity: that may include your SSN, name, address, and other personal information requested by the consumer reporting company.

When a business sees the alert on your credit report, they must verify your identity before issuing you credit. As part of this verification process, the business may try to contact you directly. This may cause some delays if you're trying to obtain credit. To compensate for possible delays, you may wish to include a cell phone number, where you can be reached easily, in your alert. Remember to keep all contact information in your alert current.

2. Close the accounts that you know, or believe, have been tampered with or opened fraudulently.

Call and speak with someone in the security or fraud department of each company. Follow up in writing, and include copies (not originals) of supporting documents. It's important to notify credit card companies and banks in writing. Send your letters by certified mail, return receipt requested, so you can document what the company received and when. Keep a file of your correspondence and enclosures.

When you open new accounts, use new personal identification numbers (PINs) and passwords. Avoid using easily available information like your mother's maiden name, your birth date, the last four digits of your SSN or your phone number, or a series of consecutive numbers.

If the identity thief has made charges or debits on your accounts, or on fraudulently opened accounts, ask the company for the forms to dispute those transactions:

- For charges and debits on existing accounts, ask the representative to send you the company's fraud dispute forms. If the company doesn't have special forms, write a letter to dispute the fraudulent charges or debits. In either case, write to the company at the address given for "billing inquiries," not the address for sending your payments.

- For new unauthorized accounts, ask if the company accepts the ID Theft Affidavit. If not, ask the representative to send you the company's fraud dispute forms. If the company already has reported these accounts or debts on your credit report, dispute this fraudulent information.

Once you have resolved your identity theft dispute with the company, ask for a letter stating that the company has closed the disputed accounts and has discharged the fraudulent debts. This letter is your best proof if errors relating to this account reappear on your credit report or you are contacted again about the fraudulent debt.

Applications or other transaction records related to the theft of your identity may help you prove that you are a victim. For example, you may be able to show that the signature on an application is not yours. These documents also may contain information about the identity thief that is valuable to law enforcement. By law, companies must give you a copy of the application or other business transaction records relating to your identity theft if you submit your request in writing. Be sure to ask the company representative where you should mail your request. Companies must provide these records at no charge to you within 30 days of receipt of your request and your supporting documents. You also may give permission to any law enforcement agency to get these records, or ask in your written request that a copy of these records be sent to a particular law enforcement officer.

The company can ask you for:

- proof of your identity. This may be a photocopy of a government-issued ID card, the same type of information the identity thief used to open or access the account, or the type of information the company usually requests from applicants or customers, and

- a police report and a completed affidavit, which may be the Identity Theft Affidavit or the company's own affidavit.

3. File a report with your local police or the police in the community where the identity theft took place.

Then, get a copy of the police report or at the very least, the number of the report. It can help you deal with creditors who need proof of the crime. If the police are reluctant to take your report, ask to file a "Miscellaneous Incidents" report, or try another jurisdiction, like your state police. You also can check with your state Attorney General's office to find out if state law requires the police to take reports for identity theft. Check the Blue Pages of your telephone directory for the phone number or check http://www.naag.org for a list of state Attorneys General.

4. File a complaint with the Federal Trade Commission.

By sharing your identity theft complaint with the FTC, you will provide important information that can help law enforcement officials across the nation track down identity thieves and stop them. The FTC can refer victims' complaints to other government agencies and companies for further action, as well as investigate companies for violations of laws the agency enforces.

You can file a complaint online at www.consumer.gov/idtheft. If you don't have internet access, call the FTC's Identity Theft Hotline, toll-free: 877-IDTHEFT (438-4338); TTY: 866-653- 4261; or write: Identity Theft Clearinghouse, Federal Trade Commission, 600 Pennsylvania Avenue, NW, Washington, DC 20580.

Be sure to call the Hotline to update your complaint if you have any additional information or problems.

An identity theft report may have two parts:

Part One is a copy of a report filed with a local, state, or federal law enforcement agency, like your local police department, your State Attorney General, the FBI, the U.S. Secret Service, the FTC, and the U.S. Postal Inspection Service. There is no federal law requiring a federal agency to take a report about identity theft; however, some state laws require local police departments to take reports. When you file a report, provide as much information as you can about the crime, including anything you know about the dates of the identity theft, the fraudulent accounts opened and the alleged identity thief.

Note: Knowingly submitting false information could subject you to criminal prosecution for perjury.

Part Two of an identity theft report depends on the policies of the consumer reporting company and the information provider (the business that sent the information to the consumer reporting company). That is, they may ask you to provide information or documentation in addition to that included in the law enforcement report which is reasonably intended to verify your identity theft. They must make their request within 15 days of receiving your law enforcement report, or, if you already obtained an extended fraud alert on your credit report, the date you submit your request to the credit reporting company for information blocking. The consumer reporting company and information provider then have 15 more days to work with you to make sure your identity theft report contains everything they need. They are entitled to take five days to review any information you give them. For example, if you give them information 11 days after they request it, they do not have to make a final decision until 16 days after they asked you for that information. If you give them any information after the 15-day deadline, they can reject your identity theft report as incomplete; you will have to resubmit your identity theft report with the correct information.

You may find that most federal and state agencies, and some local police departments, offer only "automated" reports a report that does not require a face-to-face meeting with a law enforcement officer. Automated reports may be submitted online, or by telephone or mail. If you have a choice, do not use an automated report. The reason? It's more difficult for the consumer reporting company or information provider to verify the information. Unless you are asking a consumer reporting company to place an extended fraud alert on your credit report, you probably will have to provide additional information or documentation when you use an automated report.

Tips for Organizing Your Case

Accurate and complete records will help you to resolve your identity theft case more quickly.

- Have a plan when you contact a company. Don't assume that the person you talk to will give you all the information or help you need. Prepare a list of questions to ask the representative, as well as information about your identity theft. Don't end the call until you're sure you understand everything you've been told. If you need more help, ask to speak to a supervisor.

- Write down the name of everyone you talk to, what he or she tells you, and the date the conversation occurred. Use Chart Your Course of Action to help you.

- Follow up in writing with all contacts you've made on the phone or in person. Use certified mail, return receipt requested, so you can document what the company or organization received and when.

- Keep copies of all correspondence or forms you send.

- Keep the originals of supporting documents, like police reports and letters to and from creditors; send copies only.

- Set up a filing system for easy access to your paperwork.

- Keep old files even if you believe your case is closed. Once resolved, most cases stay resolved, but problems can crop up.

Resolving Specific Problems

While dealing with problems resulting from identity theft can be time-consuming and frustrating, most victims can resolve their cases by being assertive, organized, and knowledgeable about their legal rights. Some laws require you to notify companies within specific time periods. Don't delay in contacting any companies to deal with these problems, and ask for supervisors if you need more help than you're getting.

Bank accounts and fraudulent withdrawals: Different laws determine your legal remedies based on the type of bank fraud you have suffered. For example, state laws protect you against fraud committed by a thief using paper documents, like stolen or counterfeit checks. But if the thief used an electronic fund transfer, federal law applies. Many transactions may seem to be processed electronically but are still considered "paper" transactions. If you're not sure what type of transaction the thief used to commit the fraud, ask the financial institution that processed the transaction.

Fraudulent electronic withdrawals: The Electronic Fund Transfer Act provides consumer protections for transactions involving an ATM or debit card, or another electronic way to debit or credit an account. It also limits your liability for unauthorized electronic fund transfers.

You have 60 days from the date your bank account statement is sent to you to report in writing any money withdrawn from your account without your permission. This includes instances when your ATM or debit card is "skimmed" that is, when a thief captures your account number and PIN without your card having been lost or stolen.

If your ATM or debit card is lost or stolen, report it immediately because the amount you can be held responsible for depends on how quickly you report the loss.

- If you report the loss or theft within two business days of discovery, your losses are limited to $50.

- If you report the loss or theft after two business days, but within 60 days after the unauthorized electronic fund transfer appears on your statement, you could lose up to $500 of what the thief withdraws.

- If you wait more than 60 days to report the loss or theft, you could lose all the money that was taken from your account after the end of the 60 days.

Note that VISA and MasterCard voluntarily have agreed to limit consumers' liability for unauthorized use of their debit cards in most instances to $50 per card, no matter how much time has elapsed since the discovery of the loss or theft of the card.

The best way to protect yourself in the event of an error or fraudulent transaction is to call the financial institution and follow up in writing by certified letter, return receipt requested so you can prove when the institution received your letter. Keep a copy of the letter you send for your records.

After receiving your notification about an error on your statement, the institution generally has 10 business days to investigate. The institution must tell you the results of its investigation within three business days after completing it and must correct an error within one business day after determining that it occurred. If the institution needs more time, it may take up to 45 days to complete the investigation but only if the money in dispute is returned to your account and you are notified promptly of the credit. At the end of the investigation, if no error has been found, the institution may take the money back if it sends you a written explanation.

Fraudulent checks and other "paper" transactions: In general, if an identity thief steals your checks or counterfeits checks from your existing bank account, stop payment, close the account, and ask your bank to notify Chex Systems, Inc. or the check verification service with which it does business. That way, retailers can be notified not to accept these checks. While no federal law limits your losses if someone uses your checks with a forged signature, or uses another type of "paper" transaction such as a demand draft, state laws may protect you. Most states hold the bank responsible for losses from such transactions. At the same time, most states require you to take reasonable care of your account. For example, you may be held responsible for the forgery if you fail to notify the bank in a timely manner that a check was lost or stolen. Contact your state banking or consumer protection agency for more information.

You can contact major check verification companies directly for the following services:

- To request that they notify retailers who use their databases not to accept your checks, call:

  - TeleCheck at 800-710-9898 or 800-927-0188

  - Certegy, Inc. (previously Equifax Check Systems) at 800-437-5120

- To find out if the identity thief has been passing bad checks in your name, call:

  - SCAN: 800-262-7771

If your checks are rejected by a merchant, it may be because an identity thief is using the Magnetic Information Character Recognition (MICR) code (the numbers at the bottom of checks), your driver's license number, or another identification number. The merchant who rejects your check should give you its check verification company contact information so you can find out what information the thief is using. If you find that the thief is using your MICR code, ask your bank to close your checking account, and open a new one. If you discover that the thief is using your driver's license number or some other identification number, work with your DMV or other identification issuing agency to get new identification with new numbers. Once you have taken the appropriate steps, your checks should be accepted.

Note:

- The check verification company may or may not remove the information about the MICR code or the driver's license/identification number from its database because this information may help prevent the thief from continuing to commit fraud.

- If the checks are being passed on a new account, contact the bank to close the account. Also contact Chex Systems, Inc., to review your consumer report to make sure that no other bank accounts have been opened in your name.

- Dispute any bad checks passed in your name with merchants so they don't start any collections actions against you.

Fraudulent new accounts: If you have trouble opening a new checking account, it may be because an identity thief has been opening accounts in your name. Chex Systems, Inc., produces consumer reports specifically about checking accounts, and as a consumer reporting company, is subject to the Fair Credit Reporting Act. You can request a free copy of your consumer report by contacting Chex Systems, Inc. If you find inaccurate information on your consumer report, follow the procedures under Correcting Credit Reports to dispute it. Contact each of the banks where account inquiries were made, too. This will help ensure that any fraudulently opened accounts are closed.

Chex Systems, Inc.
800-428-9623
http://www.chexhelp.com
Fax: 602-659-2197

Chex Systems, Inc.
Attn: Consumer Relations
7805 Hudson Road, Suite 100
Woodbury, MN 55125

Where to Find Help

If you have trouble getting a financial institution to help you resolve your banking-related identity theft problems, including problems with bank-issued credit cards, contact the agency that oversees your bank (see list). If you're not sure which of these agencies is the right one, call your bank or visit the National Information Center of the Federal Reserve System at www.ffiec.gov/nic and click on "Institution Search."

Federal Deposit Insurance Corporation (FDIC) (http://www.fdic.gov): The FDIC supervises state-chartered banks that are not members of the Federal Reserve System, and insures deposits at banks and savings and loans. Call the FDIC Consumer Call Center toll-free: 800-934-3342; or write: Federal Deposit Insurance Corporation, Division of Compliance and Consumer Affairs, 550 17th Street, NW, Washington, DC 20429.

FDIC publications:

- Classic Cons... And How to Counter Them
- A Crook Has Drained Your Account. Who Pays?
- Your Wallet: A Loser's Manual

Federal Reserve System (Fed) (http://www.federalreserve.gov): The Fed supervises state-chartered banks that are members of the Federal Reserve System. Call: 202-452-3693; or write: Division of Consumer and Community Affairs, Mail Stop 801, Federal Reserve Board, Washington, DC 20551; or contact the Federal Reserve Bank in your area. The Reserve Banks are located in Boston, New York, Philadelphia, Cleveland, Richmond, Atlanta, Chicago, St. Louis, Minneapolis, Kansas City, Dallas, and San Francisco.

National Credit Union Administration (NCUA) (http://www.ncua.gov): The NCUA charters and supervises federal credit unions and insures deposits at federal credit unions and many state credit unions. Call: 703-518-6360; or write: Compliance Officer, National Credit Union Administration, 1775 Duke Street, Alexandria, VA 22314.

Office of the Comptroller of the Currency (OCC) (http://www.occ.treas.gov): The OCC charters and supervises national banks. If the word "national" appears in the name of a bank, or the initials "N.A." follow its name, the OCC oversees its operations. Call toll-free:

1-800-613-6743 (business days 9:00 a.m. to 4:00 p.m. CST); fax: 713-336-4301; or write: Customer Assistance Group, 1301 McKinney Street, Suite 3710, Houston, TX 77010. OCC publications:

- Check Fraud: A Guide to Avoiding Losses
- How to Avoid Becoming a Victim of Identity Theft
- Identity Theft and Pretext Calling Advisory Letter 2001–4

Office of Thrift Supervision (OTS) (www.ots.treas.gov): The OTS is the primary regulator of all federal, and many state-chartered, thrift institutions, including savings banks and savings and loan institutions. Call: 202-906-6000; or write: Office of Thrift Supervision, 1700 G Street, NW, Washington, DC 20552.

Bankruptcy Fraud

U. S. Trustee (UST) (www.usdoj.gov/ust): If you believe someone has filed for bankruptcy in your name, write to the U.S. Trustee in the region where the bankruptcy was filed. A list of the U.S. Trustee Programs' Regional Offices is available on the UST website, or check the Blue Pages of your phone book under U.S. Government Bankruptcy Administration.

In your letter, describe the situation and provide proof of your identity. The U.S. Trustee will make a criminal referral to law enforcement authorities if you provide appropriate documentation to substantiate your claim. You also may want to file a complaint with the U.S. Attorney or the FBI in the city where the bankruptcy was filed. The U.S. Trustee does not provide legal representation, legal advice, or referrals to lawyers. That means you may need to hire an attorney to help convince the bankruptcy court that the filing is fraudulent. The U.S. Trustee does not provide consumers with copies of court documents. You can get them from the bankruptcy clerk's office for a fee.

Correcting Fraudulent Information in Credit Reports

The Fair Credit Reporting Act (FCRA) establishes procedures for correcting fraudulent information on your credit report and requires that your report be made available only for certain legitimate business needs.

Under the FCRA, both the consumer reporting company and the information provider (the business that sent the information to the consumer reporting company), such as a bank or credit card company, are responsible for correcting fraudulent information in your report. To protect your rights under the law, contact both the consumer reporting company and the information provider.

Consumer reporting company obligations: Consumer reporting companies will block fraudulent information from appearing on your credit report if you take the following steps: Send them a copy of an identity theft report and a letter telling them what information is fraudulent. The letter also should state that the information does not relate to any transaction that you made or authorized. In addition, provide proof of your identity that may include your SSN, name, address, and other personal information requested by the consumer reporting company.

The consumer reporting company has four business days to block the fraudulent information after accepting your identity theft report. It also must tell the information provider that it has blocked the information. The consumer reporting company may refuse to block the information or remove the block if, for example, you have not told the truth about your identity theft. If the consumer reporting company removes the block or refuses to place the block, it must let you know.

The blocking process is only one way for identity theft victims to deal with fraudulent information. There's also the "reinvestigation process," which was designed to help all consumers dispute errors or inaccuracies on their credit reports.

Information provider obligations: Information providers stop reporting fraudulent information to the consumer reporting companies once you send them an identity theft report and a letter explaining that the information that they're reporting resulted from identity theft. But you must send your identity theft report and letter to the address specified by the information provider. Note that the information provider may continue to report the information if it later learns that the information does not result from identity theft.

If a consumer reporting company tells an information provider that it has blocked fraudulent information in your credit report, the information provider may not continue to report that information to the consumer reporting company. The information provider also may not hire someone to collect the debt that relates to the fraudulent account, or sell that debt to anyone else who would try to collect it.

Sample Blocking Letter Consumer Reporting Company

Date
Your Name
Your Address
Your City, State, Zip Code

Complaint Department
Name of Consumer Reporting Company
Address
City, State, Zip Code

Dear Sir or Madam:

I am a victim of identity theft. I am writing to request that you block the following fraudulent information in my file. This information does not relate to any transaction that I have made. The items also are circled on the attached copy of the report I received. (Identify item(s) to be blocked by name of source, such as creditors or tax court, and identify type of item, such as credit account, judgment, etc.)

Enclosed is a copy of the law enforcement report regarding my identity theft. Please let me know if you need any other information from me to block this information on my credit report.

Sincerely,
Your name
Enclosures: (List what you are enclosing.)

Credit Cards

The Fair Credit Billing Act establishes procedures for resolving billing errors on your credit card accounts, including fraudulent charges on your accounts. The law also limits your liability for unauthorized credit card charges to $50 per card. To take advantage of the law's consumer protections, you must:

- write to the creditor at the address given for "billing inquiries," not the address for sending your payments. Include your name, address, account number, and a description of the billing error, including the amount and date of the error. See Sample Letter.

- send your letter so that it reaches the creditor within 60 days after the first bill containing the error was mailed to you. If an identity thief changed the address on your account and you didn't receive the bill, your dispute letter still must reach the creditor within 60 days of when the creditor would have mailed the bill. This is one reason it's essential to keep track of your billing statements, and follow up quickly if your bills don't arrive on time.

You should send your letter by certified mail, and request a return receipt. It becomes your proof of the date the creditor received the letter. Include copies (not originals) of your police report or other documents that support your position. Keep a copy of your dispute letter.

The creditor must acknowledge your complaint in writing within 30 days after receiving it, unless the problem has been resolved. The creditor must resolve the dispute within two billing cycles (but not more than 90 days) after receiving your letter.

Sample Dispute Letter for Existing Accounts

Date
Your Name
Your Address
Your City, State, Zip Code
Your Account Number

Name of Creditor
Billing Inquiries
Address
City, State, Zip Code

Dear Sir or Madam:

I am writing to dispute a fraudulent (charge or debit) on my account in the amount of $_____. I am a victim of identity theft, and I did not make this (charge or debit). I am requesting that the (charge be removed or the debit reinstated), that any finance and other charges related to the fraudulent amount be credited, as well, and that I receive an accurate statement.

Enclosed are copies of (use this sentence to describe any enclosed information, such as a police report) supporting my position. Please investigate this matter and correct the fraudulent (charge or debit) as soon as possible.

Sincerely,
Your name
Enclosures: (List what you are enclosing.)

96

Criminal Violations

Procedures to correct your record within criminal justice databases can vary from state to state, and even from county to county. Some states have enacted laws with special procedures for identity theft victims to follow to clear their names. You should check with the office of your state Attorney General, but you can use the following information as a general guide.

If wrongful criminal violations are attributed to your name, contact the police or sheriff's department that originally arrested the person using your identity, or the court agency that issued the warrant for the arrest. File an impersonation report with the police/sheriff's department or the court, and confirm your identity: Ask the police department to take a full set of your fingerprints, photograph you, and make copies of your photo identification documents, like your driver's license, passport, or travel visa. To establish your innocence, ask the police to compare the prints and photographs with those of the impostor.

If the arrest warrant is from a state or county other than where you live, ask your local police department to send the impersonation report to the police department in the jurisdiction where the arrest warrant, traffic citation, or criminal conviction originated.

The law enforcement agency should then recall any warrants and issue a "clearance letter" or "certificate of release" (if you were arrested/booked). You'll need to keep this document with you at all times in case you're wrongly arrested again. Ask the law enforcement agency to file the record of the follow-up investigation establishing your innocence with the district attorney's (D.A.) office and court where the crime took place. This will result in an amended complaint. Once your name is recorded in a criminal database, it's unlikely that it will be completely removed from the official record. Ask that the "key name" or "primary name" be changed from your name to the impostor's name (or to "John Doe" if the impostor's true identity is not known), with your name noted as an alias.

You'll also want to clear your name in the court records. To do so, you'll need to determine which state law(s) will help you with this and how. If your state has no formal procedure for clearing your record, contact the D.A.'s office in the county where the case was originally prosecuted. Ask the D.A.'s office for the appropriate court records needed to clear your name. You may need to hire a criminal defense attorney to help you clear your name. Contact Legal Services in your state or your local bar association for help in finding an attorney.

Finally, contact your state Department of Motor Vehicles (DMV) to find out if your driver's license is being used by the identity thief. Ask that your files be flagged for possible fraud.

Debt Collectors

The Fair Debt Collection Practices Act prohibits debt collectors from using unfair or deceptive practices to collect overdue bills that a creditor has forwarded for collection, even if those bills don't result from identity theft.

You can stop a debt collector from contacting you in two ways:

- Write a letter to the collection agency telling them to stop. Once the debt collector receives your letter, the company may not contact you again with two exceptions: They can tell you there will be no further contact, and they can tell you that the debt collector or the creditor intends to take some specific action.

- Send a letter to the collection agency, within 30 days after you received written notice of the debt, telling them that you do not owe the money. Include copies of documents that support your position. Including a copy (not original) of your police report may be useful. In this case, a collector can renew collection activities only if it sends you proof of the debt.

If you don't have documentation to support your position, be as specific as possible about why the debt collector is mistaken. The debt collector is responsible for sending you proof that you're wrong. For example, if the debt you're disputing originates from a credit card you never applied for, ask for a copy of the application with the applicant's signature. Then, you can prove that it's not your signature.

If you tell the debt collector that you are a victim of identity theft and it is collecting the debt for another company, the debt collector must tell that company that you may be a victim of identity theft.

While you can stop a debt collector from contacting you, that won't get rid of the debt itself. It's important to contact the company that originally opened the account to dispute the debt, otherwise that company may send it to a different debt collector, report it on your credit report, or initiate a lawsuit to collect on the debt.

Driver's License

If you think your name or SSN is being used by an identity thief to get a driver's license or a non-driver's ID card, contact your state

DMV. If your state uses your SSN as your driver's license number, ask to substitute another number.

Investment Fraud

U.S. Securities and Exchange Commission (SEC) (http://www.sec.gov): The SEC's Office of Investor Education and Assistance serves investors who complain to the SEC about investment fraud or the mishandling of their investments by securities professionals. If you believe that an identity thief has tampered with your securities investments or a brokerage account, immediately report it to your broker or account manager and to the SEC.

You can file a complaint with the SEC's Complaint Center at www.sec.gov/complaint.shtml. Include as much detail as possible. If you don't have internet access, write to the SEC at: SEC Office of Investor Education and Assistance, 450 Fifth Street, NW, Washington DC, 20549-0213. For answers to general questions, call 202-942-7040.

Mail Theft

U.S. Postal Inspection Service (USPIS) (www.usps.gov/websites/depart/inspect): The USPIS is the law enforcement arm of the U.S. Postal Service, and investigates cases of identity theft. The USPIS has primary jurisdiction in all matters infringing on the integrity of the U.S. mail. If an identity thief has stolen your mail to get new credit cards, bank or credit card statements, pre-screened credit offers, or tax information, or has falsified change-of-address forms or obtained your personal information through a fraud conducted by mail, report it to your local postal inspector.

You can locate the USPIS district office nearest you by calling your local post office, checking the Blue Pages of your telephone directory, or visiting www.usps.gov/websites/depart/inspect.

Passport Fraud

United States Department of State (USDS) (www.travel.state.gov/passport/passport_1738.html): If you've lost your passport, or believe it was stolen or is being used fraudulently, contact the USDS through their website, or call a local USDS field office. Local field offices are listed in the Blue Pages of your telephone directory.

Phone Fraud

If an identity thief has established phone service in your name, is making unauthorized calls that seem to come from and are billed to your cellular phone, or is using your calling card and PIN, contact your service provider immediately to cancel the account or calling card. Open new accounts and choose new PINs. If you're having trouble getting fraudulent phone charges removed from your account or getting an unauthorized account closed, contact the appropriate agency below.

For local service, contact your state Public Utility Commission.

For cellular phones and long distance, contact the Federal Communications Commission (FCC) at http://www.fcc.gov. The FCC regulates interstate and international communications by radio, television, wire, satellite, and cable. Call: 888-CALL-FCC; TTY: 888-TELL-FCC; or write: Federal Communications Commission, Consumer Information Bureau, 445 12th Street, SW, Room 5A863, Washington, DC 20554. You can file complaints online at http://www.fcc.gov, or e-mail your questions tomailto:fccinfo@fcc.gov.

Social Security Number Misuse

Social Security Administration (SSA) (http://www.ssa.gov): If you have specific information of SSN misuse that involves the buying or selling of Social Security cards, may be related to terrorist activity, or is designed to obtain Social Security benefits, contact the SSA Office of the Inspector General. You may file a complaint online at www.socialsecurity.gov/oig, call toll-free: 800-269-0271, fax: 410-597-0118, or write: SSA Fraud Hotline, P.O. Box 17768, Baltimore, MD 21235.

You also may call SSA toll-free at 800-772-1213 to verify the accuracy of the earnings reported on your SSN, request a copy of your Social Security Statement, or get a replacement SSN card if yours is lost or stolen. Follow up in writing.

SSA publications:

- SSA Fraud Hotline for Reporting Fraud

- Social Security: Your Number and Card (SSA Pub. No. 05-10002)

- Identity Theft And Your Social Security Number (SSA Pub. No. 05-10064)

Student Loans

Contact the school or program that opened the student loan to close the loan. At the same time, report the fraudulent loan to the U.S. Department of Education. Call the Inspector General's Hotline toll-free at 800-MIS-USED; visit www.ed.gov/about/offices/list/oig/hotline .html?src=rt; or write: Office of Inspector General, U.S. Department of Education, 400 Maryland Avenue, SW, Washington, DC 20202-1510.

Tax Fraud

Internal Revenue Service (IRS) (http://www.treas.gov/irs/ci): The IRS is responsible for administering and enforcing tax laws. Identity fraud may occur as it relates directly to your tax records. Visit http://www.irs.gov and type in the IRS key word "Identity Theft" for more information.

If you have an unresolved issue related to identity theft, or you have suffered or are about to suffer a significant hardship as a result of the administration of the tax laws, visit the IRS Taxpayer Advocate Service website www.irs.gov/advocate or call toll-free: 877-777-4778.

If you suspect or know of an individual or company that is not complying with the tax law, report it to the Internal Revenue Service Criminal Investigation Informant Hotline by calling toll-free: 800-829-0433 or visit http://www.irs.gov/and type in the IRS key word "Tax Fraud."

For More Information

Federal Trade Commission (FTC) (http://www.ftc.gov): The FTC wants consumers and businesses to know about the importance of personal information privacy. To request free copies of brochures, visit www.consumer.gov/idtheft or call 877-FTC-HELP (382-4357).

FTC publications:

- ID Theft: What's It All About?

- Avoiding Credit and Charge Card Fraud

- Credit and ATM Cards: What to Do If They're Lost or Stolen

- Credit Card Loss Protection Offers: They're The Real Steal

- Electronic Banking

- Fair Credit Billing

- Your Access to Free Credit Reports

- Fair Debt Collection
- How to Dispute Credit Report Errors
- Identity Crisis... What to Do If Your Identity Is Stolen

Department of Justice (DOJ) (www.usdoj.gov): The DOJ and its U.S. Attorneys prosecute federal identity theft cases. Information on identity theft is available at www.usdoj.gov/criminal/fraud/idtheft.html.

Federal Bureau of Investigation (FBI) (http://www.fbi.gov): The FBI, a criminal law enforcement agency, investigates cases of identity theft. The FBI recognizes that identity theft is a component of many crimes, including bank fraud, mail fraud, wire fraud, bankruptcy fraud, insurance fraud, fraud against the government, and terrorism. Local field offices are listed in the Blue Pages of your telephone directory.

U.S. Secret Service (USSS) (http://www.treas.gov/usss): The U.S. Secret Service investigates financial crimes, which may include identity theft. Although the Secret Service generally investigates cases where the dollar loss is substantial, your information may provide evidence of a larger pattern of fraud requiring their involvement. Local field offices are listed in the Blue Pages of your telephone directory.

Financial Crimes Division (http://www.treas.gov/usss/financial_crimes.shtml)

Staying Alert

Once resolved, most cases of identity theft stay resolved. But occasionally, some victims have recurring problems. To help stay on top of the situation, continue to monitor your credit reports and read your financial account statements promptly and carefully. You may want to review your credit reports once every three months in the first year of the theft, and once a year thereafter. And stay alert for other signs of identity theft, like:

- failing to receive bills or other mail. Follow up with creditors if your bills don't arrive on time. A missing bill could mean an identity thief has taken over your account and changed your billing address to cover his tracks.

- receiving credit cards that you didn't apply for.

102

- being denied credit, or being offered less favorable credit terms, like a high interest rate, for no apparent reason.

- getting calls or letters from debt collectors or businesses about merchandise or services
you didn't buy.

Minimizing Recurrences

When it comes to identity theft, you can't entirely control whether you will become a victim. But there are certain steps you can take to minimize recurrences.

What to Do Today

- Place passwords on your credit card, bank, and phone accounts. Avoid using easily available information like your mother's maiden name, your birth date, the last four digits of your SSN or your phone number, or a series of consecutive numbers. When opening new accounts, you may find that many businesses still have a line on their applications for your mother's maiden name. Ask if you can use a password instead.

- Secure personal information in your home, especially if you have roommates, employ outside help, or are having work done in your home.

- Ask about information security procedures in your workplace or at businesses, doctor's offices, or other institutions that collect your personally identifying information. Find out who has access to your personal information and verify that it is handled securely. Ask about the disposal procedures for those records as well. Find out if your information will be shared with anyone else. If so, ask how your information can be kept confidential.

Active Duty Alerts for Military Personnel

If you are a member of the military and away from your usual duty station, you may place an active duty alert on your credit reports to help minimize the risk of identity theft while you are deployed. Active duty alerts are in effect on your report for one year. If your deployment lasts longer, you can place another alert on your credit report.

When you place an active duty alert, you'll be removed from the credit reporting companies' marketing list for pre-screened credit card offers for two years unless you ask to go back on the list before then.

See Consumer Reporting Companies for contact information. The process for getting and removing an alert, and a business's response to your alert, are the same as that for an initial alert. You may use a personal representative to place or remove an alert.

Maintaining Vigilance

- Don't give out personal information on the phone, through the mail, or on the internet unless you've initiated the contact or are sure you know who you're dealing with. Identity thieves are clever, and have posed as representatives of banks, internet service providers (ISPs), and even government agencies to get people to reveal their SSN, mother's maiden name, account numbers, and other identifying information. Before you share any personal information, confirm that you are dealing with a legitimate organization. Check an organization's website by typing its URL in the address line, rather than cutting and pasting it. Many companies post scam alerts when their name is used improperly. Or call customer service using the number listed on your account statement or in the telephone book.

- Treat your mail and trash carefully.

  - Deposit your outgoing mail in post office collection boxes or at your local post office, rather than in an unsecured mailbox. Promptly remove mail from your mailbox. If you're planning to be away from home and can't pick up your mail, call the U.S. Postal Service at 800-275-8777 to request a vacation hold. The Postal Service will hold your mail at your local post office until you can pick it up or are home to receive it.

  - To thwart an identity thief who may pick through your trash or recycling bins to capture your personal information, tear or shred your charge receipts, copies of credit applications, insurance forms, physician statements, checks and bank statements, expired charge cards that you're discarding, and credit offers you get in the mail. To opt out of receiving offers of credit in the mail, call: 888-5-OPTOUT (888-567-8688). The three nationwide consumer reporting companies use the same toll-free number to let consumers choose not to receive credit offers based on their lists. Note that you will be asked to provide your SSN which the consumer reporting companies need to match you with your file.

- Don't carry your SSN card; leave it in a secure place.

- Give your SSN only when absolutely necessary, and ask to use other types of identifiers. If your state uses your SSN as your driver's license number, ask to substitute another number. Do the same if your health insurance company uses your SSN as your policy number.

- Carry only the identification information and the credit and debit cards that you'll actually need when you go out.

- Be cautious when responding to promotions. Identity thieves may create phony promotional offers to get you to give them your personal information.

- Keep your purse or wallet in a safe place at work; do the same with copies of administrative forms that have your sensitive personal information.

- When ordering new checks, pick them up from the bank instead of having them mailed to your home mailbox.

A Special Word about Social Security Numbers

Your employer and financial institutions will need your SSN for wage and tax reporting purposes. Other businesses may ask you for your SSN to do a credit check if you are applying for a loan, renting an apartment, or signing up for utilities. Sometimes, however, they simply want your SSN for general record keeping. If someone asks for your SSN, ask:

- Why do you need my SSN?

- How will my SSN be used?

- How do you protect my SSN from being stolen?

- What will happen if I don't give you my SSN?

If you don't provide your SSN, some businesses may not provide you with the service or benefit you want. Getting satisfactory answers to these questions will help you decide whether you want to share your SSN with the business. The decision to share is yours.

The Doors and Windows Are Locked, But...

You may be careful about locking your doors and windows, and keeping your personal papers in a secure place. Depending on what you use your personal computer for, an identity thief may not need to set foot in your house to steal your personal information. You may store your SSN, financial records, tax returns, birth date, and bank account numbers on your computer. These tips can help you keep your computer—and the personal information it stores—safe.

- Virus protection software should be updated regularly, and patches for your operating system and other software programs should be installed to protect against intrusions and infections that can lead to the compromise of your computer files or passwords. Ideally, virus protection software should be set to automatically update each week. The Windows XP operating system also can be set to automatically check for patches and download them to your computer.

- Do not open files sent to you by strangers, or click on hyperlinks or download programs from people you don't know. Be careful about using file-sharing programs. Opening a file could expose your system to a computer virus or a program known as "spyware," which could capture your passwords or any other information as you type it into your keyboard.

- Use a firewall program, especially if you use a high-speed internet connection like cable, DSL or T-1 that leaves your computer connected to the internet 24 hours a day. The firewall program will allow you to stop uninvited access to your computer. Without it, hackers can take over your computer, access the personal information stored on it, or use it to commit other crimes.

- Use a secure browser—software that encrypts or scrambles information you send over the internet—to guard your online transactions. Be sure your browser has the most up-to-date encryption capabilities by using the latest version available from the manufacturer. You also can download some browsers for free over the internet. When submitting information, look for the "lock" icon on the browser's status bar to be sure your information is secure during transmission.

- Try not to store financial information on your laptop unless absolutely necessary. If you do, use a strong password—a combination of letters (upper and lower case), numbers, and symbols.

A good way to create a strong password is to think of a memorable phrase and use the first letter of each word as your password, converting some letters into numbers that resemble letters. For example, "I love Felix; he's a good cat," would become 1LFHA6c. Don't use an automatic log-in feature that saves your user name and password, and always log off when you're finished. That way, if your laptop is stolen, it's harder for a thief to access your personal information.

• Before you dispose of a computer, delete all the personal information it stored. Deleting files using the keyboard or mouse commands or reformatting your hard drive may not be enough because the files may stay on the computer's hard drive, where they may be retrieved easily. Use a "wipe" utility program to overwrite the entire hard drive.

• Look for website privacy policies. They should answer questions about maintaining accuracy, access, security, and control of personal information collected by the site, how the information will be used, and whether it will be provided to third parties. If you don't see a privacy policy—or if you can't understand it— consider doing business elsewhere.

It's The Law

Federal Law

The Identity Theft and Assumption Deterrence Act, enacted by Congress in October 1998 (and codified, in part, at 18 U.S.C. §1028) makes identity theft a federal crime.

Under federal criminal law, identity theft takes place when someone "knowingly transfers, possesses or uses, without lawful authority, a means of identification of another person with the intent to commit, or to aid or abet, or in connection with, any unlawful activity that constitutes a violation of federal law, or that constitutes a felony under any applicable state or local law."

Under this definition, a name or Social Security number is considered a "means of identification." So is a credit card number, cellular telephone electronic serial number, or any other piece of information that may be used alone or in conjunction with other information to identify a specific individual.

Violations of the federal crime are investigated by federal law enforcement agencies, including the U.S. Secret Service, the FBI, the U.S.

Postal Inspection Service, and the Social Security Administration's Office of the Inspector General. Federal identity theft cases are prosecuted by the U.S. Department of Justice.

For the purposes of the law, the FCRA defines identity theft to apply to consumers and businesses.

State Laws

Many states have passed laws making identity theft a crime or providing help in recovery from identity theft; others are considering such legislation. Where specific criminal identity theft laws do not exist, the practices may be prohibited under other laws. Contact your state Attorney General (for a list of state offices, visit http://www.naag.org) or local consumer protection agency for laws related to identity theft, or visit www.consumer.gov/idtheft.

Privacy Policy

When you contact the Federal Trade Commission (FTC) with complaints or requests for information, you can do it online at www.consumer.gov/idtheft; by telephone, toll-free at 877-ID-THEFT (438-4338); or by mail: Federal Trade Commission, Identity Theft Clearinghouse, 600 Pennsylvania Avenue, NW, Washington, DC 20580. Before you contact FTC, there are a few things you should know.

FTC enters the information you send into the Identity Theft Clearinghouse, an electronic database. The Clearinghouse is a system of records covered under the Privacy Act of 1974. In general, the Privacy Act prohibits unauthorized disclosures of the records it protects. It also gives individuals the right to review records about themselves. Learn more about your Privacy Act rights and the FTC's Privacy Act procedures by contacting the FTC's Freedom of Information Act Office: 202-326-2430; www.ftc.gov/foia/privacy_act.htm.

The information you submit is shared with FTC attorneys and investigators. It also may be shared with employees of various federal, state, or local law enforcement or regulatory authorities. The FTC also may share your information with some private entities, such as consumer reporting companies and any companies you may have complained about, where it believes that doing so might help resolve identity theft-related problems. You may be contacted by the FTC or any of the agencies or private entities to whom your complaint has been referred. In some limited circumstances, including requests from Congress, the FTC may be required by law to disclose information you submit.

You have the option to submit your information anonymously. However, if you do not provide your name and contact information, law enforcement agencies and other organizations will not be able to contact you for more information to help in identity theft investigations and prosecutions.

Part Two

Banking and Bank Services

Chapter 11

Banking Basics

You Can Bank on It: A safe and convenient place to keep your money

Banks—including commercial banks, savings and loan associations and savings banks—and credit unions are companies that keep your money safe and provide you with easy ways to access it. A bank account can also help you keep track of how you spend your money.

Banks are for-profit companies—their income comes from charging fees and lending money. Account balances in banks are insured by the federal government. Your basic insurance depends on the size of your balance—up to $100,000 per person at the same bank is covered. But you may have more than $100,000 insurance coverage if you also have different kinds of accounts at the same bank, such as a joint account with another person or an Individual Retirement Account (IRA). Insured institutions must display an official sign showing they are covered by the Federal Deposit Insurance Corporation (FDIC).

A credit union is a non-profit cooperative financial institution owned and controlled by its members. Credit unions serve groups that share something in common, such as where they work or live or their place of worship. Credit unions provide checking and savings accounts and loans, often at better rates than commercial banks.

The National Credit Union Share Insurance Fund, administered by the National Credit Union Administration, an agency of the federal government, insures credit union deposits for up to $100,000 per account.

To find a credit union that you can join, call the Credit Union National Association at 800-358-5710, or visit its website (http://www.cuna.org).

Checking Up on New Customers

If you apply to open a bank account and you're rejected, it's probably because your name is listed in the database of ChexSystems, the major national account verification company. Account verification services help banks screen out applicants who have mishandled bank accounts in the past. If you ever overdrew your checking account and then abandoned it while you still had a negative balance, your name might be included in ChexSystems' database.

ChexSystems is by federal law considered a "specialty credit reporting bureau" and must comply with the Fair Credit Reporting Act (FCRA), enforced by the Federal Trade Commission (FTC). Reports about individuals remain on file for five years, unless the bank or credit union that filed the report removes it sooner. The decision to delete a report is up to the bank or credit union that provided the information.

As of December 2004, you have the right to one free copy of your ChexSystems report each year (http://www.chexhelp.com or 800-428-9623). Your report is free if you have been denied a bank account in the past 60 days or if you are a victim of bank fraud. An example of bank fraud is when someone steals your checks and forges your signature in order to use them.

Your ChexSystems report includes instructions for disputing inaccurate information. The company must investigate your claim and notify you of the results within 30 days.

Checking Accounts

Checking accounts let you deposit and withdraw money and write checks to pay for purchases and bills. Joint accounts allow co-owners, such as a husband and wife, to have equal access to the account.

With most checking accounts, you will be given a card that allows you to withdraw cash and make deposits at your bank's automated teller machines (ATMs) and withdraw cash at machines owned by other banks. Your card will have a personal identification number (PIN). You also may be able to use your ATM card and PIN to buy things and get cash back at stores.

Banks and credit unions may offer various types of checking accounts:

- Free checking—with no monthly maintenance fees and no minimum balance requirements—is often available if you agree to have your paycheck or benefits check deposited directly into the account electronically. Direct deposit has the added benefits of safety and security (your check can't be lost or stolen) and convenience (you don't have to go to the bank or ATM to make a deposit). Free checking also may be available if you agree to use ATMs for deposits and withdrawals and avoid teller visits.

- Electronic transfer accounts (ETAs) may be available if you receive federal benefits, such as Social Security or Supplemental Security Disability Income (SSDI). The low-cost government-sponsored account offers an ETA debit card and four free withdrawals per month. Withdrawals can be made at your bank's or credit union's ATMs or at point-of-sale (POS) terminals at stores. There are no check writing privileges with an ETA. To find out if a bank or credit union near you offers ETAs, call 888-382-3311 or visit the ETA website (http://www.eta-find.gov).

- Basic or Lifeline accounts tend to have no (or very low) minimum balance requirements—which means you won't get hit with a monthly fee if your account balance dips too low. Some states require that banks offer basic checking to accommodate low-income customers. These accounts sometimes have limited check writing privileges.

- Internet banking allows you to access your bank account from your computer. If you set up an account with an internet-only bank, you will have to mail your deposits to the bank and use local ATMs for cash withdrawals. Many internet-only banks give you a credit for ATM fees you will be charged when you use other banks' ATMs.

- Senior or student accounts offer no (or very low) minimum balance requirements. Check writing may be limited on these accounts, with a per-check fee if you exceed the monthly allowance.

Using a Debit Card

If your bank issues you an automated teller machine (ATM) card with a MasterCard or Visa logo on it, you have a debit card. A debit card is connected directly to your bank account. When you use it, money goes from your account to the company you are paying. It can be used wherever MasterCard or Visa cards are accepted, even overseas.

You can use debit cards in two ways:

- To use your card at an ATM or a point-of-sale (POS) terminal at a store, you have to provide your personal identification number (PIN).

- You can also use your debit card at stores and restaurants that accept credit cards, without providing a PIN. You will be asked to sign a receipt.

Be careful with your debit card.

Keep a close eye on your debit card. To avoid any liability for losses arising from its unauthorized use, tell the bank right away if your card is lost or stolen.

When your debit card is lost or stolen, it could be easy for others to use because a PIN is not always required. You are liable for a small amount—or maybe nothing at all—when your card is used without your authorization. But it can take time and effort to prove your case to the bank and get your money back.

Always report a lost or stolen card right away. Your liability may be limited to zero if you report the loss within two business days, and to $50 if you report it more than two business days after realizing your card is missing. However, you could lose all the money in your bank account and the unused portion of your line of credit for overdrafts if you fail to report an unauthorized transfer or withdrawal within 60 days after your bank statement is mailed to you.

If you give your card and your PIN to someone, you are responsible for any withdrawals, even if you didn't authorize them. Guard your PIN carefully—never write it on the card or give it to anyone else.

Savings Accounts

A savings account is a safe place to keep your money while earning interest on it.

When you open a savings account, you might be given a passbook in which the bank will record your deposits and withdrawals. Some banks don't use passbooks—they send you a monthly or quarterly transaction record (statement). You can request an ATM card that can be used for deposits and withdrawals. (You also can use the bank's deposit and withdrawal slips and go to a teller.) Depending on the bank and the type of savings account, the number of free ATM withdrawals may be limited to a few each month.

Money in a savings account earns interest—a return on your money. Most banks do not pay much interest on savings accounts—usually 1% or 2%. Interest is expressed as an annual percentage rate (APR)—the amount your money would earn if left on deposit for one year. Currently most banks pay 1% interest on savings accounts. If you have $1,000 on deposit for a year, it would earn $10.

There are two kinds of interest, simple and compound. Compound interest is better, because it allows you to earn interest not only on your initial deposit but also on the interest you earn.

Certificates of Deposit

Certificates of deposits, or CDs, offer a guaranteed interest rate for a specified term, such as one year.

You can choose the length of time that your money is on deposit—from a few months to several years. The longer the term, the higher the interest rate. If you withdraw your money before the term ends (maturity), you will lose interest. Many banks charge a penalty for early withdrawal. A penalty could cost you some of the money you deposited.

Safe Deposit Boxes

Safe deposit boxes can be a good place to store paperwork or items that would be difficult to replace in case of fire, flood, or theft.

Because only the box holder has access to the contents, they also offer privacy. Some insurance companies charge lower insurance premiums on valuables kept in a safe deposit box instead of at your home. Don't keep the original copy of your will or life insurance policy in a safe deposit box because it might be sealed at the time of death and your survivors will need a court's permission to open it.

Opening a Bank Account

To open an account, go to a bank branch or credit union office. Bring identification with your photo and signature on it and your Social

Security number. If you don't have a driver's license, state identification card or passport, call before you go to ask what you could use instead.

Bring money—cash or a check—to deposit when you open an account. Call beforehand to find out what the minimum opening deposit requirement is.

To help you find the right bank or credit union, make some calls in advance.

If you think you qualify, ask about a Lifeline or ETA account. Describe your needs to the bank representative. For instance, explain that you write only a few checks each month or that you are not comfortable using an ATM. Ask these important questions:

- What is the minimum I need to open an account?

- What is the interest rate on the account?

- Is there a monthly fee?

- Is there any way to avoid monthly fees?

- What happens if my account balance falls below the minimum requirement?

- Is there a maximum number of checks I can write each month?

- Is there a fee for using your ATMs?

You can buy personalized checks from the bank (some banks charge as much as $25 for a box of 200) or from a mail-order check printing service which offers lower-cost checks. Two sources for low-cost checks are:

Checks in the Mail, 877-397-1541, http://www.citm.com

Checks Unlimited, 800-426-0822, http://www.checksunlimited.com

Balancing Your Checkbook

The bank will send you statements. Check your statement as soon as it arrives to verify that all deposits, withdrawals, debits and checks are accurate.

Keep a running balance of all deposits, withdrawals, debits and checks in your checkbook register. When your monthly statement arrives, reconcile your account by following the step-by-step instructions in the statement.

Tips for Keeping Bank Costs Down

- Ask if you can combine the balances in your checking and savings accounts to meet the minimum balance requirement and avoid maintenance fees.

- Save on ATM fees by using your own bank's machines or those owned by banks that don't charge fees to non-customers. If you can't avoid a fee, take out larger sums less frequently to avoid repeat fees on numerous smaller withdrawals.

- Use direct deposit for your paycheck or government benefits check. The money is sent to your account electronically. Direct deposit is faster, safer and more convenient and may make you eligible for a free account.

- Buy checks from a mail-order company instead of your bank.

- Ask the bank to reverse occasional late fees or bounced check fees.

- An optional bank service called overdraft protection saves you from bouncing checks. Transfer fees and/or interest usually apply but are a lot lower than bounced check fees.

Resolving Problems

Mixed-up deposits, no-show bill payments or double debits—mistakes like this don't happen every day. But when they do occur, complain as soon as possible. The law may limit the window of opportunity for filing complaints.

If you have a complaint, start by calling a customer service representative or visiting your bank.

Ask for the person's name and write it down. During the conversation, offer a solution and ask the representative to correct the problem by a certain date. Don't lose your temper. Raising your voice or making threats will not gain the cooperation of bank employees.

Summarize your discussion with the representative in a letter and send it to the bank. Attach documentation of your complaint. (Make copies for the bank—do not give away your originals.) The letter may help prove you took timely action.

If you are not satisfied with the bank's response, you can complain to the bank's regulator.

- Banks with "national" in the name or "N.A." after the name are regulated by the Comptroller of the Currency, 800-613-6743 (http://www.occ.treas.gov).

- Federal savings and loans and savings banks are regulated by the Office of Thrift Supervision, 800-842-6929 (http://www .ots.treas.gov).

- State-chartered banks are regulated by state banking authorities. To find your state agency, look in the government section of your white pages directory or on the internet (http://consumer action.gov/caw_state_resources.shtml).

- Federally chartered credit unions are regulated by the National Credit Union Administration, 703-518-6330 (http://www.ncua.gov).

If you don't think your bank falls into any of these categories, contact the FDIC at 800-934-3342, which co-regulates any bank that is covered by FDIC insurance.

Chapter 12

Internet Banking

There is a lot you should know about internet banking. It can save you time, money, and effort, but it's important to protect yourself from potential pitfalls. Below is information on banking options, different types of online banking, services and advantages, protecting your privacy, "cookies" and privacy, security, regulations that protect consumers, and filing a complaint against a financial institution.

Banking Consumers' Options

- You can go to a traditional "brick and mortar" institution that has a building and personal service representatives, but doesn't offer internet banking services.

- Or you can bank at a "brick and click" financial institution that has a physical structure, and also offers internet banking services.

- Or you can choose a "virtual" bank or financial institution that has no public building and exists only online.

Internet banking, and other types of online banking, offer advantages such as speed and convenience. But since the internet is a public network, it presents some privacy and security issues. Knowing the

Reprinted from "What You Should Know about Internet Banking," an online financial education publication of the Federal Reserve Bank of Chicago, http://www.chicagofed.org, 2006.

"Do's and Don'ts" of internet banking can help make your online banking experience more productive, safe, and enjoyable.

Two Different Types of Online Banking

Internet banking is usually conducted through a personal computer (PC) that connects to a banking website via the internet. For example, a consumer at home accesses a financial institution's website via a modem and phone line or other telecommunications connection, and an internet service provider such as America Online, Microsoft's MSN Network, Earthlink, Juno, or AT&T WorldNet.

Internet banking also can be conducted via wireless technology through both personal digital assistants (PDAs) or cellular phones.

Electronic banking is conducted by using automatic teller machines (ATMs), telephones (not via the internet), or debit cards. Debit cards look like a credit card. But unlike a credit card, using a debit card removes funds from your bank account immediately.

What Internet Banking Offers—Services and Advantages

As a consumer, you can use internet banking to:

• Access account information, review bills, pay bills, transfer funds, apply for credit, or trade securities.

• You can find out if a check has cleared or when a bill is due.

• You can apply for mortgages, shop for the best loan rates, and compare insurance policies and prices.

• And you can do all of these things anytime you want to—day or night.

Some people like to tie banking functions into personal financial software such as Intuit's Quicken or Microsoft's Money. This can make record-keeping and tax preparation quicker and easier. Many consumers also like the idea of not waiting in line to do their banking, and paying their bills without shuffling papers and buying stamps.

Protecting Your Privacy

You need to be concerned about privacy and security. Consider this: When you bank via the internet, your personal and financial information may be shared with others without your knowledge.

A financial institution may want to share information about you to help market products specific to your needs and interests. For example, it might share information about your average checking account balance with an affiliate selling life insurance or securities.

Financial institutions have policies about what information they collect, how they use this information and with whom they will share it. Financial institutions are required to provide customers with a copy of their privacy policy. Reviewing this policy can tell you what information your financial institution keeps about you, and what information, if any, it shares with its affiliates or others.

You have the right to tell your financial institution not to share your personal information with others without your consent. You should be given a choice to "opt out," allowing you to limit sharing of your personal information.

- Do check for an "opt out" option.

How "Cookies" Could Affect Your Privacy

Internet technology allows financial institutions and other websites to track your browsing habits while at their site. This may be done using a small file stored on your PC called a "cookie." Tracking your browsing gives financial institutions information about your apparent interests and preferences. It helps them to potentially market goods and services to you based on these interests and preferences.

- Do check your financial institution's website privacy statement. Determine if the website uses cookies or otherwise tracks your browsing habits. If this tracking practice concerns you, your PC's web browser may offer useful options.

A web browser is a program on your PC that enables you to browse websites over the internet (Internet Explorer and Netscape are two examples of browsers). Check the Preferences or Tools areas of your browser to look for cookies. Your browser may offer the option to notify you before a cookie is created, identifying who is attempting to place the cookie and giving you the option to accept or reject it. Your browser also may offer you the option to reject all cookies, or to accept all cookies.

Just be aware that some websites are designed to function properly only when their cookies are accepted. Blocking cookies may prevent normal access to certain websites or to some of their online options. If this happens, you can easily begin accepting cookies again.

• Do check your browser's options for accepting or rejecting cookies.

Security Tips—How to Protect Your Personal Information

Since the internet is a public network, it's important to safeguard your banking information, credit card numbers, Social Security number, and other personal information.

Some consumers have had credit card numbers and Social Security numbers stolen and used fraudulently. Of course, this can happen even if you don't bank online. By taking reasonable steps to protect your personal information, you can reduce the chances that it may be stolen.

• Do ask your financial institution about its security practices. How does it safeguard your information during transmission and on their website?

Websites use uniform resource locators (URL) as a kind of internet street address. You can tell your browser which website you want to go to with the URL. When a URL begins with http plus an "s", it identifies the site as "secure," meaning that it encrypts or scrambles transmitted information. This prevents others from seeing your information when it travels over the internet.

Also, most browsers and web pages display a small icon of a locked padlock or a key to show that the site is encrypting your information during transmission. Your browser may also notify you when you are entering a "secure" website.

• Do make sure your transmissions are encrypted before doing any online transactions or sending personal information.

Is E-Mail Safe?

E-mail is usually not secure. It's not a good idea to send personal information such as your Social Security number, personal identification number (PIN) or account numbers via e-mail, unless you know it is encrypted.

• Don't send personal information by ordinary e-mail.

• Do change any passwords or PINs you receive via e-mail that are not encrypted.

Other Security Tips

Do

- Do make sure you are on the right website. Impostors have created websites with similar names to trick unsuspecting consumers into revealing personal information.

- Do make sure that the financial institution is properly insured. It should be insured by the Federal Deposit Insurance Corporation (FDIC). FDIC coverage only applies to deposit products such as savings accounts, checking accounts and Certificates of Deposit (CDs). The coverage does not apply to transactions involving mutual funds, stocks, bonds, and annuities.

- Do be "password smart." When possible, use a mix of letters and numbers for added safety. Change your password regularly. Keep your password or PIN to yourself. Avoid easy-to-guess passwords like first names, birthdays, anniversaries, or Social Security numbers.

- Do check bank, debit, and credit card statements thoroughly every month. Keep good records. Save information about banking transactions. Check this information for agreement with account statements, debit card bills, and credit card bills. Look for any errors or discrepancies.

- Do report errors, problems, or complaints promptly.

- Do keep virus protection software up-to-date. Back-up key files regularly.

- Do exit the banking site immediately after completing your banking.

Don't

- Don't have other browser windows open at the same time you are banking online.

- Don't disclose personal information such as credit card and Social Security numbers unless you know whom you are dealing with, why they want this information and how they plan to use it.

- Don't download files sent by strangers or click on hyperlinks from people or sites you don't know. Sometimes doing this can infect your computer with viruses that can damage hardware or software.

Consumer Regulations that Protect You

There are federal regulations that protect consumers against unauthorized transactions, including internet bank transactions as well as those conducted via an automated teller machine (ATM) or using a debit card.

The Electronic Fund Transfer Act, or Regulation E, says a consumer's liability for an unauthorized transaction is determined by how soon the financial institution is notified. A consumer could be liable for the entire amount unless the unauthorized transaction is reported within 60 days of receipt of the financial institution's statement detailing the unauthorized transaction. The sooner the unauthorized transaction is reported, the less the level of liability; therefore, it's important to report unauthorized transactions immediately to limit loss. It's also important to remember that it might take time while the unauthorized transaction is being investigated for money deducted from your account to be credited back to it.

The Truth-in-Lending Act, or Regulation Z, governs illegal credit card use. While bank transactions conducted over the internet are governed by Regulation E, credit card purchases over the internet are governed by Regulation Z. When making purchases via the internet, it's smart to use a credit card. That's because if a credit card is stolen or used by an unauthorized party, liability should be no more than $50 if proper notice is given to the credit card vendor. The vendor can be telephoned, but it's best to follow up the call with a letter stating that the transaction was made by an unauthorized user, and detailing the account number and the dollar amount of the unauthorized transaction. Consumers do not have to pay the disputed amount during investigation.

All financial institutions are also subject to Regulation P covering privacy and the Interagency Guidelines for Safeguarding Consumer Information.

All federally-insured financial institutions are subject to federal regulations concerning the distribution of personal information. These institutions must comply with established guidelines for safeguarding this information. They are also subject to onsite examinations to ensure compliance with consumer laws and regulations.

How to File a Complaint

It's best to contact a customer service representative or senior manager at your financial institution and discuss the problem first. The problem may simply be a misunderstanding.

But if you are still not satisfied, you can file a written complaint containing the following information:

- Your name, address, and daytime telephone number, and the name and address of the financial institution involved in your complaint or inquiry.

- Your account number, type of account, the names of the people you talked to, and a description of the problem.

- Describe exactly what happened and the dates involved. Include copies of any letters or other documents that may help to investigate the complaint; however, don't send originals. Sign and date your letter.

You may write directly to the financial institution with which you experienced the problem, or to the authority that regulates that institution. If you don't know the right regulatory authority, call the institution and ask. Or contact one or more of the following:

Federal Reserve System
Regulates state-chartered banks that are members of the Federal Reserve System
202-452-3693

Federal Deposit Insurance Corporation (FDIC)
Regulates state-chartered, non-member banks
800-934-3342

Office of Thrift Supervision
Regulates savings and loans, as well as savings banks
800-842-6929

Office of Comptroller of the Currency (OCC)
Regulates national banks
800-613-6743

National Credit Union Administration
Regulates credit unions
703-518-6330

Chapter 13

Automated Teller Machines (ATMs)

ATMs and You: Tips on Self-Service Banking

The ATM—short for "automated teller machine"—has been a part of our life since the mid-1960s. The first ATMs were strictly for getting cash. Today's machines do much more. You can probably go to one of your bank's ATMs and make a deposit or loan payment, transfer funds between accounts, or inquire about your account balance.

You may use your ATM card to get money on a trip, even in a foreign country. That way you won't have to carry extra cash that can be lost or stolen. You can even go to some ATMs to buy postage stamps or add money to a pre-paid cell phone service. ATM cards also may be used to make purchases at stores, with the payment automatically coming from your bank account.

While ATMs are very common and very beneficial, "a few people are hesitant about using ATMs and others just have a lot of questions or concerns, especially when they hear the occasional horror story," says Janet Kincaid, Federal Deposit Insurance Corporation (FDIC) Senior Consumer Affairs Officer. She adds, though, that "the more people learn how ATMs can meet their needs, the more they can use ATMs to take away some of life's hassles."

"ATMs and You: Tips on Self-Service Banking," "Tips for Avoiding or Resolving an ATM Problem," "ATM Safety: Common Sense Tips for Combating Crooks," "Simple Ways to Avoid Unnecessary Fees at the ATM," "Paying for Purchases with Your ATM Card," and "Laws Protecting ATM Users," *FDIC Consumer News*, Federal Deposit Insurance Corporation (FDIC), Spring 2004.

Tips for Avoiding or Resolving an ATM Problem

ATMs in the United States handle more than 10 billion transactions a year, and the overwhelming majority go smoothly. But sometimes things don't go the way you want or expect. Here are some problems that ATM users can encounter, plus tips for avoiding or resolving them.

ATM fraud can occur if a thief steals an existing ATM card or makes a counterfeit card, and obtains your personal identification number (PIN), which is needed to authorize transactions.

To limit your liability for any losses, it's important to immediately report the problem to your ATM card issuer. Your bank may ask you to sign an affidavit or other notice of the theft. Important: Under the Electronic Fund Transfer Act (EFTA), if you report that your ATM card is lost or stolen within two business days after you realize your card is missing, your losses are limited to a maximum of $50 for any unauthorized use. If you wait more than two business days to report a lost or stolen ATM card, your potential liability goes up significantly.

Depending on the circumstances, if it is clear that you are an innocent victim of fraud and you promptly reported the loss or theft of the card or an unauthorized transaction, many banks will voluntarily hold you to no liability.

- **My bank statement shows an incorrect amount for an ATM withdrawal:** Always save your ATM receipts until you compare them to your monthly statement or you verify your transactions online. Promptly report any error. FDIC attorney Susan van den Toorn says to be fully protected under the EFTA "you must notify your financial institution orally or in writing no later than 60 days after it sends your periodic statement."

- **The ATM ate my card:** This can happen if, for example, the card was defective or your bank suspects it may be involved in some type of fraudulent activity, according to Denise Davis, an FDIC Consumer Affairs Specialist. "Immediately contact the financial institution that issued your card," she says. Don't expect to receive your original ATM card back—you'll probably get a replacement card. The process can occur fairly quickly if you notify your bank immediately.

- **The machine cheated me:** What should you do if the ATM gives you too little cash, or no cash at all, and the receipt says you got exactly what you asked for? Immediately contact your bank to report the problem, even if the machine belongs to another financial institution or company (although it's wise to alert that other entity, too, if possible). Make sure to keep a record of the conversation. It also never hurts to follow up in writing. The next step is for the ATM's owner to determine if the machine has too much or too little cash, and why.

- **What happened to my deposit?:** When making a deposit at the ATM, record the transaction in your checkbook, including information about each check. Keep the ATM receipt and verify the deposit by reviewing your account statement or checking your account online, which is faster. If you believe some or all of your deposit was mishandled, immediately contact your bank and follow up with a letter. If a check is missing, you might have to ask the check issuer to stop payment. Also remember that deposited funds are not immediately available for you to withdraw; they will be subject to your bank's funds availability policy and federal schedules.

If you can't resolve any of these problems directly with the financial institution that issued your ATM card, consider calling or writing its federal regulator.

ATM Safety: Common Sense Tips for Combating Crooks

ATM manufacturers and financial institutions go to great lengths to prevent robberies and fraud at cash dispensing machines. They place ATMs in safe locations, light them well, and use a variety of security measures. Many banks also limit the amount of cash that can be withdrawn each day so that a thief can't quickly clean out an account. Even so, not all ATM crimes can be prevented.

Protect your ATM card: Know where it is at all times and keep it secure. Carry only the cards—debit or credit—you think you'll need. The fewer cards you carry, the less likely they'll be lost or stolen and used in a fraud attempt. Destroy old or expired ATM cards. Be sure to cut through the account number and magnetic strip before disposing of a card.

Safeguard your personal identification number (PIN): Never write your PIN on your card or on a piece of paper you keep near your card. Memorize it instead. "If a thief finds or steals your ATM card and

131

your PIN, it's like you've opened up your bank account and offered free samples," says Janet Kincaid, FDIC Senior Consumer Affairs Officer.

Don't share your PIN with anyone—not even a relative who isn't a co-owner of your account. Beware of deceptive calls or e-mails from crooks claiming to be from your bank or the police asking you to "verify" (divulge) your PIN. Make sure that no one can easily see your PIN as you enter it at the ATM keypad.

Choose an ATM carefully and use common sense: Be aware of your surroundings, particularly at night. Avoid ATMs in dark or remote areas or where people seem to be loitering.

Walk away if you notice something suspicious. Michael Benardo, a manager in the FDIC's Technology Supervision Branch, gives these examples of fraudulent recording devices found at ATMs: unusual-looking devices attached over the card slots of machines for "skimming" or gathering information from the magnetic strip on the back of the card; transparent overlays on ATM keypads that can record PINs; and tiny cameras hidden behind innocent-looking brochure holders and focused on where ATM users enter their PINs. Also go elsewhere if you see a sign directing you to only one of multiple ATMs—it could be the machine that was tampered with by a crook.

There are even reports of crooks installing "card cleaners" at an ATM. "These are really just skimming devices that capture account information, and the only cleaning they're used for is to clean out someone's account," says Benardo.

Also protect your ATM card when you use it to make purchases at retail establishments. For example, if you give an employee your card and you notice that he or she swipes it through two devices instead of one, that second device could be recording your account information for use in making a fraudulent card. Report that situation to a manager and your card issuer.

Note that some ATMs belong to non-banking companies or even individuals, not to banks or other depository institutions. While a privately owned ATM may be safe to use, "for the consumer, there's more uncertainty about who these companies are, whether they are legitimate or whether they're being audited or regulated by the government on an ongoing basis," Benardo says. He notes, for example, reports of dishonest ATM owners collecting card numbers for use in making duplicate cards and committing fraud. In general, your safest bet is to use an ATM owned by a federally insured banking institution. If you are considering using a private ATM, stick to one at a trusted merchant and make sure the ATM's owner is clearly identified.

Withdraw cash safely: Have your ATM card in your hand as you approach the ATM. When you collect your cash, immediately put it into your pocket or purse and count it later in private. Take your receipt and keep moving. The idea is to give a would-be robber less time to target you and steal your cash, wallet or purse.

What if you drive to an ATM? It's a good idea to use a drive-up ATM at a bank office or branch. Keep the engine running, lock all doors and roll up the passenger-side windows. If it's night-time and a drive-up machine isn't available, park in a well-lit area close to the ATM and, if possible, take another person with you.

Promptly report anything suspicious: Immediately notify your bank if your ATM card is lost or stolen; you notice a recording device or something else suspicious at a machine; or you receive an unsolicited call or e-mail asking for personal information, such as your account number and PIN. Also, immediately notify your card issuer about an unauthorized ATM or debit card transaction on your account. Remember that the faster you report a problem, the greater your federal protections are. Early notice also may be key in catching the crooks.

Simple Ways to Avoid Unnecessary Transaction Fees at the ATM

With ATMs, convenience is the name of the game. But as with pretty much everything in today's marketplace, convenience sometimes comes with a cost. For example, withdrawing cash from an ATM that doesn't belong to your bank or that's not part of its multi-bank ATM "network" can cost you anywhere from $1 to $4 per transaction. "The amounts may seem small but fees can add up over time," says Denise Davis, an FDIC Consumer Affairs Specialist.

What can you do to get the best of both worlds—convenient service and little or nothing in the way of fees? Here are some suggestions:

Use your own bank's ATMs whenever possible: Practically all banks offer accounts with free ATM transactions to their own customers. However, some institutions also have accounts that do charge their own customers an ATM fee. So, look carefully at the fees and choose the type of account that best fits your needs. If you plan to use ATMs a lot, consider an account with free withdrawals from an institution with many convenient locations. And if the account you choose is subject to ATM fees, you'll still pay less using your own bank's machine compared to going elsewhere and paying a second fee.

Take precautions before using another institution's ATM. Look for an ATM indicating that it doesn't impose an "access fee" or "surcharge" to non-customers. Your bank might be able to provide the names of other institutions that won't charge you a fee. Or, go to one of several internet sites that list surcharge-free ATMs. Also become familiar with your own bank's fees for using another institution's ATMs. Some banks, for example, have agreements not to charge ATM fees to each others' customers. Remember that if you're unable to use a surcharge-free machine, you'll probably face two charges—one from the ATM's owner, and the second from your own institution. Note that federal law requires that an ATM alert a non-customer about a surcharge before a transaction is completed.

Consider withdrawing larger sums each time: For example, make a single $100 or $200 ATM withdrawal instead of several $20 or $40 withdrawals. "You'll save time, energy, and the cash that you would have spent on transaction fees," says Davis.

Get cash back when using your ATM/debit card to make a purchase: "Many folks are unaware that you often can get cash back for free when you use your debit card to make purchases at the grocery store, the pharmacy or other businesses," says Elizabeth Kelderhouse, an FDIC Community Affairs Officer. Some stores also will cash a check free of charge or for a fee that would be less than what you'd pay at an ATM.

Avoid ATM-related mistakes that can trigger bounced-check fees: Immediately deduct your cash withdrawals and store purchases, including any fees, in your checkbook. Also don't rely on the ATM for information about how much money is in your checking account. "The balance shown on the ATM screen or receipt wouldn't include checks you've written that haven't been paid yet or debit card transactions that haven't been posted to the account," cautions Howard Herman, an FDIC Consumer Affairs Specialist. "Accurately maintaining your checkbook is the best way to know if you have funds available.

Paying for purchases with your ATM card: Your ATM card also is a type of debit card that may be used for purchases at "point of sale" terminals at stores, with the payment coming automatically from your bank account. Contact your financial institution if you have questions about using your ATM card or debit card for purchases.

Laws Protecting ATM Users

If you believe there's an accounting error involving an ATM trans-action: The federal Electronic Fund Transfer Act (EFTA) offers pro-tections, especially if you contact your financial institution within 60 days after the statement containing the problem was sent. Your in-stitution also must promptly investigate the matter.

If your ATM card is lost or stolen and is being used by a thief: Notify your financial institution within two business days af-ter learning that your ATM or debit card has been lost or stolen and the EFTA limits your losses to $50 or the amount of the unauthorized transfers, whichever is less. If you wait more than two business days to report a lost or stolen ATM or debit card, you could be liable for losses up to $500. And if you wait more than 60 days after receiving a bank statement that includes an unauthorized transfer—for ex-ample, a withdrawal made with a counterfeit card—the law doesn't require your bank to reimburse you for any losses due to unautho-rized transfers made after the 60-day period. After you notify your bank about a lost or stolen card, under most circumstances you will limit your liability for unauthorized transactions from that point on.

Rights to information: The EFTA also requires that you be told about ATM fees and other matters regarding transactions. Also, any ATM owner that imposes a surcharge for using its machine must disclose the amount of the fee and allow the user to cancel the transaction.

Note that some states may have greater consumer protections than those under the EFTA.

Chapter 14

Checking Accounts

Chapter Contents

137

Section 14.1

Finding the Right Checking Account

"A Shopper's Guide to Bank Products and Services—Checking Accounts: Finding the Right Balance," *FDIC Consumer News*, Federal Deposit Insurance Corporation, Summer 2005.

Most banks offer several types of checking accounts whose features and costs can vary widely. How can you know which bank and which checking account may be best for you?

Start by determining how you plan to use your checking account. Your goal should be to find the right mix of features at the right costs, preferably without a monthly maintenance fee.

Will you be writing a lot of checks each month? If so, you'll want an account that doesn't impose fees based on the number of checks you write.

Are you interested in paying bills over the internet instead of writing and mailing checks? Make sure online banking services are provided and ask about the costs.

Do you expect to make a lot of automated teller machine (ATM) withdrawals? Consider a bank with conveniently located ATMs and free withdrawals from its own machines. (Depending on the bank and the account, your bank may charge a fee for using another bank's ATM—in addition to the fee the other institution may impose.)

Review the potential costs for other services you expect to use and compare one bank's accounts with a few others. That's easy to do because the federal Truth in Savings Act requires banks to provide a written disclosure of their fees before an account is opened.

Also remember that just because an account is advertised as "free" or "no cost" it doesn't mean you'll never run up a charge. Under Federal Reserve Board rules, an institution can't advertise a "free" checking account if you could be charged a maintenance or activity fee (such as for going below a required minimum balance). But, your bank can offer a free account and still impose charges for certain services, such as check printing, ATM use, or overdrafts.

Howard Herman, a Federal Deposit Insurance Corporation (FDIC) Consumer Affairs Specialist, added that while it's important to consider an account's costs and limitations those may not always be the deciding factors. "For some people, the convenience of doing all their banking in one place may be enough to outweigh the costs or minimum balance requirements," he said. "These are personal decisions that only you can make."

Of course, you're probably not planning to overdraw your checking account, but mistakes do happen. For example, some people accidentally overdraw their checking account when using a debit card for a purchase or making an ATM withdrawal for more than the balance in their account. For each bounced check there may be a bank fee of about $25 to $35 plus charges from merchants. A bounced check that is not repaid in a timely fashion also may become part of your record and you may have difficulties opening a new checking account or getting a merchant to accept your checks.

Questions to Ask About a Checking Account

What are the fees?

The Truth in Savings Act requires institutions to disclose fees before you open a deposit account. If there is a monthly fee, ask about ways to reduce or eliminate it, such as by having your paycheck or Social Security check directly deposited to your account or by maintaining a minimum balance. Also ask about other fees, such as for using ATMs or overdrawing your account. As you shop around, consider only the fees you expect to incur and don't worry about the rest.

Is there a minimum balance requirement? What is the penalty for going below the minimum?

You may be able to meet the requirement or reduce the penalty if you have other accounts at the same bank or if you use direct deposit.

Will the account earn interest? If so, how much and what factors can raise or reduce the interest rate?

Some checking accounts pay interest, others don't. "Even if the account pays an attractive interest rate you should consider the fees and other factors so you can determine whether the overall deal is best for you," said Howard Herman, an FDIC Consumer Affairs Specialist.

If I overdraw my account, what are my options for avoiding fees for insufficient funds?

Example: Banks offer overdraft lines of credit, which work like a loan. Keep in mind that these programs typically come with their own

139

costs. Of course, the best way to avoid overdrawing your account is to keep your checkbook up-to-date by recording all transactions and regularly balancing your account.

Will the bank and the account be convenient for me?

If you make frequent visits to the bank or to ATMs, their locations (and the fees paid for ATM withdrawals) may be the most important consideration in deciding where to open a checking account.

Section 14.2

Deposited Checks Subject to Temporary Hold

"Reminder: Deposited Checks Subject to Temporary 'Hold'," *FDIC Consumer News*, Federal Deposit Insurance Corporation, Winter 2005/2006.

Federal rules allow banking institutions to put a temporary "hold" on certain deposits as a way of protecting against losses, primarily from checks drawn against accounts with insufficient funds. Depending on the type of deposit—electronic direct deposit, Treasury check, local check, large check and so on—you may have to wait anywhere from one business day to 11 business days before you can withdraw your deposit. Many consumers do not understand when their deposited funds can be made available to them. To raise awareness of the rules, we are providing responses to two common questions consumers have about holds on checks.

I deposited into my bank account in Maine a $6,000 check drawn on a bank in Texas. The next day, I received a notice from my bank that part of my deposit was being held for 11 business days because it is a "large deposit." Is my bank allowed to do this?

Yes. Federal Reserve Board (Fed) rules governing funds availability permit a bank to hold a large check ($5,000 or more) for up to seven business days if it's a local check and up to 11 business days if it's a non-local check.

First, be aware that $100 of the deposit must be made available after one business day as a way of getting some of the funds to you quickly. In addition, the bank must make the first $5,000 of the deposit available for withdrawal according to the bank's policy for non-local checks (which should be no later than the fifth business day after the deposit). For the remaining $1,000 of the $6,000 deposit, the bank is permitted under the rules to withhold the money up to 11 business days. The rules issued by the Fed also specify how and when you must be informed of the hold being imposed.

A friend says that her bank never places a hold on her deposited checks. My bank always places holds on my checks. Aren't banks supposed to use the same schedule for making funds available?

No. While all banks are subject to the same maximum hold periods established by law and the rules issued by the Fed, each bank may make deposits available sooner. Each bank determines what its policy will be. It can make all of the funds available immediately or delay availability up to the maximums permitted by law. There is no requirement that banks uniformly provide the same availability schedule.

Finally, if you need funds from a deposit quickly or if you're unsure about your bank's check-hold policies, talk with a manager at your bank.

Section 14.3

Protect Yourself from Bounced-Check Fees

"Protecting Yourself from Overdraft and Bounced-Check Fees," Federal
Reserve Board of Governors, 2005.

How do overdrafts and bounced checks happen?

When you write a check, withdraw money from an ATM, use your
debit card to make a purchase, or make an automatic bill payment or
other electronic payment for more than the amount in your checking
account, you overdraw your account. Your bank (or your savings and
loan or credit union) has the choice to either pay the amount or not. If
it pays even though you don't have the money in your account, you may
be charged an "overdraft" fee. If your bank returns your check without paying it, you may be charged a "bounced-check" or "nonsufficient
funds" fee. The person or company that you wrote the check to—for
example, a store, your landlord, or the phone company—may charge
you a "returned-check" fee in addition to the fee your bank charges you.

How can you avoid overdraft and bounced-check fees?

The best way to avoid overdraft and bounced-check fees is to manage your account so you don't overdraw it.

- Keep track of how much money you have in your checking account by keeping your account register up-to-date. Record all
  checks when you write them and other transactions when you
  make them. Don't forget to subtract any fees.

- Pay special attention to your electronic transactions. Record
  your ATM withdrawals and fees, debit card purchases, and
  online payments.

- Don't forget about automatic bill payments you may have set
  up for utilities, insurance, or loan payments.

- Keep an eye on your account balance. Remember that some
  checks and automatic payments may not have cleared yet.

- Review your account statements each month. Between statements, you can find out which payments have cleared and check your balance by calling your bank or by checking online or at an ATM. Be sure to find out the actual amount in your account—your account balance not including any funds available to you through "courtesy overdraft-protection," or "bounce coverage," plans.

Sometimes mistakes happen. If you do overdraw your account, deposit money into the account as soon as possible to cover the overdraft amount plus any fees and daily charges from your bank. Depositing money into your account can help you avoid additional overdrafts and fees.

What are "courtesy overdraft-protection" or "bounce coverage" plans?

Many banks (as well as savings and loans and credit unions) offer "courtesy overdraft-protection" or "bounce coverage" plans so that your checks do not bounce and your ATM and debit card transactions go through. With these plans, you'll still pay an overdraft fee or a bounce coverage fee to the bank for each item. But you will avoid the merchant's returned-check fee and will stay in good standing with the people you do business with.

How much do courtesy overdraft-protection, or bounce coverage, plans cost?

Plans vary, but most banks charge a flat fee (often $20 to $30) for each item they cover. And many set a dollar limit on the total amount your account may be overdrawn at any one time. For example, the bank might cover overdrafts up to a total of $300, including all the fees. In addition, some banks charge a daily fee—say $5 a day—for every day your account is overdrawn.

Example: Suppose you forgot that you had only $15 in your account and wrote a check for $25, used an ATM to get $40 cash, and used your debit card to buy $30 worth of groceries. In these three transactions you've spent a total of $95—and overdrawn your account by $80 ($95 − $15 = $80). How much will your forgetfulness cost you?

If you have a courtesy overdraft-protection plan, your bank may decide to cover all three transactions. And each of the three overdrafts will trigger a fee. You will owe your bank the $80 that you spent even though it wasn't in your account, plus the three overdraft fees. If your overdraft fee is $25 per overdraft, you will owe your bank $155: $80 + $75 (3 x $25).

What are some other ways to cover overdrafts?

Banks, savings and loans, and credit unions may provide other ways of covering overdrafts that may be less expensive. Ask your bank about these options before making your choice. You may be able to:

- Link your checking account to a savings account you have with the bank. If you overdraw your checking account, the bank can transfer funds from your savings account to your checking account. Ask your bank about transfer fees.

- Set up an overdraft line of credit with the bank. You need to apply for a "line of credit" just as you would apply for a regular loan. If you overdraw your account, the bank will lend you the funds by using your line of credit to cover the overdraft. You will pay interest on this loan, and there may be an annual fee. But the overall costs may be less than the costs for courtesy overdraft-protection plans.

- Link your account to a credit card you have with the bank. If you link your account to a credit card, any overdraft amount becomes a cash advance on your credit card. You will probably be charged a cash-advance fee, and interest charges on the advance will start immediately. The cost of this option depends on the interest rate on your credit card and how long you take to pay back the advance.

Table 14.1. Ways to cover your overdrafts

Ways to cover your overdrafts	Example of possible cost for each overdraft*
Good account management	$0
Link to savings account	$5 transfer fee
Overdraft line of credit	$15 annual fee + 12% APR
Link to cash advance on credit card	$3 cash-advance fee + 18% APR
Courtesy overdraft-protection plan	$20 to $30
Bounced check	$40 to $60 ($20 to $30 bank fee + $20 to $30 merchant fee)

*These costs are only examples. Ask your bank, savings and loan, or credit union about its fees.

The choice is yours. Consider the ways to cover your overdrafts as shown in Table 14.1.

What do you need to know about courtesy overdraft-protection, or bounce coverage, plans?

- Avoid using these plans as short-term loans—they are costly forms of credit.

- If you overdraw your account, get money back into your account as soon as possible. Remember that you need to put enough money back into your account to cover both the amount of your overdraft and any bank fees.

- Even if you have one of these plans, there is no guarantee that your bank will cover your checks, ATM withdrawals, and debit card and other electronic transactions that overdraw your account.

- Good account management is the lowest-cost way to protect your hard-earned money. If you need overdraft protection every now and then, ask your bank about the choices and services that are right for you.

What should you do if you have a problem or complaint about courtesy overdraft-protection, or bounce coverage, plans?

If you have a complaint, first try to resolve the problem directly with your bank, savings and loan, or credit union. If you are unable to resolve the problem, you may want to file a complaint with one of the state or federal agencies responsible for enforcing consumer banking laws.

For more information, contact the federal agency responsible for regulating your financial institution.

Section 14.4

Protect Yourself against Check Fraud

"Check Fraud," an undated document produced by Federal Reserve Financial Services (www.frbservices.org); accessed July 18, 2006.

Check fraud affects every financial institution, every business, and every individual throughout the United States and around the world. Industry sources estimate that check fraud and counterfeiting costs our nation between $10 and $14 billion per year.

This section offers a look at the various forms of check fraud and what each of us can do to prevent it. If you have any questions or concerns, please contact your local Federal Reserve Bank.

Forms of Check Fraud

Forged signatures: Forged signatures usually involve the use of legitimate blank checks, with a false imitation of the payor signature on the signature line. Many cases of forged signatures are perpetrated by a person known to the valid payor. "Employees gone bad" are one source of forged signatures. In other cases, signatures are forged on blank checks stolen from the mail while being shipped from the check printer to the account holder. The theft of blank check stock from the mail tends to increase following natural disasters when account holders have to replace destroyed check stock.

Forged endorsements: Forged endorsements often involve the theft of valid checks which are then endorsed and cashed or deposited by someone other than the payee. Marital partners involved in separation or divorce proceedings are a common source for forged endorsements. Forged endorsements can also appear on checks made payable to more than one party when one party endorses the check for all parties.

Counterfeit checks: Counterfeit checks are the fastest growing source of fraudulent checks. Check counterfeiters use today's sophisticated color copiers to copy valid checks. Exact imitations of genuine

146

checks can be created with readily available desktop publishing capabilities. Scanning a real check into a computer, and then using desktop publishing software to change some of the check information, allows the counterfeiter to include many valid check components into the imitation. When this counterfeit check is printed on a high quality laser printer, extremely authentic looking "bad" checks can be created. Some of these counterfeit checks even include MICR (magnetic ink character recognition) line characters. As computer technology continues to become more widespread, this form of check fraud has the potential for explosive growth in the near future. Almost any kind of check can be counterfeited, including cashier's, payroll, government, and traveler's checks.

Altered checks: Altered checks are defined as valid check stock with certain fields changed. When the payee name is changed, payment is made to the wrong person. The courtesy and/or written amount can be increased, resulting in overpayment to the payee. Some checks have had the MICR line altered with bogus information (such as the routing/transit (ABA) number or the account number) to slow down the clearing/return process. Checks can be altered to include information that assists the criminal in negotiating the check. For example, bank officer approval stamps have been lifted from one check and included on another check of higher value.

Check kiting: Check kiting requires multiple bank accounts and the movement of moneys between accounts. The check kiter takes advantage of the time required by a bank to clear a check. A check drawn on one bank is deposited in a second bank without having proper funds to cover the check. When the deposit is made, the bank grants the depositor a conditional credit, and will allow the customer to draw checks against uncollected funds. The customer then writes a check on the second bank and deposits it in the first bank to cover the original check. Unless detected, this process can continue indefinitely, covering one check written against insufficient funds with another check.

Third-party bill paying services: Third-party bill are often misused to commit check fraud. The checks produced by these service providers do not include the payor signature. Instead, the signature line reflects something such as "signature on file." Unauthorized checks produced by third-party payment services are usually not detected until the customer reviews the monthly bank statement. By

147

the time the customer identifies the unauthorized check, it is often too late to recover the funds, since the "24-hour window" (actually until midnight of the next banking day) for the timely return of checks has long since passed. These checks usually sail right through the check sorting operation, since they include good account information and sometimes even include good serial numbers. Too often, both business and individual account holders seem unaware of how their account information, given too freely to a requesting party, can be used for fraudulent purposes.

Demand drafts: Demand drafts can be misused to commit check fraud. This practice involves the misuse of account information to obtain funds from a person's bank account without that person's signature on a negotiable instrument. Other terms for demand drafts are "preauthorized drafts" and "telephone drafts." While there are many legitimate business uses of demand drafts, such as quick-turnaround telephone transactions initiated by airlines and car rental companies, demand drafts have been used by deceptive telemarketers who obtain bank account information and withdraw unauthorized funds from consumers' bank accounts, without their realizing that such withdrawals are occurring.

The Federal Trade Commission has published a "Telemarketing Sales Rule," effective December 31, 1995, which is designed to offer some protection to consumers and banks against deceptive telemarketing practices. Among other things, the rule requires "verifiable authorization," such as written consent or express oral authorization which is tape recorded. While rules and laws help, consumers (and businesses) still need to use demand drafts cautiously and provide account information only to known reputable payees.

Other forms of check fraud: Check fraud has also been committed by individuals opening fraudulent bank accounts or making fraudulent deposits through the automatic teller machine (ATM) network. Others have ordered checks directly from check printers using bogus names, addresses, routing numbers, and account numbers. Still others have counterfeit money orders cashed by check cashing operations.

Another scheme involves the deposit of fraudulent checks, followed by quick funds withdrawal before actual check clearing. This form of fraud is actually made easier by the fact that most banks, for competitive reasons, make funds available sooner than required by federal regulations.

Elements of a Check

Recognizing a fraudulent check is easier when you are familiar with the components that make up a good check. All parties who participate in check transactions should be aware of the following elements of a check:

Perforation: Look for at least one perforated side on the check.

Bank address: The address of the bank should correspond to the appropriate Federal Reserve District. For example, if you receive a check drawn on a bank in California, the routing/transit number generally should depict the Twelfth Federal Reserve District (12). Note, however, that some banks with offices in several Federal Reserve Districts are using a routing/transit number for one Federal Reserve District and a bank address in a different Federal Reserve District.

Federal Reserve district and office: The first two digits of field 5 (shown in Figure 14.1), the routing/transit number in the MICR line, indicate the Federal Reserve district.

- 01: Boston
- 02: New York
- 03: Philadelphia
- 04: Cleveland
- 05: Richmond
- 06: Atlanta
- 07: Chicago
- 08: St. Louis
- 09: Minneapolis
- 10: Kansas City
- 11: Dallas
- 12: San Francisco

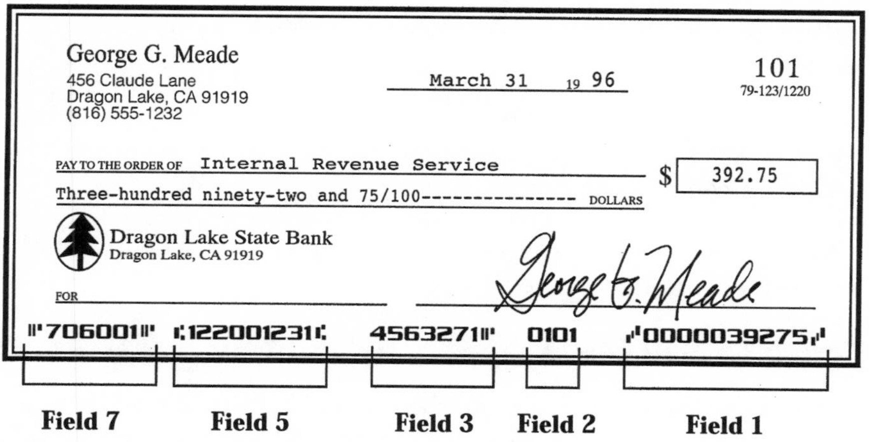

Figure 14.1. Elements of a Check.

The third digit indicates the particular District office. As an example, in the Sixth District (Atlanta), the numbers and the offices are:

- 1: Atlanta
- 2: Birmingham
- 3: Jacksonville
- 4: Nashville
- 5: New Orleans
- 6: Miami Field

In the Tenth District (Kansas City), the numbers and the offices are:

- 1: Kansas City
- 2: Denver
- 3: Oklahoma City
- 4: Omaha

In the Twelfth District (San Francisco), the **1220** depicted in Figure 14.1. would indicate the Los Angeles Office.

Bank ID number: Positions 5 through 8 of field 5 of the MICR line (see Figure 14.1) identify the issuing bank. MICR symbols (⑂ , ⑂) surround the routing/transit number in the MICR line.

Account number: Field 3 in the MICR line (see Figure 14.1) identifies the customer's account number. A MICR symbol (⑊) follows the account number in the MICR line.

Serial number: Field 2 in the MICR line (see Figure 14.1) generally identifies the check number on personal checks. The serial number in the MICR line should match the serial number at the top right corner of the check.

Auxiliary number: Field 7 in the MICR line (see Figure 14.1) identifies the auxiliary number, generally on commercial checks only. The auxiliary number generally matches the number in the top right corner of a commercial check.

Fractional routing/transit number: The fraction on the top of the check should match the bank ID in the MICR line.

Signs of a Bad Check

There are a few key signs that can tip you off to a "bogus" check. The first is perforation. Most checks produced by check printing companies have at least one perforated edge. Although some companies produce their own legitimate checks using blank check stock and laser printers with MICR-printing capabilities, the lack of a perforation often is the first signal of a phony check.

Inconsistent routing and fractional routing numbers also can indicate a counterfeit check. Many check forgers alter the routing/transit number in the MICR line to gain additional clearing time while the check is misrouted to an incorrect, distant Reserve Bank or paying bank. Forgers also print an incorrect fractional routing number to further delay presentment of the item and print a bank location on the check that is inconsistent with routing/transit and/or fractional routing numbers.

Check Security Features

As those who commit check fraud become more sophisticated, so must those who combat them. The following features are helping to make fraud more difficult.

- **Watermarks:** Since watermarks are designed to be viewed at a 45-degree angle, scanners and photocopiers are not able to reproduce them.

- **Void pantographs:** Pantograph technology protects documents from being illegally duplicated. When documents containing pantographs are copied, words like "copy" or "void" appear.

- **Warning bands:** Warning bands call attention to the security features that protect the document.

- **Laid lines:** Laid lines are unevenly spaced lines on the check that make it difficult to electronically cut and paste information on the check from a scanned image.

- **Chemically sensitive paper:** Chemically sensitive paper reveals attempts at altering the paper with eradicator chemicals. When the eradicator comes in contact with the paper, the word "void" will appear.

- **Prismatic printing:** Prismatic printing is designed to make it difficult to reproduce intricate colored backgrounds on color copies.

- **Micro printing:** Micro printing is a group of words so small that it becomes unreadable and appears as a line when copied or scanned.

Section 14.5

Check 21 and Substitute Checks

"Consumer Guide to Check 21 and Substitute Checks," Federal Reserve
Board of Governors, February 2004.

How does Check 21 affect you?

Because of Check 21 and other check-system improvements, your
checks may be processed faster—which means money may be deducted from your checking account faster. Before you write a check,
make sure that your checking account has enough money in it to cover
the check.

You may be one of the majority of consumers who do not receive
their canceled checks with their account statements. Instead, you may
receive "pictures" (known as digital images) of your checks, a list of
your paid checks, or a combination of these items. Check 21 will have
little or no effect on these practices.

On the other hand, if you do get your canceled checks back in your
regular account statements, you may notice some changes under
Check 21. For example, your bank may start sending you a combination of original checks and substitute checks in your account statements. You may use a canceled substitute check as proof of payment
just as you would use a canceled original check.

The account agreement you have with your bank governs whether
you receive canceled checks with your account statements. If you currently get canceled checks back with your statements, you will continue to receive your checks unless your bank notifies you that it is
changing your account agreement.

You may receive substitute checks in other limited circumstances.
For example, your bank may give you a substitute check if you ask to
have a particular canceled check back to prove a payment. Also, your
bank might provide a substitute check to you when returning a
"bounced" check that you deposited into your account.

By law, your bank may not pay a check from your account unless
you authorized that payment. In other words, you are protected from
having your bank pay the same check from your account more than

152

once or from having your bank pay the wrong amount for a check. Check 21 does not change these protections. However, Check 21 does give you special rights if you receive a substitute check from your bank. This text explains your rights regarding substitute checks. For your rights in other situations, contact your bank.

What is a substitute check?

A substitute check is a special paper copy of the front and back of an original check. The substitute check may be slightly larger than the original check. Substitute checks are specially formatted so they can be processed as if they were original checks. The front of a substitute check should state: "This is a legal copy of your check. You can use it the same way you would use the original check." Figure 14.2 and Figure 14.3 show what a substitute check looks like.

Figure 14.2. Front of a substitute check

Figure 14.3. Back of a substitute check

Not all copies of a check are substitute checks. For example, pictures of multiple checks printed on a page (also known as an image statement) that is returned to you with your monthly statement are not substitute checks. Online check images and photocopies of original checks are not substitute checks either. You can use image statements and other copies of checks to verify that your bank has paid a check.

Why do banks create substitute checks?

Some banks find that exchanging electronic images of checks with other banks is faster and more efficient than physically transporting paper checks. In certain circumstances, however, banks may need to use a paper check. To address this need, Check 21 allows a bank to create and send a substitute check that is made from an electronic image of the original check.

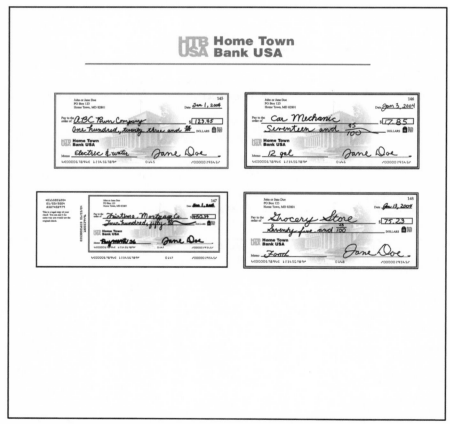

Figure 14.4. Image Statement

Can I require my bank to return my original check?

No. In general, the law does not require your bank to return your original check. Many banks destroy original paper checks. Other banks may store original checks for some period of time and then destroy them. Check 21 ensures that you have the same legal protections when you receive a substitute check from your bank as you do when you receive an original check.

What should I do if I receive a substitute check and there is a problem?

Check 21 provides a special process that allows you to claim a refund (also known as an expedited recredit) when you receive a substitute check from a bank and you think there is an error because of the substitute check. For example, you may think that you were charged twice for the same check.

You may use the special process to get a refund of the money you lost. The amount of your refund under the special process is limited to the amount of your loss or the amount of the substitute check that you received, whichever is less, plus interest on that amount if your account earns interest. If your loss is more than the amount of the substitute check, you may have the right under other laws to recover additional amounts of money.

If your bank finds that your claim is valid, you should receive your refund by the next business day after the bank's finding. Unless your bank finds that your claim is not valid, you should receive up to $2,500 of your refund (plus interest if your account earns interest) within 10 business days after your bank receives your claim. You should receive the rest of your refund (plus interest if your account earns interest) no later than 45 days after your bank receives your claim. If your bank finds that your claim is not valid, it will send you a notice explaining why.

Your bank may reverse the refund (including any interest on the refund) if it can show that the substitute check did not cause an error in your account.

How do I file a claim under the special refund procedure for substitute checks?

If you notice a problem with a substitute check, you should contact your bank as soon as possible. In general, to use the special refund procedure for substitute checks, you should contact your bank no later than 40 days from the date your bank provided the substitute check or from the date of the statement that shows the problem.

In general, you must take the following steps:

- Describe why you think the charge to your account is incorrect.

- Describe why you believe the original check or a better version of the substitute check is needed to determine whether the substitute check should have been deducted from your account.

- Estimate how much money you lost because of the substitute check. (Include any fees you were charged as a result of the substitute check. Also, alert your bank to any interest you lost, if your account earns interest.)

- Provide a copy of the substitute check, or give your bank information that will help it identify the substitute check and investigate your claim.

What if I have more questions about substitute checks?

- Contact your bank.
- Visit the online information about Check 21 at http://www.federalreserve.gov/paymentsystems/truncation.
- Contact your state's consumer protection agency or attorney general's office for information on state laws that apply to checks and substitute checks.

Remember

- When a bank uses substitute checks, your checks may be processed faster. Be sure you have enough money in your account to cover the checks that you write.

- Always review your account statement to make sure the charges are correct.

- If you receive something other than a substitute check, be aware of your rights to resolve errors under other state and federal laws.

- Contact your bank right away if you notice an error in your account.

Section 14.6

Electronic Check Conversion

"When Is Your Check Not a Check? Electronic Check Conversion,"
Federal Reserve Board of Governors, August 2006.

Suppose you're at a store making a purchase and decide to pay by check—at least, that's what you believe you're doing.

The clerk asks you for a check that is completely filled out, partially filled out, or even blank. The clerk then runs the check through a machine and hands the voided check back to you with your receipt.

What just happened? Did you pay by check? Why did the clerk return the check to you? The answer is, you just experienced electronic check conversion.

The following questions and answers explain how electronic check conversion works and what your rights are as a consumer.

What is electronic check conversion?

Electronic check conversion is a process in which your check is used as a source of information—for the check number, your account number, and the number that identifies your financial institution. The information is then used to make a one-time electronic payment from your account—an electronic fund transfer. The check itself is not the method of payment.

How will I know that my check is being used for electronic check conversion?

When you provide your check, you must be given notice that information from your check will be used to make an electronic payment from your account. The notice is required by the federal law that applies to electronic fund transfers—the Electronic Fund Transfer Act and the Federal Reserve Board's Regulation E. Notice may be provided in different ways. For example, a merchant may post a sign at the register or may give you a written notice that you'll be asked to sign.

157

What are some of the differences between electronic check conversion and using my check as payment?

- Your electronic transaction may be processed faster than a check. Be sure you have enough money in your account at the time you make the purchase.

- You have different consumer rights with an electronic check conversion transaction than when you use your check as payment. For example, with electronic check conversion, you have the right to an investigation by your financial institution when an error occurs.

What are my rights in electronic check conversion transactions?

- You have the right to receive notice when you provide your check telling you that information from the check will be used to make an electronic payment from your account.

- You have the right to receive notice when you provide your check telling you of any fee that the merchant will collect from your account electronically if you do not have enough money in your account to cover the transaction. This fee is similar to a "bounced check" fee.

- You have the right to receive a receipt when you make a purchase at a store. The receipt will contain information about the transaction, including the following:

  - Date
  - Location
  - Amount
  - Name of merchant

- You have the right to have this same information included as part of the regular account statement from your financial institution.

- You have the right to ask your financial institution to investigate any electronic fund transfers from your account that you believe are unauthorized or incorrect.

What should I do if I have a problem with an electronic check conversion transaction?

Always review your regular account statement from your financial institution. You should immediately contact your financial institution if you see a problem. Were you charged the wrong amount? Were you charged

158

twice for the same transaction? You have only 60 days (from the date your statement was sent) to tell the financial institution about the problem. Depending on the circumstances, the financial institution may take up to 45 days from the time you notify it to complete its investigation.

With electronic check conversion, may I use the same check more than once?

No. An electronic check conversion transaction is a one-time electronic payment from your account. If you were to use the same check for more than one transaction and you had a problem with one of the transactions, your financial institution might have difficulty investigating the problem because the same check number would appear more than once on your statement.

Can electronic check conversion occur if I mail a check to pay a bill?

Yes. For example, let's assume that each time you get your insurance bill there is a notice. It tells you that when you mail a check, information from that check will be used to make an electronic payment from your account. If you then send a check, you have agreed to electronic check conversion. Unlike what happens when you make a purchase at a store, however, you won't receive a receipt. Your check won't be returned to you with your account statement from your financial institution because the transaction was processed as an electronic fund transfer, not as a check transaction.

As with electronic check conversions in stores, be sure you have enough money in your account when you mail your check, keep records of your payments, and check your account statements from your financial institution to make sure the amounts charged are correct.

What if I don't want my check to be used for electronic check conversion?

If you don't want your check to be used for electronic check conversion, you may have to provide another form of payment (for example, cash, debit card, or credit card).

What if I have a question or problem with an electronic check conversion?

Contact your financial institution. For information on state laws that may apply to electronic check conversion, contact your state's consumer protection agency or attorney general's office.

159

Where can I file a complaint about a merchant or someone else I paid by electronic check conversion?

Federal Trade Commission
Consumer Response Center
600 Pennsylvania Ave., NW
Washington, DC 20580
Toll-free: 877-FTC-HELP or 877-382-4357
Website: http://www.ftc.gov

Please also send a copy of your complaint to:

Board of Governors of the Federal Reserve System
Division of Consumer and Community Affairs
Washington, DC 20551
Phone: 202-452-3693
Website: www.federalreserve.gov

Remember

Before you agree to electronic check conversion, you should first ask yourself:

- Do I understand that the information from my check will be used to make an electronic payment from my account?

- Do I have enough money in my account to cover the payment?

Before you leave the store, you should ask yourself:

- Did I receive a receipt?

- Does the amount on the receipt match the amount of my purchase?

- Was my check returned to me and voided?

When you receive your statement from your financial institution, you should:

- Make sure that the charges on your statement match your records.

- Contact your financial institution right away if you notice a problem.

Section 14.7

Key Laws Governing Checking Accounts

FDIC Consumer News, Federal Deposit Insurance Corporation, Summer 2004.

Funds availability: One way depository institutions protect themselves against losses from bad checks is to put a "hold" on certain deposits. The Expedited Funds Availability Act of 1987 sets the maximum time periods that financial institutions may hold funds deposited by check before making the money available for withdrawal. Also, the Check Clearing for the 21st Century Act (called Check 21), which became effective on October 28, 2004, speeds up the check clearing process.

Erroneous or fraudulent payments: In general, most of the protections against improper payments are covered by state laws, which can vary significantly. Typically, a bank is liable to its customer if it charges its customer's account for a check that is not "properly payable," although state laws also generally require customers to review monthly account statements and report any unauthorized transactions promptly. The new federal Check 21 law, which authorizes banks to pay based on a substitute check instead of an original check, includes provisions for "expedited recrediting" in cases of improper payment. And the Electronic Fund Transfer Act, which governs consumer rights and responsibilities for debit cards, also puts a premium on prompt notification of an unauthorized transfer using your card. Important: If you wait longer than 60 days after the date the bank mails the statement containing the debit card error, you could be liable for the full balance in your account plus any overdraft line of credit.

If you need proof of a payment: Your original canceled check or substitute check with endorsements provides proof of payment, although images of checks are also accepted often. Under Check 21, your bank may provide you a substitute check that is the legal equivalent of the original check.

Chapter 15

Debit Cards vs. Credit Cards

Chapter Contents

Section 15.1

Payment Cards: The Basics

"What You Need to Know About Payment Cards," © 2004; reprinted with permission from the Federal Reserve Bank of Philadelphia, http://www.philadelphiafed.org.

What is a payment card?

A payment card is typically a 3 3/8" by 2 1/8" plastic card with either a magnetic stripe or a computer chip that stores the card user's data, including card number and expiration date. The most familiar types of payment cards have a magnetic stripe and include credit, charge, debit, and prepaid cards.

Credit card: Any card that may be used to borrow money or buy products and services on credit. The balance can be paid in full by a set due date or paid over time with interest, as long as the borrower makes monthly minimum payments in amounts specified by the issuer. Credit cards are issued by banks, retail stores, and other businesses.

Charge card: Operates similarly to a credit card as a way to make purchases except you have to pay the total balance each month.

Debit card: A payment card that debits a designated bank account upon settlement of a transaction, such as a retail purchase or automated teller machine (ATM) withdrawal. The transaction can be authorized by the card user either with a signature or by entering a personal identification number (PIN).

Prepaid card: Also called stored-value card; contains or represents an amount of pre-loaded value. The card holder may use the balance over time or all at once. Examples of prepaid cards include retailers' gift cards, payroll cards, phone cards, and travel cards.

What is a balance transfer fee?

A balance transfer fee is a special one-time fee charged for paying off other credit card balances. While some issuers do not impose this fee, many do. It is usually a percentage of the amount transferred up to a maximum amount and is in addition to any interest charges that may accrue on the balance. Today, consumers use many different types of payment cards.

Are APR and interest rate the same thing?

They are the same. APR stands for annual percentage rate (of interest) and represents the annual interest rate that cardholders pay to borrow funds using a credit card's revolving line of credit. The APR may vary depending on the credit card and on the individual. The APR can change over time, but card issuers are required to tell consumers about any such change, either as part of the Cardholder Agreement, which governs the credit card product, or through a "Change in Terms" notice.

If I pay my balance in full each month, will I be charged interest?

Typically, no. Cardholders who pay their balances in full each month are eligible for an interest-free grace period, during which no interest is charged on their current balance until the next payment is due. It is important for cardholders to carefully read their Cardholder Agreements to understand exactly the policies and procedures governing their payment card product.

What is a credit limit?

A credit limit is the amount established by the card issuer as the maximum amount you may borrow to pay for purchases or cash advances; it is based on your creditworthiness.

Is it bad to have several credit cards?

Not necessarily. It is more important to borrow responsibly and to pay bills when they are due. Most consumers need only two credit cards: one for small purchases they pay off each month, and one for larger purchases they spread out over time. A third card for emergencies or business purposes might also be appropriate.

165

What is a minimum finance charge?

If you have a very low balance, the finance charges will be very low and may be subject to a minimum finance charge set by the card issuer. For example, if you have a $25 balance and pay an annual interest rate of 15 percent, the finance charge for one month will be approximately 32 cents. Many issuers have a minimum finance charge of 50 cents. Therefore, you would be charged 50 cents, not 32 cents, for the billing cycle.

What is the minimum payment, and how is it calculated?

The minimum payment is the amount a cardholder must pay against an outstanding balance in order to keep an account in good standing. Typically, it represents 2 percent to 3 percent of the outstanding balance but can vary by issuer and by level of outstanding balance. It is important to review your Cardholder Agreement or to check with your card issuer to confirm its minimum payment policy.

Making only the minimum payment will greatly extend the time it takes to pay off the balance. As an example, making only the minimum payment, a cardholder with a $5,000 balance and an interest rate of 15 percent will repay a total of $12,653, in principal and interest, over a period of 27 years and 11 months before the entire balance is paid off. This also assumes that no new purchases are added to the balance.

What is a cash advance?

These are funds advanced to you from your credit card line. By using your credit card and its PIN at an ATM or in person at a bank, you can receive cash. However, cash advances on credit cards are typically charged special fees and higher interest rates than when the card is used for purchases. Cash advances on credit cards are typically charged special fees and higher interest rates than when the card is used for purchases.

What is a secured credit card?

It is a credit card that requires a cash deposit as security for the account. Generally, consumers with no credit history or a poor credit history can obtain credit cards from some issuers under a secured card program. The cash deposit can start as low as $50 or $100; however, most secured card issuers require a minimum deposit in the $300 to $500 range. The security deposit generally earns interest. The deposit may be returned after satisfactory credit has been established with the issuer.

If my credit or debit cards are used without my authorization, how much could I lose?

It is very important to notify your card issuer by phone and in writing as soon as you suspect that unauthorized charges have been made using your payment card. For credit cards, federal law limits consumer liability to $50 per card for unauthorized purchases. If you report the loss before your credit cards are used, the card issuer cannot hold you responsible for any unauthorized charges.

For debit cards, federal law also limits consumer liability for unauthorized use, but in this case, the limits depend on how quickly the victim reports the fraudulent activity to the card issuer. If unauthorized activity is reported within two business days, the liability limit is $50. If reported within 60 days, the liability limit is $500. If the fraud is reported more than 60 days after the customer received the statement showing the fraudulent activity, the liability is potentially unlimited.

Many payment card issuers offer better liability protection for their customers than is required by law for either credit or debit cards, and you should check with your issuer or refer to your Cardholder Agreement to review the issuer's policies regarding unauthorized card use.

Section 15.2

Debit Cards: Beyond Cash and Checks

Debit cards are also known as check cards. Debit cards look like
credit cards or ATM (automated teller machine) cards, but operate like
cash or a personal check. Debit cards are different from credit cards.
While a credit card is a way to "pay later," a debit card is a way to
"pay now." When you use a debit card, your money is quickly deducted
from your checking or savings account.

Debit cards are accepted at many locations, including grocery stores,
retails stores, gasoline stations, and restaurants. You can use your card
anywhere merchants display your card's brand name or logo, even on
the internet. They offer an alternative to carrying a checkbook or cash.

Do You Have a Debit Card?

You may not realize that you have a debit card. Many banks are
replacing their standard ATM cards with upgraded ATM cards that
have a debit feature. You may also receive in the mail what looks like
a credit card when in fact it is a debit card.

What Is the Difference Between a Debit Card and a Credit Card?

It's the difference between "debit" and "credit." Debit means "subtract." When you use a debit card, you are subtracting your money
from your own bank account. Debit cards allow you to spend only what
is in your bank account. It is a quick transaction between the merchant and your personal bank account.

Credit is money made available to you by the bank or other financial institution, like a loan. The amount the issuer allows you to use
is determined by your credit history, income, debts, and ability to pay.
You may use the credit with the understanding that you must repay

the charges, plus interest, if you do not pay the account in full each month. You will receive a monthly statement detailing your charges and payment requirements.

Two Ways Debit Cards Work

With a PIN: You provide your personal identification number, or PIN, at the time of sale. Without a PIN, or PIN-less: You sign a receipt for the purchase, as you would with a credit card.

Some debit cards are designed to work only with a PIN, others can be used with either a PIN or a signature. PIN-only debit cards offer greater security because it's more difficult for unauthorized people to use them. Cards that can work both in the PIN and PIN-less methods offer more flexibility, especially when dealing with merchants who do not have the equipment needed to process PIN transactions.

In either case, the funds are automatically deducted from your account within a short time.

What You Should Know about Debit Cards

- Obtaining a debit card is often easier than obtaining a credit card.

- Using a debit card instead of writing checks saves you from showing identification or giving out personal information at the time of the transaction.

- Using a debit card frees you from carrying cash or a checkbook.

- Using a debit card means you may no longer have to stock up on traveler's checks or cash when you travel.

- Debit cards may be more readily accepted by merchants than checks, even when you travel.

- The debit card is a quick, "pay now" product, giving you no grace period.

- As with credit cards, you may dispute unauthorized charges or other mistakes within 60 days. You should contact the card issuer if a problem cannot be resolved with the merchant. However, using a debit card may mean you have less protection than with credit card purchase for items which are never delivered, are defective, or were misrepresented.

- Returning goods or canceling services purchased with a debit card is treated as if the purchases were made with cash or a check.

169

Be Aware

If your debit card works with either a PIN or a signature and the store accepts both, you choose which way to use it at the point of sale.

If you choose "debit" on the merchant's terminal and "swipe" your card through, you will be asked for your PIN. If you choose "credit" on the terminal and swipe your card through, you will be asked to sign a receipt. "Credit" does not mean that you will be billed, as with a credit card. The money will be debited from your account automatically.

What You Should Know before You Use a Debit Card

1. Know if it is a credit card or a debit card. Also, decide whether you want a PIN-only debit card or one that can be used with either a PIN or a signature. Ask the card issuer about your options.

2. Know if there are fees applied to using the card. Some financial institutions charge a monthly fee or a per-transaction fee, others do not. These fees are set by the card issuer and must be disclosed to consumers.

3. Know about your liability for the unauthorized use, theft, or loss of your debit card. Ask if the issuer has any special liability policies and how they work.

4. Know how problems with non-delivery, defective merchandise, or misrepresentation will be handled. This is especially important when you use a debit card to purchase goods or services for future delivery, rather than on a "cash and carry" basis. Ask the issuer about its policies for these types of disputes.

Seven Tips for Using Debit Cards Responsibly

1. If your card is lost or stolen, report the loss immediately to your financial institution.

2. If you suspect your card is being fraudulently used, report this immediately to your financial institution.

3. Take your receipts. Don't leave them for others to see. Your account number may be all someone needs to order merchandise through the mail or over the phone at your expense, especially if the card can be used without a PIN.

4. If you have a PIN number, memorize it. Do not keep your PIN number with your card. Also, don't choose a PIN number that a smart thief could figure out, such as your phone number or birthday.

5. Never give your PIN number to anyone. Keep your PIN private.

6. Always know how much money you have available in your account. Don't forget to consider money that you have set aside to cover a check that has not yet cleared your bank.

7. Deduct debits and any transaction fees from the balance in your check register immediately. Keep the receipts in one place in case you need them later.

What If My Card Is Lost or Stolen?

In the event that your card is lost or stolen, you need to know the extent of your protection. Government regulations require debit card issuers to set a maximum liability of $50 if the debit card is reported lost or stolen within two days of discovery. Liability increases to $500 if the lost or stolen debit card is reported within 60 days. Neglect to notify the bank of the theft within 60 days after a bank statement is sent, and you could lose everything in your checking and overdraft accounts.

Check with your financial institution about your liability. Many debit card issuers offer consumers better protection than the government regulations require. Some even offer consumers "zero liability" in cases of fraud, theft, or other unauthorized card use if the cardholder reports the problem within a certain time.

If a problem arises, remember that it is your money that is at stake.

• Under government regulations, financial institutions may have up to 20 days to provide provisional credit to consumers for losses due to debit card theft or unauthorized use of the card.

• In cases where a cardholder's debit card has been used fraudulently, some issuers promise even faster provisional credit for lost funds, in as few as five business days after notification.

• You may not know that your debit card or its number has been stolen until checks you have written have bounced. Be aware that the issuer is not required to waive bounced check charges or cover any fees that may be imposed by the recipients of checks that unintentionally bounced because a debit card was stolen. Many banks do, however, refund these fees as a measure of good customer service.

171

Debit cards offer the consumer many conveniences. They are more readily accepted by merchants than checks, especially when you are out of your own state or in other countries. You are not required to provide identification or give personal information when using a debit card. This makes the transaction quicker and allows you to keep personal information to yourself.

However, because the money spent using a debit card comes directly from your bank account, you need to be careful in order to prevent fraudulent use of your card number.

Section 15.3

Debit or Credit: Which Is Better?

Excerpted from "Debit or Credit? Which is Better?" by Rebecca Lindsey, updated December 2006, available at www.cardratings.com. © 2006 U.S. Citizens for Fair Credit Card Terms, Inc. All rights reserved. Reprinted with permission.

Many people know they have an option to use a debit card, but don't take advantage of it because they have a lack of knowledge or interest, or simply are in the habit of writing checks. While checks, ATM cards, and credit cards are fairly self-explanatory, many people fail to see much difference between a credit card and a debit card. So the questions are, is there a significant difference, and is one better than the other?

What's the Difference?

Credit: Every time you use a credit card, you are actually borrowing money that is made available to you by a bank or other financial institution. The institution pays the debt to the vendor, and in turn, you pay the money back to the institution. By signing up for a credit card, you agree to pay back the money that you borrowed, in addition to any interest drawn on the amount you borrowed.

Debit: Odds are, you have a debit card in your wallet or purse right now, since many ATM cards are programmed to have debit options. Issued by your bank, debit cards take funds directly from the money that you have in your bank account—in a sense acting like a check, just faster. With a debit card, you don't have to carry cash or checks, and it is very convenient to shop at a variety of places including gas stations, grocery stores, restaurants, and retail stores. They provide instant access to your money and are accepted worldwide.

Debit cards are used much like credit cards, meaning that the store you are shopping at 'swipes' them, and you are normally given the option of signing your receipt instead of using a required PIN number (you can enter your PIN number if your prefer). You also typically don't have to show a picture ID.

Which Is Better?

Maybe you still don't see much of a difference, besides where the money comes from and when you have to pay up. So which one is better to use? It depends upon how careful you are with your card and what you are using the card for.

The features that make debit cards convenient—instant access to your money, lack of a required PIN number, and not having to drag out your photo ID when you use it—make fraud that much easier. Unless reported quickly, theft of your debit card can quickly devastate your bank account. This is where you begin to see a difference between credit and debit cards.

Credit card companies are held to strict liability laws; the law limits consumer liability for credit card fraud to $50 and many credit cards, including all Visa and MasterCard credit cards, now have zero liability policies (your liability for unauthorized transactions is $0). In addition, if you notice suspicious charges on your credit card statement such as double billing or an incorrect charge, the credit card company is obligated to investigate if you send in a written request within 60 days.

For debit card fraud, your liability is $50 if you notify the bank within two days of noticing the fraudulent charges. After two days, your liability increases to $500, and up to your entire account balance after 60 days. So if you notice that your card is missing within two days and report it, you can only be made to pay up to $50. However if you report the theft after two days, you can be held responsible for paying for purchases or charges that you didn't make. Although many banks have started to implement voluntary plans to limit customer's liability to $50, there is no federal law regarding this issue. Finally,

Visa and MasterCard do extend limited zero liability protection to debit cards branded with the Visa or MasterCard logo, but this protection has certain restrictions.

The key to protecting yourself when you suspect that your stuff has been stolen is acting fast! The Federal Trade Commission offers an excellent resource that can help you respond quickly in case your wallet or purse is stolen.

In addition to stricter liability laws, credit cards also offer more consumer protection on purchases made. Use credit cards for very large or fragile purchases, and for objects that will be delivered to your home after the purchase; this gives you added insurance in case the purchase is damaged in route.

One final advantage of credit cards is that they are a great tool for consumers that are seeking to establish or reestablish an attractive credit history. Responsible credit card usage can improve one's credit rating. Credit cards typically report account activity to at least one of the three major credit bureaus on a monthly basis. An attractive credit rating will improve your chances of obtaining favorable credit terms (low interest rates and low fees) for all types of loans, including automobile loans, mortgages, and personal loans.

Discipline Yourself

One pitfall that many consumers fall into is not keeping up with their debit transactions. This is like writing checks and not recording your purchases—you may end up trying to spend money that you don't have. If you're not good at recording your check transactions, you will need to discipline yourself to keep up with your transaction receipts.

Probably the main thing to remember if you are using a debit card regularly is that it's not just a card; it's ready access to your money. Be as careful with it as you would with your wallet if it had the contents of your entire bank account in it. The National Consumers League is a good resource if you would like even more information on debit cards. It offers information and tips for responsible use of debit cards, including record keeping and theft report.

Section 15.4

Card Blocking:
A Concern with Both
Debit and Credit Cards

"Credit and Debit Card Blocking," U.S. Federal Trade Commission
(www.ftc.gov); June 2003.

Have you ever been told you were over your credit card limit, or
had your debit card declined, even though you knew you had available credit, or money in your bank account? If this happened shortly
after you stayed in a hotel or rented a car, the problem could have
been card "blocking."

What's Blocking?

When you use a credit or debit card to check into a hotel or rent a
car, the clerk usually contacts the company that issued your card to
give an estimated total. If the transaction is approved, your available
credit (credit card) or the balance in your bank account (debit card)
is reduced by this amount. That's a "block." Some companies also call
this placing a "hold" on those amounts.

Here's how it works: Suppose you use a credit or debit card when
you check into a $100-a-night hotel for five nights. At least $500 would
likely be blocked. In addition, hotels and rental car companies often
add anticipated charges for "incidentals" like food, beverages, or gasoline to the blocked amount. These incidental amounts can vary widely
among merchants.

If you pay your bill with the same card you used when you
checked in, the final charge on your credit card, or final amount on
your debit card, probably will replace the block in a day or two. However, if you pay your bill with a different card, or with cash or a check,
the company that issued the card you used at check-in might hold
the block for up to 15 days after you've checked out. That's because
they weren't notified of the final payment and didn't know you paid
another way.

175

Why Blocking Can Be a Problem

Blocking is used to make sure you don't exceed your credit line (credit card) or overdraw your bank account (debit card) before checking out of a hotel or returning a rental car, leaving the merchant unpaid. Blocking is sometimes also used by restaurants for anticipated sizable bills (like large groups at dinner or a party), by companies cleaning your home, and other businesses to ensure credit or account money will be available to complete payment.

If you're nowhere near your credit limit or don't have a low balance in your bank account, blocking probably won't be a problem. But if you're reaching that point, be careful. Not only can it be embarrassing to have your card declined, it also can be inconvenient, especially if you have an emergency purchase and insufficient credit or money in your bank account. On debit cards, depending on the balance in your bank account, blocking could lead to charges for insufficient funds while the block remains in place.

How to Avoid Blocking

To avoid the aggravation that blocking can cause, follow these tips:

- When you check into a hotel or rent a car—or if a restaurant or other business asks for your card in advance of service—ask if the company is "blocking," how much will be blocked, how the amount is determined, and how long the block remains in place.

- Consider paying hotel, motel, rental car, or other "blocked" bills with the same credit or debit card you used at the beginning of the transaction. Ask the clerk when the prior block will be removed.

- If you pay with a different card, by cash, or by check, remind the clerk you're using a different form of payment and ask them to remove the prior block promptly.

- Ask your current debit card issuer if they permit blocks, for how long, and from what types of merchants. If they do, you may want to consider getting an overdraft line of credit from your bank. Ask about a plan that always automatically covers the overdraft and does not involve a separate bank decision on whether or not to pay it each time. Although you might incur some interest on this plan if you don't pay off the amount fairly quickly, you would not have an overdraft that is not paid. Ask your bank if they offer an overdraft line of credit, how it would work, and how much it costs.

In addition, if you are considering a credit or debit card, shop around. When comparing credit and debit card offers, ask issuers if they permit blocks, for how long, and from what types of merchants. You may want to consider an issuer that uses shorter blocks.

Chapter 16

Plastic Fraud: Protect Yourself

State-of-the-art thieves are concentrating on plastic cards. In the past, this type of fraud was not very common. Today, it is a big business for criminals. Plastic cards bring new convenience to your shopping and banking, but they can turn into nightmares in the wrong hands. This chapter describes credit and debit cards and some common schemes involving card fraud with tips to help you avoid them.

Credit and Debit Cards

Although they may look the same, all plastic cards do not work the same. In fact, there are two very different kinds of cards in use today: credit cards and debit cards. As the names imply, credit cards allow the extension of credit and the delay of payment while debit cards charge or debit your account at the moment of the transaction.

Credit cards: Many credit cards work as follows: You charge goods or services and the merchant who accepts your credit card sends the transaction information to the card-issuing institution. The institution then bills you, usually on a monthly basis. In many cases, payment may be made by the due date with no interest assessed. If the total bill is not paid by the due date, you often can pay off your debt in monthly payments that include finance charges.

"Plastic Fraud," reprinted with permission from the Federal Reserve Bank of San Francisco, http:www.frbsf.org. This undated document is from http://www.frsb.org/publications/consumer/plastucfraud.pdf; accessed July 2006.

Debit cards: Debit cards, unlike credit cards, automatically withdraw funds from your account at the time you make a transaction. Debit cards are used most commonly at automated teller machines (ATMs) and for purchasing goods directly in stores. The machine-readable plastic card contains a magnetic strip indicating your account number, bank number, and type of account. Debit card users gain access to the issuing institution's computer by using a secret code, their personal identification number (PIN). The PIN should only be known to the card holder.

Avoiding Card Fraud

Although credit and debit card fraud can take many forms, the following examples explain some situations to watch for.

Stolen cards at the office: Over the lunch hour when you leave your office for lunch, you could be the target of a credit card thief. Credit card thieves often gain illegal access to the offices of employees who are away in order to search unattended. Most times, they leave the offices and immediately go on a shopping spree, charge credit cards to their limits, and withdraw cash on debit cards. Protect your credit cards as you would cash. Never write your PIN number on your debit card. Instead, always commit your PIN number to memory.

Extra copies of charge slips: When processing your credit card, a dishonest merchant may decide to imprint a few extra copies of the charge slip. Later, the merchant can submit these copies to the issuing institution for payment on phony charges. Keep your eye on your credit card whenever it is in use. Watch clerks process your credit payments. Open your credit card bills promptly each month. Make sure that you made the listed purchases. Also, report any charges that you did not make to the credit card company.

Discarded charge slips: Sometimes, people may collect copies of your discarded charge slips from the wastebasket. Dishonest people could use the information from the copies to order merchandise by mail and ship it to a phony address. In addition, they could also sell the copies to counterfeiters who would take the account numbers and use them to alter cards or make new ones. After signing a credit card slip, ask for your receipt or duplicates. After you have compared them to the charges listed on your monthly credit card statement, tear them up and throw them away.

Unsigned credit cards: Stealing and using credit cards that have not been signed is another potential fraud. In other words, credit card thieves could steal your unsigned credit cards and then sign your name on the card in their handwriting. By doing so, they take your name as an alias and they will never have a problem writing and verifying their own signature. Protect your credit cards. When you receive a new or replacement card, sign the back of it as soon as it is activated. Always be sure to store it in a safe place. Cut up expired cards before disposing of them.

Loss of multiple cards: While shopping, you can easily be targeted by pickpockets. If your purse or wallet is stolen, you may lose all your credit cards at one time. Separate your cards. Only carry those cards with you that you plan to use. Also, check your cards from time to time and put aside those cards you don't use very often.

Strange requests for your PIN [personal identification number]: This form of fraud involves thieves who find creative ways to steal your credit or debit cards when you don't know about it. For example, sometimes people crawl behind rows in movie theaters and steal pocketbooks while you are watching a movie. When you return home they call you, identify themselves as bank security agents, and ask for your PIN. If you hesitate, they simply ask you to phone their supervisor and give you an accomplice's phone number to call. By doing so, they are able to get your PIN and use the stolen debit cards to withdraw cash and make purchases. Again, never reveal your PIN to anyone. Also, never keep your PIN in your purse or wallet. Don't write your PIN on your card either. Always try to memorize it.

Recognizing Counterfeit Cards

Legitimate cards: Legitimate cards follow standard specifications as to color, tint, quality, and style. Stamped letters and numbers are spaced evenly and sized equally. The signature panel is uniform in size and is almost impossible to scrape off.

Altered cards: Altered cards are made from actual cards. The original stamped data is melted down or pressed out. Then, the card is re-stamped with legitimate account numbers, names, and expiration dates, which have been illegally obtained. On altered cards, the letters do not line up well and are usually irregular in size. Some credit card companies help merchants identify altered cards by making an authenticator machine available to merchants. The machine authenticates or verifies certain information that is encoded on the back stripe on the back of the card.

Counterfeit cards: Counterfeiters make most counterfeit cards by silk-screening or painting the card logo and issuing institution's name onto a blank piece of card plastic. Because they are silk-screened, the cards don't look exactly like the real thing. Real credit cards are printed. Also, the signature panel on silk-screened cards may be glued or painted on and can be easily lifted or chipped. This panel may also appear uneven in size or placement.

New Technology

New technology is making it more difficult for criminals to use, alter, or counterfeit credit and debit cards. Some of the innovations are already in use.

These security features have been added to major credit cards:

1. **Holograph:** A three-dimensional, laser produced optical device that changes its color and image as the card is tilted.

2. **Fine-line printing:** A repeated pattern of the card company name positioned as background for the company logo.

3. **Ultra-violet ink:** Special ink that is visible only under ultra-violet light, which will display the credit card company's logo.

"Smart Cards" may be the credit cards of the future. Each card has a built-in computer microprocessor. Signatures have been replaced with personal identification numbers and verification is handled only by computers. Eventually these cards may provide information on investments, charge accounts, and money market accounts. We may someday think of the credit card as a pocket-sized computer memory bank. Improved verification methods are also being developed and tested. These include fingerprinting, retinal eye scanners, and computerized signature cards.

On the Internet

While using the internet, you can learn about any number of topics and buy almost anything. Be aware, though, that internet shopping, like traditional shopping, may carry some risk. Software to protect you and your privacy is often a part of most websites. In fact, when ordering online, it would be wise to check if you are on a secure server by looking for a security symbol such as an unbroken key or padlock symbol at the bottom of your internet browser window. These symbols indicate that any information you may send to the website, including your credit card numbers, is encrypted or put into computer code prior to transmission.

Consumer Liability

It is important to keep a personal list of your credit and debit card numbers, the issuing banks, and their phone numbers so that you can contact them in case of loss or theft.

Credit Cards

If your credit card is lost or stolen, contact your bank or issuing institution immediately. Your monthly statement should list the phone number of whom to contact.

You do not have to pay for any unauthorized charges made after you have notified the issuing bank or institution. The most you will have to pay for unauthorized charges is $50 on each account. But this can add up if several cards are lost or stolen at the same time.

If you think that you did not make some or all of the purchases listed on your statement, you can take action. The Fair Credit Billing Act, an addition to the Truth-in-Lending law, requires prompt correction of billing mistakes. Within 60 days after the bill was mailed, you must notify the creditor in writing. You do not have to pay the amount in question while you are waiting for an answer.

Debit Cards

If your debit card is lost or stolen, notify the issuing bank or institution immediately. According to the Electronic Fund Transfer Act, if notification is given within two business days of discovery of the loss or theft, you may only be liable for $50. If you do not notify them within the two-day limit, you could lose up to $500. Finally, if notification is not given within 60 days after receiving a statement showing unauthorized withdrawals, you could be liable for everything.

What Is the Law?

The Credit Card Fraud Act imposes prison sentences and stiff fines on persons convicted of unauthorized or counterfeit use of credit cards

183

and debit cards. Also, the law makes it a federal crime to use any unauthorized card, plate, code, or account number to obtain money, goods, or services. The Secret Service is authorized to investigate violations under this act.

Part Three

Building and Using Credit

Chapter 17

Building and Keeping Good Credit

What Is Your Credit History?

When you ask for a loan or apply for a credit card, lenders look at your "credit history" to see how reliable you have been in repaying loans or credit.

If you've never been granted credit, such as a credit card, store account, car loan or mortgage, you may not have a credit history.

Good credit can help you:

- Buy a home.
- Get a job.
- Set up telephone, gas and electric, water or heating oil accounts.
- Rent an apartment.
- Buy "big ticket" items (furniture, electronics or appliances) without paying cash.
- Finance a car.
- Qualify for insurance coverage.
- Borrow money.
- Obtain a credit card.

Reprinted with permission from "Building and Keeping Good Credit," a brochure created by Consumer Action in partnership with Capital One Services, Inc. © 2005 Consumer Action. All rights reserved.

Good Credit Versus Negative Credit

If you have had credit cards or loans and made all required payments on time, you probably have a good credit history. A positive credit record results from using credit wisely.

People with good credit have:

- Established credit—they have borrowed money or used a credit card.

- A proven record of making at least the minimum payments on time—by the due date—and staying within their credit limits.

- Only obtained loans or credit cards that they are capable of paying back. (Don't overextend yourself—apply for only the credit you can afford.)

Negative credit results from failing to pay bills as agreed. Your credit can be negatively affected by:

- Late payments.

- Paying less than the minimum.

- Having too many credit cards with large balances or large amounts of available credit—even if you make on-time payments.

- Overdue accounts that have been referred to a collection agency.

- Declaring bankruptcy.

- Having court-ordered withdrawals from your paycheck to pay debts (garnishment).

What Is a Credit Report?

Your credit report is a record of your loans, credit cards, payments and outstanding debts. The information is supplied by companies that have given you credit or loaned you money (lenders).

Lenders give regular reports about your credit accounts to companies called credit reporting bureaus. These companies are in the business of collecting information about consumers from lenders (such as banks, savings and loans, credit unions, finance companies and stores). Credit reporting bureaus keep this information in computer databases and provide it to lenders when you apply for a new credit card or loan. Credit reporting bureaus do not make lending decisions.

When you apply for a credit card or loan, lenders use your credit report to decide if you are responsible enough to handle additional credit. Your credit report contains:

- Current and past payment information—whether your payments have been on time or late.

- Outstanding balances—the balances on your credit cards and the amounts of your outstanding loans.

- Information about you from public records, such as a bankruptcy or overdue property taxes.

- Overdue child support payments.

- The names of everyone who recently asked for a copy (inquiries).

Your credit report does not have:

- Information about your race, religion, political party, medical history, lifestyle, background, or criminal record.

How Do I Get My Credit Report?

Under federal law, every year you can get a free copy of your credit report from the three biggest companies that provide credit reports. These companies are:

- **Experian:** 888-397-3742 http://www.experian.com

- **Equifax:** 800-685-1111 http://www.equifax.com

- **TransUnion:** 800-916-8800 http://www.transunion.com

These three companies have created the "Annual Credit Report" site (http://www.annualcreditreport.com) for you to get the free annual credit reports required under federal law. You can order your reports online, by phone at 877-322-3228, or by mail. To order your reports by mail you must visit the website and download an order form and send it to the address given on the website.

You are entitled to a free credit report annually from each of the three companies. You can order all three reports at the same time, or you can stagger your reports. Ordering individual company reports at different times during the year gives you a chance to monitor your credit report more frequently without having to pay for your additional reports.

You will need to supply the credit bureaus with information so they can identify you. This usually includes your:

- Full name, including your middle initial and suffix (Jr., Sr. or III) if applicable.

- Current address and previous addresses for two to five years, depending on the bureau.

- Social Security number.

- Date of birth.

- Current employer.

- Phone number.

Your report is free if you've been denied credit in the last 60 days based on your credit report or are a victim of fraud.

Why Was My Credit Application Denied?

Many people who apply for credit are denied. If this happens, the lender must tell you why your application was denied. In most cases, the denial will be for one of the following reasons:

You have no credit history: If you've never had credit, if you've just begun to use credit or if you haven't used credit recently, lenders may deny you credit because you do not have a credit history. Without this information, lenders are less able to determine if you are a good credit risk.

If you've never had credit, or haven't used credit in a long time, you can begin to build a credit history. (See "How can I establish good credit?")

You have too much outstanding credit: Lenders are reluctant to give you new credit if you already have a large amount of outstanding credit. When lenders evaluate your application, they consider your income, current credit limits (if available) and debt payments to decide how much debt you can pay. Lenders often imagine the worst case scenario—if you suddenly used all your credit accounts up to the limits, would your income cover the payments? If the answer is no, your application might be rejected.

You did not handle credit responsibly in the past: Have you been granted credit but did not handle it appropriately? If you made

190

payments late, did not pay back a loan or filed for bankruptcy, lenders will not want to give you a new credit card or loan. To improve your credit report, you must settle old debts and make on-time payments for months, even years, before you will again be considered a good credit risk.

You are a victim of fraud: A dishonest person may try to set up credit in your name—this is called identity theft. Some people only find out they are victims when they apply for credit and are denied. You are not responsible, but it will be hard to prove you are a good credit risk until you clear your name.

One way to guard against identity fraud and credit fraud is to check your credit report at least once a year. If you find any accounts you do not recognize, call the credit bureau's fraud department immediately. To prevent fraud, keep a close eye on your credit cards and billing statements.

What If My Credit Application Is Denied?

The lender's explanation of why your application was denied will also tell you which credit reporting bureau supplied your credit report.

If you've been turned down, you are entitled to a free copy for up to 60 days. Contact the credit reporting company by telephone to get one.

If you've never had credit and the reason for the denial is insufficient credit history, contacting the reporting bureau won't help you.

After reviewing your report, if you feel a mistake has been made, contact the credit reporting bureau. You have a right to point out any inaccurate information in your credit report and to dispute it. The dispute process is simple—it usually can be done by calling the customer service number given on your credit report.

The credit reporting agency will contact the creditor who supplied negative or inaccurate information about you. Meanwhile the disputed information will be removed from your credit report, but it might be put back on if the lender tells the bureau it is accurate.

If that happens, you have the right to add up to a 100-word explanation to your credit report giving your side of the story. When you apply for credit, lenders may consider your statement.

How Can I Establish Good Credit?

Below are three ideas for establishing credit. If you are successful in establishing an account, and use it responsibly for a year or two, you will begin to build a good credit history.

Ask local companies for credit: Try your bank, credit union or a local department store. But make sure that the company sends the information on your credit account to one or more credit reporting bureaus so that it will help you establish a credit history.

Find a co-signer: Ask a relative or friend with good credit to co-sign your credit application. A co-signer promises to pay if you don't. If you don't make payments on time, the co-signer will be responsible for the loan. By failing to pay, you could damage your relative's or friend's credit.

Get a secured credit card: A secured credit card is a bank credit card backed by money you deposit in a bank account. If you don't pay off your credit card bill, the money in your account may be used to cover that debt.

Shop around to find a good deal. You can compare current information about secured cards at http://www.bankrate.com on the internet. Before you apply, make sure the card issuer will send the information on your credit account to a credit reporting bureau. Look for a secured card with:

- A low annual fee.

- No up-front application, processing or membership fees.

- An interest-bearing account for your deposit.

"Unsecured" Credit Cards

Many companies offer unsecured credit cards for people with no credit history or damaged credit. These can be expensive credit options, because many of them have:

- Low credit lines.

- High interest rates.

- Up front application, processing, and reservation fees, usually charged to your first statement.

- Annual or monthly membership fees.

- A fee for line-of-credit increases.

If you are considering one of these cards, shop around among lenders. Compare fees and interest rates. Because the fees often equal the credit limit on these cards, you may have no available credit until you pay the fees.

Optional Credit Card Services

Your credit card company may offer you services and products for a fee:

- Credit insurance—a service that helps pay your monthly minimum payments for a short time if you become ill or disabled.

- Credit monitoring services that charge to watch your credit report and let you know about any negative changes.

- Magazines and coupon books.

These services are optional—you do not have to accept them. If you say no to optional offers, it should not affect your application for a credit card.

Your Rights

The Fair Credit Reporting Act is a federal law that regulates credit reporting bureaus and prohibits inaccurate or obsolete information from being reported in credit files.

You are entitled to a free credit report annually from each of the three national credit reporting companies. (See "How do I get my credit report?") When you receive it, carefully check all the information, including all account numbers and payment records. Make sure that old accounts you closed are listed properly with the words "closed at the consumer's request."

You have the right to correct errors in your credit report. Enclosed with your credit report will be a form or letter explaining what to do if you find inaccurate information or items you do not agree with. Always dispute inaccurate information.

After you begin the dispute process, the credit bureau must check with the source of the information and send you an update. It must respond to your dispute in a timely way. In most cases, you should receive a response in 30 to 45 days.

If, after hearing from the bureau, you disagree with its response, you can add up to a 100-word statement to your credit report giving your side of the story.

Where to Complain

To complain about a credit bureau, department store or other non-FDIC (Federal Deposit Insurance Corporation) insured financial institution, write to the Consumer Response Center, Federal Trade Commission (FTC), Washington, DC 20580. You may also file a complaint online at the FTC website (http://www.ftc.gov).

To complain about a lender or credit card company, call the company and ask for the name and address of its regulatory agency. Send your complaint letter there, and forward a copy to your state Attorney General.

Chapter 18

Questions and Answers about Credit Reports

What information is included in my credit report?

Your personal credit report contains:

- Federal district bankruptcy records and state and county court records of tax liens and monetary judgments. This information comes from public records.

- Specific information about each account, such as the date opened, credit limit or loan amount, balance, monthly payment, and payment pattern during the past several years. This information comes from companies that do business with you.

- The names of those who have obtained a copy of your credit report. (On your copy of your Experian credit report, addresses are included.) This information comes from the credit reporting agency.

- Your name, current and previous addresses, phone number, Social Security number, date of birth, and current and previous employers. Your spouse's name may appear on your version of the credit report, but it will not appear on the version that is provided to others. This information comes in part from your credit applications, so its accuracy depends on your filling out the forms clearly, completely, and consistently each time you apply for credit.

- Statements of dispute, which allow both consumers and creditors to report the factual history of an account. Statements of dispute are added after a consumer officially disputes the status of an account, the account has been reinvestigated, and the consumer and creditor cannot agree about the account status. Both the consumer's and creditor's statements of the account status will appear on the credit report.

Most of the data Experian has on file is positive, indicating that most people pay their bills on time.

How often should I check my credit report?

Your credit history plays a major role when you apply for any type of credit or loan, such as a credit card, auto loan, mortgage, employment screening, utilities deposits, and insurance. It is a good idea to know what is included in your credit history before applying for credit or a loan. Creditors and lenders use your credit history to determine if you are a credit risk. The most important thing you can do to demonstrate you are a good credit risk is to pay your bills on time.

Why aren't my spouse's accounts displayed on my credit report?

The credit reporting agencies maintain individual credit files for each U.S. resident. They do not maintain combined files for spouses. Therefore, your credit report is separate and different from your spouse's. Joint credit accounts you have with your spouse will appear on both credit reports.

What information is not in a credit report?

Your Experian credit report does not contain—and Experian does not collect—data about race, religious preference, medical history, personal lifestyle, political preference, friends, criminal record, or any other information unrelated to credit.

How can I get a copy of my credit report besides online?

To purchase a copy of your credit report via telephone, call 800-311-4769. Please have your address, ZIP code, and Social Security number on hand when you call. In addition, review the fee information. [Note: For information about your eligibility to receive a free annual credit report, see Chapter 23—How to Get a Copy of Your Credit Report.]

What should I do if I find an error in my credit report?

First, get a copy of your report and review it carefully. If you find an error, you may dispute it online. You can also call the telephone number on your credit report for assistance if you feel any information is inaccurate or incomplete.

Please be specific by including the account number of an item you feel is in error and explain exactly why you feel it is inaccurate. Simply saying an item is wrong does not give enough detail to help resolve the issue. Investigations of disputed items can take up to 30 days, or up to 45 days for items disputed on an annual free credit report.

Can credit repair clinics fix my bad credit?

Some consumers pay so-called credit clinics hundreds and even thousands of dollars to fix their credit report, but only time can heal bad credit. Experian credit reports contain easy-to-follow instructions for disputing information at no charge. Information proven to be inaccurate will be changed or deleted. Federal and state laws mandate the amount of time that various credit information remains on a credit report.

If you need help repaying creditors, managing debt, or setting up a personal budget, consider contacting a nonprofit credit counseling organization that offers budgeting and credit management training.

How does a credit bureau help me?

If you're like most consumers in the United States, your ability to own a home, purchase a car, fund a college education, travel, and make routine purchases hinges on your responsible use of credit. Because an automated credit reporting system run by national consumer credit reporting agencies works quietly in the background, you have unlimited options in your financial life. For example, you can:

- Purchase a home in one area of the country based on the good credit record you established while living in another part of the country.

- Shop for and be offered financial services from institutions in other regions of the country.

- Negotiate a deal for a new car and drive it off the lot within a few hours.

Credit reporting also helps foster intense competitive marketing battles among financial services providers. This competition provides you with:

- Lower interest rates.

- Reduced annual fees.

- Special toll-free customer service phone numbers.

- Customer recognition programs.

- Purchase protection plans, and many other benefits.

How long does information remain on the credit report?

Experian stores information from credit grantors and public records, including bankruptcies, judgments, and liens. Missed payments and most public record items remain on the credit report for seven years, with the exception of Chapter 7, 11, and 12 bankruptcies, which remain for 10 years, and unpaid tax liens, which remain for up to 15 years.

Active positive information may remain on the report indefinitely.

Requests for your credit history remain on the credit report for up to two years.

Why can't information be deleted from the credit report?

Experian stores information from credit grantors and public records in compliance with the Fair Credit Reporting Act. When you use credit, a record of your payment history is reported to credit reporting agencies.

If you believe the information in the credit report is inaccurate, you may dispute it and we will investigate and correct or remove any inaccurate information or information that cannot be verified.

Does Experian approve or deny credit?

Experian does not grant or deny credit. Each credit grantor makes that decision based on its own guidelines. Experian only stores information from credit grantors and public records and supplies this information to other creditors.

How does a collection account appear on the credit report?

While you make payments on your collection account, the status will remain "collection account." Once you pay the account in full, then it will show "paid collection." A paid collection account will remain on the credit report for seven years from the initial missed payment that led to the collection.

Why does student loan information appear more than once on the credit report?

Student loans are reported individually by enrollment periods; therefore, the loans cannot be combined.

How do I contact the national consumer reporting agencies?

You may call TransUnion at (800) 888-4213. You may call Equifax at (800) 685-1111. You may call Experian at (888) 397-3742.

How can I contact a customer service representative?

The national consumer reporting agencies can best assist a consumer who has first obtained a copy of their personal credit report. To obtain a copy contact one of the agencies with the previously listed numbers. Once you receive your report, it will display the appropriate contact phone number or address for consumers, should you believe any information is incorrect.

What's the difference between a consumer disclosure and a credit report?

A consumer disclosure contains a comprehensive history of your credit information, including all inquiries. A credit report contains the same type of credit information and inquiries that a lender or creditor will see when they check your credit. The key difference is the consumer disclosure includes some inquiries, such as account monitoring and those resulting in pre-approved offers, and some address and demographic information that are not displayed on the credit report viewed by lenders.

How can I order a copy of my personal credit report?

For fast and efficient access to your personal credit report, order your credit report online or call one of the national consumer reporting agencies to request a copy of your personal credit report to be delivered by U.S. mail.

All consumers are also eligible to obtain one statutory free annual credit file disclosure from each of the national credit reporting companies every twelve months.

I hear I can get a free copy of my credit report if I've been turned down for a loan. How does that work?

Under the Fair Credit Reporting Act (FCRA), you may be entitled to receive a free copy of your personal credit report if you have received notice within the past 60 days that you have been declined credit, employment or housing, or if adverse action has been taken against you based on information from Experian. You can order your free report online at http://www.experian.com/reportaccess, or by calling 866-200-6020. If not eligible, some state laws require a free credit report or a lesser fee for consumers in their states.

Chapter 19

Getting Credit: Tips for Young Adults

What's Credit?

Being out on your own can be fun and exciting, but it also means taking on new financial responsibilities. The decisions you make now about how you manage your finances and borrow money will affect you in the future—for better or worse.

Did you know that there are companies that keep track of whether you pay your debts and if you make payments on time? Then these companies make this information available in the form of a credit report and score.

A bad credit history can haunt you for a long time—seven years or more. That's why the best thing to do is learn how to maintain good credit before there's a problem. While this might seem complicated at first, it gets easier once you understand the basics of credit and how it works.

Credit is more than just a plastic card you use to buy things—it is your financial trustworthiness. Good credit means that your history of payments, employment, and salary make you a good candidate for a loan, and creditors—those who lend money or services—will be more willing to work with you. Having good credit usually translates into lower payments and more ease in borrowing money. Bad credit, however, can be a big problem. It usually results from making payments late or borrowing too much money, and it means that

"Getting Credit: What You Need to Know about Your Credit," Federal Trade Commission (www.ftc.gov), July 2003.

you might have trouble getting a car loan, a credit card, a place to live, and, sometimes, a job.

Your Credit

Most creditors use credit scoring to evaluate your credit record. This involves using your credit application and report to get information about you, such as your annual income, outstanding debt, bill-paying history, and the number and types of accounts you have along with how long you have had them. Potential lenders use your credit score to help predict whether you are a good risk to repay a loan and make payments on time.

Many people just starting out have no credit history and may find it tough to get a loan or credit card, but establishing a good credit history is not as difficult as it seems.

- You might apply for a credit card issued by a local store, because local businesses are more willing to extend credit to someone with no credit history. Once you establish a pattern of making your payments on time, major credit card issuers might be more willing to extend credit to you.

- You might apply for a secured credit card. Basically, this card requires you to put up the money first and then lets you borrow 50 to 100 percent of your account balance.

- You might ask other people who have an established credit history to co-sign on an account. By co-signing, the person is agreeing to pay back the loan if you don't.

What a Difference a Word Makes

Credit card: You can use a credit card to buy things and pay for them over time. But remember, buying with credit is a loan—you have to pay the money back. What's more, if the credit card company sends you a check, it's not a gift. It's a loan you have to pay back. In addition to the cost of what you bought, you will owe a percentage of what you spent (interest) and sometimes an annual fee.

Charge card: If you use a charge card, you must pay your balance in full when you get your regular statement.

Debit card: This card allows you to access the money in your checking or savings account electronically to make purchases.

The Fine Print

When applying for credit cards, it's important to shop around. Fees, charges, interest rates, and benefits can vary drastically among credit card issuers. And, in some cases, credit cards might seem like great deals until you read the fine print and disclosures. When you're trying to find the credit card that's right for you, look at the:

- **Annual percentage rate (APR):** The APR is a measure of the cost of credit, expressed as a yearly interest rate. Usually, the lower the APR, the better for you. Be sure to check the fine print to see if your offer has a time limit. Your APR could be much higher after the initial limited offer.

- **Grace period:** This is the time between the date of the credit card purchase and the date the company starts charging you interest.

- **Annual fees:** Many credit card issuers charge an annual fee for giving you credit, typically $15 to $55.

- **Transaction fees and other charges:** Most creditors charge a fee if you don't make a payment on time. Other common credit card fees include those for cash advances and going beyond the credit limit. Some credit cards charge a flat fee every month, whether you use your card or not.

- **Customer service:** Customer service is something most people don't consider, or appreciate, until there's a problem. Look for a 24-hour toll-free telephone number.

- **Other options:** Creditors may offer other options for a price, including discounts, rebates, and special merchandise offers. If your card is lost or stolen, federal law protects you from owing more than $50 per card—but only if you report that it was lost or stolen within two days of discovering the loss or theft. Paying for additional protection may not be a good value.

Your Personal Financial Information

Banks and other financial companies may share your personal financial information with their subsidiaries and other companies. But you can limit some of that sharing if you want to. "Opting out" can help keep much of your financial information private and reduce unsolicited offers that come in the mail. But it also means you may not see offers that could interest you. Your financial institutions will send you a privacy notice once a year in your statement or as a separate mailing. Be sure to read these notices carefully. Get answers to your questions from these companies. If you decide you want to opt out, follow the company's instructions—you may need to call them, return a form, or go online. You can shop around for a financial institution with the privacy policy you want.

Do the Math

Keep in mind that credit card interest rates and minimum monthly payments affect how long it will take to pay off your debt and how much you'll pay for your purchase over time.

Suppose when you're 22, you charge $1,000 worth of clothes and CDs on a credit card with a 19 percent interest rate. If you pay $20 every month, you'll be over 30 by the time you pay off the debt. You'll have paid an extra $1,000 in interest. And that's if you never charge anything else on that card!

Keep Your Credit Record Clean

Good credit is important, now and in the future. In most cases, it takes seven years for accurate, negative information to be deleted from a credit report. Bankruptcy information takes even longer to be deleted—10 years.

Know What Creditors Look for on Credit Reports

Understanding what types of information most creditors evaluate is important. Your credit report is a key part of your credit score, but it is not the only factor. You get points for other things like these:

- Your bill-paying history
- How many accounts you have and what kind
- Late payments
- Longevity of accounts
- The unused portions of lines of credit
- Collections actions
- Outstanding debt

Where to Obtain a Copy of Your Credit Report

Credit reporting agencies don't share files, so you'll need to contact each reporting agency to make sure the information about you is correct. The three major credit reporting agencies are:

- Equifax
  - 800-685-1111
  - http://www.equifax.com

- Experian
  - 888-397-3742
  - http://www.experian.com

- TransUnion
  - 800-888-4213
  - http://www.transunion.com

For information about obtaining a copy of your credit report, see Chapter 23— How to Get a Copy of Your Credit Report.

Keep Credit Cards Under Control

Whether you shop online, by telephone, or by mail, a credit card can make buying many things much easier; but when you use a credit card, it's important to keep track of your spending. Incidental and impulse purchases add up, and each one you make with a credit card is a separate loan. When the bill comes, you have to pay what you owe. Owing more than you can afford to repay can damage your credit rating.

Keeping good records can prevent a lot of headaches, especially if there are inaccuracies on your monthly statement. If you notice a problem, promptly report it to the company that issued the card. Usually the instructions for disputing a charge are on your monthly statement. If you order by mail, by telephone, or online, keep copies and printouts with details about the transaction.

These details should include the company's name, address, and telephone number; the date of your order; a copy of the order form you sent to the company or a list of the stock codes of the items ordered; the order confirmation code; the ad or catalog from which you ordered (if applicable); any applicable warranties; and the return and refund policies.

Finally, if you have a credit card, take the following precautions:

- Never lend it to anyone.

- Never sign a blank charge slip. Draw lines through blank spaces on charge slips above the total so the amount can't be changed.

- Never put your account number on the outside of an envelope or on a postcard.

- Always be cautious about disclosing your account number on the telephone unless you know the person you're dealing with represents a reputable company.

- Always carry only the cards you anticipate using to prevent the possible loss or theft of all your cards or identification.

- Always report lost or stolen ATM and credit cards to the card issuers as soon as possible. Follow up with a letter that includes your account number, when you noticed the card was missing, and when you first reported the loss.

Protect Your Identity

Identity theft involves someone else using your personal information to create fraudulent accounts, charge items to another person's existing accounts, or even get a job. You can minimize the risks by managing your personal information wisely and cautiously. Here are some ways to protect yourself from identity theft:

- Before you reveal any personally identifying information, find out how it will be used and whether it will be shared.

- Pay attention to your billing cycles. Follow up with creditors if your bills don't arrive on time.

- Guard your mail from theft. Deposit outgoing mail in post office collection boxes or at your local post office. Promptly remove mail from your mailbox after it has been delivered. If you're planning to be away from home and can't pick up your mail, call the U.S. Postal Service toll-free at 800-275-8777, or visit http://www.usps.gov to request a vacation hold.

- When possible, put passwords on your credit card, bank, and phone accounts. Avoid using easily available information like your mother's maiden name, your birth date, the last four digits of your Social Security number or telephone number, or a series of consecutive numbers. It's a good idea to keep a list of your credit card issuers and their telephone numbers.

- Don't give out personal information on the telephone, through the mail, or over the internet unless you've initiated the contact or you know whom you're dealing with.

- Protect personal information in your home. For example, tear or shred documents like charge receipts, copies of credit offers and applications, insurance forms, physician's statements, discarded bank checks and statements, and expired credit cards before you throw them away. Be cautious about leaving personal information in plain view, especially if you have roommates, employ outside help, or are having service work done.

- Find out who has access to your personal information at work and verify that the records are kept in a secure location.

- Never carry your Social Security card; leave it in a secure place at home. Give out your Social Security number only when absolutely necessary.

- Order your credit report from each of the three major credit reporting agencies every year to make sure it is accurate and includes only those activities you've authorized.

- Carry only the identification that you actually need.

What to Do If You Are a Victim of Identity Theft

If your cards, bills or identification have been misused to open new accounts in your name, file a complaint with the Federal Trade Commission. Call toll-free 877-ID-THEFT (877-438-4338); TDD: 202-326-2502, or visit www.consumer.gov/idtheft.

Improve Your Credit Record

A lot of people spend more than they can afford and pay less toward their debts than they should. To get control over your finances and to manage your debt, try:

Budgeting: In many cases, people design and then stick to a budget to get their debt under control. A budget is a plan for how much money you have and how much money you spend. Sticking to a realistic budget allows you to pay off your debts and save for the proverbial rainy day.

Credit counseling: Many universities, military bases, credit unions, and housing authorities operate nonprofit financial counseling programs. Some charge a fee for their services. Creditors may be willing to accept reduced payments if you're working with a reputable program to create a debt repayment plan. When you choose a credit counselor, be sure to ask about fees you will have to pay and what kind of counseling you'll receive. A credit counseling organization isn't necessarily legitimate just because it says it's nonprofit. You may want to check with the Better Business Bureau for any complaints against a counselor or counseling organization. Visit http://www.bbbonline.org for your local Better Business Bureau's telephone number.

Bankruptcy: Bankruptcy is considered the credit solution of last resort. Unlike negative credit information that stays on a credit report for seven years, bankruptcies stay on a credit report for 10 years. Bankruptcy can make it difficult to rent an apartment, buy a house or a condo, get some types of insurance, get additional credit, and, sometimes, get a job. In some cases, bankruptcy may not be an easily available option.

When to Contact Creditors

If you're having trouble paying your bills, contact your creditors immediately. Tell them why it's difficult for you, and try to work out a modified plan that reduces your payments to a more manageable level. Don't wait until your accounts have been turned over to a debt collector. Take action immediately and keep a detailed record of your conversations and correspondence.

Use Caution

Turning to a business that offers help in solving debt problems may seem like a reasonable solution when your bills become unmanageable. Be cautious. Before you do business with any company, check it out with your local consumer protection agency or the Better Business Bureau in the company's location. One rule to remember is that if a credit repair offer seems too easy or just too good to be true, it probably is too good to be true. And knowing your rights can help you steer clear of rip-offs. For example, according to state and federal laws, companies that help people improve their credit rating cannot do the following:

- Make false claims about their services.

- Charge you until the services are completed.

- Perform services until the waiting period has passed. After you sign the written contract, you have three days to change your mind and cancel the services.

If you've had a problem, the Federal Trade Commission (FTC) works for the consumer to prevent fraudulent, deceptive, and unfair business practices in the marketplace and to provide information to help consumers spot, stop, and avoid them. To file a complaint or to get free information on consumer issues, call toll-free, 877-FTC-HELP (877-382-4357), or visit www.ftc.gov/ftc/consumer.htm. The FTC enters internet, telemarketing, identity theft, and other fraud-related complaints into Consumer Sentinel, a secure, online database available to hundreds of civil and criminal law enforcement agencies in the United States and abroad.

It's a good idea to contact your local consumer protection agency, state attorney general, or Better Business Bureau, too. Many attorneys general have toll-free consumer hotlines. To find the number for your state's attorney general, check with your local directory assistance.

Avoid Advance Fee Loan Scams

Offers that guarantee you a credit card for a fee—before you even apply—are against the law. These scams often target consumers with credit problems. If someone calls you making that kind of promise, tell the caller not to call you anymore and hang up.

Ads Promising "Debt Relief" Actually May Be Offering Bankruptcy

As you try to take control of your debt, be on the lookout for advertisements that offer quick fixes. While ads pitch the promise of debt relief, they rarely mention that this relief comes in the form of bankruptcy. Because bankruptcy stays on your credit report for 10 years and hinders your ability to get credit, it's important to ask for details before agreeing to any debt-relief services.

Don't Be Lost

A lost or stolen wallet or purse is a gold mine of information for identity thieves. If your wallet or purse is lost or stolen:

- File a report with the police immediately and keep a copy.

- Cancel your credit cards. Call the issuer(s) immediately. Many companies have 24-hour toll-free numbers to deal with such emergencies. The number is on your monthly statement.

- Get new cards with new account numbers.

- Call the fraud departments of the major credit reporting agencies, and ask each agency to put a "fraud alert" on your account:

    - Equifax: 800-525-6285

    - Experian 888-397-3742

    - TransUnion 800-680-7289

- Report the loss to the fraud department of the bank where you have your checking and savings accounts. Ask about the next steps regarding your accounts, including your ATM or debit card.

- Review your credit reports regularly and have them corrected when necessary.

- Report a missing driver's license to your state department of motor vehicles.

- Change your home and car locks, if your keys were taken.

Chapter 20

Personal Life Events and Your Credit

Marriage

Managing your credit can be tricky, even when you're the only person involved in your financial decisions. Add a new spouse to the mix, and you have to be extra careful to ensure your credit remains in good standing.

For many engaged couples, talking about finances takes a back seat to the excitement of wedding planning. But, before saying "I do," you need to be aware of the credit issues that could arise with a new marriage.

First of all, both you and your spouse should put all your financial records—savings, salaries, investments, real estate, and especially credit—on the table. If one of you has a less-than-glowing credit history, it will affect the other as soon as you start applying for credit together and opening joint accounts. In addition, your new joint accounts will appear on both spouses' credit reports in the future, so be sure to pay careful attention to your bills and pay them on time.

Once you've aired your credit laundry, you'll need to decide whether or not to merge all of your financial accounts. Many couples do this because consolidated accounts often make for easier record keeping. Just remember, both of you are responsible for all debt incurred in any joint credit accounts. So, regardless of who's incurring debt, a missed payment on a joint account will negatively affect both of your records. The same is true in community property states, where virtually any debt entered into during marriage is automatically considered joint. Consider also if you miss a payment on an individual account, that payment may very well impact your ability to open joint accounts because both credit histories will be considered.

The best way to keep your record clean starts with a solid understanding of the terms of your joint accounts. That means paying attention to interest rates, credit limits, annual or late payment fees, and cash advance limits. If you decide to consolidate your accounts, you might want to keep at least one credit account in your own name as a safeguard in the event of an emergency. Keeping an individual account can also be a good thing in the event of divorce to reestablish an individual credit history.

Women who take their husband's surname after getting married need to notify the Social Security Administration and their current creditors of this change. You do not need to notify the credit reporting agencies of a name change. They will automatically update the name on a credit report when creditors report it.

The key to successful credit management as a couple is understanding that your individual credit behavior affects both you and your partner. To ensure that you are able to quickly get credit at the best possible terms, be sure you both understand all the implications that accompany a joint account. In addition, consider how the payments stemming from a major credit purchase will affect your overall budget.

Divorce

With divorce and separation come new experiences and responsibilities. Suddenly words like "child support payments" and "100 percent liable for bills" enter the picture. If you ignore your increased financial obligations or fail to separate your accounts, it may be hard to open new accounts and obtain new loans in your name. But there are many moves you can make to protect and restore the good credit that took years to build.

Get Your Credit Report and Protect Your Good Credit

Before you begin, get an idea of what your credit report looks like.

Your divorce decree does not relieve you from joint debts you incurred while married. You are responsible for joint accounts, from credit cards and car loans to home mortgages. Even when a divorce judge orders your ex-spouse to pay a certain bill, you're still legally responsible for making sure it is paid because you promised—both as a couple and as individuals—to do so.

The credit grantor (a bank, credit card issuer, mortgage company, or other credit-lending business) also has a legal right to report negative information to a credit reporting agency if your ex-spouse pays late on a joint account. If your ex-spouse doesn't pay at all, you'll probably have to pay—or the grantor can take legal action against you.

- Close or separate joint accounts. If you can talk to your ex-spouse, you can save a lot of grief. Analyze all your debts and decide who should be responsible for each. Call your creditors and ask them how to transfer your joint accounts to the person who is solely responsible for payments. However, you still might have legal responsibility to pay existing balances unless the creditor agrees to release you from the debt.

- Take stock of your properties. You may have to refinance your home to get one name off the mortgage. Or you might need to sell your home and divide the proceeds.

- Keep paying all bills. Until you can separate your accounts, neither of you can afford to miss a turn paying bills. During divorce negotiations, send in at least the minimum payment due on all joint bills. Miss even one payment and it stays on your credit profile for up to seven years, making it hard to obtain new credit in your own name. Beware of well-meaning friends and relatives who may tell you to ignore making payments or to run up debts. Always make all payments with at least the minimum due.

Establish Credit Independently

Start small and build up. Get a credit card that has a small credit limit, perhaps from a local department store or financial institution. Then always pay your bills on time so your credit history will be excellent. After six months, apply for another card and continue paying bills consistently. Don't run your debt up beyond what you can afford to pay. It's a winning strategy that's easy to master.

Ask a family member or friend to co-sign. Perhaps a relative or friend with an established credit history can cosign your loan or credit application—provided you repay that cosigned debt on time. Remember, any transaction also will show up on the cosigner's credit profile. After a few months, try again to get credit on your own.

Consider applying for a secured credit card. You must open and maintain a savings account as security for your line of credit. Your credit line is a percentage of your deposit. Beware of the extra fees you may have to pay for secured credit.

Rebuild Positive Credit History

You can pick up your pieces and start fresh with a positive credit report—if you pay your bills on time. After all, your credit profile is always evolving.

Your recent bill-paying pattern is critical. Your behavior (during the next 18–24 months) is most important in deciding whether you're a good credit risk. Even one late payment can affect your ability to get a mortgage.

Help is available if you're having difficulty paying bills. The nonprofit National Foundation for Credit Counseling (NFCC), (800) 388-2227, can help you establish a budget and repay creditors. Other organizations offer quality credit counseling as well. Be sure the organization you work with is non-profit and provides budgeting and financial management training in addition to any debt management plan, and does so at little or no cost. Be very cautious of any organization that claims it can provide a quick fix to your credit problems, provides you with no financial management education, or that charges substantial fees for its services.

Bankruptcy Is a Last Resort

Bankruptcy should be the last move to make if you get in over your head.

- It's not an easy way out. Filing for bankruptcy is no guarantee that it will be granted because a court judgment must be made. Even if all you do is file your bankruptcy papers with the court, it gets reported on your credit profile.

- Not all debts are included in bankruptcy. Things like alimony, child support, student loans, and taxes secured by liens still must be paid consistently.

- Bankruptcy remains on your credit history up to 10 years. While a declaration of bankruptcy removes many debts, any reference to filing, dismissal, or discharge still appears on your credit history for up to 10 years. During this time, you'll find it more difficult if not impossible to get a new mortgage, personal loan, or a credit card.

Consider Mediation

Mediation can make things much fairer by helping you and your ex-spouse work out a reasonable and equitable divorce agreement. If you'd like help finding a mediator, contact the American Arbitration Association. To locate an attorney, check with your state or local Bar Association.

Death of a Spouse

If you've lost a spouse, you're already going through one of the most emotionally draining experiences possible. When a loved one dies, there are also numerous financial matters to deal with, including credit and debt issues. There are, however, some simple steps you can take now to help down the road.

Stabilizing your credit in the event of a death can be difficult, especially if your spouse held all of the credit in his or her name. Keep in mind that in community property states, credit accounts opened during marriage are automatically joint. That means you are still responsible for any debt that your deceased spouse incurred.

By law, a creditor cannot automatically close a joint account or change the terms because of the death of one spouse. Generally, the creditor will ask the survivor to file a new credit application in his or her own name. After reviewing the new information, the creditor will then decide to continue to extend credit or alter the credit limit. You might want to open a new credit account in your name. In doing so, keep in mind that you must use your name only when applying. Including your deceased spouse's name will result in a joint account. Experian automatically updates its records with periodic reports from the Social Security Administration. When the update is made, your spouse's credit history will be flagged to show that he or she has passed away and their name will be removed from any pre-approved credit offer mailing lists.

Chapter 21

Getting Credit when You're over 62

Credit is an important money management tool for both young and older consumers. Yet the elderly, particularly older women, may find it difficult to get credit.

If you're an older consumer who has paid with cash all your life, you may find it difficult to open a credit account. That's because you have "no credit history" of how you paid on credit. If your income has decreased, you may find it harder to get a loan because you have "insufficient income." Or, if your spouse dies, you may find creditors trying to close joint accounts. A "joint account" is one for which both spouses applied and signed the credit agreement.

Under the federal Equal Credit Opportunity Act (ECOA), it's against the law for a creditor to deny you credit or terminate existing credit simply because of your age. This chapter explains your rights and offers tips for applying for and maintaining credit.

Applying for Credit

Applying for credit used to mean asking your neighborhood banker for a loan. Now, with national credit cards and computerized applications, the day of personal evaluations may be over. Instead, computer evaluations look at, among other things, your income, payment history, credit card accounts, and any outstanding balances. Paying in

"Getting Credit When You're Over 62," Federal Trade Commission (www.ftc.gov), April 2006.

cash and in full may be sound financial advice, but they won't give you a payment history that helps you get credit.

A major indicator of your ability to repay a loan is your current income. Those who consider income must include types of income that are likely to be received by older consumers. This includes salaries from part-time employment, Social Security, pensions, and other retirement benefits.

You also may want to tell creditors about assets or other sources of income, such as your home, additional real estate, savings and checking accounts, money market funds, certificates of deposit, and stocks and bonds.

If you're age 62 or over, you have certain other protections. You can't be denied credit because credit-related insurance is not available based on your age. Credit insurance pays off the creditor if you should die or become disabled.

On the other hand, a creditor can consider your age for these reasons:

- Favor applicants who are age 62 or older

- Determine other elements of creditworthiness. For example, a creditor could consider whether you're close to retirement age and a lower income.

While a creditor cannot take your age directly into account, a creditor may consider age as it relates to certain elements of creditworthiness. If, for example, at the age of 70, you apply for a 30-year mortgage, a lender might be concerned that you may not live to repay the loan. However, if you apply for a shorter loan term, increase your down payment, or do both, you might satisfy the creditor's concerns.

Checking Your Credit History

A credit report includes information on where you live, how you pay your bills, and whether you've been sued, arrested, or filed for bankruptcy. Nationwide consumer reporting companies sell the information in your report to creditors, insurers, employers, and other businesses that use it to evaluate your applications for credit, insurance, employment, or renting a home.

You may find that your file doesn't list all of your credit accounts. That's because not all creditors report to consumer reporting companies. You may ask that additional accounts be reported to your file. Some bureaus may charge for this service.

Credit information about shared accounts should be reported in your name and your spouse's. If it's not, ask the creditor in writing to report the account in both names.

The Fair Credit Reporting Act (FCRA) requires each of the major nationwide consumer reporting companies to provide you with a free copy of your credit report, at your request, once every 12 months.

To order your free annual report from one or all the national consumer reporting companies, visit: http://www.annualcreditreport.com; call toll-free: 877-322-8228; or complete the Annual Credit Report Request Form and mail it to: Annual Credit Report Request Service, P.O. Box 105281, Atlanta, GA 30348-5281. You can print the form from http://www.ftc.gov/credit. Do not contact the three nationwide consumer reporting companies individually; they provide free annual credit reports only through http://www.annualcreditreport.com, 877-322-8228, and Annual Credit Report Request Service, P.O. Box 105281, Atlanta, GA 30348-5281.

Other Rights to Free Reports

Under federal law, you're also entitled to a free report if a company takes adverse action against you, such as denying your application for credit, insurance or employment, and you request your report within 60 days of receiving notice of the action. The notice will give you the name, address, and phone number of the consumer reporting company that supplied the information about you. You're also entitled to one free report a year if you're unemployed and plan to look for a job within 60 days; if you're on welfare; or if your report is inaccurate because of fraud. Otherwise, a consumer reporting company may charge you up to $9.50 for additional copies of your report.

To buy a copy of your report, contact:

- Equifax: 800-685-1111; http://www.equifax.com

- Experian: 888-EXPERIAN (888-397-3742); http://www.experian.com

- TransUnion: 800-916-8800; http://www.transunion.com

Under state law, consumers in Colorado, Georgia, Maine, Maryland, Massachusetts, New Jersey, and Vermont already have free access to their credit reports.

If you ask, only the last four digits of your Social Security number will appear on your credit reports.

Establishing a Credit History

If you're denied a loan or credit card because you have no credit history, consider establishing one. The best way is to apply for a small line of credit from your bank or a credit card from a local department store. Make sure you list your best financial references. Make payments regularly and make certain the creditor reports your credit history to a credit bureau.

If Your Spouse Dies

Under the ECOA, a creditor cannot automatically close or change the terms of a joint account solely because of the death of your spouse. A creditor may ask you to update your application or reapply. This can happen if the account was originally based on all or part of your spouse's income and if the creditor has reason to believe your income alone cannot support the credit line.

After you submit a re-application, the creditor will determine whether to continue to extend you credit or change your credit limits. Your creditor must respond in writing within 30 days of receiving your application. During that time, you can continue to use your account with no new restrictions. If you're application is rejected, you must be given specific reasons, or told of your right to get this information.

These protections also apply when you retire, reach age 62 or older, or change your name or marital status.

Kinds of Accounts

It's important to know what kind of credit accounts you have, especially if your spouse dies. There are two types of accounts—individual and joint. You can permit authorized persons to use either type.

Individual: An individual account is opened in one person's name and is based only on that person's income and assets. If you're concerned about your credit status if your spouse should die, you may want to try to open one or more individual accounts in your name. That way, your credit status won't be affected.

When you're applying for individual credit, ask the creditor to consider the credit history of accounts reported in your spouse's or former spouse's name, as well as those reported in your name. The creditor must consider this information if you can prove it reflects positively and accurately on your ability to manage credit. For example, you may be able to show through canceled checks that you made payments on an account, even though it's listed in your spouse's name only.

Joint: A joint account is opened in two people's names, often a husband and wife, and is based on the income and assets of both or either person. Both people are responsible for the debt.

Account "Users"

If you open an individual account, you may authorize another person to use it. If you name your spouse as the authorized user, a creditor who reports the credit history to a credit bureau must report it in your spouse's name as well as in yours (if the account was opened after June 1, 1977). A creditor also may report the credit history in the name of any other authorized user.

If You're Denied Credit

The ECOA does not guarantee you'll get credit. But if you're denied credit, you have the right to know why. There may be an error or the computer system may not have evaluated all relevant information. In that case, you can ask the creditor to reconsider your application.

If you believe you've been discriminated against, you may want to write to the federal agency that regulates that particular creditor. Your complaint letter should state the facts. Send it, along with copies (not originals) of supporting documents. You also may want to contact an attorney. You have the right to sue a creditor who violates the ECOA.

Regulators

For National Banks
Comptroller of the Currency
Customer Assistance Group
1301 McKinney Street, Suite 3710
Houston, TX 77010

For State Member Banks of the Reserve System
Federal Reserve Board
Division of Consumer and Community Affairs
Mail Stop 801
Washington, DC 20551

For Federal Credit Unions
National Credit Union Administration
1775 Duke Street
Alexandria, VA 22314

For Non-Member Federally Insured Banks
Federal Deposit Insurance Corporation
Office of Consumer Programs
550 Seventeenth St., NW
Washington, DC 20429

For Federally Insured Savings and Loans, and Federally Chartered
State Banks
Office of Thrift Supervision
Consumer Affairs Program
1700 G St., NW
Washington, DC 20552

For Other Creditors (includes retail, gasoline, finance, and mort-
gage companies)
Federal Trade Commission
Consumer Response Center
600 Pennsylvania Ave, NW
Washington, DC 20580

Chapter 22

Understanding Your Credit Score

A credit score is a number that helps lenders and others predict how likely you are to make your credit payments on time. Each score is based on the information then in your credit report.

Why Do Your Scores Matter?

Credit scores affect whether you can get credit and what you pay for credit cards, auto loans, mortgages, and other kinds of credit. For most kinds of credit scores, higher scores mean you are more likely to be approved and pay a lower interest rate on new credit.

Want to rent an apartment? Without good scores, your apartment application may be turned down by the landlord. Your scores also may determine how big a deposit you will have to pay for telephone, electricity, or natural gas service.

Lenders look at your scores all the time. They look at your scores when deciding, for example, whether to change your interest rate or credit limit on a credit card, or whether to send you an offer through the mail. Having good credit scores makes your financial dealings a lot easier and can save you money in lower interest rates. That's why they are a vital part of your financial health.

Consider a couple who is looking to buy their first house. Let's say they want a thirty-year mortgage loan and their FICO [Fair Isaac

Corporation] credit scores are 720. They could qualify for a mortgage with a low 5.5 percent interest rate. But if their scores are 580, they probably would pay 8.5 percent or more—that's at least 3 full percentage points more in interest. On a $100,000 mortgage loan, that 3 point difference will cost them $2,400 dollars a year, adding up to $72,000 dollars more over the loan's 30-year lifetime. Your credit scores do matter.

What Is a Good Score?

When lenders talk about "your score," they usually mean the FICO® score developed by Fair Isaac Corporation. It is today's most commonly used scoring system. FICO scores range from 300–850, and most people score in the 600s and 700s (higher FICO scores are better). Lenders buy your FICO score from three national credit reporting agencies (also called credit bureaus): Equifax, Experian, and TransUnion.

In the eyes of most lenders, FICO credit scores above 700 are very good and a sign of good financial health. FICO scores below 600 indicate high risk to lenders and could lead lenders to charge you much higher rates or turn down your credit application.

Not Just One Score

There are many types of credit scores. They are developed by independent companies, credit reporting agencies, and even some lenders. As a rule, the higher the score, the better.

- Each credit reporting agency calculates your score and each score may be different because the credit history each agency has about you may be different. Lenders may make a credit card or auto loan decision based on a single agency's score, although others such as mortgage lenders often will look at all three scores.

- Your credit score changes when your information changes at that credit reporting agency. This is good news. It means you can improve a poor score over time by improving how you handle credit.

- Many insurance companies use something similar when setting your insurance rates, called a "credit-based insurance score." You may be able to improve your insurance score by improving how you handle credit, which in turn may lower your premium payments on auto or homeowners insurance.

- Some credit scores offered to consumers are just estimates and are different from the credit risk scores lenders actually use, although they may appear similar. Consumer reporting agencies and other companies sometimes use an estimated score to illustrate a consumer's general level of credit risk. How might you tell whether a score is estimated? Ask the company if the score is used by most lenders. If it isn't, it is likely to be an estimated score.

Five Parts to Your FICO Credit Scores

As a rule, credit scores analyze the credit-related information on your credit report. How they do this varies. Since FICO scores are frequently used, here is how these scores assess what is on your credit report.

1. **Your payment history—about 35% of a FICO score:** Have you paid your credit accounts on time? Late payments, bankruptcies, and other negative items can hurt your credit score. But a solid record of on-time payments helps your score.

2. **How much you owe—about 30% of a FICO score:** FICO scores look at the amounts you owe on all your accounts, the number of accounts with balances, and how much of your available credit you are using. The more you owe compared to your credit limit, the lower your score will be.

3. **Length of your credit history—about 15% of a FICO score:** A longer credit history will increase your score. However, you can get a high score with a short credit history if the rest of your credit report shows responsible credit management.

4. **New credit—about 10% of a FICO score:** If you have recently applied for or opened new credit accounts, your credit score will weigh this fact against the rest of your credit history. FICO scores distinguish between a search for a single loan and a search for many new credit lines, in part by the length of time over which inquiries occur. If you need a loan, do your rate shopping within a focused period of time, such as 30 days, to avoid lowering your FICO score.

5. **Other factors—about 10% of a FICO score:** Several minor factors also can influence your score. For example, having a mix of credit types on your credit report—credit cards, installment loans such as a mortgage or auto loan, and personal lines of credit—is normal for people with longer credit histories and can add slightly to their scores.

What's Not in Your Scores

By law, credit scores may not consider your race, color, religion, national origin, sex and marital status, and whether you receive public assistance or exercise any consumer right under the federal Equal Credit Opportunity Act or the Fair Credit Reporting Act.

Learn Your Scores Soon

It's now easy to get your credit scores to check your financial health. Different sources provide credit scores to consumers via the internet, telephone or U.S. mail. For most scores, you will need to pay a small amount. You also will be asked to prove your identity to make sure your financial information isn't given to the wrong person.

Recommended Places Where You Can Get Your Scores

Annual Credit Report Service: Congress recently established this outlet to make it easier for consumers to get their credit reports and credit scores from the three national credit reporting agencies.
Website: https://www.annualcreditreport.com
Phone: 877-322-8228
U.S. Mail: Annual Credit Report Request Service
P. O. Box 105281
Atlanta, GA 30348-5281

- Cost: One free credit report per year from each credit reporting agency is available, but it does not include your credit score.

Myfico.com: The consumer internet site of Fair Isaac Corporation which developed the FICO score.
Web: http://www.myfico.com

- Cost: $14.95 for one FICO score and credit report. $44.85 for all three FICO scores and credit reports from the three credit reporting agencies (2005 pricing).

- Description: This score is most often used by lenders. It lets you see how prospective lenders would evaluate your credit history.

- Score range: FICO score from Equifax, Experian, and/or Trans Union 300–850

Individual Credit Reporting Agencies:

Equifax
Web: www.equifax.com
Phone: 800-685-1111

Experian
Web: www.experian.com
Phone: 866-200-6020

TransUnion
Web: www.transunion.com
Phone: 800-888-4213

- Prices for credit scores with credit reports vary from $14.95 to $34.95 (2005 pricing).

- Each credit reporting agency offers a different type of credit score to consumers.

- FICO score via: Equifax 300–850; Experian score 330–830; TransUnion score 150–934

Mortgage Lenders:

- Credit score is free when applying for mortgage or home equity loan.

- This score will likely be the actual score used to evaluate your application.

- Ask your lender to be sure. FICO score from Equifax, Experian, or Trans Union 300–850

Credit Score Examples

Vera, A Single Mother

Behavior/Action: As of March 2004, Vera and husband Dave have been married for 10 years. They have one daughter April, age 4. Financially they are making payments on time for two car loans, one mortgage, and four credit cards which have low balances. But sadly, their marriage has deteriorated and they agree to divorce. In the settlement Vera retains custody of April. Dave takes one of the cars and responsibility for its loan. He also takes two of their four credit cards, and agrees to pay 50 percent of the monthly mortgage payments.

227

- *Vera's current FICO score:* 780

Behavior/Action: In May, Dave struggles financially following the divorce and runs up his two credit cards to nearly their limit. Vera doesn't realize her name is still on the card accounts Dave is using.

- *Change in Vera's score:* -80
- *Vera's current FICO score:* 700

Behavior/Action: In July, Dave continues to struggle and misses payments on both cards. Both cards still are nearly maxed out.

- *Change in Vera's score:* -100
- *Vera's current FICO score:* 600

Behavior/Action: In August, Vera gets a call from her bank about the missed payments. Once she understands what has happened, she contacts Dave and asks him to roll over the balances on both cards to a new card that he opens in his name only, which he does. Paying off the two accounts improves her score.

- *Change in Vera's score:* +80
- *Vera's current FICO score:* 680

Behavior/Action: In February, 2005, Vera continues to manage her money carefully, paying her bills on time and keeping her two card balances low. Meanwhile the two missed payments get older on her credit file and have less impact to her score. Dave lands a better job and makes his part of the mortgage payments on time.

- *Change in Vera's score:* +40
- *Vera's current FICO score:* 720

Behavior/Action: In March, Vera's car breaks down. Since she relies on it to get to work and to take April to preschool, she has no choice but to have it repaired. To pay the garage she maxes out one of her credit cards.

- *Change in Vera's score:* -80
- *Vera's current FICO score:* 640

Behavior/Action: In April, Vera decides she needs a reliable car, she asks her bank about auto loan rates. They tell her that her credit score is too low to qualify her for their best rate. Since money is tight, she waits to buy a car.

- *Change in Vera's score:* None
- *Vera's current FICO score:* 640

July: Vera has steadily paid down her high credit card balance and monitored her score. When her score has improved, Vera applies and is approved for an excellent rate on an auto loan. She buys a used car and feels good about how she has managed her credit.

- *Change in Vera's score:* +40
- *Vera's current FICO score:* 680

Don and Doris, A Married Couple

Behavior/Action: As of March 2004, Don and Doris are married and in their 50s. They have twin sons who graduated from college a year ago, have good jobs, and live in different states. Don and Doris have been managing their money carefully for 30 years. They are making payments on a mortgage, three credit cards with large balances, and a $50,000 bank loan that paid for their sons' college. Now that their sons are on their own financially, Don and Doris focus on paying down their credit card balances by making larger monthly payments and using their cards sparingly. (Don and Doris have separate FICO scores, but in this example, they would rise and fall together.)

- *Doris and Don's current FICO score:* 690

Behavior/Action: By March 2005, after a year of steady payments, their credit card balances are significantly lower. They continue to manage their credit well and haven't opened any new accounts.

- *Change in Doris and Don's FICO score:* +50
- *Doris and Don's current FICO score:* 740

Behavior/Action: In June, the couple decides to go on an extended vacation, taking leaves of absence from their jobs to so they can tour the U.S. in a motor home. They buy their motor home with help from a new bank loan at a favorable rate, thanks to their good credit scores. But opening the new loan lowers their scores a bit. Since their plans will keep them on the road for three months, they put one of their sons in charge of paying their monthly bills.

- *Change in Doris and Don's FICO score: -20*
- *Doris and Don's Current FICO score: 720*

Behavior/Action: They have a wonderful vacation. When they return in September, they find they had neglected to tell their son about the bank loan. He didn't open the invoices they received from the bank thinking they were monthly account statements. Now their bank loan payment is 60 days late.

- *Change in Doris and Don's FICO score: -75*
- *Doris and Don's current FICO score: 645*

Behavior/Action: In October, Doris calls the bank, explains the mix-up and sends in the overdue payments immediately. A couple of weeks later their bank conveys their new account information to the credit reporting agencies, where it is available to influence their credit scores.

- *Change in Doris and Don's FICO score: +20*
- *Doris and Don's current FICO score: 665*

Behavior/Action: By April 2006, after six more months of on-time payments, their credit scores have steadily improved. Although the late payment will remain on their credit reports for seven years, it will impact their scores less as time passes. Don and Doris are on track once again to regain their good FICO credit scores in the 700s.

- *Change in Doris and Don's FICO score: +30*
- *Doris and Don's current FICO score: 695*

Helpful Tips

1. When you get your credit scores, make sure you also learn the highest and lowest scores possible, as well as the most important factors that influenced your scores. These factors can give you an idea of how you can improve your scores.

2. Getting your own credit scores or credit reports won't affect your scores, as long as you order them from one of the sources listed in this chapter.

3. Review your credit reports for accuracy. Mistakes and omissions on your credit reports probably will affect your credit scores. If you spot an error, contact the credit reporting agency and the creditor whose information is wrong.

4. If you have questions or problems with your credit scores, contact the company that provided them to you.

Boosting Your Scores

Your credit scores change when new information is reported by your creditors. So your scores will improve over time when you manage your credit responsibly. Here are some general ways to improve your credit scores:

- Pay your bills on time. Delinquent payments and collections can really hurt your score.

- Keep balances low on credit cards. High debt levels can hurt your score.

- Pay off debt rather than moving it between credit cards. The most effective way to improve your score in this area is to pay down your revolving credit.

- Apply for and open new credit accounts only when you need them.

- Check your credit report regularly for accuracy and contact the creditor and credit reporting agency to correct any errors.

- If you have missed payments, get current and stay current. The longer you pay your bills on time, the better your score.

Improving your credit scores can help you:

- Lower your interest rates.
- Speed up credit approvals.
- Reduce deposits required by utilities.
- Get approved for apartments.
- Get better credit card, auto loan, and mortgage offers.

Chapter 23

How to Get a Copy of Your Credit Report

Your Access to Free Credit Reports

The Fair Credit Reporting Act (FCRA) requires each of the nationwide consumer reporting companies—Equifax, Experian, and TransUnion—to provide you with a free copy of your credit report, at your request, once every 12 months. The FCRA promotes the accuracy and privacy of information in the files of the nation's consumer reporting companies. The Federal Trade Commission (FTC), the nation's consumer protection agency, enforces the FCRA with respect to consumer reporting companies.

A credit report includes information on where you live, how you pay your bills, and whether you've been sued, arrested, or filed for bankruptcy. Nationwide consumer reporting companies sell the information in your report to creditors, insurers, employers, and other businesses that use it to evaluate your applications for credit, insurance, employment, or renting a home.

Here are the details about your rights under the FCRA and the Fair and Accurate Credit Transactions (FACT) Act, which established the free annual credit report program.

This chapter includes information from "Your Access to Free Credit Reports," Federal Trade Commission (FTC), September 2005; and "Fake Credit Report Sites: Cashing in on Your Personal Information," FTC, September 2003.

233

How do I order my free report?

The three nationwide consumer reporting companies have set up a central website, a toll-free telephone number, and a mailing address through which you can order your free annual report.

To order, visit annualcreditreport.com, call 877-322-8228, or complete the Annual Credit Report Request Form and mail it to the following address:

Annual Credit Report Request Service
P.O. Box 105281
Atlanta, GA 30348-5281

You can print the form from ftc.gov/credit. Do not contact the three nationwide consumer reporting companies individually. They are providing free annual credit reports only through www.annualcreditreport.com, 877-322-8228, and Annual Credit Report Request Service at the previously listed address.

You may order your reports from each of the three nationwide consumer reporting companies at the same time, or you can order your report from each of the companies one at a time. The law allows you to order one free copy of your report from each of the nationwide consumer reporting companies every 12 months.

A warning about "impostor" websites: Only one website is authorized to fill orders for the free annual credit report you are entitled to under law—www.annualcreditreport.com. Other websites that claim to offer "free credit reports," "free credit scores," or "free credit monitoring" are not part of the legally mandated free annual credit report program. In some cases, the "free" product comes with strings attached. For example, some sites sign you up for a supposedly "free" service that converts to one you have to pay for after a trial period. If you don't cancel during the trial period, you may be unwittingly agreeing to let the company start charging fees to your credit card.

Some "impostor" sites use terms like "free report" in their names; others have URLs that purposely misspell www.annualcreditreport.com in the hope that you will mistype the name of the official site. Some of these "impostor" sites direct you to other sites that try to sell you something or collect your personal information.

Annualcreditreport.com and the nationwide consumer reporting companies will not send you an e-mail asking for your personal information. If you get an e-mail, see a pop-up ad, or get a phone call from someone claiming to be from Annualcreditreport.com or any of the three nationwide consumer reporting companies, do not reply or click on any link in the message. It's probably a scam. Forward any such e-mail to the FTC at spam@uce.gov.

What information do I need to provide to get my free report?

You need to provide your name, address, Social Security number, and date of birth. If you have moved in the last two years, you may have to provide your previous address. To maintain the security of your file, each nationwide consumer reporting company may ask you for some information that only you would know, like the amount of your monthly mortgage payment. Each company may ask you for different information because the information each has in your file may come from different sources.

Why do I want a copy of my credit report?

Your credit report has information that affects whether you can get a loan—and how much you will have to pay to borrow money. You want a copy of your credit report for these reasons:

* Make sure the information is accurate, complete, and up-to-date before you apply for a loan for a major purchase like a house or car, buy insurance, or apply for a job.

* Help guard against identity theft. That's when someone uses your personal information—like your name, your Social Security number, or your credit card number—to commit fraud. Identity thieves may use your information to open a new credit card account in your name. Then, when they don't pay the bills, the delinquent account is reported on your credit report. Inaccurate information like that could affect your ability to get credit, insurance, or even a job.

How long does it take to get my report after I order it?

If you request your report online at www.annualcreditreport.com, you should be able to access it immediately. If you order your report by calling toll-free 877-322-8228, your report will be processed and mailed to you within 15 days. If you order your report by mail using the Annual Credit Report Request Form, your request will be processed and mailed to you within 15 days of receipt.

Whether you order your report online, by phone, or by mail, it may take longer to receive your report if the nationwide consumer reporting company needs more information to verify your identity.

There also may be times when the nationwide consumer reporting companies receive a high volume of requests for credit reports. If that happens, you may be asked to re-submit your request. Or, you may be told that your report will be mailed to you sometime after 15 days from your request. If either of these events occurs, the nationwide consumer reporting companies will let you know.

Are there any other situations where I might be eligible for a free report?

Under federal law, you're entitled to a free report if a company takes adverse action against you such as denying your application for credit, insurance, or employment and you ask for your report within 60 days of receiving notice of the action. The notice will give you the name, address, and phone number of the consumer reporting company. You're also entitled to one free report a year if you're unemployed and plan to look for a job within 60 days; if you're on welfare; or if your report is inaccurate because of fraud, including identity theft. Otherwise, a consumer reporting company may charge you up to $9.50 for another copy of your report within a 12-month period.

To buy a copy of your report, contact the credit reporting company directly:

- Equifax: 800-685-1111; http://www.equifax.com

- Experian: 888-EXPERIAN (888-397-3742); http://www.experian.com

- Trans Union: 800-916-8800; http://www.transunion.com

Under state law, consumers in Colorado, Georgia, Maine, Maryland, Massachusetts, New Jersey, and Vermont already have free access to their credit reports.

Should I order a report from each of the three nationwide consumer reporting companies?

It's up to you. Because nationwide consumer reporting companies get their information from different sources, the information in your report from one company may not reflect all, or the same, information in your reports from the other two companies. That's not to say that the information in any of your reports is necessarily inaccurate; it just may be different.

Should I order my reports from all three of the nationwide consumer reporting companies at the same time?

You may order one, two, or all three reports at the same time, or you may stagger your requests. It's your choice. Some financial advisors say staggering your requests during a 12-month period may be a good way to keep an eye on the accuracy and completeness of the information in your reports.

What if I find errors—either inaccuracies or incomplete information—in my credit report?

Under the FCRA, both the consumer reporting company and the information provider (that is, the person, company, or organization that provides information about you to a consumer reporting company) are responsible for correcting inaccurate or incomplete information in your report. To take full advantage of your rights under this law, contact the consumer reporting company and the information provider.

1. Tell the consumer reporting company, in writing, what information you think is inaccurate. Consumer reporting companies must investigate the items in question—usually within 30 days—unless they consider your dispute frivolous. They also must forward all the relevant data you provide about the inaccuracy to the organization that provided the information. After the information provider receives notice of a dispute from the consumer reporting company, it must investigate, review the relevant information, and report the results back to the consumer reporting company. If the information provider finds the disputed information is inaccurate, it must notify all three nationwide consumer reporting companies so they can correct the information in your file.

    When the investigation is complete, the consumer reporting company must give you the written results and a free copy of your report if the dispute results in a change. (This free report does not count as your annual free report under the FACT Act.) If an item is changed or deleted, the consumer reporting company cannot put the disputed information back in your file unless the information provider verifies that it is accurate and complete. The consumer reporting company also must send you written notice that includes the name, address, and phone number of the information provider.

2. Tell the creditor or other information provider in writing that you dispute an item. Many providers specify an address for disputes. If the provider reports the item to a consumer reporting company, it must include a notice of your dispute. And if you are correct—that is, if the information is found to be inaccurate—the information provider may not report it again.

What can I do if the consumer reporting company or information provider won't correct the information I dispute?

If an investigation doesn't resolve your dispute with the consumer reporting company, you can ask that a statement of the dispute be included in your file and in future reports. You also can ask the consumer reporting company to provide your statement to anyone who received a copy of your report in the recent past. You can expect to pay a fee for this service.

If you tell the information provider that you dispute an item, a notice of your dispute must be included any time the information provider reports the item to a consumer reporting company.

How long can a consumer reporting company report negative information?

A consumer reporting company can report most accurate negative information for seven years and bankruptcy information for 10 years. There is no time limit on reporting information about criminal convictions; information reported in response to your application for a job that pays more than $75,000 a year; and information reported because you've applied for more than $150,000 worth of credit or life insurance. Information about a lawsuit or an unpaid judgment against you can be reported for seven years or until the statute of limitations runs out, whichever is longer.

Can anyone else can get a copy of my credit report?

The FCRA specifies who can access your credit report. Creditors, insurers, employers, and other businesses that use the information in your report to evaluate your applications for credit, insurance, employment, or renting a home are among those that have a legal right to access your report.

Can my employer get my credit report?

Your employer can get a copy of your credit report only if you agree. A consumer reporting company may not provide information about you to your employer, or to a prospective employer, without your written consent.

Fake Credit Report Sites: Cashing in on Your Personal Information

You may have seen websites or received unsolicited e-mail offering credit reports, sometimes for free. Be aware that some of these online operators may not actually provide credit reports, but may be using these sites as a way to capture your personal information. From there, they may sell your information to others who may use it commit fraud, including identity theft.

This is a variation on "phishing," also called "carding," a high-tech scam that uses spam or fraudulent websites to deceive consumers into disclosing their credit card numbers, bank account information, Social Security numbers, passwords, and other sensitive information.

The Federal Trade Commission (FTC), the nation's consumer protection agency, urges you to take the following precautions when visiting sites or responding to e-mail that offer credit reports:

- If you get an e-mail offering a credit report, don't reply or click on the link in the e-mail. Instead, contact the company cited in the e-mail using a telephone number or website address you know to be genuine.

- Be skeptical of unsolicited e-mail offering credit reports. Keep an eye out for e-mail from an atypical address, like XYZ123@website.net, or an e-mail address ending in a top level domain other than .com, like .ru or .de.

- Check whether the company has a working telephone number and legitimate address. You can check addresses at websites like http://www.switchboard.com, and phone numbers through reverse lookup search engines like http://www.anywho.com.

- Check for misspellings and grammatical errors. Silly mistakes and sloppy copy—for example, an area code that doesn't match an address—often are giveaways that the site is a scam. Look at the company's web address: is it a real company's address or it is a misspelled version of a legitimate company's web address?

- Check to see whether the e-mail address matches the website address. That is, when you enter the company's web address into the browser, does it go to the sender's site or re-direct you to a different web address? If it re-directs you, that's a red flag that you should cease the transaction.

- Find out who owns the website by using a "Whois" search such as the search at http://www.networksolutions.com.

- Exit from any website that asks for unnecessary personal information, like a personal identification number (PIN) for your bank account, the three-digit code on the back of your credit card, or your passport number and issuing country. Legitimate sites don't ask for this information.

- All legitimate sites will want to verify who you are and will respond to an electronic request for a credit report by asking you for an additional piece of information. If a site does not ask a follow-up question, the site is almost certainly a fake.

- Use only secure websites. Look for the "lock" icon on the browser's status bar, and the phrase "https" in the URL address for a website, to be sure your information is secure during transmission. All real sites are secure.

- Watch your mailbox and credit card statements: If you've responded to a bogus site, you may never receive the credit report they offered for free. If you paid one of these sites for a credit report, your credit card may never be charged. If you find that you have unauthorized charges, contact your financial institutions and credit card issuers immediately.

- Report suspicious activity to the FTC and the U.S. Secret Service. Send the actual spam to the Los Angeles Electronic Crimes Task Force at LA.ECTF.reports@usss.dhs.gov and to the FTC at spam@uce.gov. If you believe you've been scammed, file your complaint at http://www.ftc.gov, and then visit the FTC's Identity Theft website (www.consumer.gov/idtheft) to learn how to minimize your risk of damage from identity theft.

For More Information and to Complain

The FTC works for the consumer to prevent fraudulent, deceptive and unfair business practices in the marketplace and to provide information to help consumers spot, stop, and avoid them. To file a complaint or to get free information on consumer issues, visit http://www.ftc.gov or call toll-free, 877-FTC-HELP (877-382-4357); TTY: 866-653-4261. The FTC enters internet, telemarketing, identity theft, and other fraud-related complaints into Consumer Sentinel, a secure, online database available to hundreds of civil and criminal law enforcement agencies in the U.S. and abroad.

Consumers also can call their local office of the Secret Service.

Chapter 24

How to Dispute Credit Report Errors

Your credit report contains information about where you live, how you pay your bills, and whether you've been sued, arrested, or filed for bankruptcy. Consumer reporting companies sell the information in your report to creditors, insurers, employers, and other businesses that use it to evaluate your applications for credit, insurance, employment, or renting a home. The federal Fair Credit Reporting Act (FCRA) promotes the accuracy and privacy of information in the files of the nation's consumer reporting companies.

Some financial advisors and consumer advocates suggest that you review your credit report periodically. Why?

- Because the information it contains affects whether you can get a loan—and how much you will have to pay to borrow money.

- To make sure the information is accurate, complete, and up-to-date before you apply for a loan for a major purchase like a house or car, buy insurance, or apply for a job.

- To help guard against identity theft. That's when someone uses your personal information—like your name, your Social Security number, or your credit card number—to commit fraud. Identity thieves may use your information to open a new credit card account in your name. Then, when they don't pay the bills, the

"How to Dispute Credit Report Errors," Federal Trade Commission (www.ftc.gov), May 2006.

delinquent account is reported on your credit report. Inaccurate information like that could affect your ability to get credit, insurance, or even a job.

Getting Your Credit Report

An amendment to the FCRA requires each of the nationwide consumer reporting companies—Equifax, Experian, and TransUnion—to provide you with a free copy of your credit report, at your request, once every 12 months.

How to Order Your Free Report

The three nationwide consumer reporting companies have set up one website, toll-free telephone number, and mailing address through which you can order your free annual report. To order, visit http://www.annualcreditreport.com, call 877-322-8228, or complete the Annual Credit Report Request Form and mail it to: Annual Credit Report Request Service, P.O. Box 105281, Atlanta, GA 30348-5281. You can use the form in this brochure, or you can print it from ftc.gov/credit. Do not contact the three nationwide consumer reporting companies individually. They are providing free annual credit reports only through http://www.annualcreditreport.com, 877-322-8228, and Annual Credit Report Request Service, P.O. Box 105281, Atlanta, GA 30348-5281.

You may order your reports from each of the three nationwide consumer reporting companies at the same time, or you can order from only one or two. The law allows you to order one free copy from each of the nationwide consumer reporting companies every 12 months.

You need to provide your name, address, Social Security number, and date of birth. If you have moved in the last two years, you may have to provide your previous address. To maintain the security of your file, each nationwide consumer reporting company may ask you for some information that only you would know, like the amount of your monthly mortgage payment. Each company may ask you for different information because the information each has in your file may come from different sources.

Other Situations Where You Might Be Eligible for a Free Report

Under federal law, you're also entitled to a free report if a company takes adverse action against you, such as denying your application for credit, insurance, or employment, based on information in your report. You must ask for your report within 60 days of receiving notice of the action. The notice will give you the name, address, and phone number of the consumer reporting company.

You're also entitled to one free report a year if you're unemployed and plan to look for a job within 60 days; if you're on welfare; or if your report is inaccurate because of fraud, including identity theft.

Otherwise, a consumer reporting company may charge you up to $9.50 for another copy of your report within a 12-month period. To buy a copy of your report, contact:

* Equifax: 800-685-1111
  http://www.equifax.com

* Experian: 888-EXPERIAN (888-397-3742)
  http://www.experian.com

* TransUnion: 800-916-8800
  http://www.transunion.com

Under state law, consumers in Colorado, Georgia, Maine, Maryland, Massachusetts, New Jersey, and Vermont already have free access to their credit reports.

Correcting Errors

Under the FCRA, both the consumer reporting company and the information provider (that is, the person, company, or organization that provides information about you to a consumer reporting company) are responsible for correcting inaccurate or incomplete information in your report. To take advantage of all your rights under this law, contact the consumer reporting company and the information provider.

Step one: Tell the consumer reporting company, in writing, what information you think is inaccurate. Include copies (not originals) of documents that support your position. In addition to providing your complete name and address, your letter should clearly identify each item in your report you dispute, state the facts and explain why you dispute the information, and request that it be removed or corrected. You may want to enclose a copy of your report with the items in question circled. Send your letter by certified mail, "return receipt requested," so you can document what the consumer reporting company received. Keep copies of your dispute letter and enclosures.

Consumer reporting companies must investigate the items in question—usually within 30 days—unless they consider your dispute frivolous. They also must forward all the relevant data you provide about the inaccuracy to the organization that provided the information. After the information provider receives notice of a dispute from the consumer reporting company, it must investigate, review the relevant information, and report the results back to the consumer reporting company. If the information provider finds the disputed information is inaccurate, it must notify all three nationwide consumer reporting companies so they can correct the information in your file.

When the investigation is complete, the consumer reporting company must give you the results in writing and a free copy of your report if the dispute results in a change. This free report does not count as your annual free report. If an item is changed or deleted, the consumer reporting company cannot put the disputed information back in your file unless the information provider verifies that it is accurate and complete. The consumer reporting company also must send you written notice that includes the name, address, and phone number of the information provider.

If you ask, the consumer reporting company must send notices of any corrections to anyone who received your report in the past six months. You can have a corrected copy of your report sent to anyone who received a copy during the past two years for employment purposes.

If an investigation doesn't resolve your dispute with the consumer reporting company, you can ask that a statement of the dispute be included in your file and in future reports. You also can ask the consumer reporting company to provide your statement to anyone who received a copy of your report in the recent past. You can expect to pay a fee for this service.

Step two: Tell the creditor or other information provider, in writing, that you dispute an item. Be sure to include copies (not originals) of documents that support your position. Many providers specify an address for disputes. If the provider reports the item to a consumer reporting company, it must include a notice of your dispute. And if you are correct—that is, if the information is found to be inaccurate—the information provider may not report it again.

Adding Accounts to Your File

Your credit file may not reflect all your credit accounts. Although most national department store and all-purpose bank credit card accounts will be included in your file, not all creditors supply information to consumer reporting companies: some travel, entertainment, gasoline card companies, local retailers, and credit unions are among the creditors that don't.

If you've been told that you were denied credit because of an "insufficient credit file" or "no credit file" and you have accounts with creditors that don't appear in your credit file, ask the consumer reporting companies to add this information to future reports. Although they are not required to do so, many consumer reporting companies will add verifiable accounts for a fee. However, understand that if these creditors do not report to the consumer reporting company on a regular basis, the added items will not be updated in your file.

When negative information in your report is accurate, only the passage of time can assure its removal. A consumer reporting company can report most accurate negative information for seven years and bankruptcy information for ten years. Information about an unpaid judgment against you can be reported for seven years or until the statute of limitations runs out, whichever is longer. There is no time limit on reporting: information about criminal convictions; information reported in response to your application for a job that pays more than $75,000 a year; and information reported because you've applied for more than $150,000 worth of credit or life insurance. There is a standard method for calculating the seven-year reporting period. Generally, the period runs from the date that the event took place.

Sample Dispute Letter

Date
Your Name
Your Address, City, State, Zip Code

Complaint Department
Name of Company
Address
City, State, Zip Code

Dear Sir or Madam:

I am writing to dispute the following information in my file. I have circled the items I dispute on the attached copy of the report I received.

This item (identify item(s) disputed by name of source, such as creditors or tax court, and identify type of item, such as credit account or judgment) is (inaccurate or incomplete) because (describe what is inaccurate or incomplete and why). I am requesting that the item be removed (or request another specific change) to correct the information.

Enclosed are copies of (use this sentence if applicable and describe any enclosed documentation, such as payment records or court documents) supporting my position. Please reinvestigate this (these) matter(s) and (delete or correct) the disputed item(s) as soon as possible.

Sincerely,
Your Name

Enclosures: (List what you are enclosing.)

Chapter 25

Credit Repair:
Self-Help May Be Best

You see the advertisements in newspapers, on TV, and on the internet. You hear them on the radio. You get fliers in the mail. You may even get calls from telemarketers offering credit repair services. They all make the same claims:

- "Credit problems? No problem!"
- "We can erase your bad credit—100% guaranteed."
- "Create a new credit identity—legally."
- "We can remove bankruptcies, judgments, liens, and bad loans from your credit file forever!"

Do yourself a favor and save some money. Don't believe these statements. Only time, a conscious effort, and a personal debt repayment plan will improve your credit report.

This chapter explains how you can improve your creditworthiness and gives legitimate resources for low or no-cost help.

The Scam

Everyday, companies nationwide appeal to consumers with poor credit histories. They promise, for a fee, to clean up your credit report so you can get a car loan, a home mortgage, insurance, or even a job.

"Credit Repair: Self-Help May Be Best," Federal Trade Commission (www.ftc.gov), December 2005.

The truth is, they can't deliver. After you pay them hundreds or thousands of dollars in fees, these companies do nothing to improve your credit report; most simply vanish with your money.

The Warning Signs

If you decide to respond to a credit repair offer, look for these telltale signs of a scam:

- Companies that want you to pay for credit repair services before they provide any services.

- Companies that do not tell you your legal rights and what you can do for yourself for free.

- Companies that recommend that you not contact a credit reporting company directly.

- Companies that suggest that you try to invent a "new" credit identity—and then, a new credit report—by applying for an Employer Identification Number to use instead of your Social Security number.

- Companies that advise you to dispute all information in your credit report or take any action that seems illegal, like creating a new credit identity. If you follow illegal advice and commit fraud, you may be subject to prosecution.

You could be charged and prosecuted for mail or wire fraud if you use the mail or telephone to apply for credit and provide false information. It's a federal crime to lie on a loan or credit application, to misrepresent your Social Security number, and to obtain an Employer Identification Number from the Internal Revenue Service under false pretenses.

Under the Credit Repair Organizations Act, credit repair companies cannot require you to pay until they have completed the services they have promised.

The Truth

No one can legally remove accurate and timely negative information from a credit report. The law allows you to ask for an investigation of information in your file that you dispute as inaccurate or incomplete. There is no charge for this. Everything a credit repair clinic can do for you legally, you can do for yourself at little or no cost. The following provisions are part of The Fair Credit Reporting Act (FCRA):

- You're entitled to a free report if a company takes adverse action against you, like denying your application for credit, insurance, or employment, and you ask for your report within 60 days of receiving notice of the action. The notice will give you the name, address, and phone number of the consumer reporting company. You're also entitled to one free report a year if you're unemployed and plan to look for a job within 60 days; if you're on welfare; or if your report is inaccurate because of fraud, including identity theft.

- Each of the nationwide consumer reporting companies—Equifax, Experian, and TransUnion—is required to provide you with a free copy of your credit report, at your request, once every 12 months.

The three companies have set up a central website, a toll-free telephone number, and a mailing address through which you can order your free annual report. To order, click on annualcreditreport.com, call 877-322-8228, or complete the Annual Credit Report Request Form and mail it to: Annual Credit Report Request Service, P.O. Box 105281, Atlanta, GA 30348-5281. You can print the form from ftc.gov/credit. Do not contact the three nationwide consumer reporting companies individually. They are providing free annual credit reports only through annualcreditreport.com, 877-322-8228, and Annual Credit Report Request Service, P.O. Box 105281, Atlanta, GA 30348-5281. You may order your reports from each of the three nationwide consumer reporting companies at the same time, or you can order your report from each of the companies one at a time. Otherwise, a consumer reporting company may charge you up to $9.50 for another copy of your report within a 12-month period.

- You can dispute mistakes or outdated items for free. Under the FCRA, both the consumer reporting company and the information provider (that is, the person, company, or organization that provides information about you to a consumer reporting company) are responsible for correcting inaccurate or incomplete information in your report. To take advantage of all your rights under this law, contact the consumer reporting company and the information provider. For detailed information about disputing credit report errors, see Chapter 24—How to Dispute Credit Report Errors.

Reporting Accurate Negative Information

When negative information in your report is accurate, only the passage of time can assure its removal. A consumer reporting company can report most accurate negative information for seven years and bankruptcy information for ten years. Information about an unpaid judgment against you can be reported for seven years or until the statute of limitations runs out, whichever is longer. There is no time limit on reporting: information about criminal convictions; information reported in response to your application for a job that pays more than $75,000 a year; and information reported because you've applied for more than $150,000 worth of credit or life insurance. There is a standard method for calculating the seven-year reporting period. Generally, the period runs from the date that the event took place.

The Credit Repair Organizations Act

By law, credit repair organizations must give you a copy of the "Consumer Credit File Rights Under State and Federal Law" before you sign a contract. They also must give you a written contract that spells out your rights and obligations. Read these documents before you sign anything. The law contains specific protections for you. For example, a credit repair company cannot perform the following actions:

- Make false claims about their services.

- Charge you until they have completed the promised services.

- Perform any services until they have your signature on a written contract and have completed a three-day waiting period. During this time, you can cancel the contract without paying any fees.

Your contract must specify these items:

- The payment terms for services, including their total cost

- A detailed description of the services to be performed

- How long it will take to achieve the results

- Any guarantees they offer

- The company's name and business address

Have You Been Victimized?

Many states have laws regulating credit repair companies. State law enforcement officials may be helpful if you've lost money to credit repair scams.

If you've had a problem with a credit repair company, don't be embarrassed to report it. While you may fear that contacting the government will only make your problems worse, remember that laws are in place to protect you. Contact your local consumer affairs office or your state Attorney General (AGs). Many AGs have toll-free consumer hotlines. Check the Blue Pages of your telephone directory for the phone number or check http://www.naag.org for a list of state Attorneys General.

Need Help? Don't Despair

Just because you have a poor credit report doesn't mean you won't be able to get credit. Creditors set their own credit-granting standards and not all of them look at your credit history the same way. Some may look only at more recent years to evaluate you for credit, and they may grant credit if your bill-paying history has improved. It may be worthwhile to contact creditors informally to discuss their credit standards.

If you're not disciplined enough to create a workable budget and stick to it, work out a repayment plan with your creditors, or keep track of mounting bills, consider contacting a credit counseling organization. Many credit counseling organizations are nonprofit and work with you to solve your financial problems. But not all are reputable. For example, just because an organization says it's "nonprofit," there's no guarantee that its services are free, affordable, or even legitimate. In fact, some credit counseling organizations charge high fees, or hide their fees by pressuring consumers to make "voluntary" contributions that only cause more debt.

Most credit counselors offer services through local offices, the internet, or on the telephone. If possible, find an organization that offers in-person counseling. Many universities, military bases, credit unions, housing authorities, and branches of the U.S. Cooperative Extension Service operate nonprofit credit counseling programs. Your financial institution, local consumer protection agency, and friends and family also may be good sources of information and referrals.

If you are considering filing for bankruptcy, you should know about one major change to the bankruptcy laws: As of October 17, 2005, you must get credit counseling from a government-approved organization within six months before you file for bankruptcy relief.

You can find a state-by-state list of government-approved organizations at www.usdoj.gov/ust. That is the website of the U.S. Trustee Program, the organization within the U.S. Department of Justice that supervises bankruptcy cases and trustees.

Reputable credit counseling organizations can advise you on managing your money and debts, help you develop a budget, and offer free educational materials and workshops. Their counselors are certified and trained in the areas of consumer credit, money and debt management, and budgeting. Counselors discuss your entire financial situation with you, and help you develop a personalized plan to solve your money problems. An initial counseling session typically lasts an hour, with an offer of follow-up sessions.

Chapter 26

Credit and Your Consumer Rights

Chapter Contents

Section 26.1

Equal Credit Opportunity Act

"Equal Credit Opportunity," Federal Trade Commission (FTC), March 1998; reviewed for currency February 2006.

Credit is used by millions of consumers to finance an education or a house, remodel a home, or get a small business loan.

The Equal Credit Opportunity Act (ECOA) ensures that all consumers are given an equal chance to obtain credit. This doesn't mean all consumers who apply for credit get it: Factors such as income, expenses, debt, and credit history are considerations for creditworthiness.

The law protects you when you deal with any creditor who regularly extends credit, including banks, small loan and finance companies, retail and department stores, credit card companies, and credit unions. Anyone involved in granting credit, such as real estate brokers who arrange financing, is covered by the law. Businesses applying for credit also are protected by the law.

When You Apply for Credit, a Creditor May Not...

- Discourage you from applying because of your sex, marital status, age, race, national origin, or because you receive public assistance income.

- Ask you to reveal your sex, race, national origin, or religion. A creditor may ask you to voluntarily disclose this information (except for religion) if you're applying for a real estate loan. This information helps federal agencies enforce anti-discrimination laws. You may be asked about your residence or immigration status.

- Ask if you're widowed or divorced. When permitted to ask marital status, a creditor may only use the terms: married, unmarried, or separated.

- Ask about your marital status if you're applying for a separate, unsecured account. A creditor may ask you to provide this information if you live in "community property" states: Arizona,

California, Idaho, Louisiana, Nevada, New Mexico, Texas, and Washington. A creditor in any state may ask for this information if you apply for a joint account or one secured by property.

- Request information about your spouse, except when your spouse is applying with you; your spouse will be allowed to use the account; you are relying on your spouse's income or on alimony or child support income from a former spouse; or if you reside in a community property state.

- Inquire about your plans for having or raising children.

- Ask if you receive alimony, child support, or separate maintenance payments, unless you're first told that you don't have to provide this information if you won't rely on these payments to get credit. A creditor may ask if you have to pay alimony, child support, or separate maintenance payments.

When Deciding to Give You Credit, a Creditor May Not...

- Consider your sex, marital status, race, national origin, or religion.

- Consider whether you have a telephone listing in your name. A creditor may consider whether you have a phone.

- Consider the race of people in the neighborhood where you want to buy, refinance or improve a house with borrowed money.

- Consider your age, unless:

  - you're too young to sign contracts, generally younger than 18 years of age;

  - you're 62 or older, and the creditor will favor you because of your age;

  - it's used to determine the meaning of other factors important to creditworthiness. For example, a creditor could use your age to determine if your income might drop because you're about to retire;

  - it's used in a valid scoring system that favors applicants age 62 and older. A credit-scoring system assigns points to answers you provide to credit application questions. For example, your length of employment might be scored differently depending on your age.

257

When Evaluating Your Income, a Creditor May Not...

- Refuse to consider public assistance income the same way as other income.

- Discount income because of your sex or marital status. For example, a creditor cannot count a man's salary at 100 percent and a woman's at 75 percent. A creditor may not assume a woman of childbearing age will stop working to raise children.

- Discount or refuse to consider income because it comes from part-time employment or pension, annuity, or retirement benefits programs.

- Refuse to consider regular alimony, child support, or separate maintenance payments. A creditor may ask you to prove you have received this income consistently.

You Also Have the Right to...

- Have credit in your birth name (Mary Smith), your first and your spouse's last name (Mary Jones), or your first name and a combined last name (Mary Smith-Jones).

- Get credit without a cosigner, if you meet the creditor's standards.

- Have a cosigner other than your husband or wife, if one is necessary.

- Keep your own accounts after you change your name, marital status, reach a certain age, or retire, unless the creditor has evidence that you're not willing or able to pay.

- Know whether your application was accepted or rejected within 30 days of filing a complete application.

- Know why your application was rejected. The creditor must give you a notice that tells you either the specific reasons for your rejection or your right to learn the reasons if you ask within 60 days.

- Acceptable reasons include: "Your income was low," or "You haven't been employed long enough." Unacceptable reasons are: "You didn't meet our minimum standards," or "You didn't receive enough points on our credit-scoring system." Indefinite and vague reasons are illegal, so ask the creditor to be specific.

- Find out why you were offered less favorable terms than you applied for—unless you accept the terms. Ask for details. Examples of less favorable terms include higher finance charges or less money than you requested.

- Find out why your account was closed or why the terms of the account were made less favorable unless the account was inactive or delinquent.

A Special Note to Women

A good credit history—a record of how you paid past bills—often is necessary to get credit. Unfortunately, this hurts many married, separated, divorced, and widowed women. There are two common reasons women don't have credit histories in their own names: they lost their credit histories when they married and changed their names; or creditors reported accounts shared by married couples in the husband's name only.

If you're married, divorced, separated, or widowed, contact your local credit bureau(s) to make sure all relevant information is in a file under your own name.

If You Suspect Discrimination...

- Complain to the creditor. Make it known you're aware of the law. The creditor may find an error or reverse the decision.

- Check with your state Attorney General to see if the creditor violated state equal credit opportunity laws. Your state may decide to prosecute the creditor.

- Bring a case in federal district court. If you win, you can recover damages, including punitive damages. You also can obtain compensation for attorney's fees and court costs. An attorney can advise you on how to proceed.

- Join with others and file a class action suit. You may recover punitive damages for the group of up to $500,000 or one percent of the creditor's net worth, whichever is less.

- Report violations to the appropriate government agency. If you're denied credit, the creditor must give you the name and address of the agency to contact. While some of these agencies don't resolve individual complaints, the information you provide helps them decide which companies to investigate. A list of agencies follows.

If a retail store, department store, small loan and finance company, mortgage company, oil company, public utility, state credit union, government lending program, or travel and expense credit card company is involved, contact:

Consumer Response Center
Federal Trade Commission (FTC)
Washington, DC 20580

The FTC cannot intervene in individual disputes, but the information you provide may indicate a pattern of possible law violations that require action by the Commission.

If your complaint concerns a nationally chartered bank (National or N.A. will be part of the name), write to:

Comptroller of the Currency
Compliance Management
Mail Stop 7-5
Washington, DC 20219

If your complaint concerns a state-chartered bank that is insured by the Federal Deposit Insurance Corporation but is not a member of the Federal Reserve System, write to:

Federal Deposit Insurance Corporation
Consumer Affairs Division
Washington, DC 20429

If your complaint concerns a federally chartered or federally insured savings and loan association, write to:

Office of Thrift Supervision
Consumer Affairs Program
Washington, DC 20552

If your complaint concerns a federally chartered credit union, write to:

National Credit Union Administration
Consumer Affairs Division
Washington, DC 20456

Complaints against all kinds of creditors can be referred to:

Department of Justice
Civil Rights Division
Washington, DC 20530

Section 26.2

Fair Credit Reporting Act

Excerpted from an undated document titled "Your Credit Rights,"
reprinted with permission from the Federal Reserve Bank of San
Francisco, http://www.frbsf.org; accessed July 18, 2006.

The Fair Credit Reporting Act promotes the accuracy and privacy
of information in consumer credit reports. It also controls the use of
credit reports and requires consumer reporting agencies to maintain
correct and complete files. According to this act, you have a right to
review your credit report and to have incorrect information corrected.

Issuing Credit Reports

Credit bureaus, the most common type of consumer reporting agency
(CRA) that compiles and issues credit reports, are required to help you
understand your report. Reports can be issued only to those with a legitimate business reason. These include creditors, employers, insurers,
and government agencies reviewing your status for licensing or benefit purposes, or any third party for whom you request a report.

Credit Report Errors

If you find an error on your report, you should notify the credit
bureau in writing immediately. The bureau is responsible for investigating and for changing or removing any incorrect data. The source
of the error must then notify all consumer reporting agencies where
they sent information. If you are not satisfied with the correction, you
have the right to add a brief statement (100 words or less) about the
issue to your credit report. The statement should be a clarification,
not an explanation, of credit problems.

Denied Credit

If your credit application is turned down because of an error on
your report, the lender is required to provide you with the name and
address of the credit bureau that issued the report. Then, you have

30 days to request a free copy from the bureau. The bureaus must disclose to you all information in the report, its source, and who has recently received the report.

You have the right to have the credit bureau re-issue corrected reports to lenders who received reports within the last six months, or to employers who received one in the past two years.

Disclosure

Consumer reporting agencies must provide you access to the information in your credit report, as well as identify those who have requested the information recently. [For more information about receiving a copy of your credit report, See Chapter 23—How to Get a Copy of Your Credit Report.]

Limiting Access

You may request that consumer reporting agencies do not distribute your name on lists used by creditors and insurers to make unsolicited offers of credit and insurance. Requests can be made by telephone or in writing by filling out a form available from each credit reporting agency.

For telephone requests, call 888-5-OPT OUT to be excluded from Experian, Equifax, and TransUnion. Telephone requests last for two years; written requests are permanent.

Consumers have the right to sue consumer reporting agencies, users, and providers in state and federal court for violations of the Fair Credit Reporting Act.

Section 26.3

Fair Credit Billing Act

"Fair Credit Billing," an undated document produced by the Federal
Trade Commission; reviewed for currency in February 2006.

Have you ever been billed for merchandise you returned or never
received? Has your credit card company ever charged you twice for
the same item or failed to credit a payment to your account? While
frustrating, these errors can be corrected. It takes a little patience and
knowledge of the dispute settlement procedures provided by the Fair
Credit Billing Act (FCBA).

The law applies to "open end" credit accounts, such as credit cards,
and revolving charge accounts—such as department store accounts.
It does not cover installment contracts—loans or extensions of credit
you repay on a fixed schedule. Consumers often buy cars, furniture
and major appliances on an installment basis, and repay personal
loans in installments as well.

What types of disputes are covered?

The FCBA settlement procedures apply only to disputes about
"billing errors." Here are some examples:

- Unauthorized charges (Federal law limits your responsibility
  for unauthorized charges to $50.)

- Charges that list the wrong date or amount

- Charges for goods and services you didn't accept or weren't
  delivered as agreed

- Math errors

- Failure to post payments and other credits, such as returns

- Failure to send bills to your current address—provided the
  creditor receives your change of address, in writing, at least 20
  days before the billing period ends

263

- Charges for which you ask for an explanation or written proof of purchase along with a claimed error or request for clarification

To take advantage of the law's consumer protections, you must take the following steps:

- Write to the creditor at the address given for "billing inquiries," not the address for sending your payments, and include your name, address, account number and a description of the billing error.
- Send your letter so that it reaches the creditor within 60 days after the first bill containing the error was mailed to you.

Send your letter by certified mail, return receipt requested, so you have proof of what the creditor received. Include copies (not originals) of sales slips or other documents that support your position. Keep a copy of your dispute letter.

The creditor must acknowledge your complaint in writing within 30 days after receiving it, unless the problem has been resolved. The creditor must resolve the dispute within two billing cycles (but not more than 90 days) after receiving your letter.

What happens while my bill is in dispute?

You may withhold payment on the disputed amount (and related charges), during the investigation. You must pay any part of the bill not in question, including finance charges on the undisputed amount.

The creditor may not take any legal or other action to collect the disputed amount and related charges (including finance charges) during the investigation. While your account cannot be closed or re-stricted, the disputed amount may be applied against your credit limit.

Will my credit rating be affected?

The creditor may not threaten your credit rating or report you as delinquent while your bill is in dispute. However, the creditor may report that you are challenging your bill. In addition, the Equal Credit Opportunity Act prohibits creditors from discriminating against credit applicants who exercise their rights, in good faith, under the FCBA. Simply put, you cannot be denied credit simply because you've disputed a bill.

What if the bill is incorrect?

If your bill contains an error, the creditor must explain to you—in writing—the corrections that will be made to your account. In addition to crediting your account, the creditor must remove all finance charges, late fees or other charges related to the error.

If the creditor determines that you owe a portion of the disputed amount, you must get a written explanation. You may request copies of documents proving you owe the money.

What if the bill is correct?

If the creditor's investigation determines the bill is correct, you must be told promptly and in writing how much you owe and why. You may ask for copies of relevant documents. At this point, you'll owe the disputed amount, plus any finance charges that accumulated while the amount was in dispute. You also may have to pay the minimum amount you missed paying because of the dispute.

If you disagree with the results of the investigation, you may write to the creditor, but you must act within 10 days after receiving the explanation, and you may indicate that you refuse to pay the disputed amount. At this point, the creditor may begin collection procedures. However, if the creditor reports you to a credit bureau as delinquent, the report also must state that you don't think you owe the money. The creditor must tell you who gets these reports.

What if the creditor fails to follow the procedure?

Any creditor who fails to follow the settlement procedure may not collect the amount in dispute, or any related finance charges, up to $50, even if the bill turns out to be correct. For example, if a creditor acknowledges your complaint in 45 days—15 days too late—or takes more than two billing cycles to resolve a dispute, the penalty applies. The penalty also applies if a creditor threatens to report—or improperly reports—your failure to pay to anyone during the dispute period.

Can I dispute the bill if I'm not satisfied with my purchase?

Disputes about the quality of goods and services are not "billing errors," so the dispute procedure does not apply. However, if you buy unsatisfactory goods or services with a credit or charge card, you can take the same legal actions against the card issuer as you can take under state law against the seller.

To take advantage of this protection regarding the quality of goods or services, you must meet these criteria:

- Have made the purchase (it must be for more than $50) in your home state or within 100 miles of your current billing address

- Make a good faith effort to resolve the dispute with the seller first

The dollar and distance limitations don't apply if the seller also is the card issuer—or if a special business relationship exists between the seller and the card issuer.

Are there any other billing rights?

Businesses that offer "open end" credit also must follow these rules:

- Give you a written notice when you open a new account—and at certain other times—that describes your right to dispute billing errors

- Provide a statement for each billing period in which you owe—or they owe you—more than one dollar

- Send your bill at least 14 days before the payment is due—if you have a period within which to pay the bill without incurring additional charges

- Credit all payments to your account on the date they're received, unless no extra charges would result if they failed to do so. Creditors are permitted to set some reasonable rules for making payments, say setting a reasonable deadline for payment to be received to be credited on the same date.

- Promptly credit or refund overpayments and other amounts owed to your account. This applies to instances where your account is owed more than one dollar. Your account must be credited promptly with the amount owed. If you prefer a refund, it must be sent within seven business days after the creditor receives your written request. The creditor must also make a good faith effort to refund a credit balance that has remained on your account for more than six months.

Can I sue the creditor?

You can sue a creditor who violates the FCBA. If you win, you may be awarded damages, plus twice the amount of any finance charge—

as long as it's between $100 and $1,000. The court also may order the creditor to pay your attorney's fees and costs.

If possible, hire a lawyer who is willing to accept the amount awarded to you by the court as the entire fee for representing you. Some lawyers may not take your case unless you agree to pay their fee—win or lose—or add to the court-awarded amount if they think it's too low.

How to I report FCBA violations?

The Federal Trade Commission (FTC) enforces the FCBA for most creditors except banks. The FTC works for the consumer to prevent fraudulent, deceptive and unfair business practices in the marketplace and to provide information to help consumers spot, stop and avoid them. To file a complaint or to get free information on consumer issues, call toll-free, 877-FTC-HELP (877-382-4357), or use the complaint form at http://www.ftc.gov. The FTC enters internet, telemarketing, identity theft and other fraud-related complaints into Consumer Sentinel, a secure, online database available to hundreds of civil and criminal law enforcement agencies in the U.S. and abroad.

Section 26.4

Fair Debt Collection Practices Act

Excerpted from an undated document titled "Your Credit Rights," reprinted with permission from the Federal Reserve Bank of San Francisco, http://www.frbsf.org; accessed July 18, 2006.

The Fair Debt Collection Practices Act promotes the fair treatment of consumers by prohibiting debt collectors from using unfair, deceptive, or abusive practices.

This act applies to professional debt collectors who collect on loans they did not originate. Though it technically does not apply to banks, department stores, and other lenders who collect their own debts, no reputable lender is permitted to use such practices.

- Debt collectors are permitted to contact people other than the debtor only to locate the debtor or make a reasonable effort to communicate with the debtor about the debt.

- After making contact, debt collectors are required to send written notice informing the debtor of the amount of the debt, the name of the creditor, and the fact that the debt will be considered valid unless disputed within 30 days.

- Debt collectors are prohibited from harassing, oppressing, or being abusive in collecting a debt. This includes using threats or obscene language, publicizing the debt, making annoying or anonymous telephone calls, and misrepresenting the identity of the collector, the status of the debt, and the consequences if it is not paid.

If debt collectors violate the Fair Debt Collection Practices Act, consumers can sue for actual and punitive damages.

Section 26.5

Opting out of Preapproved Offers

"Prescreened Offers of Credit and Insurance," Federal Trade Commission, July 2005.

Mail call: Bills, a letter from your Aunt Mary, a circular from a local department store, your monthly bank statement, and an offer for a new credit card that says you've been "prescreened" or "prequalified."

A "prescreened" offer of credit? What's that?

Many companies that solicit new credit card accounts and insurance policies use prescreening to identify potential customers for the products they offer. Prescreened offers—sometimes called "preapproved" offers—are based on information in your credit report that indicates you meet criteria set by the offeror. Usually, prescreened solicitations come via mail, but you also may get them in a phone call or in an e-mail.

How does prescreening work?

Prescreening works in one of two ways:

- A creditor or insurer establishes criteria, like a minimum credit score, and asks a consumer reporting company for a list of people in the company's database who meet the criteria; or

- A creditor or insurer provides a list of potential customers to a consumer reporting company and asks the company to identify people on the list who meet certain criteria.

Can prescreening hurt my credit report or credit score?

No. There will be "inquiries" on your credit report showing which companies obtained your information for prescreening, but those inquiries will not have a negative effect on your credit report or credit score.

269

Can I reduce the number of unsolicited credit and insurance offers I get?

If you decide that you don't want to receive prescreened offers of credit and insurance, you have two choices: You can opt out of receiving them for five years or opt out of receiving them permanently. Call toll-free 888-5-OPTOUT (888-567-8688) or visit http://www.optoutprescreen.com for details. The telephone number and website are operated by the major consumer reporting companies. When you call or visit the website, you'll be asked to provide certain personal information, including your home telephone number, name, Social Security number, and date of birth. The information you provide is confidential and will be used only to process your request to opt out.

Remember that if you have joint credit relationships, like a mortgage or a car loan with a spouse, partner, or other adult, you may continue to receive some prescreened solicitations until both of you exercise your opt-out right.

Why would someone opt out—or not?

Some people prefer not to receive these kinds of offers in the mail, especially if they are not in the market for a new credit card or insurance policy. They may prefer to opt out to limit access to their credit report information for credit and insurance solicitations, or to reduce some mailbox "clutter." However, some companies send offers that are not based on prescreening, and your federal opt-out right will not stop those kinds of solicitations.

As you consider opting out, you should know that prescreened offers can provide many benefits, especially if you are in the market for a credit card or insurance. Prescreened offers can help you learn about what's available, compare costs, and find the best product for your needs. Because you are pre-selected to receive the offer, you can be turned down only under limited circumstances. The terms of prescreened offers also may be more favorable than those that are available to the general public. In fact, some credit card or insurance products may be available only through prescreened offers.

Does opting out hurt my credit score?

Removing your name from prescreened lists has no effect on your ability to apply for or obtain credit or insurance.

If I decide to opt out, how long will it be before I stop getting prescreened offers?

Requests to opt out are processed within five days, but it may take up to 60 days before you stop receiving prescreened offers.

What if I opt out and then change my mind?

You can use the same toll-free telephone number or website to opt back in.

Will calling 888-5-OPTOUT or visiting www.optoutprescreen.com stop all unsolicited offers of credit and insurance?

Calling the opt-out line or visiting the website will stop the prescreened solicitations that are based on lists from the major consumer reporting companies. You may continue to get solicitations for credit and insurance based on lists from other sources. For example, opting out won't end solicitations from local merchants, religious and charitable associations, professional and alumni associations, and companies with which you already conduct business. To stop mail from groups like these—as well as mail addressed to "occupant" or "resident"—you must contact each source directly.

What other opt-out programs should I know about?

The federal government has created the National Do Not Call Registry—a free, easy way to reduce the telemarketing calls you get at home. To register your phone number or to get information about the registry, visit www.donotcall.gov, or call 888-382-1222 from the phone number you want to register. You will get fewer telemarketing calls within 31 days of registering your number. Your number will stay on the registry for five years, until it is disconnected, or until you take it off the registry. After five years, you will be able to renew your registration.

The Direct Marketing Association (DMA), a trade association for businesses in direct, database, and interactive global marketing, maintains a Mail Preference Service that lets you opt out of receiving direct mail marketing from many national companies for five years. When you register with this service, your name will be put on a "delete" file and made available to direct-mail marketers. However, your

271

registration will not stop mailings from any organizations that are not registered with the DMA's Mail Preference Service. To register with DMA, send a letter to:

Direct Marketing Association
Mail Preference Service
PO Box 643
Carmel, NY 10512
Online registration:
http://www.the-dma.org/consumers/offmailinglist.html

The DMA also has an e-Mail Preference Service to help you reduce unsolicited commercial e-mails. To "opt-out" of receiving unsolicited commercial e-mail from DMA members, visit www.dmaconsumers.org/offemaillist.html. Your online request will be effective for one year.

Part Four

Borrowing Money

Chapter 27

Manage Credit Wisely

Learning to Manage Credit

Borrowing can help you meet your long-term goals for an education, car, or home. But borrowing for day-to-day needs and wants gets many people into financial trouble. Before using your credit card, getting a payday loan, renting-to-own, or borrowing against your home's equity, ask yourself if you really need to borrow the money.

- Avoid spur-of-the-moment purchases.
- Set a monthly limit on credit card charges.
- Pay more than the minimum on your credit card bill.

The minimum payment trap: It would take 61 years to pay off a $5,000 credit card balance if you make only the minimum monthly payment. You would pay almost $16,000 in interest (assuming a 14% interest rate and minimum payment of 1.5% of the outstanding balance).

Protect Your Credit Rating

Lenders use credit reports to decide whether to loan money. Insurance companies, landlords, and employers also check credit reports.

This chapter begins with "Learning to Manage Credit," excerpted from "There's a Lot to Learn About Money," Federal Reserve Board of Governors, November 2002. Additional text under the heading "Banking and Credit" is excerpted from "2006 Consumer Action Handbook," Federal Citizen Information Center, U.S. General Services Administration, 2006.

A report that shows defaults or late payments—even 30 days late—can mean not getting a loan or paying a higher interest rate.

Get the Best Deal

When you borrow money, you have a right and a responsibility to know all the loan's terms and conditions. Ask questions and compare interest rates and fees. Know what's at stake if you don't make your payments. Before you borrow money, ask these questions:

- What is the interest rate?

- What are all the fees?

- How much will I have paid in interest when the loan is paid off?

- Can I pay it off early without penalty?

- Shop around and compare. Don't get taken.

- Question an offer that makes borrowing sound too good to be true.

- Always read and understand the fine print.

- Seek help if you need it.

Banking and Credit

ATM/Debit cards: With a debit card and personal identification number (PIN), you can use an Automated Teller Machine (ATM), to withdraw cash, make deposits, or transfer funds between accounts. Some ATMs charge a fee if you are not a member of the ATM network or are making a transaction at a remote location. Retail purchases can also be made with a debit card. You enter your PIN or sign for the purchase. Some banks that issue debit cards are charging customers a fee for debit card purchases made with a PIN. Although a debit card looks like a credit card, the money for the purchase is transferred immediately from your bank account to the store's account. The purchase will be shown on your bank account statement.

Credit: Like everything else you buy, credit has a price tag and it pays to comparison shop. With the internet, you can now compare local credit offers with those from financial institutions around the nation. For up-to-date interest rate reports on mortgages, auto loans, credit cards, home equity loans, and other banking products visit www.bankrate.com. For a listing of credit cards visit www.cardlocator.com.

Installment loans: Before you sign an agreement for a loan to buy a house, a car or other large purchase, make sure you fully understand all the lender's terms and conditions:

- The dollar amount you are borrowing

- The payment amounts and when they are due

- The total finance charge—the total of all the interest and fees you must pay to get the loan

- The Annual Percentage Rate (APR)—the rate of interest you will pay over the full term of the loan

- Penalties for late payments

- What the lender will do if you can't pay back the loan

- Penalties if you pay the loan back early

Table 27.1. Save Money with the Right Loan

Get the Lowest Rate

$15,000 Car Loan for 5 Years

Lender	Interest rate	Total interest
Pixley Bank	6.5%	$ 2,609.53
ABC Car loan	7.5%	$ 3,034.15
XYZ Finance Company	8.75%	$ 3,573.51

Choose the Shortest Term

$15,000 Car Loan at 10 Percent Interest

	3-year	4-year	5-year
Number of payments	36	48	60
Payment	$484	$380	$318
Total paid	$17,424	$18,261	$19,122
Interest saved	$1,698	$861	$0

Source: Federal Reserve Board of Governors

Fortunately, the Truth in Lending Act requires lenders to give you this information so you can compare different offers.

Payday and tax refund loans: With a typical payday loan, you might write a personal check for $115 to borrow $100 for two weeks—until payday. The annual percentage rate (APR) in this example is 390 percent. Payday loans are illegal in some states.

Another high cost way to borrow money is a tax refund loan. This type of credit lets you get an advance on a tax refund. APRs as high as 774% have been reported. If you are short of cash, avoid both of these loans by asking for more time to pay a bill or seeking a traditional loan. Even a cash advance on your credit card may cost less.

Home equity loans: Consider carefully before taking out a home equity loan. Although this type of loan might let you take tax deductions that you could not take with other types of loans, they reduce the equity you have built up in your house. If you are unable to make payments, you could lose your home.

Home equity loans can either be a revolving line of credit or a one-time, closed-end loan. Revolving credit lets you choose when and how often to borrow against the equity in your home. In a closed-end loan, you receive a lump sum for a particular purpose, such as remodeling or tuition. Apply for a home equity loan through a bank or credit union first. These loans are likely to cost less than those offered by finance companies.

Credit cards: Chances are you've gotten your share of "pre-approved" credit card offers in the mail. Examine the fine print carefully before you accept any offer for a credit or charge card.

- The Annual Percentage Rate (APR). If the interest rate is variable, how is it determined and when can it change?

- The periodic rate. This is the interest rate used to figure the finance charge on your balance each billing period.

- The annual fee. While some cards have no annual fee, others expect you to pay an amount each year for being a cardholder.

- The grace period. This is the number of days you have to pay your bill before finance charges start. Without this period, you may have to pay interest from the date you use your card or when the purchase is posted to your account.

- The finance charges. Most lenders calculate finance charges using an average daily account balance—this is the average of what you owed each day in the billing cycle. Look for offers that use an adjusted balance, which subtracts your payment from your beginning balance. The finance charges you will pay are usually lower. Stay away from offers that use the previous balance in calculating what you owe; this method has the highest finance charge. Also don't forget to check if there is a minimum finance charge.

- Other fees. Ask about special fees when you get a cash advance, make a late payment, or go over your credit limit. Some companies charge a monthly fee regardless of whether you use your card.

The Fair Credit and Charge Card Disclosure Act requires credit and charge card issuers to include this information on credit applications.

Chapter 28

Understanding Loan Contracts

Understanding the Contract

When you sign or co-sign an application for credit you are agreeing to all of its terms. If you are approved, the application becomes a contract and you are legally bound to the terms. It is important to understand the terms used in a contract before you sign on the dotted line.

By law, a creditor must disclose all the terms of the agreement in writing on the application. This is called the Truth in Lending Disclosure. The type of credit applied for will determine the terms that must be disclosed. Two types of credit are available to consumers: closed-end and open-end. Closed-end credit includes installment loans and mortgages. Credit cards and home equity lines of credit are examples of open-end credit.

Closed-end credit is a loan which requires the same payment each month for a specified amount of time, at a specified interest rate. This type of credit is often used to purchase cars, furniture and appliances and for personal loans. The following disclosures must be made in writing prior to the loan closing:

- Name of the company financing the loan.

- The amount financed and a list of what is and is not included in the amount financed (purchase price, down payment, taxes).

- The finance charge which includes interest and other fees, expressed in a dollar amount.

- The annual percentage rate (APR). This is the cost of the credit expressed as a yearly rate.

- The payment schedule which includes the number of payments, the amount of each, and when they are due.

- The total amount of the payments.

- The prepayment penalty, if applicable. This is a charge for paying the loan in full before the end of the loan period.

- The late payment charge if the payments are not made on time. The consequences of not making payments on time is also explained.

- The security interest, if any. For example, with a car loan, the car becomes the security for the loan. If payments are not made as agreed, the creditor can take the car.

- Insurance charges, if any. For example, credit life insurance will pay the loan in full if the borrower dies. This coverage is optional, at the borrower's choice, and is an expensive way to buy life insurance.

Open-end credit allows consumers to incur new debt before paying off old debt. The borrower receives a line of credit and agrees to repay at least a partial amount each month. Most credit cards are this form of credit. The disclosures are different than those required for closed-end credit. Look for the following terms in an application for open-end credit:

- **Annual fee:** An amount charged to you once a year for the opportunity to use the credit. Not all open-end accounts have annual fees.

- **Annual percentage rate:** The annual percentage rate (APR) is the annual interest rate you will be charged on any unpaid balance. Some creditors offer set or fixed rates, while others may have a variable rate (a rate that may change from month to month).

- **Minimum payment:** The minimum amount which must be paid by the payment due date; usually between 1.5–4% of the unpaid balance.

- **Late and over limit fees**: The amount that you will be charged if you are late with a payment or go over the credit limit.

- **Grace period:** The number of days you have to pay off your bill before interest is charged. Typically grace periods are 20–25 days in length. The grace period only exists if you do not have a previous balance. Not all open-end credit has a grace period.

- **Cash advance:** The cash advance feature allows you to make cash withdrawals against your line of credit. Withdrawals can be made through an ATM, at a bank or by cashing special checks. Interest rates on cash advances are usually higher than those on purchases. Moreover, there is no grace period on cash advances.

- **Default rate:** If your payment is late, you miss a minimum payment, pay with a check that bounces, or exceed your credit limit, your APR may increase. This new rate is called the default rate. If the agreement also says that the "rate will increase if you fail to make payment to another creditor when due," this is a universal default policy. Your rate can increase dramatically based on your poor payment history with other creditors, even if your payment record with the creditor who uses the universal default policy is perfect.

Before You Sign or Co-Sign

- Read the contract carefully and completely.

- If you do not understand the contract or if a particular item is unclear, have someone who is knowledgeable read and explain each item to you. Do not sign the application or contract unless you understand everything to which you are agreeing.

- Make sure that all spaces are filled in. Do not sign the contract if there are blank spaces. Fill in blank spaces or draw a line through them if they are not applicable.

- Make a copy of the final contract after you sign it. Keep this copy for your records.

Chapter 29

How Is Interest Calculated?

Although Shakespeare cautioned "neither a borrower nor a lender be," using and providing credit has become a way of life for many individuals in today's economy. Examples of borrowing by individuals are numerous: home mortgages, car loans, credit cards, etc. While perhaps more commonly thought of as investing, many examples of lending by individuals can be identified. By opening a savings account, an individual makes a loan to the bank; by purchasing a savings bond, an individual makes a loan to the government.

As with goods and services that an individual might buy or sell, the use or extension of credit has a price attached to it, namely the interest paid or earned. And, just as consumers shop for the best price on a particular item of merchandise, so too should consumers "comparison shop" for credit—whether borrowing or lending. But comparing prices for credit can, at times, be confusing. Although the price of credit is generally stated as a rate of interest, the amount of interest paid or earned depends on a number of other factors, including the method used to calculate interest.

Two federal laws have been passed to minimize some of the confusion consumers face when they borrow or lend money. The Truth in Lending Act, passed in 1968, has made it easier for consumers

Reprinted from "The ABCs of Figuring Interest," an online financial education publication of the Federal Reserve Bank of Chicago, http://www.chicagofed.org, 2006.

to comparison shop when they borrow money. Similarly, the purpose of the Truth in Savings Act, passed in 1991, is to assist consumers in comparing deposit accounts offered by depository institutions.

Provisions of the Truth in Lending Act have been implemented through the Federal Reserve's Regulation Z, which defines creditor responsibilities. Most importantly, creditors are required to disclose both the Annual Percentage Rate (APR) and the total dollar finance charge to the borrowing consumer. Simply put, the APR is the relative cost of credit expressed in percentage terms on the basis of one year. Just as "unit pricing" gives the consumer a basis for comparing prices of different-sized packages of the same product, the APR enables the consumer to compare the prices of different loans regardless of the amount, maturity, or other terms.

Similarly, provisions of the Truth in Savings Act have been implemented through the Federal Reserve's Regulation DD. These provisions include a requirement that depository institutions disclose an annual percentage yield (APY) for interest-bearing deposit accounts. Like the APR, an APY will provide a uniform basis for comparison by indicating, in percentage terms on the basis of one year, how much interest a consumer receives on a deposit account.

While federal laws make it easier to comparison shop for credit and deposit accounts, a variety of methods continue to be used to calculate the amount of interest paid or earned by a consumer. To make an informed decision, it is useful to understand the relationships between these different methods.

Interest Calculations

Interest represents the price borrowers pay to lenders for credit over specified periods of time. The amount of interest paid depends on a number of factors: the dollar amount lent or borrowed, the length of time involved in the transaction, the stated (or nominal) annual rate of interest, the repayment schedule, and the method used to calculate interest.

If, for example, an individual deposits $1,000 for one year in a bank paying 5 percent interest on savings, then at the end of the year the depositor may receive interest of $50, or some other amount, depending on the way interest is calculated. Alternatively, an individual who borrows $1,000 for one year at 5 percent and repays the loan in one payment at the end of a year may pay $50 in interest, or some other amount, again depending on the calculation method used.

Simple Interest

The various methods used to calculate interest are basically variations of the simple interest calculation method. The basic concept underlying simple interest is that interest is paid only on the original amount borrowed for the length of time the borrower has use of the credit. The amount borrowed is referred to as the principal. In the simple interest calculation, interest is computed only on that portion of the original principal still owed.

- *Example 1:* Suppose $1,000 is borrowed at 5 percent and repaid in one payment at the end of one year. Using the simple interest calculation, the interest amount would be 5 percent of $1,000 for one year, or $50, since the borrower had use of $1,000 for the entire year.

When more than one payment is made on a simple interest loan, the method of computing interest is referred to as "interest on the declining balance." Since the borrower only pays interest on that amount of original principal that has not yet been repaid, interest paid will be smaller the more frequent the payments. At the same time, of course, the amount of credit at the borrower's disposal is also smaller.

- *Example 2:* Using simple interest on the declining balance to compute interest charges, a 5 percent, $1,000 loan repaid in two payments—one at the end of the first half-year and another at the end of the second half-year would accumulate total interest charges of $37.50. The first payment would be $500 plus $25 (5 percent of $1,000 for one-half year), or $525; the second payment would be $500 plus $12.50 (5 percent of $500 for one-half year), or $512.50. The total amount paid would be $525 plus $512.50, or $1,037.50. Interest equals the difference between the amount repaid and the amount borrowed, or $37.50. If four quarterly payments of $250 plus interest were made, the interest amount would be $31.25; if 12 monthly payments of $83.33 plus interest were made, the interest amount would be $27.08.

- *Example 3:* When interest on the declining balance method is applied to a 5 percent, $1,000 loan that is to be repaid in two equal payments, payments of $518.83 would be made at the end of the first half-year and at the end of the second half-year. Interest due at the end of the first half-year remains $25;

therefore, with the first payment the balance is reduced by $493.83 ($518.83 less $25), leaving the borrower $506.17 to use during the second half-year. The interest for the second half-year is 5 percent of $506.17 for one-half year, or $12.66. The final $518.83 payment, then, covers interest of $12.66 plus the outstanding balance of $506.17. Total interest paid is $25 plus $12.66, or $37.66, slightly more than in Example 2.

The equal payment variation is commonly used with mortgage payment schedules. Each payment over the duration of the loan is split into two parts. Part one is the interest due at the time the payment is made, and part two—the remainder—is applied to the balance or amount still owed. In addition to mortgage lenders, credit unions typically use the simple interest/declining balance calculation method for computing interest on loans. A number of banks also offer personal loans using this method.

Other Calculation Methods

Add-on interest, bank discount, and compound interest calculation methods differ from the simple interest method as to when, how, and on what balance interest is paid. The "effective annual rate" for these methods is that annual rate of interest which, when used in the simple interest rate formula, equals the amount of interest payable in these other calculation methods. For the declining balance method, the effective annual rate of interest is the stated or nominal annual rate of interest. For the methods described below, the effective annual rate of interest differs from the nominal rate.

Add-on interest: When the add-on interest method is used, interest is calculated on the full amount of the original principal. The interest amount is immediately added to the original principal, and payments are determined by dividing principal plus interest by the number of payments to be made. When only one payment is involved, this method produces the same effective interest rate as the simple interest method. When two or more payments are to be made, however, use of the add-on interest method results in an effective rate of interest that is greater than the nominal rate. True, the interest amount is calculated by applying the nominal rate to the total amount borrowed, but the borrower does not have use of the total amount for the entire time period if two or more payments are made.

- *Example 4:* Consider, again, the two-payment loan in Example 3. Using the add-on interest method, interest of $50 (5 percent of $1,000 for one year) is added to the $1,000 borrowed, giving $1,050 to be repaid; half (or $525) at the end of the first half-year and the other half at the end of the second half-year.

Recall that in Example 3, where the declining balance method was used, an effective rate of 5 percent meant two equal payments of $518.83 were to be made. Now with the add-on interest method each payment is $525. The effective rate of this 5 percent add-on rate loan, then, is greater than 5 percent. In fact, the corresponding effective rate is 6.631 percent. This rate takes into account the fact that the borrower does not have use of $1,000 for the entire year, but rather use of $1,000 for the first half-year and use of about $500 for the second half-year.

To see that a one-year, two equal-payment, 5 percent add-on rate loan is equivalent to a one-year, two equal-payment, 6.631 percent declining balance loan, consider the following. When the first $525 payment is made, $33.15 in interest is due (6.631 percent of $1,000 for one-half year). Deducting the $33.15 from $525 leaves $491.85 to be applied to the outstanding balance of $1,000, leaving the borrower with $508.15 to use during the second half-year. The second $525 payment covers $16.85 in interest (6.631 percent of $508.15 for one-half year) and the $508.15 balance due.

In Example 4, using the add-on interest method means that no matter how many payments are to be made, the interest will always be $50. As the number of payments increases, the borrower has use of less and less credit over the year. For example, if four quarterly payments of $262.50 are made, the borrower has the use of $1,000 during the first quarter, around $750 during the second quarter, around $500 during the third quarter, and around $250 during the fourth and final quarter. Therefore, as the number of payments increases, the effective rate of interest also increases. For instance, in the current example, if four quarterly payments are made, the effective rate of interest would be 7.922 percent; if 12 monthly payments are made, the effective interest rate would be 9.105 percent. The add-on interest method is sometimes used by finance companies and some banks in determining interest on consumer loans.

Bank discount: When the bank discount calculation method is used, interest is calculated on the amount to be paid back, and the borrower receives the difference between the amount to be paid back and the interest amount. The bank discount method is also referred to as the discount basis.

- *Example 5:* Consider the loan in Example 1 where a 5 percent, $1,000 loan is to be repaid at the end of one year. If the bank discount method is used, the interest amount of $50 would be deducted from the $1,000, leaving the borrower with $950 to use over the year. At the end of the year, the borrower pays $1,000. The interest amount of $50 is the same as in Example 1. The borrower in Example 1, however, had the use of $1,000 over the year. Thus, the effective rate of interest here would be 5.263 percent— $50 divided by $950—compared to an effective rate of 5 percent in Example 1. Forms of borrowing that use the bank discount method often have no intermediate payments. For example, the bank discount method is used for Treasury bills sold by the U.S. government and commercial paper issued by businesses. In addition, U. S. savings bonds are sold on a discount basis, that is, at a price below their face value.

How Many Days in a Year?

In the above examples, a year was assumed to be 365 days long. Historically, in order to simplify interest calculations, lenders and borrowers often assumed that each year had twelve 30-day months, resulting in a 360-day year. For any given nominal rate of interest, the effective rate of interest will be greater when a 360-day year is used in the interest calculation than when a 365-day year is used.

- *Example 6:* Suppose that a $1,000 loan is discounted at 5 percent and payable in 365 days. This is the situation in Example 5 where, based on a 365-day year, the effective rate of interest was 5.263 percent. If the bank discount calculation assumes a 360-day year, then the length of time is computed to be 365/360 or 1 1/72 years instead of exactly one year; the interest deducted (the discount) equals $50.69 instead of $50; and the effective annual rate of interest is 5.34 percent. Some of the examples cited earlier that use the bank discount method, namely Treasury bills sold by the U.S. government and commercial paper issued by businesses, assume a 360-day year in calculating interest.

Compound Interest

When the compound interest calculation is used, interest is calculated on the original principal plus all interest accrued to that point in time. Since interest is paid on interest as well as on the amount borrowed, the effective interest rate is greater than the nominal interest rate. The compound interest rate method is often used by banks and savings institutions in determining interest they pay on savings deposits "loaned" to the institutions by the depositors.

- *Example 7:* Suppose $1,000 is deposited in a bank that pays a 5 percent nominal annual rate of interest, compounded semiannually (twice a year). At the end of the first half-year, $25 in interest (5 percent of $1,000 for one-half year) is payable. At the end of the year, the interest amount is calculated on the $1,000 plus the $25 in interest already paid, so that the second interest payment is $25.63 (5 percent of $1,025 for one-half year). The interest amount payable for the year, then, is $25 plus $25.63, or $50.63. The effective rate of interest is 5.063 percent, which is greater than the nominal 5 percent rate.

The more often interest is compounded within a particular time period, the greater will be the effective rate of interest. In a year, a 5 percent nominal annual rate of interest compounded four times (quarterly) results in an effective annual rate of 5.0945 percent; compounded 12 times (monthly), 5.1162 percent; and compounded 365 times (daily), 5.1267 percent. When the interval of time between compoundings approaches zero (even shorter than a second), then the method is known as continuous compounding. Five percent continuously compounded for one year will result in an effective annual rate of 5.1271 percent.

When Repayment Is Early

In the above examples, it was assumed that periodic loan payments were always made exactly when due. Often, however, a loan may be completely repaid before it is due. When the declining balance method for calculating interest is used, the borrower is not penalized for prepayment since interest is paid only on the balance outstanding for the length of time that amount is owed. When the add-on interest calculation is used, however, prepayment implies that the lender obtains some interest that is unearned. The borrower then is actually paying an even higher effective rate since the funds are not available for the length of time of the original loan contract.

Some loan contracts make provisions for an interest rebate if the loan is prepaid. One method used in determining the amount of the interest rebate is referred to as the Rule of 78. Application of the Rule of 78 yields the percentage of the total interest amount that is to be returned to the borrower in the event of prepayment. The percentage figure is arrived at by dividing the sum of the integer numbers (digits) from one to the number of payments remaining by the sum of the digits from one to the total number of payments specified in the original loan contract. For example, if a five-month loan is paid off by the end of the second month (that is, there are three payments remaining), the percentage of the interest that the lender would rebate is (1+2+3) divided by (1+2+3+4+5). This equals 6 divided by 15, or 40 percent. The name derives from the fact that 78 is the sum of the digits from one to 12 and, therefore, is the denominator in calculating interest rebate percentages for all 12-period loans.

Application of the Rule of 78 results in the borrowers paying somewhat more interest than would have been paid with a comparable declining balance loan. How much more depends on the total number of payments specified in the original loan contract and the effective rate of interest charged. The greater the specified total number of payments and the higher the effective rate of interest charged, the more the amount of interest figured under the Rule of 78 exceeds that under the declining balance method.

The difference between the Rule of 78 interest and the declining balance interest also varies depending upon when the prepayment occurs. This difference over the term of the loan tends to increase up to about the one-third point of the term and then decrease after this point. For example, with a 12-month term, the difference with prepayment occurring in the second month would be greater than the difference that would occur with prepayment in the first month; the third-month difference would be greater than the second-month difference; the fourth month (being the one-third point) would be greater than both the third month-difference and the fifth-month difference. After the fifth month, each succeeding month's difference would be less than the previous month's difference.

- *Example 8:* Suppose that there are two $1,000 loans that are to be repaid over 12 months. Interest on the first loan is calculated using a 5 percent add-on method, which results in equal payments of $87.50 due at the end of each month ($1,000 plus $50 interest divided by 12 months). The effective annual rate of interest for this loan is 9.105 percent. Any interest rebate due because of prepayment is to be determined by the Rule of 78. Interest on the second loan is calculated using a declining balance method where the annual rate of interest is the effective annual rate of interest from the first loan, or 9.105 percent. Equal payments of $87.50 are also due at the end of each month for the second loan. Suppose that repayment on both loans occurs after one-sixth of the term of the loan has passed, that is, at the end of the second month, with the regular first month's payment being made for both loans. The interest paid on the first loan will be $14.74, while the interest paid on the second loan will be $14.57, a difference of 17 cents. If the prepayment occurs at the one-third point, that is, at the end of the fourth month (regular payments having been made at the end of the first, second, and third months), interest of $26.92 is paid on the first loan and interest of $26.69 on the second loan, a difference of 23 cents. If the prepayment occurs later, say at the three-fourths point, that is, at the end of the ninth month (regular payments having been made at the end of the first through eighth months), $46.16 in interest is paid on the first loan and $46.07 in interest is paid on the second loan, a difference of but 9 cents.

Charges Other than Interest

In addition to the interest that must be paid, loan agreements often will include other provisions that must be satisfied. Two examples of these provisions are mortgage points and required (compensating) deposit balances.

Mortgage points: Mortgage lenders will sometimes require the borrower to pay a charge in addition to the interest. This extra charge is calculated as a percentage of the mortgage amount and is referred to as mortgage points. For example, if 2 points are charged on a $100,000 mortgage, then 2 percent of $100,000, or $2,000, must be paid in addition to the stated interest. The borrower, therefore, is paying a higher price than if points were not charged—that is, the effective rate of interest is increased. In order to determine what the effective rate of interest is when points are charged, it is necessary to deduct the dollar amount resulting from the point calculation from the mortgage amount and add it to the interest amount to be paid. The borrower is viewed as having use of the mortgage amount less the point charge amount rather than the entire mortgage amount.

- *Example 9:* Suppose that 2 points are charged on a 20-year, $100,000 mortgage where the rate of interest (declining balance calculation) is 7 percent. The payments are to be $775.30 per month. Once the borrower pays the $2,000 point charge, there is $98,000 to use. With payments of $775.30 a month over 20 years, the result of the 2-point charge is an effective rate of 7.262 percent. The longer the time period of the mortgage, the lower will be the effective rate of interest when points are charged because the point charge is spread out over more payments. In the above example, if the mortgage had been for 30 years instead of 20 years, the effective rate of interest would have been 7.201 percent.

Required (compensating) deposit balances: A bank may require that a borrower maintain a certain percentage of the loan amount on deposit as a condition for obtaining the loan. The borrower, then, does not have the use of the entire loan amount but rather the use of the loan amount less the amount that must be kept on deposit. The effective rate of interest is greater than it would be if no compensating deposit balance were required

- *Example 10:* Suppose that $1,000 is borrowed at 5 percent from a bank to be paid back at the end of one year. Suppose, further, that the lending bank requires that 10 percent of the loan amount be kept on deposit. The borrower, therefore, has the use of only $900 ($1,000 less 10 percent) on which an interest amount of $50 (5 percent of $1,000 for one year) is charged. The effective rate of interest is, therefore, 5.556 percent as opposed to 5 percent when no compensating balance is required.

Summary

Although not an exhaustive list, the methods of calculating interest described here are some of the more common methods in use. They indicate that the method of interest calculation can substantially affect the amount of interest paid, and that savers and borrowers should be aware not only of nominal interest rates but also of how nominal rates are used in calculating total interest charges.

Through time, the level of interest rates may fluctuate, but the methods of calculation remain constant. Thus, the concepts of figuring interest explained here apply regardless of whether the specific numerical examples used are representative of today's market rates.

Chapter 30

Has Someone Asked You to Cosign a Loan?

What would you do if a friend or relative asked you to cosign a loan? Before you answer, make sure you understand what cosigning involves. Under federal law, creditors are required to give you a notice that explains your obligations. The cosigner's notice states:

- You are being asked to guarantee this debt. Think carefully before you do. If the borrower does not pay the debt, you will have to. Be sure you can afford to pay if you have to, and that you want to accept this responsibility.

- You may have to pay up to the full amount of the debt if the borrower does not pay. You may also have to pay late fees or collection costs, which increase this amount.

- The creditor can collect this debt from you without first trying to collect from the borrower. Depending on your state, this may not apply. If state law forbids a creditor from collecting from a cosigner without first trying to collect from the primary debtor, this sentence may be crossed out or omitted altogether. The creditor can use the same collection methods against you that can be used against the borrower, such as suing you, or garnishing your wages. If this debt is ever in default, that fact may become a part of your credit record.

- This notice is not the contract that makes you liable for the debt.

"Cosigning a Loan," Federal Trade Commission (www.ftc.gov), March 1997; reviewed for currency in February 2006.

Cosigners Often Pay

Studies of certain types of lenders show that for cosigned loans that go into default, as many as three out of four cosigners are asked to repay the loan. When you're asked to cosign, you're being asked to take a risk that a professional lender won't take. If the borrower met the criteria, the lender wouldn't require a cosigner.

In most states, if you cosign and your friend or relative misses a payment, the lender can immediately collect from you without first pursuing the borrower. In addition, the amount you owe may be increased—by late charges or by attorneys' fees—if the lender decides to sue to collect. If the lender wins the case, your wages and property may be taken.

If You Do Cosign

Despite the risks, there may be times when you want to cosign. Your child may need a first loan, or a close friend may need help. Before you cosign, consider this information:

- Be sure you can afford to pay the loan. If you're asked to pay and can't, you could be sued or your credit rating could be damaged.

- Even if you're not asked to repay the debt, your liability for the loan may keep you from getting other credit because creditors will consider the cosigned loan as one of your obligations.

- Before you pledge property to secure the loan, such as your car or furniture, make sure you understand the consequences. If the borrower defaults, you could lose these items.

- Ask the lender to calculate the amount of money you might owe. The lender isn't required to do this, but may if asked. You also may be able to negotiate the specific terms of your obligation. For example, you may want to limit your liability to the principal on the loan, and not include late charges, court costs, or attorneys' fees. In this case, ask the lender to include a statement in the contract similar to: "The cosigner will be responsible only for the principal balance on this loan at the time of default."

- Ask the lender to agree, in writing, to notify you if the borrower misses a payment. That will give you time to deal with the problem or make back payments without having to repay the entire amount immediately.

- Make sure you get copies of all important papers, such as the loan contract, the Truth-in-Lending Disclosure Statement, and warranties—if you're cosigning for a purchase. You may need these documents if there's a dispute between the borrower and the seller. The lender is not required to give you these papers; you may have to get copies from the borrower.

- Check your state law for additional cosigner rights.

Chapter 31

Credit Cards: Borrowing Money for Every-Day Purchases

Chapter Contents

Section 31.1

Thinking about a Credit Card?

From "A Shopper's Guide to Bank Products and Services: Credit Cards:
Understand Your Needs...and the Fine Print," *FDIC Consumer News*,
Federal Deposit Insurance Corporation, Summer 2005.

First, think about how you plan to use the card. Ask yourself when you expect to pay for all that you charge—by the due date each month or over several months? This is a crucial question. Many Americans carry a balance on their credit card and pay interest on it each month. Yet many of these same people chose their card because it has no annual fee, without considering whether they could get a better interest rate on a different card. In the long run, they could pay far more in interest than what they save by not paying an annual fee.

Other people sign up for a card because of cash rebates, bonus points toward airline travel, free T-shirts, and other giveaways—but they, too, could end up paying more in fees or interest than the value of their reward.

Generally speaking, if you expect to pay your credit card bill in full each month, your best bet is a card with no annual fee and with the kinds of rebates or rewards that fit your lifestyle. If you don't expect to pay off your card balance in full most months, go for a card with a low interest rate and the right mix of rebates or rewards to justify any fees.

Before you sign up for a card, carefully review the terms and conditions, including the potential fees or penalties, all of which must be disclosed to you before you incur any charges on the account. These terms, by law, must be easy to spot. For example, the most important terms must be in a specially highlighted box or near the box. Don't overlook them.

Among the key terms and conditions to know: the interest rate and when and how it could change (low introductory "teaser" rates typically only last for six months to a year); the "grace period" (the number of days before the card company starts charging you interest on purchases); and the interest calculation method, which is crucial for consumers who routinely carry a balance on their credit card.

Another term to watch for is a "default rate," which is a higher interest rate that you could be charged if you pay late on this or another credit card, or for other actions that the credit card issuer considers too risky.

Staff at the Federal Deposit Insurance Corporation (FDIC) cite various examples of consumers running into problems with new credit cards simply because they didn't take the time to read key details. One consumer whose new credit card came with a zero-percent initial interest rate decided to "write himself a loan" with one of the blank "convenience" checks provided by the card company. Unfortunately, he failed to take note of the fact that the interest rate on that loan was different than what it was for his card—in fact, the loan had an Annual Percentage Rate (APR) of 24 percent, compounded daily.

Another person signed up for a new card every four or five months so she could transfer the balance from an old card and take advantage of the super-low introductory interest rate. She later discovered that having a lot of credit cards hurt her credit rating, which resulted in a higher interest rate when she applied for a mortgage.

Section 31.2

Choosing a Credit Card

Excerpted from "Choosing a Credit Card," Federal Reserve Board of Governors, October 2004.

Shopping around for a credit card can save you money on interest and fees. You'll want to find one with features that match your needs.

What are the APRs?

The annual percentage rate—APR—is the way of stating the interest rate you will pay if you carry over a balance, take out a cash advance, or transfer a balance from another card. The APR states the interest rate as a yearly rate.

Multiple APRs: A single credit card may have several APRs:

- One APR for purchases, another for cash advances, and yet another for balance transfers. The APRs for cash advances and balance transfers often are higher than the APR for purchases (for example, 14% for purchases, 18% for cash advances, and 19% for balance transfers).

- Tiered APRs. Different rates are applied to different levels of the outstanding balance (for example, 16% on balances of $1–$500 and 17% on balances above $500).

- A penalty APR. The APR may increase if you are late in making payments. For example, your card agreement may say, "If your payment arrives more than ten days late two times within a six-month period, the penalty rate will apply."

- An introductory APR. A different rate will apply after the introductory rate expires.

- A delayed APR. A different rate will apply in the future. For example, a card may advertise that there is "no interest until next March." Look for the APR that will be in effect after March.

If you carry over a part of your balance from month to month, even a small difference in the APR can make a big difference in how much you will pay over a year.

Fixed vs. variable APR: Some credit cards are "fixed rate"—the APR doesn't change, or at least doesn't change often. Even the APR on a "fixed rate" credit card can change over time. However, the credit card company must tell you before increasing the fixed APR.

Other credit cards are "variable rate"—the APR changes from time to time. The rate is usually tied to another interest rate, such as the prime rate or the Treasury bill rate. If the other rate changes, the rate on your card may change, too. Look for information on the credit card application and in the credit card agreement to see how often your card's APR may change (the agreement is like a contract—it lists the terms and conditions for using your credit card).

How long is the grace period?

The grace period is the number of days you have to pay your bill in full without triggering a finance charge. For example, the credit card company may say that you have "25 days from the statement date, provided you paid your previous balance in full by the due date." The statement date is given on the bill. The grace period usually applies only to new purchases. Most credit cards do not give a grace period for cash advances and balance transfers. Instead, interest charges start right away.

If you carried over any part of your balance from the preceding month, you may not have a grace period for new purchases. Instead, you may be charged interest as soon as you make a purchase (in addition to being charged interest on the earlier balance you have not paid off). Look on the credit card application for information about the "method of computing the balance for purchases" to see if new purchases are included or excluded.

How is the finance charge calculated?

The finance charge is the dollar amount you pay to use credit. The amount depends in part on your outstanding balance and the APR.

Credit card companies use one of several methods to calculate the outstanding balance. The method can make a big difference in the finance charge you'll pay. Your outstanding balance may be calculated:

- Over one billing cycle or two,

- Using the adjusted balance, the average daily balance, or the previous balance, and

- Including or excluding new purchases in the balance.

Depending on the balance you carry and the timing of your purchases and payments, you'll usually have a lower finance charge with one-cycle billing and either:

- The average daily balance method excluding new purchases,

- The adjusted balance method, or

- The previous balance method.

Minimum finance charge: Some credit cards have a minimum finance charge. You'll be charged that minimum even if the calculated amount of your finance charge is less. For example, your finance charge may be calculated to be 35¢—but if the company's minimum finance charge is $1.00, you'll pay $1.00. A minimum finance charge usually applies only when you must pay a finance charge—that is, when you carry over a balance from one billing cycle to the next.

What are the fees?

Most credit cards charge fees under certain circumstances:

- Annual fee (sometimes billed monthly): charged for having the card

- Cash advance fee: charged when you use the card for a cash advance; may be a flat fee (for example, $3.00) or a percentage of the cash advance (for example, 3%)

- Balance-transfer fee: charged when you transfer a balance from another credit card (Your credit card company may send you "checks" to pay off the other card. The balance is transferred when you use one of these checks to pay the amount due on the other card.)

- Late-payment fee: charged if your payment is received after the due date

- Over-the-credit-limit fee: charged if you go over your credit limit

- Credit-limit-increase fee: charged if you ask for an increase in your credit limit

- Set-up fee: charged when a new credit card account is opened

- Return-item fee: charged if you pay your bill by check and the check is returned for non-sufficient funds (that is, your check bounces)

- Other fees: some credit card companies charge a fee if you pay by telephone (that is, if you arrange by phone for payment to be transferred from your bank to the company) or to cover the costs of reporting to credit bureaus, reviewing your account, or providing other customer services. Read the information in your credit card agreement to see if there are other fees and charges.

What are the cash advance features?

Some credit cards let you borrow cash in addition to making purchases on credit. Most credit card companies treat these cash advances and your purchases differently. If you plan to use your card for cash advances, look for information about:

- **Access:** Most credit cards let you use an ATM to get a cash advance. Or the credit card company may send you "checks" that you can write to get the cash advance.

- **APR:** The APR for cash advances may be higher than the APR for purchases.

- **Fees:** The credit card company may charge a fee in addition to the interest you will pay on the amount advanced.

- **Limits:** Some credit cards limit cash advances to a dollar amount (for example, $200 per cash advance or $500 per week) or a portion of your credit limit (for example, 75% of your available credit limit).

- **How payments are credited:** Many credit card companies apply your payments to purchases first and then to cash advances. Read your credit card agreement to learn how your payments will be credited.

How much is the credit limit?

The credit limit is the maximum total amount—for purchases, cash advances, balance transfers, fees, and finance charges—you may charge on your credit card. If you go over this limit, you may have to pay an "over-the-credit-limit fee."

What kind of card is it?

Most credit card companies offer several kinds of cards:

- Secured cards, which require a security deposit. The larger the security deposit, the higher the credit limit. Secured cards are usually offered to people who have limited credit records—people who are just starting out or who have had trouble with credit in the past.

- Regular cards, which do not require a security deposit and have just a few features. Most regular cards have higher credit limits than secured cards but lower credit limits than premium cards.

- Premium cards (gold, platinum, titanium), which offer higher credit limits and usually have extra features—for example, product warranties, travel insurance, or emergency services.

Does the card offer incentives and other features?

Many credit card companies offer incentives to use the card and other special features:

- Rebates (money back) on the purchases you make

- Frequent flier miles or phone-call minutes

- Additional warranty coverage for the items you purchase

- Car rental insurance

- Travel accident insurance or travel-related discounts

- Credit card registration, to help if your wallet or purse is lost or stolen and you need to report that all your credit cards are missing

Credit cards may also offer, for a price:

- Insurance to cover the payments on your credit card balance if you become unemployed or disabled, or die. Premiums are usually due monthly, making it easy to cancel if the payments are higher than you want to pay or you decide you don't need the insurance any longer.

- Insurance to cover the first $50 of charges if your card is lost or stolen. Under federal law, you are not responsible for charges over $50.

- Before you sign up to pay for any of these features, think carefully about whether it will be useful for you. Don't pay for something you don't want or don't need.

How do I find information about credit cards?

You can find lists of credit card plans, rates, and terms on the internet, in personal finance magazines, and in newspapers. The Federal Reserve System surveys credit card companies every six months. You'll need to get the most recent information directly from the credit card company—by phoning the company, looking on the company's website, or reading a solicitation or application.

Under federal law, all solicitations and applications for credit cards must include certain key information, in a disclosure box similar to the one shown in Figure 31.1.

Annual percentage rate (APR) for purchases	2.9% until 11/1/08 after that, **14.9%**
Other APRs	Cash-advance APR: 15.9% Balance-transfer APR: 15.9% Penalty rate: 23.9% See explanation below. *
Variable-rate information	Your APR for purchase transactions may vary. The rate is determined monthly by adding 5.9% to the Prime Rate **
Grace period for repayment of balances for purchases	25 days on average
Method of computing the balance for purchases	Average daily balance (excluding new purchases)
Annual fees	None
Minimum finance charge	$.50
Transaction fee for cash advances: 3% of the amount advanced Balance-transfer fee: 3% of the amount transferred Late-payment fee: $25 Over-the-credit-limit fee: $25	
* Explanation of penalty. If your payment arrives more than ten days late two times within a six-month period, the penalty rate will apply. ** The Prime Rate used to determine your APR is the rate published in the *Wall Street Journal* on the 10th day of the prior month.	

Figure 31.1 Credit card disclosure box.

APR for purchases: The annual percentage rate you'll be charged if you carry over a balance from month to month. If the card has an introductory rate, you'll see both that rate and the rate that will apply after the introductory rate expires.

Other APRs: The APRs you'll be charged if you get a cash advance on your card, transfer a balance from another card, or are late in making a payment. More information about the penalty rate may be stated outside the disclosure box—for instance, in a footnote. In this example, if you make two payments that are more than ten days late within six months, the APR will increase to 23.9%.

Variable-rate information: Information about how the variable rate will be determined (if relevant). More information may be stated outside the disclosure box—for instance, in a footnote.

Grace period for repayment of balances for purchases: The number of days you'll have to pay your bill for purchases in full without triggering a finance charge.

Method of computing the balance for purchases: The method that will be used to calculate your outstanding balance if you carry over a balance and will pay a finance charge.

Annual fees: The amount you'll be charged each twelve-month period for simply having the card.

Minimum finance charge: The minimum, or fixed, finance charge that will be imposed during a billing cycle. A minimum finance charge usually applies only when a finance charge is imposed, that is, when you carry over a balance.

Transaction fee for cash advances: The charge that will be imposed each time you use the card for a cash advance.

Balance-transfer fee: The fee that will be imposed each time you transfer a balance from another card.

Late-payment fee: The fee that will be imposed when your payment is late.

Over-the-credit-limit fee: The fee that will be imposed if your charges exceed the credit limit set for your card.

What are your liability limits?

If your credit card is lost or stolen—and then is used by someone without your permission—you do not have to pay more than $50 of those charges. This protection is provided by the federal Truth in Lending Act. You do not need to buy "credit card insurance" to cover amounts over $50.

If you discover that your card is lost or stolen, report it immediately to your credit card company. Call the toll-free number listed on your monthly statement. The company will cancel the card so that new purchases cannot be made with it. The company will also send you a new card.

Make a list of your account numbers and the companies' phone numbers. Keep the list in a safe place. If your wallet or purse is lost or stolen, you'll have all the numbers in one place. Take the list of phone numbers—not the account numbers—with you when you travel, just in case a card is lost or stolen.

What can you do about billing errors?

The federal Fair Credit Billing Act covers billing errors. Examples of billing error are:

- A charge for something you didn't buy.

- A bill for an amount different from the actual amount you charged.

- A charge for something that you did not accept when it was delivered.

- A charge for something that was not delivered according to agreement.

- Math errors.

- Payments not credited to your account.

- A charge by someone who does not have permission to use your credit card.

If you think your credit card bill has an error, take the following steps:

1. Write to the credit card company within 60 days after the statement date on the bill with the error. Use the address for "billing inquiries" listed on the bill. Tell the company:

- Your name and account number,

- That you believe the bill contains an error, and why you believe it's wrong, and

- The date and amount of the error (the "disputed amount").

2.   Pay all the other parts of the bill. You do not have to pay the "disputed amount" or any minimum payments or finance charges that apply to it.

If there is an error, you will not have to pay any finance charges on the disputed amount. Your account must be corrected.

If there is no error, the credit card company must send you an explanation and a statement of the amount you owe. The amount will include any finance charges or other charges that accumulated while you were questioning the bill.

What if the item you purchase is damaged?

The federal Fair Credit Billing Act allows you to withhold payment on any damaged or poor-quality goods or services purchased with a credit card—even if you have accepted the goods or services—as long as you have made an attempt to solve the problem with the merchant.

The sale must have been for more than $50 and must have taken place in your home state or within 100 miles of your home address. You should notify the credit card company in writing and explain why you are withholding your payment.

You may withhold the payment while the credit card company investigates your claim. If you pay the charges for the goods on your credit card bill before the dispute is resolved, you will lose your right to make a claim.

Section 31.3

A Reader's Guide to the Fine Print in Credit Card Mailings

"A Reader's Guide to Credit Card Mailings (and the Fine Print)," *FDIC Consumer News*, Federal Deposit Insurance Corporation, Fall 2002.

Card Solicitations

You're pre-approved: This doesn't mean you're guaranteed a card. It means that you have received a firm offer of credit based on criteria established by the company for what it wants in a customer. You must apply for the card and the company will conduct a full credit check. Tip: If you don't receive the card or the terms you were offered, ask the bank for the reasons.

APR (annual percentage rate): The interest rate charged if you carry a balance on your card. Tip: If you usually carry a balance, shop around for a card with a low APR. If you pay off your balance in full every month, the APR is less important than a card's other costs or features. Also, find out if the interest rate is fixed or variable and whether different interest rates apply to different events (such as if you get a cash advance from a teller machine or pay your credit card bill late).

Introductory rates: Also known as "teaser rates," these are very low interest rates offered to entice you to open a new account. But as explained in the fine print, the introductory rate may increase dramatically after six months or so. Tip: Understand the terms of the offer. That low introductory rate may only apply to balances you transfer to your card from other loans or cards you have and not to any new purchases.

Grace period: The number of days before the card company starts charging you interest on purchases. Tip: If you plan to avoid interest charges by paying your balance in full most months, make sure your card's terms permit that. It's getting harder to find credit cards that give several weeks of interest-free purchases. Some cards have no grace period, meaning you'd always pay interest from the date of purchase.

Balance computation method: How the card company will determine the balance on which you may be charged interest. Tip: If you expect to carry a balance most months or if your card offers a short or no grace period, the balance calculation method could be a big factor in your finance charges. Perhaps the most common method is the "average daily balance" approach, where finance charges are calculated on the daily average for the billing period. Other calculation methods may be more costly, including one called the "two-cycle" system where, if you pay in full one month but only pay part of the bill the next month, you'll be charged interest for both months instead of just one.

Annual fee: Yearly charge for use of the credit card. Tip: If you expect to pay your balance in full most months, look for a card with a full grace period and no annual fee. However, if you plan on carrying a balance or you're looking for club perks, then a card with an annual fee and low APR may be a better choice.

Other fees: May include fees for late payments, charges above your credit limit, cash advances, balance transfers from another card, and certain purchases. Tip: Shop around for the features you want and for the lowest cost.

Rewards: Incentives for using the card, such as cash back or bonus points toward airline travel or the purchase of a car. Tip: Be aware of the rules and restrictions, including limits on how much you can earn or deadlines for taking advantage of a reward. Also, compare the likely value of the bonuses with the potential costs of the card.

Stopping Solicitations

Some people want to be on marketers' lists for new product offers, but others don't. If you want to reduce the number of offers for credit cards and other financial products, call toll-free 888-5-OPTOUT (888-567-8688) to remove your name from marketing lists provided to creditors and other companies.

Card Statements

Transactions: Open your bill immediately and check your transactions. If there is a mistake, you can dispute the charge and withhold payment for that specific amount. Tip: To be protected by the Fair Credit Billing Act, you must send a letter to the creditor that is received within 60 days after the creditor sent you the statement with the inaccuracy. Your letter also must be sent to the address the creditor has specified for billing inquiries.

Periodic interest rate: If you carry a balance, check the periodic interest rate on the statement, to make sure what you are being charged is what was disclosed to you. Tip: Pay close attention. Notice of a change is usually provided in your monthly statements, so read the fine print.

Records: Retain your credit card statements and any significant inserts received with your statement. You never know when you might need to refer to them. Tip: Note the date a payment was mailed, the check number and the amount paid.

Section 31.4

Credit Card Fees

"Credit Card Fees Often Go Unnoticed Even As They Increase,"
FDIC Consumer News, Spring 2001.

Credit cards offer great convenience to consumers, but that convenience comes at a price. In recent years, card issuers have raised or added new fees for their products and services. While these costs are described in the mailings and card agreements (contracts) consumers receive from card companies, too many people forget about these fees or aren't aware of them until after they've run up a sizable bill. *FDIC (Federal Deposit Insurance Corporation) Consumer News* asked Janet Kincaid, a credit card specialist with the FDIC in Kansas City, for examples of fees that are becoming more common or more costly, yet still go unnoticed by many cardholders:

Monthly maintenance fees: Rather than charge an annual fee, some lenders impose a monthly fee, often from $6 to $12 a month, whether you use the card that month or not. "Many people don't blink twice over $6 a month—it doesn't seem so bad," Kincaid says. "But if they stopped to think that they're paying $72 a year just to be able to carry a card, they'd realize they could have done better by paying a lower annual fee."

Balance transfer fees: You've probably received mail from a credit card issuer trumpeting a "can't-beat-this" low Annual Percentage Rate (APR) of, say, 2.9 percent on any balance you transfer to that card from a competitor's card. But, there also could be a fee for the balance transfer that could outweigh the benefit of the low interest rate. In addition, there may be no grace period on the balance you transfer. "Interest often begins accruing the moment the balance transfer is completed," Kincaid explains. "Even if you paid off the balance by the due date, you may still incur interest charges."

Suppose you transfer a $100 balance at a special 2.9 percent APR to a card that otherwise charges a 15 percent APR, and you already have a $200 balance on that card from your previous purchases. Then let's say you send in a $50 card payment at the end of the month. It's important to know how that $50 payment will be applied. Will the payment go to reduce the "old" high-rate $200 balance or the "new" low-rate $100 balance you transferred? "The card issuer can decide how to allocate your payment, and unless you know the card issuer's policy by calling the company or checking your card agreement, you can assume the procedures will benefit the card issuer," Kincaid says.

Cash advance fees: When you use your credit card to get cash from an ATM, that's considered a loan, and you will incur interest charges immediately, without a grace period. But in addition, you may be charged a transaction fee by both the financial institution that holds your credit card and by the bank that owns the ATM you're using. The fee can either be a flat dollar amount or a percentage (perhaps three percent) of the cash advance. The fee can make a simple cash withdrawal fairly expensive.

Fees for late payments: If you mail in your payment too close to the due date and miss the deadline, you could face a late-payment fee. These fees have increased in recent years from about $15 to as much as $29. You may face other penalties, such as having your interest rate raised or your card canceled. Here's another alternative to mailing a payment late: Consider calling your card company to authorize it to "debit" (deduct) your payment directly from your bank account before the deadline. "This convenience will cost you more than a postage stamp, usually as much as $10," says Kincaid, "but it's usually a better, cheaper option than paying late and incurring a penalty."

Fees for sending in less than the minimum monthly payment: Suppose you're expected to pay at least $50 for a card payment but you only have $25 available, so you send it in anyway. "Yes, you've made a payment," Kincaid says, "but anything less than the minimum can be considered a late payment, subject to a late-payment fee." Again, those fees have increased to as much as $29 at many institutions. And, because an insufficient payment is considered a late payment, you could be subject to other penalties, such as having your interest rate raised or your card canceled.

The lesson here? Read and understand a credit card offer before you commit to anything. And, monitor your monthly billings or other mailings for notices of fee increases or rule changes by your card company. New rules from the Federal Reserve Board also will make it easier to see and understand key information about the card's costs on the applications and solicitations. Example: Card companies for years have been generally required to clearly disclose the APR for purchases charged to a credit card, but they must present this information in 18-point type. Compliance with the new rules became mandatory October 1, 2001.

Section 31.5

Minimum Payments Equal Maximum Costs

"Minimum Payments, Maximum Costs on Credit Cards," *FDIC Consumer News*, Federal Deposit Insurance Corporation, Summer 2003.

One of the great things about using a credit card is that you can buy now and pay later. But some consumers take the pay-later concept to an extreme—they pay only the minimum amount due on their card's outstanding balance each month and end up paying the maximum costs. (The minimum payment is set by each card issuer—typically it's about two percent of your outstanding balance—and it is shown on your monthly bill.) While it might appear to be a good deal to pay only $20 a month to buy a $1,000 computer, *FDIC (Federal Deposit Insurance Corporation) Consumer News* wants you to know just how much that computer will really cost when you add in the interest charges.

"Many people think if they only make the minimum payment shown on the statement they can keep their account current, keep charging, and have extra cash for other bills," says Janet Kincaid, a Senior Consumer Affairs Officer with the Federal Deposit Insurance Corporation (FDIC). "This is generally true, but what people also need to think about is the long-term cost of this alternative." She adds that if you pay only the minimum amount, "it will take you a very long time to pay off the balance, and the interest costs can be shocking."

How shocking? Take a look at the two examples provided in Table 31.1. The first one shows what would happen if you have a $5,000 out-standing balance on your credit card (to keep things simple, we as-sume you make no additional purchases), an Annual Percentage Rate of 18 percent, and you make only the minimum payment due ($100 initially but gradually declining each month because minimum pay-ments usually are based on a percentage of the balance, which will decrease.) Using this example, it will take 46 years and cost $13,926 in interest charges before you've paid the $5,000, putting the total cost at $18,926. If instead you pay $100 the first month and every month—which would be more than the minimum due—the balance would be paid off in eight years and the interest charges would be cut from $13,926 to $4,311.

316

The second example shows that if you pay only the minimum due (set at two percent of the outstanding balance or $10, whichever is greater), a $500 television will cost $939 and require eight years of payments, a $1,000 computer will cost $2,899 and take 19 years of payments (about 15 years longer than you'll probably own the computer), and furniture purchased for $2,500 will cost $8,781 and take 34 years to pay off.

Table 31.1. Making Only the Minimum Payment Adds to Costs

$5,000 at 18%

Starting Balance	Interest Rate (APR)	Monthly Payment	Years to Pay Off	Total Interest Paid	Total Cost
$5,000	18%	The minimum ($100 the first month, then gradually declines)	46	$13,926	$18,926
$5,000	18%	$100	8	$4,311	$9,311
$5,000	18%	$250	2	$986	$5,986

Note: The minimum payment is assumed to be two percent of the outstanding balance or $10, whichever is greater. Years are rounded to the nearest whole year.

Sample Purchases

Item	Price	Interest Rate (APR)	Years to Pay Off	Total Interest Paid	Total Cost
TV	$500	18%	8	$439	$939
Computer	$1,000	18%	19	$1,899	$2,899
Furniture	$2,500	18%	34	$6,281	$8,781

Note: All payments are the monthly minimum of two percent of the outstanding balance or $10, whichever is greater. Years are rounded to the nearest whole year.

How can you protect yourself?

Pay as much as you can on your charge card each month—pay the entire balance, if possible—in order to avoid interest charges. The FDIC and other bank regulators have taken steps to ensure that minimum card payments are reasonable, "but because there is no law or regulation requiring that minimum payments be a certain dollar amount or percentage, card issuers have a lot of flexibility in setting low minimum payments," says FDIC Consumer Affairs Specialist Howard Herman. "As credit card interest rates are often quite high, consumers need to take charge of the situation and pay as much of their card balance as they can afford. The amount you pay toward your credit card bill each month can have greater long-term consequences for your finances than how much money you save or invest each month."

And if you can't pay most or all of your credit card bill, try to pay as much above the minimum as possible. "Depending on your balance," Kincaid says, "even stretching to pay an extra $50 a month can make a big difference in reducing your total interest costs."

If all you can afford is the minimum amount, pay that...and pay it on time. "Many consumers are not aware that if they pay less than the minimum, the bank may still assess a late fee of $35 or more and could report the account to the credit bureaus as delinquent," says FDIC Supervisory Consumer Affairs Specialist Lynne Gottesburen. This kind of negative information in your credit file could result in your card issuer increasing the interest rate or even canceling your card.

If you plan to carry a balance each month, look for a card that has a low interest rate and a grace period. The grace period is the number of days before the card company starts charging interest on new purchases. Remember that grace periods can vary. With most cards, if you don't pay your bill in full you can be charged interest immediately on new purchases. Many cards have no grace period, which means you always pay interest on new purchases from the day you make the purchase.

Kincaid and Herman agree that one of the worst financial moves a consumer can make is to pay only the minimum due on credit card balances. They and other FDIC officials say that while it takes discipline to pay most or all of your credit card bill each month, the sooner you pay off your balance, the less you pay in interest and the more you have available to save for a home, college education, retirement, or something else that truly benefits you.

Section 31.6

Card "Clubs" and Other Extras: A Good Deal or Not?

FDIC Consumer News, Federal Deposit Insurance Corporation, Fall 2002.

You see them advertised by your bank or credit card company—special credit card or debit card "clubs," memberships and other extras you can sign up for, sometimes free of charge, but often for a fee added to your account or credit card bill. These offers may include services that monitor your credit reports for possible signs of fraud or identity theft, auto club membership and other travel programs, and even discounts on health care products and services. The ads make it all sound so good...but is it a good deal for you? *FDIC (Federal Deposit Insurance Corporation) Consumer News* offers the following suggestions:

Read and understand the fine print before agreeing to anything. Federal laws require credit and debit card issuers to disclose the fees and terms of their programs, including clubs. But too many people don't review this information until they need a particular good or service, and by then it may be too late to take full advantage of the program. "Even if something is being offered for free, you still should understand the terms of the program before you sign up," says Joni Creamean, a Senior Consumer Affairs Specialist with the FDIC. She notes, for example, that an extra service may be available free for a year, but if you don't cancel after that, the cost of the program for the next year automatically could be charged to your account, and you may end up paying for a program you no longer want.

Think about whether you really need the service and, if you do, shop for the best deal. Example: If you travel a lot by car or airplane, you may benefit from programs that offer emergency roadside assistance or lost luggage insurance. But first research whether you already get travel protection under a different program or if you can buy it for less elsewhere. Also, services that monitor your credit reports and alert you to potential fraud may be beneficial but other good options may cost less.

If you sign up for a program, make sure it continues to meet your needs. Keep copies of the application you sign and send in as well as any promotional literature and updates you receive. "This documentation may be crucial to your case if the program doesn't fulfill its disclosed purpose," Creamean explains. And, if you decide to cancel, be sure to follow the procedures specified by the company in its literature in order to avoid delays that can trigger membership or other costs.

Section 31.7

Frequently Encountered Problems with Plastic

"Problems with Plastic: Our Tips for Tackling Your Top Five Concerns," *FDIC Consumer News*, Federal Deposit Insurance Corporation, Fall 2002.

What are the most common problems reported with credit or debit cards, according to FDIC staffers who respond to consumer inquiries? Here they are, along with guidance on how to prevent and resolve those problems.

Billing errors and other disputed transactions: Billing errors include a charge on your credit card bill that isn't yours or an incorrect dollar amount on a credit or debit card transaction. Other problems might include a payment that didn't show up on your statement or a dispute with a merchant over something you purchased.

To reduce the odds that you'll be charged for something inappropriately, promptly review your monthly statements. With your credit card, the Fair Credit Billing Act (FCBA) protects you from paying for a purchase that wasn't yours or that you didn't agree to. But you must write the creditor (a call isn't sufficient) using the address given for billing inquiries (not the payment address), and your letter (or any complaint form provided with your bill) must reach the creditor within 60 days after the first bill containing the error was mailed to you. "I recommend that you send your dispute by certified mail, with a return-receipt requested, so that you have proof that the creditor received it on time," says FDIC Senior Consumer Affairs Officer Janet Kincaid. Also include copies—not originals—of any sales slips or other relevant documentation, and keep a copy of your request.

The FCBA also allows you to withhold payment for defective goods or services purchased with a credit card until the problem has been corrected, under certain conditions. In general, the purchase must be for more than $50 from a merchant in your home state or within 100 miles of your home. Your card issuer may offer additional protections.

Even though debit card transaction amounts are deducted from your bank account immediately—or within a few days—you have protections against errors and defective purchases under the Electronic Fund Transfer Act (EFTA) and industry practices. So, notify your financial institution immediately if there is a problem involving your debit card. While the EFTA does not require you to put your complaint in writing, it's a good idea to do so.

In an important development, Congress in November 2003 passed a new law that can help you ensure the accuracy of your credit information and monitor your credit files for signs you may be a victim of identity theft. The law enables you to obtain a free copy of your credit report once a year from each of the three major credit bureaus. Nationwide as of December 1, 2004, you have the right to learn your credit scores, which are designed to help predict how likely you are to repay a loan or make payments on time. As of that same date, merchants also must notify you if they plan to report negative information about you to a credit bureau. The Federal Trade Commission (http://www.ftc.gov) and the Federal Reserve Board (http://www.federalreserve.gov) have issued rules to put the new law into effect.

Application Denied or Downgraded: Consumers get upset when they apply for a credit card and, because of incorrect information in their credit report, their request is denied or they are offered less favorable credit terms than they expected. Credit report errors can happen, so periodically get a copy of your credit report to make sure everything is correct. It's especially smart to review your credit report before applying for a mortgage, credit card or other important loan, so that an error doesn't slow down your credit approval. And if you do find an error in your credit record, write to the credit bureau that prepared the report and provide copies of relevant documentation.

You can get your credit record by contacting any of the three major credit bureaus: Equifax (call 800-685-1111 or go to http://www.equifax.com on the internet); Experian (866-200-6020, which is toll free, or go to http://www.experian.com); and TransUnion (800-888-4213 or http://www.transunion.com). Their reports can vary, so some experts suggest that you review your credit report from all three credit bureaus. Your report is free in some cases but can cost no more than $9 under current law. If a creditor rejects your card application based on your credit report, you must be told so and given a chance to correct inaccurate information. That is one situation where you may be eligible for a free credit report.

Late Payment Fees: You say you mailed your credit card payment on time or you paid through your bank's electronic bill payment service...and you still got hit with a $30 late fee. Why? Financial institutions mark credit card payments as "paid" on the day they are received, not the day you mailed it. While the federal Truth in Lending Act (TILA) says a card issuer must credit your payment as of the date of receipt, most card issuers suggest that consumers allow seven to ten days for payments to be received and credited. Find out your bank's cutoff time for card payments. Some have a 10:00 a.m. deadline for payments to be credited that day. Also, send your payment to the address indicated by your card company. Mailing to the wrong address can cause late or even missed payments. And if you know your "late" payment arrived on time, contact your card issuer to resolve the matter.

Consumers using their bank's electronic bill payment service also should recognize that it still may take two or more days for their credit card company to receive the funds. To be safe, pay a few days in advance.

Changes in Terms: Credit card companies have the right to change interest rates or terms, as outlined in the card member agreement. However, FDIC attorney Mark Mellon explains that "if your card contract permits a change in rate or terms, a notice must be mailed or delivered to you at least 15 days prior to the effective date." Carefully read the information in your monthly statement or other mailings from your card company. If you don't want to accept a rate increase or other change, you can contact the card issuer and try to negotiate a better deal but there's no guarantee it will agree. If you decide to close the account, Kincaid says, do so in writing, "and know the rules for canceling the card, such as how long can you continue using the card and making payments under the existing terms."

With debit cards, federal rules generally require that a notice of changes in fees or terms be mailed or delivered at least 21 days before the effective date. Again, read the information that is sent to you and, if you disagree, try to negotiate or shop around for a better deal.

Confusion Over Promotional Offers: You're probably familiar with deals like "zero percent interest" on a credit card or "no payment on merchandise until next year" if you put your purchase on your charge card. These offers usually are for limited purposes and time periods, something many consumers don't focus on until they run up unexpected charges. "These offers can be good, but you've got to read the fine print and do the math," adds Kincaid. Example: Some offers may require you to pay the balance in full by the due date or you'll be charged interest on the entire balance, starting with the date of purchase, even if you have been making payments throughout the term of the promotion.

Chapter 32

Federal Loans for Education

There are three types of federal student aid:

- **Grants:** Financial aid that doesn't have to be repaid (unless, for example, you withdraw from school and owe a refund).

- **Work-Study:** Allows you to earn money for your education.

- **Loans:** Allow you to borrow money for school. You must repay your loans, with interest.

Student loans, unlike grants and work-study, are borrowed money that must be repaid, with interest, just like car loans and mortgages. You cannot have these loans canceled because you didn't like the education you received, didn't get a job in your field of study or because you're having financial difficulty. Loans are legal obligations, so before you take out a student loan, think about the amount you'll have to repay over the years.

Types of Loans

Federal Perkins Loans

- Made through participating schools to undergraduate, graduate, and professional degree students.

Excerpted from "Funding Education Beyond High School," Federal Student Aid, U.S. Department of Education, December 2006.

- Offered by participating schools to students who demonstrate financial need.

- Made to students enrolled full-time or part-time.

- Repaid by you to your school.

Stafford Loans

Stafford loans are for undergraduate, graduate, and professional degree students. You must be enrolled as at least a half-time student to be eligible for a Stafford Loan.

There are two types of Stafford Loans: subsidized and unsubsidized. You must have financial need to receive a subsidized Stafford Loan. Financial need is not a requirement to obtain an unsubsidized Stafford Loan. The U.S. Department of Education will pay (subsidize) the interest that accrues on subsidized Stafford Loans during certain periods. These loans are made through one of two U.S. Department of Education programs:

- **William D. Ford Federal Direct Loan (Direct Loan) Program:** Loans made through this program are referred to as Direct Loans. Eligible students and parents borrow directly from the U.S. Department of Education at participating schools. Direct Loans include subsidized and unsubsidized Direct Stafford Loans (also known as Direct Subsidized Loans and Direct Unsubsidized Loans), Direct PLUS Loans, and Direct Consolidation Loans. You repay these loans directly to the U.S. Department of Education.

- **Federal Family Education Loan (FFEL) Program:** Loans made through this program are referred to as FFEL Loans. Private lenders provide funds that are guaranteed by the federal government. FFEL Loans include subsidized and unsubsidized FFEL Stafford Loans, FFEL PLUS Loans, and FFEL Consolidation Loans. You repay these loans to the bank or private lender that made you the loan.

PLUS Loans

PLUS Loans are loans parents can obtain to help pay the cost of education for their dependent undergraduate children. In addition, graduate and professional degree students may obtain PLUS Loans to help pay for their own education. These loans are made through both the Direct Loan and FFEL programs mentioned above.

Loan Program	Eligibility	Award Amounts	Interest Rates	Lender/Length of Repayment
Federal Perkins Loans	Undergraduate and graduate students	Undergraduate—up to $4,000 a year (maximum of $20,000 as an undergraduate) Graduate—up to $6,000 a year (maximum of $40,000, including undergraduate loans) Amount actually received depends on financial need, amount of other aid, availability of funds at school	5 percent	Lender is your school Repay your school or its agent Up to 10 years to repay, depending on amount owed
FFEL Stafford Loans (subsidized and unsubsidized)	Undergraduate and graduate students; must be enrolled at least half-time*	Depends on grade level in school and dependency status Financial need is required for subsidized loans Financial need not necessary for unsubsidized loans	Fixed rate of 6.8 percent for loans first disbursed on or after July 1, 2006 Government pays interest on subsidized loans during school and certain other periods	Lender is a bank, credit union or other participating private lender Repay the loan holder or its agent Between 10 and 25 years to repay, depending on amount owed and type of repayment plan selected
Direct Stafford Loans (subsidized and unsubsidized)	Same as above	Same as above	Same as above	Lender is the U.S. Department of Education; repay Department Between 10 and 25 years to repay, depending on amount owed and type of repayment plan selected
FFEL PLUS Loans	Parents of dependent undergraduate students enrolled at least half-time* (see dependency status); and graduate or professional degree students. Must not have negative credit history	Student's Cost of Attendance* – Other aid student receives = Maximum loan amount	Fixed rate at 8.5 percent for loans first disbursed on or after July 1, 2006; borrower pays all interest	Same as for FFEL Stafford Loans above
Direct PLUS Loan	Same as above	Same as above	Fixed rate at 7.9 percent for loans first disbursed on or after July 1, 2006; borrower pays all interest	Same as for Direct Stafford Loans above, except that Income Contingent Repayment Plan is not an option

Figure 32.1. Student Loan Comparison Chart

327

Consolidation Loans (Direct or FFEL)

These loans allow student or parent borrowers to combine multiple federal education loans into one loan with one monthly payment.

Questions and Answers about Federal Loans for Education

How do I apply for a Perkins or Stafford Loan?

As with all federal student financial aid, you apply for a Perkins or Stafford Loan by completing the FAFSA (Free Application for Federal Student Aid). A separate loan application is not required. However, you'll need to sign a promissory note, which is a binding legal contract that says you agree to repay your loan according to the terms of the promissory note. Read this note carefully before signing it and save a copy for your records.

How much can I borrow?

Perkins Loans: The Student Loan Comparison Chart on in Figure 32.1 shows the maximum Perkins Loan funds you can receive, depending on whether you're an undergraduate, graduate or professional degree student. However, the amount you can borrow might be less than the maximum available.

- Each school participating in the Federal Perkins Loan program receives a certain amount of Perkins funds each year from the U.S. Department of Education.

- When all available funds for that award year have been distributed, no more awards can be made for that year.

- Submit your FAFSA early so you can be considered for these funds.

Stafford Loans (Direct and FFEL): Your loan limits depend on:

- What year you are in school.

- Whether you are a dependent or independent student.

Other than interest, are there any fees or charges required to get these loans?

- **Federal Perkins Loans:** No.

- **Direct Loans and FFEL Loans:** Yes, for loans first disbursed on or after July 1, 2006, and before July 1, 2007, you'll pay an origination fee of up to 3 percent of the loan amount, deducted proportionately from each loan disbursement. For loans disbursed in subsequent years, the maximum loan fee will be reduced on a gradual basis. Because the loan is reduced by the origination fee, the loan amount that you receive will be slightly less than the amount you've borrowed and must repay.

How will I be paid?

For Perkins Loans:

- Your school will either pay you directly (usually by check) or credit your account.

- Generally, you'll receive the loan in at least two payments during the academic year.

For Stafford Loans:

- Your school will disburse your loan in at least two installments.

- No installment will be greater than half the amount of your loan.

- If you're a first-year undergraduate student and a first-time borrower, your first disbursement can't be made until 30 days after the first day of your enrollment period.

- If you're a first-time borrower you must complete entrance counseling before you receive your first loan disbursement.

Student loan money must first be used to pay for your tuition, fees, and room and board. If loan funds remain, you'll receive them by check or in cash, unless you give the school written permission to hold the funds until later in the enrollment period.

Can I cancel my student loan if I change my mind, even if I have signed the promissory note agreeing to the terms of the loan?

Yes. Before your loan money is disbursed, you may cancel all or part of your loan at any time by notifying your school. After your loan is disbursed, you may cancel all or part of the loan within certain timeframes. Your promissory note and additional information you receive from your school will explain the procedures and timeframes for canceling your loan.

Can parents and graduate and professional degree students receive both a Direct PLUS Loan and a FFEL PLUS Loan?

No. The borrowers (parents borrowing for their undergraduate children and graduate and professional degree students borrowing for themselves) can apply for either loan, but not both, during the same enrollment period. Parents could, however, apply for a Direct PLUS Loan for one child and a FFEL PLUS Loan for another dependent child.

What are the eligibility requirements for PLUS Loans?

PLUS applicants must meet the general eligibility requirements for federal student financial aid. If a parent is borrowing on behalf of a dependent undergraduate student, the student must also meet these general eligibility requirements. For example, the PLUS applicant and the student must:

- Be a United States citizen or eligible noncitizen.

- Not be in default on a federal student loan.

- Not owe a refund on a federal education grant.

- A PLUS Loan applicant must not have an adverse credit history. (A credit check will be conducted.) A PLUS Loan applicant who has an adverse credit history still may be able to receive a loan by documenting existing extenuating circumstances or by obtaining an endorser who does not have an adverse credit history. An endorser is someone who agrees to repay the loan if the borrower fails to do so.

If a parent obtains a PLUS Loan to help pay for a dependent student's education, who receives the loan money—the parent or the student?

- The school will first apply the PLUS Loan funds to the student's school account to pay for tuition, fees, room and board and other school charges.

330

- If any loan funds remain, they will be sent to the parent borrower, unless the parent authorizes the school to hold the funds or release them to the student.

- Any remaining loan funds must be used for your education expenses.

Other than interest, are there any fees or charges to get a PLUS Loan?

Yes. There is a fee of up to 4 percent of the loan amount.

Borrower's Responsibilities

When you obtain a federal student loan you have certain responsibilities. Here are some important ones:

Think about how much you're borrowing.

- Think about what your repayment obligation means before you take out a student loan.

- If you don't repay your student loan on time or according to the terms in your promissory note, you could default on this legal obligation, which has serious consequences and will adversely affect your credit rating.

Signing a promissory note means you agree to repay the loan.

- When you sign a promissory note, you're agreeing to repay the loan according to the terms of the note.

- The note states that except in cases of loan discharge (cancellation), you must repay the loan, even if you don't complete your education (in some cases, you may not have to repay a loan if you were unable to complete your education because the school closed).

- Also, you must repay your loan even if you can't get a job after you complete the program or you didn't like the education you paid for.

The U.S. Department of Education does not guarantee the quality of education you receive or that you will find a job in your field of study.

Make payments regardless of receiving billing notices.

- You must make payments on your loan even if you don't receive a bill or repayment notice.

- Billing statements (or coupon books) are sent to you as a convenience. You're obligated to make payments even if you don't receive any reminders.

- You must also make monthly payments in the full amount required by your repayment plan. Partial payments do not fulfill your obligation to repay your student loan on time.

Continue to pay while waiting for deferment or forbearance approval.

- If you apply for a deferment or forbearance, you must continue to make payments until you have been notified that your request has been approved.

- If you don't, you might end up in default.

- Keep a copy of any request form you submit, and document all contact you have with the holder of your loan.

Notify your lender or loan servicing agency of these events.

- If you graduate.

- If you withdraw from school.

- If you drop below half-time status.

- If you change your name, address, or Social Security number. (New Social Security numbers are issued only in very rare circumstances.)

- If you transfer to another school.

Receive entrance and exit counseling.

For Direct or FFEL Stafford Loans, you must complete an entrance counseling session before you're given your first loan disbursement, unless you've previously borrowed a Stafford Loan. This session provides you with useful tips and tools to help you develop a budget for managing your educational expenses and helps you to understand your loan responsibilities.

For most federal student loans, you must receive exit counseling before you leave school to make sure you understand your rights and responsibilities as a borrower. You will receive information about repayment and your loan provider will notify you of the date loan repayment begins (usually six months after you graduated, leave school or drop below half-time enrollment).

Loan Repayment

This section gives you basic information about loan repayment. For more information, go online to http://www.FederalStudentAid.ed.gov. In addition, see the U.S. Department of Education publication "Repaying Your Student Loans." You can get the latest version online at http://www.FederalStudentAid.ed.gov/pubs. Or, you can request a paper copy from the Federal Student Aid Information Center by calling 800-4-FED-AID (800-433-3243).

When do I start paying back my student loans?

- **Federal Perkins Loans:** The grace period is nine months. However, if you're attending less than half-time, check with your financial aid administrator to determine your grace period. During the grace period, you don't have to pay any principal, and you won't be charged interest.

- **Direct or FFEL Stafford Loans:** The grace period is six months.

Your lender will send you information about repayment, and you'll be notified of the date repayment begins. However, you're responsible for beginning repayment on time, even if you don't receive this information. Failing to make payments on your loan can lead to default. Default occurs when you fail to meet the terms and conditions of the promissory note, such as not making timely payments on the loan.

How much time do I have to repay my student loans?

- **Federal Perkins Loans:** Up to 10 years.

- **Direct and FFEL Stafford Loans:** Your repayment period varies from 10 to 25 years, depending on which repayment plan you choose.

You'll get more information about repayment choices before you leave school (exit counseling), and later, during your grace period, from the holder of your loan(s).

When do parents and graduate and professional degree students begin repaying a PLUS Loan?

Generally, within 60 days after the loan is fully disbursed (paid out). There is no grace period for these loans. This means interest starts to accrue as soon as the first disbursement is made. Your parents and graduate and professional degree students must begin repaying both principal and interest while in school. However, a graduate and professional degree student PLUS Loan borrower could get an in-school deferment while he or she is enrolled at least half-time.

How much will I have to repay and how often do I make payments?

Direct or FFEL Stafford Loan: Usually, you'll make monthly payments. Your repayment amount will depend on the size of your debt, the length of your repayment period, and the repayment plan you choose.

Direct Stafford Loan: You'll make payments to the U.S. Department of Education through its Direct Loan Servicing Center. Direct Loan borrowers can view and pay their bills online using their PIN at: http://www.dl.ed.gov.

FFEL Stafford Loan: You'll repay the private lender that made you the loan.

Federal Perkins Loans: You'll make monthly payments to the school that loaned you the money. You'll have up to 10 years to repay your loan. Federal Perkins Loans do not have different repayment plans.

Do I have repayment options?

Yes. Repayment plans offered for Direct Stafford Loans are generally the same as those offered for FFEL Stafford Loans. However, the Direct Loan program will continue to offer an income contingent repayment plan and the FFEL program will continue to offer an income-sensitive repayment plan.

The repayment periods for Stafford Loans vary from 10 to 25 years. When it comes time to repay, you can pick a repayment plan that's best-suited to your financial situation. The following repayment plans will be available to Direct Loan borrowers who started repaying their loans on or after July 1, 2006:

- A standard plan with a fixed annual repayment amount paid over a fixed period of time not to exceed 10 years.

- A graduated plan paid over a fixed period of time not to exceed 10 years. With this plan, your payments start with a relatively low amount and then increase, generally every two years.

- An extended plan (for new borrowers on or after Oct. 7, 1998, with more than $30,000 in outstanding loans accumulated on or after that date) with a fixed annual or graduated repayment amount to be paid over a period not to exceed 25 years.

- A plan that bases the monthly payment amount on how much money you make. For Direct Stafford Loans, this plan is called the Income Contingent Repayment Plan (Direct PLUS Loans may not be repaid under the Income-Contingent Repayment Plan). For FFEL Stafford Loans and FFEL PLUS Loans, this plan is called the Income-Sensitive Repayment Plan. The terms of these plans vary.

- For Direct Loans, the U.S. Department of Education may offer alternative repayment plans to a borrower who demonstrates that other available repayment plans are not adequate and cannot accommodate the borrower's exceptional circumstances.

For a Perkins Loan, your school is the lender. Your school or its agent will provide you with the exact repayment amounts.

Are there tax incentives while paying back student loans?

Yes. Tax benefits are available for certain higher education expenses, including a deduction for student loan interest for certain borrowers. This benefit applies to all loans used to pay for post-secondary education costs, including PLUS Loans.

The maximum deduction is $2,500 a year. Internal Revenue Service (IRS) Publication 970, Tax Benefits for Higher Education, explains these credits and other tax benefits. You can get more information online at www.irs.gov or by calling the IRS at 800-829-1040. TTY callers can call 800-829-4059.

What is loan consolidation?

Student and parent borrowers can consolidate (combine) multiple federal student loans with various repayment schedules into one loan:

335

either a FFEL Consolidation Loan or a Direct Consolidation Loan, making a single monthly payment. With a consolidation loan:

- Your monthly payment might be lower.

- You can take a longer time to repay (up to 25 years).

- You will receive a fixed interest rate on your Direct or FFEL Consolidation Loan.

Compare the cost of repaying your unconsolidated loans with the cost of repaying a consolidation loan. Things to consider are:

- Whether you'll lose any borrower benefits if you consolidate, such as interest rate discounts or principal rebates, as these benefits can significantly reduce the cost of repaying your loans.

- Whether you might lose some discharge and cancellation benefits if you include a Perkins Loan in your consolidation loan.

Carefully review your consolidation options before you apply. Talk to the holder of your loan(s) for more information before you consolidate.

If you're in default on a federal student loan, you still might be able to consolidate if you make satisfactory repayment arrangements on the defaulted loan or agree to repay the consolidation loan under the Income-Contingent or Income Sensitive Repayment Plans, provided the defaulted loan is not subject to a judgment or wage garnishment.

Chapter 33

Financing a Vehicle: Loans and Leases

Understanding Vehicle Financing

With prices averaging more than $20,000 for a new vehicle and $9,500 for a four-year-old vehicle, most consumers need financing or leasing to acquire a vehicle. In some cases, buyers use "direct lending": they obtain a loan directly from a finance company, bank, or credit union. In direct lending, a buyer agrees to pay the amount financed, plus an agreed-upon finance charge, over a period of time. Once a buyer and a vehicle dealership enter into a contract and the buyer agrees to a vehicle price, the buyer uses the loan proceeds from the direct lender to pay the dealership for the vehicle.

Consumers also may arrange for a vehicle loan over the internet.

The most common type of vehicle financing, however, is "dealership financing." In this arrangement, a buyer and a dealership enter into a contract where the buyer agrees to pay the amount financed, plus an agreed-upon finance charge, over a period of time. The dealership may retain the contract, but usually sells it to an assignee (such as a bank, finance company or credit union), which services the account and collects the payments.

This chapter includes "Understanding Vehicle Financing," U.S. Federal Trade Commission (www.ftc.gov), February 2003; "Kicking the Tires on an Auto Loan: Don't Kick Yourself for Paying Too Much," *FDIC Consumer News*, Federal Deposit Insurance Corporation (www.fdic.gov), Summer 2004; and "Keys to Vehicle Leasing," Federal Reserve Board of Governors (www.federalreserve.gov), February 2005.

For the vehicle buyer, dealership financing offers the following benefits:

- **Convenience:** Dealers offer buyers vehicles and financing in one place.

- **Multiple financing relationships:** The dealership's relationships with a variety of banks and finance companies mean they can offer buyers a range of financing options.

- **Special programs:** From time to time, dealerships may offer manufacturer-sponsored, low-rate programs to buyers.

This chapter explains dealership financing and can serve as a guide as you evaluate your own financial situation before you finance a new or used vehicle. It will also help you understand vehicle leasing.

Before You Arrive at a Dealership

Do some research:

- Determine how much you can afford to finance and spend on a monthly payment.

- Get a copy of your credit report so you are aware of what creditors will see. Errors or accurate negative information can impact your ability to get credit and/or your finance rate.

- Identify your transportation needs.

- Check auto buying guides, the internet, and other sources to find out the price range and other information for the vehicle you want to buy.

- Compare current finance rates being offered by contacting various banks, credit unions or other lenders. Compare bank quotes and dealer quotes; there may be restrictions on the most attractive rates or terms from any credit source.

What Happens when You Apply for Financing

Most dealerships have a Finance and Insurance (F&I) Department, which provides one-stop shopping for financing. The F&I Department manager will ask you to complete a credit application. Information on this application may include: your name; Social Security number; date of birth; current and previous addresses and length of stay;

current and previous employers and length of employment; occupation; sources of income; total gross monthly income; and financial information on existing credit accounts.

The dealership will obtain a copy of your credit report, which contains information about current and past credit obligations, your payment record, and data from public records (for example, a bankruptcy filing obtained from court documents). For each account, the credit report shows your account number, the type and terms of the account, the credit limit, the most recent balance, and the most recent payment. The comments section describes the current status of your account, including the creditor's summary of past due information and any legal steps that may have been taken to collect.

Dealers typically sell your contract to an assignee, such as a bank, finance company or credit union. The dealership submits your credit application to one or more of these potential assignees to determine their willingness to purchase your contract from the dealer.

These finance companies or other potential assignees will usually evaluate your credit application using automated techniques such as credit scoring, where a variety of factors, like your credit history, length of employment, income, and expenses may be weighted and scored.

Since the bank, finance company, or credit union does not deal directly with the prospective vehicle purchaser, it bases its evaluation upon what appears on the individual's credit report and score, the completed credit application, and the terms of the sale, such as the amount of the down payment. Each finance company or other potential assignee decides whether it is willing to buy the contract, notifies the dealership of its decision and, if applicable, offers the dealership a wholesale rate at which the assignee will buy the contract, often called the "buy rate."

Your dealer may be able to offer manufacturer incentives, such as reduced finance rates or cash back on certain models. You may see these specials advertised in your area. Make sure you ask your dealer if the model you are interested in has any special financing offers or rebates. Generally, these discounted rates are not negotiable, may be limited by a consumer's credit history, and are available only for certain models, makes, or model-year vehicles.

When there are no special financing offers available, you can negotiate the annual percentage rate (APR) and the terms for payment with the dealership, just as you negotiate the price of the vehicle. The APR that you negotiate with the dealer is usually higher than the wholesale rate described earlier. This negotiation can occur before or after the dealership accepts and processes your credit application.

What Influences Your APR

Your credit history, current finance rates, competition, market conditions, and special offers are among the factors that influence your APR.

Co-Signers

You may be allowed by the creditor to have a co-signer sign the finance contract with you in order to make up for any deficiencies in your credit history. A co-signer assumes equal responsibility for the contract, and the account history will be reflected on the co-signer's credit history as well. For this reason, you should exercise caution if asked to co-sign for someone else. Since many co-signers are eventually asked to repay the obligation, be sure you can afford to do so before agreeing to be someone's co-signer.

Considering a Vehicle Lease

If you are considering leasing, there are several things to keep in mind. The monthly payments on a lease are usually lower than monthly finance payments on the same vehicle because you are paying for the vehicle's expected depreciation during the lease term, plus a rent charge, taxes, and fees. But at the end of a lease, you must return the vehicle unless the lease lets you buy it, and you agree to the purchase costs and terms. To be sure the lease terms fit your situation: Consider the beginning, middle, and end of lease costs. Compare different lease offers and terms, including mileage limits, and also consider how long you may want to keep the vehicle.

When you lease a vehicle, you have the right to use it for an agreed number of months and miles. At lease end, you may return the vehicle, pay any end-of-lease fees and charges, and "walk away." You may buy the vehicle for the additional agreed-upon price if you have a purchase option, which is a typical provision in retail lease contracts. Keep in mind that in most cases, you will be responsible for an early termination charge if you end the lease early. That charge could be substantial.

Another important consideration is the mileage limit—most standard leases are calculated based on a specified number of miles you can drive, typically 15,000 or fewer per year. You can negotiate a higher mileage limit, but you will normally have an increased monthly payment since the vehicle's depreciation will be greater during your lease term. If you exceed the mileage limit set in the lease agreement, you'll probably have to pay additional charges when you return the vehicle.

340

When you lease, you are also responsible for excess wear and damage and missing equipment. You must also service the vehicle in accordance with the manufacturer's recommendations. Finally, you will have to maintain insurance that meets the leasing company's standards. Be sure to find out the cost of this insurance.

Determining How Much You Can Afford

Before financing or leasing a vehicle, make sure you have enough income to cover your current monthly living expenses. Then, finance new purchases only when you can afford to take on a new monthly payment.

The only time to consider taking on additional debt is when you're spending less each month than you take home. The additional debt load should not cut into the amount you've committed to saving for emergencies and other top priorities or life goals. Saving money for a down payment or trading in a vehicle can reduce the amount you need to finance. In some cases, your trade-in vehicle will take care of the down payment on your vehicle.

Know the Terms of Financing before You Sign

Amount financed: The dollar amount of the credit that is provided to you.

Annual percentage rate (APR): The cost of credit for one year expressed as a percentage.

Assignee: The bank, finance company or credit union that purchases the contract from the dealer.

Credit insurance: Optional insurance that pays the scheduled unpaid balance if you die or scheduled monthly payments if you become disabled. As with most contract terms, the cost of optional credit insurance must be disclosed in writing, and, if you want it, you must agree to it and sign for it.

Down payment: An initial amount paid to reduce the amount financed.

Extended service contract: Optional protection on specified mechanical and electrical components of the vehicle available for purchase to supplement the warranty coverage provided with the new or used vehicle.

Finance charge: The total dollar amount you pay to use credit.

Fixed rate financing: The finance rate remains the same over the life of the contract.

Guaranteed auto protection (GAP): Optional protection that pays the difference between the amount you owe on your vehicle and the amount you receive from your insurance company if the vehicle is stolen or destroyed before you have satisfied your credit obligation.

Monthly payment amount: The dollar amount due each month to repay the credit agreement.

Negotiated price of the vehicle: The purchase price of the vehicle agreed upon by the buyer and the dealer.

Variable rate financing: The finance rate varies and the amount you must pay changes over the life of the contract.

Remember... When Visiting the Dealership

- Stay within the price range that you can afford.

- Negotiate your finance or lease arrangements and terms.

- Consider carefully whether the transaction is best for your budget and transportation needs.

- Understand the value and cost of optional products such as an extended service contract, credit insurance, or guaranteed auto protection, if you agree to purchase. If you don't want these products, don't sign for them.

- Read the contract carefully before you sign. You are obligated once you have signed a contract.

After Completing the Vehicle Purchase or Lease

- Be aware that if you financed the vehicle, the assignee (bank, finance company, or credit union that purchases the contract) holds a lien on the vehicle's title (and in some cases the actual title) until you have paid the contract in full.

- Make your payments on time. Late or missed payments incur late fees, appear on your credit report and impact your ability to get credit in the future.

If You Encounter Financial Difficulty

- Talk to your creditors if you experience difficulties making your monthly payments. Explain your situation and the reason your payment will be late. Work out a repayment schedule with your creditors and, if necessary, seek the services of a non-profit credit counseling agency.

- Know your obligations. A creditor or assignee may take the vehicle in full satisfaction of the credit agreement or may sell the vehicle and apply the proceeds from the sale to the outstanding balance on the credit agreement. This second option is more common. If the vehicle is sold for less than what is owed, you may be responsible for the difference.

- Be aware that repossession can occur if you fail to make timely payments. It does not relieve you of your obligation to pay for the vehicle. The law in some states allows the creditor or assignee to repossess your vehicle without going to court.

Federal Laws

Familiarize yourself with laws that authorize and regulate vehicle dealership financing and leasing.

- **Truth in Lending Act:** Requires that, before you sign the agreement, creditors give you written disclosure of important terms of the credit agreement such as APR, total finance charges, monthly payment amount, payment due dates, total amount being financed, length of the credit agreement, and any charges for late payment.

- **Federal Consumer Leasing Act (FCLA):** Requires the leasing company (dealership, for example) to disclose certain information before a lease is signed, including: the total amount of the initial payment; the number and amounts of monthly payments; all fees charged, including license fees and taxes; and the charges for default or late payments. For an automobile lease, the lessor must additionally disclose the annual mileage allowance and charges for excessive mileage; whether the lease can be terminated early; whether the leased automobile can be purchased at the end of the lease; the price to buy at the end of the lease; and any extra payments that may be required at the end of the lease.

343

- **Credit Practices Rule:** Requires creditors to provide a written notice to potential co-signers about their liability if the other person fails to pay; prohibits late charges in some situations; and prohibits creditors from using certain contract provisions that the government found to be unfair to consumers.

- **Equal Credit Opportunity Act:** Prohibits discrimination related to credit because of your gender, race, color, marital status, religion, national origin, or age. It also prohibits discrimination related to credit based on the fact that you are receiving public assistance or that you have exercised your rights under the federal Consumer Credit Protection Act.

For more information on federal credit regulations and consumer rights, contact:

Federal Trade Commission
Washington, DC 20580
Phone: 877-FTC-HELP (382-4357)
Website: www.ftc.gov

Federal Reserve System
Washington, DC 20551
Phone: 202 452-3693
Website: http://www.federalreserve.gov

State Laws

Some state laws may provide you with additional rights. For information on these laws, contact your state's consumer protection agency or Attorney General's office. The National Association of Attorneys General website (http://www.naag.org) can help you identify the name and address of your state's Attorney General.

Kicking the Tires on an Auto Loan: Don't Kick Yourself for Paying Too Much

Buying a new vehicle is stressful enough without having to make a decision about how to pay for it. Zero-percent financing, rebate offers of thousands of dollars, small down payments, bank financing, dealer financing—so many choices are enough to make your head spin even before you've taken your dream purchase out for a spin. The Federal Deposit Insurance Corporation (FDIC) offers these tips to help you save time and money when it comes to shopping for an auto loan.

Review your credit report: Review your credit report long before you intend to apply for a loan. A credit report is a summary of your financial reliability—for the most part, your history of paying debts and other bills—as compiled by a company called a credit bureau. Why should you see your credit report before applying for a car loan? To correct any error before it slows down your credit approval or prevents you from getting the best possible loan terms. "Erroneous information can cost you hundreds of dollars because you could be disqualified from the best financing terms available," says Joni Creamean, a Senior Consumer Affairs Specialist with the FDIC. "You will be considered a riskier borrower and charged higher rates or be required to provide a larger down payment." Creamean adds that it could take months to correct errors in your credit history.

It's also smart to review your credit report from each of the three major credit bureaus that operate nationwide: Equifax (http://www.equifax.com), Experian (http://www.experian.com), and TransUnion (http://www.transunion.com). Credit report content may vary significantly among the credit bureaus, so that's why experts suggest you request copies from all three companies. The costs of these reports can vary, however, you are be entitled to a free credit report annually under the provisions of the new Fair and Accurate Credit Transactions Act (for more details, see Chapter 23—How to Get a Copy of Your Credit Report).

Shop for a loan: Shop for a loan before you visit a dealership or bid for a car over the internet. Contact your bank and several other local lenders. Ask about the loans they offer—the number of months for which you can borrow, the interest rates being offered, whether there are penalties if you pay the loan off early, and so on. Ask about other options for financing the car.

For example, some homeowners may want to consider a home equity loan or line of credit instead of a traditional auto loan. "A loan tied to your home may be available with very attractive terms," says Creamean. A home equity loan also may come with tax benefits (but consult your tax advisor). Important to remember, however, is that if you pledge your home as collateral for a loan, and you can't repay, you could lose your home (for more information about home equity loans, see Chapter 35—Home Equity Loans).

Janet Kincaid, FDIC Senior Consumer Affairs Officer, points to yet another reason to shop for a loan before you shop for a car: "Knowing what your spending limit is and sticking to it permits you to focus only on the vehicles within that range," she says. "This also helps you avoid taking on more debt than you are comfortable with in the long run."

Also consider getting pre-approved for a loan, meaning a lender evaluates your creditworthiness and explains your loan options and likely costs before you buy a car. "Getting pre-approved doesn't mean you have a loan in hand but it does give you the benefit of knowing what you can afford and what it will cost you in the way of a loan," Kincaid explains. "You'll also know you won't be surprised with news that you've been denied credit or charged a higher rate due to your credit record." (Consumer advocates also suggest that you not tell the dealer if you've been pre-approved elsewhere for a loan until after you've negotiated the best price on a car. Some dealers may be less flexible on the price of the vehicle if it's clear that the dealership won't be earning money on a loan.)

After you know what's available in the marketplace, including the interest rates, consider learning what the dealers are offering by reading their advertisements, making phone calls, or checking the internet. Find out if only certain models are eligible for zero-percent financing from the dealer or if a manufacturer's rebate isn't available if you opt for zero-percent financing. Having this information helps you make a good decision about financing when you're face-to-face with a sales person or finance officer at the dealership. For example, "In some situations, it may be best to accept the dealer's rebate and pass up the zero-percent financing in favor of a loan from a bank that does charge interest," says Creamean. "You'll have to do the math and decide what is best for you."

Watch your debt load: Be careful figuring out how much to borrow and for how long. Of course, the dollar amount of your loan largely will be determined by the sale price of the vehicle minus your down payment, any rebates, and the value of any trade-in. But there are other costs that you should consider when deciding how much of a car you can afford and how much of a loan you need. Those costs include auto insurance, sales taxes, annual property taxes on the car (if any), and options you may be inclined to buy, such as an extended warranty. Also remember that every item you add to your loan instead of paying up-front will add to the total cost of the loan because you will be paying interest on the amount financed.

After you determine how big a loan you need, try to pick a repayment period that makes sense for you. For example, a $15,000 loan at 4 percent interest for 36 months equals a monthly payment of $443. Stretch the same loan out to 48 months and the monthly payment drops to $339. While it's tempting to go with a longer loan to reduce your payment, be careful. "Don't make the common mistake

of thinking only in terms of monthly payments rather than the total cost of the loan," warns Creamean. "In the end, extending a loan
term will cost you more since you will be paying interest on the loan
another year or more."

Creamean says to be especially cautious before taking an auto loan
term of five years or more. "First," she says, "if you have little cash
for a down payment and you have to take on a loan of five or seven
years, you might be trying to buy more car than you can really afford. Also, in the later years of the loan, you'll still be making payments on what is an older vehicle that may have a lot of repair and
maintenance costs."

Creamean also cautions that, in five or seven years, you may still
owe more on the loan than the trade-in value of the car, and that puts
you in a difficult financial position. "Just when you need or want a
new vehicle," she says, "problems with your old car may require you
to come up with extra cash to pay off the old loan or you might have
to roll the old loan into a new loan, which may push up your interest
rate. It can become a vicious cycle."

Understand the contract: Know what you are signing and speak
up if you think there's a problem. A variety of laws provide consumer
protections in the context of auto loans. Among them: the federal Truth
in Lending Act, which requires lenders to disclose to borrowers the
terms of a loan (including the Annual Percentage Rate and the total
cost of the loan), and federal and state laws that prohibit unfair or
deceptive business practices. However, you have a responsibility for
protecting yourself, too.

"One of the most important things a borrower can do is to carefully review the loan document before signing it, because this is a contract legally binding you to repay according to the terms of the
document," says FDIC attorney Mark Mellon. While the Truth in
Lending Act gives consumers the right to cancel certain mortgage
contracts up to three business days after signing the contract, Mellon
says, "there may or may not be a similar protection for your auto loan
depending on your circumstances and state law, so it's best to be comfortable with your decision before you sign on the dotted line."

If you have a question or a concern about an auto loan and you
can't resolve the matter with the lender or auto dealer directly, contact the appropriate federal regulator if the situation involves a banking institution or the Federal Trade Commission (877-382-4357 or
http://www.ftc.gov) for a nonbank lender, such as an auto dealer or
finance company.

Keys to Vehicle Leasing

Under the federal Consumer Leasing Act, you, the consumer, have a right to information about the costs and terms of a vehicle lease. This information will help you compare lease offers and negotiate a lease that best fits your needs, budget, and driving patterns.

The information in this chapter is for a closed-end lease, the most common type of vehicle lease. With a closed-end lease, you may return the vehicle at the end of the lease term, pay any end-of-lease costs, and walk away.

Leasing Is Different from Buying

Ownership

- *Leasing:* You do not own the vehicle. You get to use it but must return it at the end of the lease unless you choose to buy it.

- *Buying:* You own the vehicle and get to keep it at the end of the financing term.

Up-Front Costs

- *Leasing:* Up-front costs may include the first month's payment, a refundable security deposit, a capitalized cost reduction (like a down payment), taxes, registration and other fees, and other charges.

- *Buying:* Up-front costs include the cash price or a down payment, taxes, registration and other fees, and other charges.

Monthly Payments

- *Leasing:* Monthly lease payments are usually lower than monthly loan payments because you are paying only for the vehicle's depreciation during the lease term, plus rent charges (like interest), taxes, and fees.

- *Buying:* Monthly loan payments are usually higher than monthly lease payments because you are paying for the entire purchase price of the vehicle, plus interest and other finance charges, taxes, and fees.

Early Termination

- *Leasing:* You are responsible for any early termination charges if you end the lease early.

- *Buying:* You are responsible for any pay-off amount if you end the loan early.

Vehicle Return

- *Leasing:* You may return the vehicle at lease-end, pay any end-of-lease costs, and "walk away."

- *Buying:* You may have to sell or trade the vehicle when you decide you want a different vehicle.

Future Value

- *Leasing:* The lessor has the risk of the future market value of the vehicle.

- *Buying:* You have the risk of the vehicle's market value when you trade or sell it.

Mileage

- *Leasing:* Most leases limit the number of miles you may drive (often 12,000–15,000 per year). You can negotiate a higher mileage limit and pay a higher monthly payment. You will likely have to pay charges for exceeding those limits if you return the vehicle.

- *Buying:* You may drive as many miles as you want, but higher mileage will lower the vehicle's trade-in or resale value.

Excessive Wear

- *Leasing:* Most leases limit wear to the vehicle during the lease term. You will likely have to pay extra charges for exceeding those limits if you return the vehicle.

- *Buying:* There are no limits or charges for excessive wear to the vehicle, but excessive wear will lower the vehicle's trade-in or resale value.

End of Term

- *Leasing:* At the end of the lease (typically 2–4 years), you may have a new payment either to finance the purchase of the existing vehicle or to lease another vehicle.

- *Buying:* At the end of the loan term (typically 4–6 years), you have no further loan payments.

Consider Beginning, Middle, and End-of-Lease Costs

At the beginning of the lease, you may have to pay your first monthly payment; a refundable security deposit or your last monthly payment; other fees for licenses, registration, and title; a capitalized cost reduction (like a down payment); an acquisition fee (also called a processing or assignment fee); freight or destination charges; and state or local taxes.

During the lease, you will have to pay your monthly payment; any additional taxes not included in the payment such as sales, use, and personal property taxes; insurance premiums; ongoing maintenance costs; and any fees for late payment. You'll also have to pay for safety and emissions inspections and any traffic tickets. If you end your lease early, you may have to pay substantial early termination charges.

At the end of the lease, if you don't buy the vehicle, you may have to pay a disposition fee and charges for excess miles and excessive wear.

Compare Lease Offers

You can compare different lease offers and negotiate some terms. Consider these items:

- The agreed-upon value of the vehicle—a lower value can reduce your monthly payment

- Up-front payments, including the capitalized cost reduction

- The length of the lease

- The monthly lease payment

- Any end-of-lease fees and charges

- The mileage allowed and per-mile charges for excess miles

- The option to purchase either at lease-end or earlier

- Whether your lease includes "gap" coverage, which protects you if the vehicle is stolen or totaled in an accident.

Also, ask for alternatives to advertised specials and other lease offerings.

Know Your Rights and Responsibilities

- When you lease a vehicle, you have the right to the following conditions:

- Use it for an agreed-upon number of months and miles
- Turn it in at lease-end, pay any end-of-lease fees and charges, and "walk away"
- Buy the vehicle if you have a purchase option
- Take advantage of any warranties, recalls, or other services that apply to the vehicle

You may be responsible for these items:

- Excess mileage charges when you return the vehicle. Your lease agreement will tell you how many miles you can drive before you must pay for extra miles and how much the per-mile charge will be.
- Excessive wear charges when you return the vehicle. The standards for excessive wear, such as for body damage or worn tires, are in your lease agreement.
- Substantial payments if you end the lease early. The earlier you end the lease, the greater these charges are likely to be.

For More Information

Contact your dealer, manufacturer, leasing company, or financial institution for more information.

The federal Consumer Leasing Act and some state laws may provide you with additional consumer rights not covered in your lease agreement. For information on these laws, contact your state's consumer protection agency or attorney general's office. You also can contact these federal agencies:

Division of Consumer and Community Affairs
Mail Stop 800
Federal Reserve Board
Washington, DC 20551

Consumer Response Center
Federal Trade Commission
6th and Pennsylvania Ave., NW
Washington, DC 20580

351

Chapter 34

What You Should Know about Mortgages

Chapter Contents

Section 34.1

Looking for the Best Mortgage

From "Looking for the Best Mortgage," Federal Reserve Board of Governors (www.federalreserve.gov), January 2004.

Shopping around for a home loan or mortgage will help you to get the best financing deal. A mortgage—whether it's a home purchase, a refinancing, or a home equity loan—is a product, just like a car, so the price and terms may be negotiable. You'll want to compare all the costs involved in obtaining a mortgage. Shopping, comparing, and negotiating may save you thousands of dollars.

Obtain Information from Several Lenders

Home loans are available from several types of lenders—thrift institutions, commercial banks, mortgage companies, and credit unions. Different lenders may quote you different prices, so you should contact several lenders to make sure you're getting the best price. You can also get a home loan through a mortgage broker. Brokers arrange transactions rather than lending money directly; in other words, they find a lender for you. A broker's access to several lenders can mean a wider selection of loan products and terms from which you can choose. Brokers will generally contact several lenders regarding your application, but they are not obligated to find the best deal for you unless they have contracted with you to act as your agent. Consequently, you should consider contacting more than one broker, just as you should with banks or thrift institutions.

Whether you are dealing with a lender or a broker may not always be clear. Some financial institutions operate as both lenders and brokers. And most brokers' advertisements do not use the word "broker." Therefore, be sure to ask whether a broker is involved. This information is important because brokers are usually paid a fee for their services that may be separate from and in addition to the lender's origination or other fees. A broker's compensation may be in the form of "points" paid at closing or as an add-on to your interest rate, or both. You should ask each broker you work with how he or she will be compensated so that you can compare the differ-ent fees. Be prepared to negotiate with the brokers as well as the lenders.

Obtain All Important Cost Information

Be sure to get information about mortgages from several lenders or brokers. Know how much of a down payment you can afford, and find out all the costs involved in the loan. Knowing just the amount of the monthly payment or the interest rate is not enough. Ask for information about the same loan amount, loan term, and type of loan so that you can compare the information. The following information is important to get from each lender and broker.

Rates

- Ask each lender and broker for a list of its current mortgage in-terest rates and whether the rates being quoted are the lowest for that day or week.

- Ask whether the rate is fixed or adjustable. Keep in mind that when interest rates for adjustable-rate loans go up, generally so does the monthly payment.

- If the rate quoted is for an adjustable-rate loan, ask how your rate and loan payment will vary, including whether your loan payment will be reduced when rates go down.

- Ask about the loan's annual percentage rate (APR). The APR takes into account not only the interest rate but also points, bro-ker fees, and certain other credit charges that you may be re-quired to pay, expressed as a yearly rate.

Points

Points are fees paid to the lender or broker for the loan and are often linked to the interest rate; usually the more points you pay, the lower the rate.

- Check your local newspaper for information about rates and points currently being offered.

- Ask for points to be quoted to you as a dollar amount—rather than just as the number of points—so that you will actually know how much you will have to pay.

355

Fees

A home loan often involves many fees, such as loan origination or underwriting fees, broker fees, and transaction, settlement, and closing costs. Every lender or broker should be able to give you an estimate of its fees. Many of these fees are negotiable. Some fees are paid when you apply for a loan (such as application and appraisal fees), and others are paid at closing. In some cases, you can borrow the money needed to pay these fees, but doing so will increase your loan amount and total costs. "No cost" loans are sometimes available, but they usually involve higher rates.

- Ask what each fee includes. Several items may be lumped into one fee.

- Ask for an explanation of any fee you do not understand.

Down Payments and Private Mortgage Insurance

Some lenders require 20 percent of the home's purchase price as a down payment. However, many lenders now offer loans that require less than 20 percent down—sometimes as little as 5 percent on conventional loans. If a 20 percent down payment is not made, lenders usually require the home buyer to purchase private mortgage insurance (PMI) to protect the lender in case the home buyer fails to pay. When government-assisted programs such as FHA (Federal Housing Administration), VA (Veterans Administration), or Rural Development Services are available, the down payment requirements may be substantially smaller.

- Ask about the lender's requirements for a down payment, including what you need to do to verify that funds for your down payment are available.

- Ask your lender about special programs it may offer.

If PMI is required for your loan:

- Ask what the total cost of the insurance will be.

- Ask how much your monthly payment will be when including the PMI premium.

- Ask how long you will be required to carry PMI.

Obtain the Best Deal That You Can

Once you know what each lender has to offer, negotiate for the best deal that you can. On any given day, lenders and brokers may offer different prices for the same loan terms to different consumers, even if those consumers have the same loan qualifications. The most likely reason for this difference in price is that loan officers and brokers are often allowed to keep some or all of this difference as extra compensation. Generally, the difference between the lowest available price for a loan product and any higher price that the borrower agrees to pay is an overage. When overages occur, they are built into the prices quoted to consumers. They can occur in both fixed and variable-rate loans and can be in the form of points, fees, or the interest rate. Whether quoted to you by a loan officer or a broker, the price of any loan may contain overages.

Have the lender or broker write down all the costs associated with the loan. Then ask if the lender or broker will waive or reduce one or more of its fees or agree to a lower rate or fewer points. You'll want to make sure that the lender or broker is not agreeing to lower one fee while raising another or to lower the rate while raising points. There's no harm in asking lenders or brokers if they can give better terms than the original ones they quoted or than those you have found elsewhere.

Once you are satisfied with the terms you have negotiated, you may want to obtain a written lock-in from the lender or broker. The lock-in should include the rate that you have agreed upon, the period the lock-in lasts, and the number of points to be paid. A fee may be charged for locking in the loan rate. This fee may be refundable at closing. Lock-ins can protect you from rate increases while your loan is being processed; if rates fall, however, you could end up with a less favorable rate. Should that happen, try to negotiate a compromise with the lender or broker.

Remember: Shop, Compare, Negotiate

When buying a home, remember to shop around, to compare costs and terms, and to negotiate for the best deal. Your local newspaper and the internet are good places to start shopping for a loan. You can usually find information both on interest rates and on points for several lenders. Since rates and points can change daily, you'll want to check your newspaper often when shopping for a home loan. But the newspaper does not list the fees, so be sure to ask the lenders about them.

357

Don't be afraid to make lenders and brokers compete with each other for your business by letting them know that you are shopping for the best deal.

Fair Lending Is Required by Law

The Equal Credit Opportunity Act prohibits lenders from discriminating against credit applicants in any aspect of a credit transaction on the basis of race, color, religion, national origin, sex, marital status, age, whether all or part of the applicant's income comes from a public assistance program, or whether the applicant has in good faith exercised a right under the Consumer Credit Protection Act.

The Fair Housing Act prohibits discrimination in residential real estate transactions on the basis of race, color, religion, sex, handicap, familial status, or national origin.

Under these laws, a consumer cannot be refused a loan based on these characteristics nor be charged more for a loan or offered less favorable terms based on such characteristics.

Credit Problems? Still Shop, Compare, and Negotiate

Don't assume that minor credit problems or difficulties stemming from unique circumstances, such as illness or temporary loss of income, will limit your loan choices to only high-cost lenders. If your credit report contains negative information that is accurate, but there are good reasons for trusting you to repay a loan, be sure to explain your situation to the lender or broker. If your credit problems cannot be explained, you will probably have to pay more than borrowers who have good credit histories. But don't assume that the only way to get credit is to pay a high price. Ask how your past credit history affects the price of your loan and what you would need to do to get a better price. Take the time to shop around and negotiate the best deal that you can.

Whether you have credit problems or not, it's a good idea to review your credit report for accuracy and completeness before you apply for a loan. To order a copy of your credit report, contact:

Equifax: 800-685-1111
TransUnion: 800-888-4213
Experian: 888-397-3742

Section 34.2

What Are Adjustable Rate Mortgages (ARMs)?

From "Consumer Handbook on Adjustable Rate Mortgages (ARM)," Federal Reserve Board of Governors (www.federalreserve.gov), June 2005.

Questions People Ask about Adjustable Rate Mortgages

What is an ARM?

With a fixed-rate mortgage, the interest rate stays the same during the life of the loan. But with an ARM, the interest rate changes periodically, usually in relation to an index, and payments may go up or down accordingly.

Lenders generally charge lower initial interest rates for ARMs than for fixed-rate mortgages. This makes the ARM easier on your pocketbook at first than a fixed-rate mortgage for the same amount. It also means that you might qualify for a larger loan because lenders sometimes make the decision about whether to extend a loan on the basis of your current income and the first year's payments. Moreover, your ARM could be less expensive over a long period than a fixed-rate mortgage—for example, if interest rates remain steady or move lower.

Against these advantages, you have to weigh the risk that an increase in interest rates would lead to higher monthly payments in the future. It's a trade-off—you get a lower rate with an ARM in exchange for assuming more risk.

Here are some questions you need to consider:

- Is my income likely to rise enough to cover higher mortgage payments if interest rates go up?

- Will I be taking on other sizable debts, such as a loan for a car or school tuition, in the near future?

- How long do I plan to own this home? (If you plan to sell soon, rising interest rates may not pose the problem they do if you plan to own the house for a long time.)

- Can my payments increase even if interest rates generally do not increase?

Some newspaper ads for home loans show surprisingly low rates. Are these loans for real, or is there a catch?

Some of the ads you see are for adjustable-rate mortgages (ARMs). These loans may have low rates for a short time—maybe only for the first year. After that, the rates may be adjusted on a regular basis. This means that the interest rate and the amount of the monthly payment may go up or down.

Will I know in advance how much my payment may go up?

With an adjustable-rate mortgage, your future monthly payment is uncertain. Some types of ARMs put a ceiling on your payment increase or interest-rate increase from one period to the next. Virtually all types must put a ceiling on rate increases over the life of the loan.

Is an ARM the right type of loan for me?

That depends on your financial situation and the terms of the ARM. ARMs carry risks in periods of rising interest rates, but they can be cheaper over a longer term if interest rates decline. You will be able to answer the question better once you understand more about ARMs.

Mortgages have changed, and so have the questions that consumers need to ask and have answered.

Shopping for a mortgage used to be a relatively simple process. Most home mortgage loans had interest rates that did not change over the life of the loan. Choosing among these fixed-rate mortgage loans meant comparing interest rates, monthly payments, fees, prepayment penalties, and due-on-sale clauses.

Today, many loans have interest rates (and monthly payments) that can change from time to time. To compare one ARM with another or with a fixed-rate mortgage, you need to know about indexes, margins, discounts, caps, negative amortization, and convertibility. You need to consider the maximum amount your monthly payment could increase. Most important, you need to compare what might happen to your mortgage costs with your future ability to pay.

How ARMs Work: The Basic Features

The Adjustment Period

With most ARMs, the interest rate and monthly payment change every year, every three years, or every five years. However, some ARMs have more frequent rate and payment changes. The period between one rate change and the next is called the "adjustment period." A loan with an adjustment period of one year is called a one-year ARM, and the interest rate can change once every year.

The Index

Most lenders tie ARM interest-rate changes to changes in an "index rate." These indexes usually go up and down with the general movement of interest rates. If the index rate moves up, so does your mortgage rate in most circumstances, and you will probably have to make higher monthly payments. On the other hand, if the index rate goes down, your monthly payment may go down.

Lenders base ARM rates on a variety of indexes. Among the most common indexes are the rates on one-, three-, or five-year Treasury securities. Another common index is the national or regional average cost of funds to savings and loan associations. A few lenders use their own cost of funds as an index, which gives them more control than using other indexes. You should ask what index will be used and how often it changes. Also ask how it has fluctuated in the past and where it is published.

The Margin

To determine the interest rate on an ARM, lenders add to the index rate a few percentage points, called the "margin." The amount of the margin may differ from one lender to another, but it is usually constant over the life of the loan. Here is the formula to calculate your interest rate:

Index rate + margin = ARM interest rate

Let's say, for example, that you are comparing ARMs offered by two different lenders. Both ARMs are for 30 years and have a loan amount of $65,000. (All the examples used in this section are based on this amount for a 30-year term. Note that the payment amounts shown here do not include taxes, insurance, or similar items.)

Both lenders use the rate on one-year Treasury securities as the index. But the first lender uses a 2% margin, and the second lender uses a 3% margin. Table 34.1 shows how that difference in the margin would affect your initial monthly payment.

In comparing ARMs, look at both the index and margin for each program. Some indexes have higher values, but they are usually used with lower margins. Be sure to discuss the margin with your lender.

Consumer Cautions

Discounts

Some lenders offer initial ARM rates that are lower than their "standard" ARM rates (that is, lower than the sum of the index and the margin). Such rates, called discounted rates, are often combined with large initial loan fees ("points") and with much higher rates after the discount expires.

Table 34.1. How Margin Affects Initial Monthly Payments

Home sale price	$ 85,000
Less down payment	- $ 20,000
Mortgage amount	= $ 65,000
Mortgage term 30 years	

First Lender

One-year index = 8%	
Margin = 2%	
ARM interest rate = 10%	
Monthly payment @ 10%	= $ 570.42

Second Lender

One-year index = 8%	
Margin = 3%	
ARM interest rate = 11%	
Monthly payment @ 11%	= $ 619.01

Very large discounts are often arranged by the seller. The seller pays an amount to the lender so that the lender can give you a lower rate and lower payments early in the mortgage term. This arrangement is referred to as a "seller buydown." The seller may increase the sales price of the home to cover the cost of the buydown.

A lender may use a low initial rate to decide whether to approve your loan, based on your ability to afford it. You should be careful to consider whether you will be able to afford payments in later years when the discount expires and the rate is adjusted. Here is how a discount might work. Let's assume that the lender's "standard" one-year ARM rate (index rate plus margin) is currently 10%. But your lender is offering an 8% rate for the first year. With the 8% rate, your first-year monthly payment would be $476.95.

But don't forget that with a discounted ARM, your initial payment will probably remain at $476.95 for only 12 months—and that any savings during the discount period may be made up during the life of the mortgage or may be included in the price of the house. In fact, if you buy a home using this kind of loan, you run the risk of payment shock.

Payment Shock

Payment shock may occur if your mortgage payment rises very sharply at the first adjustment. For example, if the index rate were to stay the same, when your discounted 8% ARM rose to the 10% "standard" rate, your monthly payment would increase from $476.95 in the first year to $568.82 in the second year.

Now, suppose that the index rate increases 2% in one year and the ARM rate rises to 12%. Your monthly payment would increase from $476.95 in the first year to year to $665.43 in the second year. That's an increase of almost $200 in your monthly payment. You can see what might happen if you choose an ARM because of a low initial rate. You can protect yourself from large increases by looking for a mortgage with features, described next, that may reduce this risk.

How Can I Reduce My Risk?

Besides offering an overall rate ceiling, most ARMs also have "caps" that protect borrowers from extreme increases in monthly payments. Others allow borrowers to convert an ARM to a fixed-rate mortgage. While they may offer real benefits, these ARMs may also cost more, or may add special features such as negative amortization.

Interest-Rate Caps

An interest-rate cap places a limit on the amount your interest rate can increase. Interest caps come in two versions:

- Periodic caps, which limit the interest-rate increase from one adjustment period to the next; and

- Overall caps, which limit the interest-rate increase over the life of the loan.

By law, virtually all ARMs must have an overall cap. Many have a periodic cap.

Let's suppose you have an ARM with a periodic interest-rate cap of 2%. At the first adjustment, the index rate goes up 3%. The example in Table 34.2 shows what happens.

Table 34.2. The Effect of a Periodic Interest-Rate Cap of 2%

ARM Interest Rate	Monthly Payment
1st year @ 10%	$ 570.42
2nd year @ 13% (without cap)	$ 717.12
2nd year @ 12% (with cap)	$ 667.30

Difference in 2nd year between payment with cap and payment without = $49.82

A drop in interest rates does not always lead to a drop in monthly payments. In fact, with some ARMs that have interest-rate caps, your payment amount may increase even though the index rate has stayed the same or declined. This may happen when an interest-rate cap has been holding your interest rate down below the sum of the index plus margin. If a rate cap holds down your interest rate, increases to the index that were not imposed because of the cap may carry over to future rate adjustments.

With some ARMs, payments may increase even if the index rate stays the same or declines.

The example in Table 34.3 shows how carryovers work. The index increased 3% during the first year. Because this ARM limits rate increases to 2% at any one time, the rate is adjusted by only 2%, to 12%

for the second year. However, the remaining 1% increase in the index carries over to the next time the lender can adjust rates. So when the lender adjusts the interest rate for the third year, the rate increases 1%, to 13%, even though there is no change in the index during the second year.

In general, the rate on your loan can go up at any scheduled adjustment date when the lender's standard ARM rate (the index plus the margin) is higher than the rate you are paying before that adjustment.

Here's an example of how a 5% overall rate cap would affect your loan: Let's say that your initial monthly payment is $570.42 at 10% and that the index rate increases 1% in each of the next nine years. With a 5% overall cap, your payment would never exceed $813.00— compared to the $1,008.64 that it would have reached in the tenth year based on a 19% interest rate.

Table 34.3. The Effect of an Interest-Rate Cap Carryover

ARM Interest Rate	Monthly Payment
1st year @ 10%	$ 570.42
If index rises 3% . . .2nd year @ 12% (with 2% rate cap)	$ 667.30
If index stays the same for the 3rd year @ 13%	$ 716.56

Even though the index stays the same in 3rd year, payment goes up $49.26

Payment Caps

Some ARMs include payment caps, which limit your monthly payment increase at the time of each adjustment, usually to a percentage of the previous payment. In other words, with a 7½% payment cap, a payment of $100 could increase to no more than $107.50 in the first adjustment period, and to no more than $115.56 in the second.

Table 34.4 shows what would happen to your payments if your rate changes in the first year by 2 percentage points but your payments can increase by no more than 7½% in any one year.

Many ARMs with payment caps do not have periodic interest-rate caps.

Table 34.4. The Effect of a 7½% Payment Cap

ARM Interest Rate	Monthly payment
1st year @ 10%	$ 570.42
2nd year @ 12% (without payment cap)	$ 667.30
2nd year @ 12% (with 7½% payment cap)	$ 613.20
Difference in monthly payment =	$54.10

Negative Amortization

If your ARM includes a payment cap, be sure to find out about "negative amortization." Negative amortization means that the mortgage balance increases. It occurs whenever your monthly mortgage payments are not large enough to pay all of the interest due on your mortgage.

Because payment caps limit only the amount of payment increases, and not interest-rate increases, payments sometimes do not cover all the interest due on your loan. This means that the interest shortage in your payment is automatically added to your debt, and interest may be charged on that amount. You might therefore owe the lender more later in the loan term than you did at the start. However, an increase in the value of your home may make up for the increase in what you owe.

Table 34.5 uses the figures from the example in Table 34.4 to show how negative amortization works during one year. Your first 12 payments of $570.42, based on a 10% interest rate, paid the balance down to $64,638.72 at the end of the first year.

The rate goes up to 12% in the second year. But because of the 7½% payment cap, your payments are not high enough to cover all the interest. The interest shortage is added to your debt (with interest on it), which produces negative amortization of $420.90 during the second year.

Table 34.5. How Negative Amortization Works

Beginning loan amount	=	$65,000.00
Loan amount at end of 1st year	=	$64,638.72
Negative amortization during 2nd year	=	$420.90
Loan amount at end of 2nd year (assuming all payments were made) ($64,638.72 + $420.90)	=	$65,059.62

If you sold your house at this point, you would owe almost $60 more than you originally borrowed despite making all of the payments.

To sum up, the payment cap limits increases in your monthly payment by deferring some of the increase in interest. Eventually, you will have to repay the higher remaining loan balance at the ARM rate then in effect. When this happens, there may be a substantial increase in your monthly payment.

Some mortgages include a cap on negative amortization. The cap typically limits the total amount you can owe to 125% of the original loan amount. When that point is reached, monthly payments may be set to fully repay the loan over the remaining term, and your payment cap may not apply. You may limit negative amortization by voluntarily increasing your monthly payment.

Be sure to discuss negative amortization with the lender to understand how it will apply to your loan.

Prepayment and Conversion

If you get an ARM and your financial circumstances change, you may decide that you don't want to risk any further changes in the interest rate and payment amount. When you are considering an ARM, ask for information about prepayment and conversion.

Prepayment: Some agreements may require you to pay special fees or penalties if you pay off the ARM early. Many ARMs allow you to pay the loan in full or in part without penalty whenever the rate is adjusted. Prepayment details are sometimes negotiable. If so, you may want to negotiate for no penalty, or for as low a penalty as possible.

Conversion: Your agreement with the lender may include a clause that lets you convert the ARM to a fixed-rate mortgage at designated times. When you convert, the new rate is generally set at the current market rate for fixed-rate mortgages.

The interest rate or up-front fees may be somewhat higher for a convertible ARM. Also, a convertible ARM may require a special fee at the time of conversion.

Section 34.3

A Consumer's Guide to Mortgage Settlement Costs

From "A Consumer's Guide to Mortgage Settlement Costs," Federal Reserve Board of Governors (www.federalreserve.gov), April 2005.

Mortgage settlement—sometimes called mortgage closing—can be confusing. A settlement may involve several people and many documents and fees. This information will help you understand all that is involved. Although the focus of this section is on settlements for home purchases, much of it will also be useful if you are refinancing a mortgage.

Settlement costs can be high, so it pays to shop around and negotiate with the seller, your lender, and your attorney or settlement agent. The less you have to pay in settlement costs, the more funds you will have for other things.

Different regions have different customs and practices regarding who pays for what at settlement. Buyers and sellers are free to negotiate certain fees. In slow-moving real estate markets, the seller may agree to pay points or fees for the buyer. In fast-moving markets, the buyer may have to agree to pay more costs to close the deal. Whatever you negotiate will become the sales contract. However, be careful; if some buyer's costs are shifted to the seller, it may increase the price you pay for the property.

You can reduce some settlement costs by shopping around for the services. The point is this: the more you know about the process, the better your chances are for saving money at settlement time.

Because practices vary significantly from area to area, it is difficult to provide estimates for settlement costs that fit everywhere. However, one rule of thumb for buyers is to figure that settlement costs will be about 3% of the price of your home. In some relatively high-tax areas of the country, 5% to 6% is more common.

Some settlement costs, such as homeowner's insurance, private mortgage insurance, or points can be more expensive if your credit rating is low. Knowing your credit score can help you understand how lenders will evaluate your applications. Beginning December 2004 your lender is required to give you a copy of your credit score.

Mortgage- and Lender-Related Settlement Costs

Most people associate settlement costs with mortgage loan charges. These fees and charges vary, so it pays to shop around for the best combination of mortgage terms and settlement costs. Mortgage-related costs that may apply to your loan include the following items.

Application Fee

Imposed by your lender or broker, this charge covers the initial costs of processing your loan request and checking your credit report.

Estimated cost: $75 to $300, including the cost of the credit report for each applicant

Loan Origination Fee

The origination fee (also called underwriting fee, administrative fee, or processing fee) is charged for the lender's work in evaluating and preparing your mortgage loan. This fee can cover the lender's attorney's fees, document preparation costs, notary fees, and so forth.

Estimated cost: 1% to 1.5% of the loan amount

Points

Points are a one-time charge imposed by the lender, usually to reduce the interest rate of your loan. One point equals 1% of the loan amount. For example, 1 point on a $100,000 loan would be $1,000. In some cases—especially in refinancing—the points can be financed by adding them to the amount that you borrow. However, if you pay the points at settlement, they are deductible on your income taxes in the year they are paid (different deduction rules apply when you refinance or purchase a second home). In your purchase offer, you may want to negotiate with the seller to have the seller pay your points.

Estimated cost: 0% to 3% of the loan amount

Appraisal Fee

Lenders want to be sure that the property is worth at least as much as the loan amount. This fee pays for an appraisal of the home you want to purchase or refinance. Some lenders and brokers include the appraisal fee as part of the application fee; you can ask the lender

369

for a copy of your appraisal. If you are refinancing and you have had a recent appraisal, some lenders may waive the requirement for a new appraisal.

Estimated cost: $300 to $700

Lender-Required Home Inspection Fees

The lender may require a termite inspection and an analysis of the structural condition of the property by an engineer or consultant. In rural areas, lenders may require a septic system test and a water test to make sure the well and water system will maintain an adequate supply of water for the house (this is usually a test for quantity, not for water quality; your county health department may require a water quality test as well, but this test may be paid for outside of the settlement). Keep in mind that this inspection is for the benefit of the lender; you may want to request your own inspection to make sure the property is in good condition.

Estimated costs: $175 to $350

Prepaid Interest

Your first regular mortgage payment is usually due about six to eight weeks after you settle (for example, if you settle in August, your first regular payment will be due on October 1; the October payment covers the cost of borrowing the money for the month of September). Interest costs, however, start as soon as you settle. The lender will calculate how much interest you owe for the part of the month in which you settle (for example, if you settle on August 16, you would owe interest for 15 days—August 16 through 31).

Estimated cost: Depends on loan amount, interest rate, and the number of days that must be paid for (a $120,000 loan at 6% for 15 days, about $300; a $142,500 loan at 6% for 15 days, about $356).

Private Mortgage Insurance (PMI)

If your down payment is less than 20% of the value of the house, the lender will usually require mortgage insurance. The insurance policy covers the lender's risk in the event that you do not make the loan payments. Typically, you will pay a monthly premium along with each month's mortgage payment. Your PMI can be canceled at your

370

request, in writing, when your reach 20% equity in your home, based on your original purchase price, if your mortgage payments are current and you have a good payment history. By federal law your PMI payments will automatically stop when you acquire 22% equity in your home, based on the original appraised value of the house, as long as your mortgage payments are current.

Estimated cost: 0.5% to 1.5% of the loan amount to prepay for the first year

Some lenders will pay for PMI—called lender's private mortgage insurance (LPMI)—and in turn will charge a higher interest rate. Unlike PMI that you pay, there is no automatic cancellation once you acquire 22% equity. To eliminate the LPMI, you must refinance the loan, which in turn means carefully considering market interest rates and settlement costs at the time to see if refinancing would be an advantage, rather than keeping your current mortgage.

FHA, VA, or RHS Fees

The Federal Housing Administration (FHA) offers insured mortgages and the Veterans Administration (VA) and the Rural Housing Service (RHS) offer mortgage guarantees. If you are getting a mortgage insured by the FHA or guaranteed by the VA or the RHS, you will have to pay FHA mortgage insurance premiums or VA or RHS guarantee fees. As with Private MI, insurance premium payments will stop when you acquire 22% equity in your home. FHA fees are about 1.5% of the loan amount. VA guarantee fees range from 1.25% to 2% of the loan amount, depending on the size of your down payment (the higher your down payment, the lower the fee percentage). RHS fees are 1.75% of the loan amount.

Homeowner's Insurance

Your lender will require that you have a homeowner's insurance policy (sometimes called hazard insurance) in effect at settlement. The policy protects against physical damage to the house by fire, wind, vandalism, and other causes. This insures that the lender's investment will be secured even if the house is destroyed. If you are buying a condominium, the hazard insurance may be part of your monthly condominium fee; you may still want homeowner's insurance for your furnishings and valuables.

Estimated cost: $300 to $1,000 (depending on the value of the home and the amount of coverage; you can estimate the cost to be about $3.50 per $1,000 of the purchase price of the home).

Flood Determination Fee

If your home is in a flood hazard area where federally subsidized flood insurance is available, lenders cannot make a mortgage loan for your home unless you buy flood insurance. Your lender may charge a fee to find out whether the home is in a flood hazard area.

Estimated cost: $15 to $50 (this is not the cost for the flood insurance; flood insurance, if required, would be in addition to your homeowners insurance and may cost from $350 to $2,800 depending on location and property value)

Escrow (or Reserve) Funds

Some lenders require that you set aside money in an escrow (reserve) account to pay for property taxes, homeowner's insurance, and flood insurance (if you need it). Lenders use escrow funds to ensure that these items are paid on time to protect their interest in your home. With an escrow account, money is held by the lender or the lender's agent, who then pays the taxes and insurance bills when they are due. At settlement, you may need to provide some payment into this account, depending on when payments will be due. For example, if you are buying your home in August and property taxes are due the following January, you will need to deposit funds into your escrow account at settlement so that you have enough to pay the taxes when they become due in January.

Survey Costs

Lenders require a survey to confirm the location of buildings and improvements on the land. Some lenders require a complete (and more costly) survey to ensure that the house and other structures are legally where you and the seller say they are.

Estimated cost: $150 to $400

Other Miscellaneous Settlement Costs

Depending upon the location and type of property, and the extra services you or your lender request, you may also have to pay some of the following fees at settlement:

- **Assumption fee:** If you are assuming (or taking over) an existing mortgage, the lender may charge a fee.

  Estimated cost: Depends on the lender, but will range from several hundred dollars to 1% of the amount of the loan you are assuming

- **Expenses prorated between the seller and the buyer:** In your purchase contract, you may agree to split some costs with the seller. In addition to prorated property taxes, some of these expenses may involve large amounts. For example, annual condominium fees, homeowners' association fees, water bills, and other lump-sum service charges may be split between you and the seller to cover your respective periods of ownership for the calendar year or tax period.

- **Inspections:** As a buyer, if you make your purchase offer contingent on the results of a home inspection—such as testing for structural damage, water quality, and radon gas emissions—you will have to pay for these inspections.

- **Escrow account funds:** In the purchase contract, you can request that the seller set up an escrow account to cover any costs for repairs, radon mitigation, house painting, or other items. For example, if you have not had a chance to test all the appliances (for instance, if you buy in the summer, you may not test the furnace), you may request an escrow account to cover repairs if they are needed in the future. The seller may agree to split the costs with you, in which case you would need these funds at settlement.

- **Fees paid to find a lender:** As a buyer, you may work with a mortgage broker or other third party to find a mortgage loan. For example, you may want to work with a broker to find a loan with nonstandard terms or conditions. Brokers arrange transactions rather than lending money directly; in other words, they find a lender for you. Brokers will generally contact several lenders regarding your application, but they are not obligated to find the best deal for you unless they have contracted with you to act as your agent.

  Estimated cost: Depends on agreement with the broker; can range from no fee to a percentage of the loan amount

Charges for Establishing and Transferring Ownership

Title Search

The goal of a title search is to assure you and your lender that the seller is the legal owner of the property and that there are no outstanding claims or liens against the property that you are buying. The title search may be performed by a lawyer, an escrow or title company, or other specialist.

Public real estate records can be spread among several local government offices, including surveyors, county courts, tax assessors, and recorders of deeds. Liens, records of deaths, divorces, court judgments, and contests over wills—all of which can affect ownership rights—must also be examined.

If real estate records are computerized, the title search can be completed fairly quickly. In some cases, however, the title search may involve visiting courthouses and examining other public records and files, which is more time-consuming.

Title Insurance

Most lenders require a title insurance policy. This policy insures the lender against an error in the results of the title search. If a problem arises, the insurance covers the lender's investment in your mortgage.

The cost of the policy (a one-time premium) is usually based on the loan amount and is often paid by the buyer. However, you may negotiate with the seller to pay all or part of the premium.

The title insurance required by the lender protects only the lender. To protect yourself against title problems, you may want to buy an "owner's" title insurance policy. Normally the additional premium cost is based on the cost of the lender's policy, but this premium can vary from area to area.

Some advice on keeping title insurance costs low: If the house you are buying was owned by the seller for only a few years, check with the seller's title company. You may be able to get a "re-issue rate," because the time between title searches was short. As well, if you are refinancing, you may be able to get a "re-issue rate" on your title insurance. The premium is likely to be lower than the regular rate for a new policy. If no claims have been made against the title since the previous title search was done, the insurer may consider the property to be a lower insurance risk.

374

Usually you will have to buy title insurance from a company acceptable to your lender. However, you can still shop around for the best premium rates (which can vary depending on how much competition there is in a market area). If you decide to buy an "owner's title policy," look for one with as few exclusions from coverage as possible. Exclusions are listed in each policy, and if a policy has many exclusions—that is, situations under which the insurer will not pay for your title problems—you may end up with little coverage. The estimated cost of title services and title insurance varies by state. For example, a lender's policy on a $100,000 loan can range from $175 in one state to $900 in another. In some states, the price can even vary by county.

Settlement Companies and Others Conducting the Settlement

Settlements are conducted by title insurance companies, real estate brokers, lending institutions, escrow companies, or attorneys. In most cases, the settlement agent is providing a service to the lender, and you may be required to pay for these services. You can also hire your own attorney to represent you at all stages of the transaction, including settlement.

You may be involved in some of the closing activities and not in others, depending on local practices and on the professionals with whom you are working. In some regions, all the people involved in the sale—the buyer; the seller; the lender; the real estate agents; attorneys for the buyer, seller, and lender; and representatives from the title firm—may meet to sign forms and transfer funds. In other regions, settlement is handled by a title or escrow firm that collects all the funding, paperwork, and signatures and makes the necessary disbursements. The firm delivers the check to the seller and the house keys to you.

Costs for settlement services vary widely, depending on the professional services involved. Regardless of the way settlement is handled in your region, shop around and ask for information on all services provided and all fees charged.

Amounts Paid to State and Local Governments

In some parts of the country transfer and recording fees are low. In other parts of the country costs of transfer fees, recording fees, and property taxes collected by local and state governments may be as much as 1.25% of the loan amount. Some of these fees, such as the recording fee and transfer fee, are one-time fees. Although there is no way to avoid paying these fees and taxes, you may be able to negotiate with the seller to pay some of these costs. But remember, you must include these terms as part of the purchase offer for the property.

Amounts for property taxes may go into an escrow account. The amount you will need depends on when property taxes are due and the timing of the settlement. The lender should be able to give you an approximation of these costs at the time you apply for the mortgage.

"All-in-One" Pricing of Settlement Costs

Some lenders have bundled most of their settlement costs into a single price. Generally, they combine the following fees:

- application
- origination
- underwriting and processing
- points
- pest inspection
- appraisal
- credit reports
- lender's attorney
- flood certification
- title search and title insurance
- recording
- and fees for other tax services

This all-in-one price, however, does not include all of the fees needed at settlement. You will also need funds for the following:

- prepaid interest (based on the day of the month you settle)
- mortgage and transfer taxes (determined by your state or local taxing agency)
- private mortgage insurance (if needed)
- homeowners (hazard) insurance
- flood insurance (if needed)
- and reserve (or escrow) funds for property taxes and homeowners insurance

Estimates of Settlement Costs

At various points in your loan application process, you are entitled to get estimates of the costs and fees associated with getting a mortgage and going through settlement.

The "Good Faith Estimate"

With such a long list of potential charges at settlement, it is important to know what to expect. The Real Estate Settlement Procedures Act (RESPA) requires your mortgage lender to give you a "good faith estimate" of all your closing costs within three business days of submitting your application for a loan, whether you are purchasing or refinancing the home. This is a good faith estimate, but the actual expenses at closing may be somewhat different.

Truth in Lending Information

For home purchases, the lender is required, under the Truth in Lending Act, to provide a statement containing "good faith estimates" of the costs of the loan within three business days of submitting your application. This estimate will include your total finance charge and the annual percentage rate (APR). The APR expresses the cost of your loan as an annual rate. This rate is likely to be higher than the stated contract interest rate on your mortgage because it takes into account discount points, mortgage insurance, and certain other fees that add to the cost of your loan. When refinancing your mortgage, you will receive the truth in lending disclosures before you settle.

The "HUD-1" Statement

When you purchase a home or refinance your mortgage, the Real Estate Settlement Procedures Act also requires the lender to give you a copy of the HUD-1 or HUD-1A Settlement Statement one day before you go to settlement, if you request it. This final statement of settlement costs will show all the fees and charges you will be expected to pay at settlement.

Fees Paid outside of Settlement

Some fees may be listed on the HUD-1 and marked as "Paid Outside of Closing" (or "POC"). You will pay some of these fees, such as for credit reports and appraisals, before settlement. Other fees, such as those to a mortgage broker, you will pay at settlement.

Section 34.4

Mortgage Lock-Ins

From "A Consumer's Guide to Mortgage Lock-Ins," Federal Reserve
Board of Governors (www.federalreserve.gov), April 2005.

When you're looking for a mortgage, you're likely to shop among lenders for the most favorable interest rate, and the lowest points and other up-front charges. When you find the most favorable terms and the lender that you want, you'll apply to that lender. But when you get to settlement, will you actually receive the terms you applied or bargained for? Or will you find that the rate has changed—and that your costs have gone up?

Lock-ins on rates and points might offer you a way to ensure that what you shop for is what you get. This section explains what these arrangements mean.

All about Lock-Ins

In most cases, the terms you are quoted when you shop among lenders only represent the terms available to borrowers settling their loan agreement at the time of the quote. The quoted terms may not be the terms available to you at settlement weeks or even months later. Therefore, you should not rely on the terms quoted to you when shopping for a loan unless a lender is willing to offer a lock-in.

What is a lock-in?

A lock-in, also called a rate-lock or rate commitment, is a lender's promise to hold a certain interest rate and a certain number of points for you, usually for a specified period of time, while your loan application is processed. (Points are additional charges imposed by the lender that are usually prepaid by the consumer at settlement but can sometimes be financed by adding them to the mortgage amount. One point equals one percent of the loan amount.) Depending upon the lender, you may be able to lock in the interest rate and number of points that you will be charged when you file your application, during processing of the loan, when the loan is approved, or later.

A lock-in that is given when you apply for a loan may be useful because it's likely to take your lender several weeks or longer to prepare, document, and evaluate your loan application. During that time, the cost of mortgages may change. But if your interest rate and points are locked in, you should be protected against increases while your application is processed. This protection could affect whether you can afford the mortgage. However, a locked-in rate could also prevent you from taking advantage of price decreases, unless your lender is willing to lock in a lower rate that becomes available during this period.

It is important to recognize that a lock-in is not the same as a loan commitment, although some loan commitments may contain a lock-in. A loan commitment is the lender's promise to make you a loan in a specific amount at some future time. Generally, you will receive the lender's commitment only after your loan application has been approved. This commitment usually will state the loan terms that have been approved (including loan amount), how long the commitment is valid, and the lender's conditions for making the loan such as receipt of a satisfactory title insurance policy protecting the lender.

Will your lock-in be in writing?

Some lenders have preprinted forms that set out the exact terms of the lock-in agreement. Others may only make an oral lock-in promise on the telephone or at the time of application. Oral agreements can be very difficult to prove in the event of a dispute.

Some lenders' lock-in forms may contain crucial information that is difficult to understand or that is in fine print. For example, some lock-in agreements may become void through some unrelated action such as a change in the maximum rate for Veterans Administration guaranteed loans. Thus, it is wise to obtain a blank copy of a lender's lock-in form to read carefully before you apply for a loan. If possible, show the lock-in form to a lawyer or real estate professional.

It is wise to obtain written, rather than verbal, lock-in agreements to make sure that you fully understand how your lender's lock-ins and loan commitments work and to have a tangible record of your arrangements with the lender. This record may be useful in the event of a dispute.

Will you be charged for a lock-in?

Lenders may charge you a fee for locking in the rate of interest and number of points for your mortgage. Some lenders may charge you a fee up-front, and may not refund it if you withdraw your application, if your credit is denied, or if you do not close the loan. Others might charge

379

the fee at settlement. The fee might be a flat fee, a percentage of the mortgage amount, or a fraction of a percentage point added to the rate you lock in. The amount of the fee and how it is charged will vary among lenders and may depend on the length of the lock-in period.

What options are available for setting the mortgage terms?

Lenders may offer different options in establishing the interest rate and points that you will be charged, such as:

- **Locked-in interest rate—locked-in points:** Under this option, the lender lets you lock in both the interest rate and points quoted to you. This option may be considered to be a true lock-in because your mortgage terms should not increase above the interest rate and points that you've agreed upon even if market conditions change.

- **Locked-in interest rate—floating points:** Under this option, the lender lets you lock in the interest rate, while permitting or requiring the points to rise and fall (float) with changes in market conditions. If market interest rates drop during the lock-in period, the points may also fall. If they rise, the points may increase. Even if you float your points, your lender may allow you to lock-in the points at some time before settlement at whatever level is then current. (For instance, say you've locked in a 10½ percent interest rate, but not the 3 points that went with that rate. A month later, the market interest rate remains the same, but the points the lender charges for that rate have dropped to 2½. With your lender's agreement, you could then lock in the lower 2½ points.) If you float your points and market interest rates increase by the time of settlement, the lender may charge a greater number of points for a loan at the rate you've locked in. In this case, the benefit you might have had by locking in your rate may be lost because you'll have to pay more in up-front costs.

- **Floating interest rate—floating points:** Under this option, the lender lets you lock in the interest rate and the points at some time after application but before settlement. If you think that rates will remain level or even go down, you may want to wait on locking in a particular rate and points. If rates go up, you should expect to be charged the higher rate.

Because practices vary, you may want to ask your lender whether there are other options available to you.

How long are lock-ins valid?

Usually the lender will promise to hold a certain interest rate and number of points for a given number of days, and to get these terms you must settle on the loan within that time period. Lock-ins of 30 to 60 days are common. But some lenders may offer a lock-in for only a short period of time (for example, seven days after your loan is approved) while some others might offer longer lock-ins (up to 120 days). Lenders that charge a lock-in fee may charge a higher fee for the longer lock-in period. Usually, the longer the period, the greater the fee.

The lock-in period should be long enough to allow for settlement, and any other contingencies imposed by the lender, before the lock-in expires. Before deciding on the length of the lock-in to ask for, you should find out the average time for processing loans in your area and ask your lender to estimate (in writing, if possible) the time needed to process your loan. You'll also want to take into account any factors that might delay your settlement. These may include delays that you can anticipate in providing materials about your financial condition and, in case you are purchasing a new house, unanticipated construction delays. Finally, ask for a lock-in with as few contingencies as possible.

Happens if the lock-in period expires?

If you don't settle within the lock-in period, you might lose the interest rate and the number of points you had locked in. This could happen if there are delays in processing whether they are caused by you, others involved in the settlement process, or the lender. For example, your loan approval could be delayed if the lender has to wait for any documents from you or from others such as employers, appraisers, termite inspectors, builders, and individuals selling the home. On occasion, lenders are themselves the cause of processing delays, particularly when loan demand is heavy. This sometimes happens when interest rates fall suddenly.

If your lock-in expires, most lenders will offer the loan based on the prevailing interest rate and points. If market conditions have caused interest rates to rise, most lenders will charge you more for your loan. One reason why some lenders may be unable to offer the lock-in rate after the period expires is that they can no longer sell the loan to investors at the lock-in rate. (When lenders lock in loan terms for borrowers, they often have an agreement with investors to buy these loans based on the lock-in terms. That agreement may expire around the same time that the lock-in expires and the lender may be unable to afford to offer the same terms if market rates have increased.) Lenders who intend to keep the loans they make may have more flexibility in those cases where settlement is not reached before the lock-in expires.

How can you speed up the approval of the loan?

While the lender has the greatest role in how fast your loan application is processed, there are certain things you can do to speed up its approval. Try to find out what documentation the lender will require from you.

Much of the information required by your lender can be brought with you when you apply for a loan. This may help to get your application moving more quickly through the process. When you first meet with your lender, be sure to bring the following documents:

- The purchase contract for the house (if you don't have the contract, check with your real estate agent or the seller).

- Your bank account numbers, the address of your bank branch and your latest bank statement, plus pay stubs, W-2 forms, or other proof of employment and salary, to help the lender check your finances.

- If you are self-employed, balance sheets, tax returns for two to three previous years, and other information about your business.

- Information about debts, including loan and credit card account numbers and the names and addresses of your creditors.

- Evidence of your mortgage or rental payments, such as canceled checks.

- Certificate of Eligibility from the Veterans Administration if you want a VA-guaranteed loan. Your lender may be able to help you obtain this.

Be sure to respond promptly to your lender's requests for information while your loan is being processed. It is also a good idea to call the lender and real estate agent from time to time. By calling occasionally, you can check on the status of your application, and offer to help contact others such as employers who may need to provide documents and other information for your loan. It is also helpful to keep notes on your contacts with the lender so that you will have a record of your conversations.

Complaints about Lock-Ins

Knowing what to look for puts you in a better position to decide whether, when, and how long to lock in mortgage terms. Also, by helping to keep the loan process moving, you can lessen the chance that your lock-in will run out before settlement.

But what if your lock-in does lapse? If you believe that the lapse was due to delays caused by the lender or someone else involved in the loan process, you should try first to reach a mutually satisfactory agreement with the lender. If that effort fails, consider writing to the appropriate state or federal regulatory agency.

Some lender actions, such as offering lock-in terms which are impossible to fulfill, failing to process your loan diligently, or causing your lock-in to expire are improper—and may even be illegal. In addition, because you may have contractual rights under your lock-in or loan commitment, you may want to consult with an attorney. Be aware, though, that complaints may not be resolved as quickly as may be necessary for a home purchase.

Depending upon their authority under applicable state or federal law, regulatory agencies may either attempt to help you resolve your complaint directly or record your complaint and recommend other action.

Section 34.5

No Money Down: 100% Mortgages

Don't have the cash for the down payment on your dream house? At some brokerage firms that offer up to 100% loan-to-value ratio mortgages or pledged-asset mortgages, that's not a problem.* In lieu of a down payment for a mortgage, customers can pledge their stocks, bonds, mutual funds, and other securities. While brokerage firm websites and brochures often tout the advantages of 100% mortgages, such as allowing investors to avoid private mortgage insurance or liquidating their securities, they may overlook or consign to the fine print the risks associated with these mortgages. (*Most brokerage firms use a subsidiary, affiliate or separate bank to administer their mortgage program. For the purposes of this text, "brokerage firm" and "firm" refer to both the brokerage firm and any other entity that administers a mortgage program offered through the brokerage firm.)

The National Association of Securities Dealers (NASD) warns that 100% mortgages are not suitable for everyone. NASD is concerned that many investors are not aware of the risks of 100% mortgages and do not understand that the securities they pledge in lieu of a down payment may be liquidated if the value of the securities drops below a certain level or they default on their mortgage.

Before you decide to apply for a 100% mortgage, make sure you understand the following risks:

- Even after you obtain your mortgage loan, you may be required to deposit more cash or securities if the value of the securities you pledged falls below the minimum required by your firm.

- Your firm can force the sale of securities in your account to meet a collateral call.

- Your firm can sell your securities to meet a collateral call without contacting you.

- You are not entitled to choose which securities in your account are sold to meet a collateral call.

- You are not entitled to an extension of time to meet a collateral call.

- If you default (stop making your monthly payments) on your mortgage, you could lose both your house and the securities you pledge.

This text will explain these risks and provide you with some basic facts about 100% mortgages.

How 100% Mortgages Work

A typical 100% mortgage or pledged-asset mortgage requires little or no cash down payment. Instead, you pledge securities in your brokerage account in lieu of a down payment, allowing you to finance up to 100% of the value of your home. The amount of securities you will have to pledge can vary depending on the type of securities you pledge and the terms of the mortgage. The amount you pledge usually exceeds the amount required, thereby allowing for some fluctuation in the value of the securities. However, if value of the securities you pledged goes down below a minimum amount set by the firm, your firm may issue a collateral call, which is a demand that you deposit additional cash or securities. If you can't do so or the value of the securities continues to decline, your firm may sell some or all of your securities, sometimes even without notifying you.

100% Mortgage Costs

Since you are borrowing more money with a 100% mortgage, you are probably paying more interest than you would have paid if you had made a cash down payment. This may make sense if you're able to achieve returns on your investments that are greater than your mortgage payments, but there can be no assurance that you will enjoy these investment returns. Moreover, if you choose an adjustable-rate 100% mortgage and interest rates rise, the returns in your investment portfolio may not keep up with your rising mortgage payments, particularly if you have bonds or other fixed instruments, which typically decline in value when interest rates rise. Even worse, with an adjustable-rate mortgage, if the securities markets decline at the same time that interest rates rise, you may be stuck with both larger mortgage payments and thousands of dollars in market losses. By contrast, if you sold your securities to come up with a cash down payment, you not only would have avoided any risk to those securities of a market decline, but you also would have a smaller mortgage and probably pay less interest.

100% Mortgage Risks

It is important that you fully understand the risks involved with 100% mortgages. These include:

- **Even after you obtain your mortgage loan, you may be required to deposit more cash or securities if the value of the securities you pledged falls below the minimum required by your firm.** A decline in the value of the securities you use as collateral for a 100% mortgage may require you to provide additional cash or securities to your firm to avoid the forced sale of those securities. Ask yourself: If I didn't have the cash in the first place for a down payment, where will I find the cash if my securities lose their value?

- **Your firm can force the sale of pledged securities to meet a collateral call.** If the value of pledged securities falls below the minimum amount set by your firm, the firm can sell the securities you pledged. The cash received from the sale of securities then remains in the account until:

    - The mortgage is repaid or refinanced;

    - You instruct the firm to use the funds to pay down the mortgage;

    - The equity in your home reaches a certain level, allowing the collateral account to be closed; or

    - The cash is applied to the outstanding mortgage balance upon default, if necessary.

- **Your firm can sell your securities without contacting you.** While most firms will attempt to notify their customers of collateral calls, they are not required to do so. Even if you're contacted and provided with a specific date to meet a collateral call, your firm may decide to sell some or all of your securities before that date without any further notice to you. For example, your firm may take this action because the market value of your securities has continued to decline.

- **You are not entitled to choose which securities are sold.** There is no provision that gives you the right to control liquidation decisions. Your firm may decide to sell any of the securities that are held as collateral for your mortgage.

- **You are not entitled to an extension of time on a collateral call.** While an extension of time to meet a collateral call may be available to you under certain conditions, you do not have a right to the extension.

- **If you default on your mortgage (stop making your monthly payments), you could lose both your home and the securities you pledge.** Some states allow your firm to immediately sell your securities if you default on your mortgage. Other states only allow your securities to be liquidated after your house is sold for a loss at a public sale.

Do Your Homework

- **Shop around for the best mortgage for you.** Mortgages are available from several types of lenders—banks, mortgage companies, and credit unions. Along with some brokerage firms, these financial institutions can offer a wide selection of mortgages and terms from which you can choose. Shop around, compare costs, and negotiate the best deal.

- **Make sure you fully understand how a 100% mortgage works.** It is important to take time to learn about the risks involved in 100% mortgages. Consult with your broker or lending officer about any concerns you may have with your mortgage.

- **Know your firm's collateral call policies.** Read your pledge agreement and other loan documents. Speak with your broker or lending officer if you don't understand these policies.

- **Consider pledging a diversified portfolio rather than a single stock.** Diversification can reduce the possibility of a collateral call because it is less likely that a variety of investments, such as stocks, bonds, and cash, will move up and down in value at the same time or at the same rate.

- **If you use securities as collateral for a mortgage, you may not want to pledge all your available securities.** Unless you have other liquid assets, you may not want to pledge all your securities; instead, retain some securities or cash so that you can promptly meet a collateral call demand to pledge additional cash or securities.

- **Manage your pledged securities.** Monitor the price of your pledged securities on a daily basis. If you see that the securities in your account are declining in value, you may want to consider depositing additional cash or securities to attempt to avoid a collateral call. If you receive a collateral call, act promptly to satisfy the call. By depositing cash or additional securities, you may be able to avoid your firm liquidating or selling the securities that it chooses.

Where to Turn for Help

If you have a problem with the brokerage firm that recommended a 100% mortgage strategy that the firm did not resolve to your satisfaction, you can file a complaint online at NASD's Investor Complaint Center at http://complaint.nasd.com.

Section 34.6

Mortgage Discrimination

From "Mortgage Discrimination," U.S. Federal Trade Commission
(www.ftc.gov), February 1998; available online at http://www.ftc.gov/
bcp/conline/pubs/homes/mortgdis.htm, accessed July 17, 2006.

The Equal Credit Opportunity Act (ECOA) and the Fair Housing
Act (FHA) protect you against discrimination when you apply for a
mortgage to purchase, refinance, or make home improvements.

Your Rights under ECOA

The ECOA prohibits discrimination in any aspect of a credit transaction based on:

- race or color;
- religion;
- national origin;
- sex;
- marital status;
- age (provided the applicant has the capacity to contract);
- the applicant's receipt of income derived from any public assistance program; and
- the applicant's exercise, in good faith, of any right under the
Consumer Credit Protection Act, the umbrella statute that includes ECOA.

Your Rights under FHA

The FHA prohibits discrimination in all aspects of residential real-
estate related transactions, including:

- making loans to buy, build, repair, or improve a dwelling;
- selling, brokering, or appraising residential real estate; and
- selling or renting a dwelling.

It also prohibits discrimination based on:

- race or color;
- national origin;
- religion;
- sex;
- familial status (defined as children under the age of 18 living with a parent or legal guardian, pregnant women, and people securing custody of children under 18); and
- handicap.

Lender Dos and Don'ts

Lenders must:

- consider reliable public assistance income in the same way as other income.
- consider reliable income from part-time employment, Social Security, pensions, and annuities.
- consider reliable alimony, child support, or separate maintenance payments, if you choose to provide this information. A lender may ask you for proof that this income is received consistently.
- if a co-signer is needed, accept someone other than your spouse. If you own the property with your spouse, he or she may be asked to sign documents allowing you to mortgage the property.

Lenders cannot:

- discourage you from applying for a mortgage or reject your application because of your race, national origin, religion, sex, marital status, age, or because you receive public assistance income.
- consider your race, national origin, or sex, although you will be asked to voluntarily disclose this information to help federal agencies enforce anti-discrimination laws. A creditor may consider your immigration status and whether you have the right to remain in the country long enough to repay the debt.
- impose different terms or conditions, such as a higher interest rate or larger down payment, on a loan based on your race, sex, or other prohibited factors.

- consider the racial composition of the neighborhood where you want to live. This also applies when the property is being appraised.

- ask about your plans for having a family. Questions about expenses related to your dependents are permitted.

- refuse to purchase a loan or set different terms or conditions for the loan purchase based on discriminatory factors.

- require a co-signer if you meet the lender's standards.

Strengthening Your Application

Not everyone who applies for a mortgage will get one. Lenders can use factors such as income, expenses, debts, and credit history to evaluate applicants.

There are steps you can take to ensure that your application gets full consideration. Give the lender all information that supports your application.

For example, stable employment is important to many lenders. Perhaps you've recently changed jobs but have been employed steadily in the same field for several years. If so, include that information on your application.

Get a copy of your credit report before you apply for a mortgage. Reports sometime contain inaccurate information. For example, accounts might be reported that don't belong to you or paid accounts might be reported as unpaid. If you find errors, dispute them with the credit bureau and tell the lender about the dispute.

If you've had past bill-paying problems, such as a lost job or high medical expenses, write a letter to the lender explaining what caused your past credit problems. Lenders must consider this information at your request.

Try for the Best Loan Terms

Some mortgage lenders may try to charge some borrowers more than others for the same loan product offered at the same time. This may include higher interest rates or origination fees or more points. Ask the lender if the rate you're being quoted is the lowest offered that day. The lender is probably basing the loan offer on the list of mortgage rates frequently issued by that institution to its loan officers. Ask to see this list. If the lender refuses and you suspect you are not being offered the lowest rates or points available, you may want to negotiate for better terms or shop for another lender. Even if you decide to accept terms that are not the lowest available, ask the lender why you did not qualify for better terms. The answer may help you to correct errors and to become more creditworthy.

If Your Application Is Rejected

If your mortgage is denied, the lender must give you specific reasons why or tell you of your right to ask for them. Under the law, you have the right to:

- Know within 30 days of the date of your completed application whether your mortgage loan is approved. The lender must make a reasonable effort to obtain all necessary information, such as credit reports and property appraisals. If your application is rejected, the lender must tell you in writing.

- Know specifically why your application was rejected. The lender must tell you the specific reason for the rejection or your right to learn the reason if you ask within 60 days. An acceptable response might be: "your income was too low" or "you haven't been employed long enough." A response of "you didn't meet our minimum standards" is not specific enough.

- Learn the specific reason why you were offered less favorable terms than you applied for, but only if you reject these terms. For example, if the lender offered you a smaller mortgage or a higher interest rate, you have the right to know why if you did not accept the lender's counter offer.

- Find out what is in your credit report. The lender may have rejected your application because of negative information in your credit report. If so, the lender must tell you this and give you the name, address, and phone number of the credit bureau. You can get a free copy of that report from the credit bureau if you request it within 60 days. Otherwise, the credit bureau can charge up to $8.

- If your report contains inaccurate information, the credit bureau is required to investigate items that you dispute. Those companies furnishing inaccurate information to the credit bureaus also must reinvestigate items that you dispute. If you still dispute the credit bureau's account after a reinvestigation, you can include your summary of the problem in your credit report.

- Get a copy of the property appraisal from the lender. Mortgage applications may be turned down because of poor appraisals. Review the appraisal. Check that it contains accurate information and determine whether the appraiser considered illegal factors, such as the racial composition of the neighborhood.

If You Suspect Discrimination

Take action if you think you've been discriminated against.

- Complain to the lender. Sometimes you can persuade the lender to reconsider your application.

- Check with your state Attorney General's office to see if the creditor violated state laws. Many states have their own equal credit opportunity laws.

- Contact a local private fair housing group and report violations to the appropriate government agency. If your mortgage application is denied, the lender must give you the name and address of the agency to contact.

- Consider suing the lender in federal district court. If you win, you can recover your actual damages and be awarded punitive damages if the court finds that the lender's conduct was willful. You also may recover reasonable lawyers' fees and court costs. You also might consider joining with others to file a class action suit.

A number of federal agencies share enforcement responsibility for the ECOA and the FHA. Determining which agency to contact depends, in part, on the type of financial institution you dealt with.

For ECOA violations involving mortgage and consumer finance companies:

Federal Trade Commission
Consumer Response Center
Washington, DC 20580
Phone: 202-326-2222
TDD: 866-653-4261

While the FTC generally does not intervene in individual disputes, the information you provide may indicate a pattern of violations requiring action by the Commission.

For violations of the FHA:

Office of Fair Housing and Equal Opportunity
US Department of Housing and Urban Development (HUD), Room 5204
Washington, DC 20410-2000
Toll-free: 800-424-8590
TDD: 800-543-8294

You have one year to file a complaint with HUD, but you should file as soon as possible. Your complaint to HUD should include:

- Your name and address;
- The name and address of the person or company who is the subject of the complaint;
- The address or other identification of the housing involved;
- A short description of the facts that caused you to believe your rights were violated; and
- The dates of the alleged violation.

HUD will notify you when it receives your complaint. Normally, HUD also will:

- Notify the alleged violator of your complaint and permit the person to submit an answer;
- Investigate your complaint and determine whether there is a reasonable cause to believe the Fair Housing Act has been violated; and
- Notify you if it cannot complete an investigation within 100 days of receiving your complaint.

For violations of the ECOA and the FHA:

- For nationally charted banks:
    Comptroller of the Currency
    Compliance Management
    Mail Stop 7-5
    Washington, DC 20219

- For state-chartered banks insured by the Federal Deposit Insurance Corporation, but not members of the Federal Reserve System:

Federal Deposit Insurance Corporation
Consumer Affairs Division
Washington, DC 20429

- For federally chartered or federally insured savings and loans:

  Office of Thrift Supervision
  Consumer Affairs Program
  Washington, DC 20552

- For federally chartered credit unions:

  National Credit Union Administration
  Consumer Affairs Division
  Washington, DC 20456

- For state member banks of the Federal Reserve System:

  Consumer and Community Affairs
  Board of Governors of the Federal Reserve System
  20th & C Streets, NW
  Washington, DC 20551

- For discrimination complaints against all kinds of creditors:

  Department of Justice
  Civil Rights Division
  Washington, DC 20530

Section 34.7

Mortgage Servicing

"Mortgage Servicing: Make Sure Your Payments Count," U.S. Federal Trade Commission (www.ftc.gov), November 2003; available online at http:// www.ftc.gov/bcp/conline/pubs/homes/mortgserv.htm, accessed July 17, 2006.

When you apply for a home mortgage, you may think that the lender will hold and service your loan until you pay it off or you sell your house. That's often not the case. In today's market, loans and the rights to service them often are bought and sold.

A home may be one of the most expensive purchases you ever make, so it's important to know who is handling your payments and that your mortgage account is properly credited. The Federal Trade Commission (FTC) wants you to know what a mortgage servicer does and what your rights are.

Mortgage Servicers: Their Responsibilities to You

A mortgage servicer is responsible for collecting your monthly loan payments and crediting your account. A servicer also handles your escrow account, if you have one.

Escrow Accounts

An escrow account is a fund held by your servicer into which you pay money to cover charges like property taxes and homeowners insurance. The escrow payments typically are included as part of your monthly mortgage payments. The servicer pays your taxes and insurance as they become due during the year. If you do not have an escrow account, you are responsible for paying your taxes and insurance and budgeting accordingly.

The Real Estate Settlement Procedures Act (RESPA), enforced by the Department of Housing and Urban Development, is the major law covering escrow accounts. If your mortgage servicer administers an escrow account for you, the servicer is generally required to make escrow payments for taxes, insurance, and any other charges in a timely manner. Within 45 days of establishing the account, the servicer must give you a statement that clearly itemizes the estimated taxes, insurance premiums, and other anticipated charges to be paid over the next 12 months, and the expected dates and totals of those payments.

Under RESPA, the mortgage servicer also is required to give you a free annual statement that details the activity of your escrow account. This statement shows your account balance and reflects payments for your property taxes, homeowners insurance, and other charges.

Transfer of Servicing

If your loan is about to be sold, you generally get two notices: one from your current mortgage servicer; the other from the new servicer. Usually, your current servicer must notify you at least 15 days before the effective date of the transfer, unless you received a written transfer notice at settlement. The effective date is when the first mortgage payment is due at the new servicer's address. The new servicer must notify you within 15 days after the transfer has occurred.

The notices must include:

- the name and address of the new servicer.

- the date the current servicer will stop accepting your mortgage payments.

- the date the new servicer will begin accepting your mortgage payments.

- toll-free or collect-call telephone numbers, for the current and new mortgage servicer, for information about the transfer.

- whether you can continue any optional insurance, such as credit life or disability insurance; what action, if any, you must take to maintain coverage; and whether the insurance terms will change.

- a statement that the transfer will not affect any terms or conditions of your mortgage, except those directly related to the servicing of the loan. For example, if your contract says you were allowed to pay property taxes and insurance premiums on your own, the new servicer cannot demand that you establish an escrow account.

- There is a 60-day grace period after the transfer: during this time you cannot be charged a late fee if you mistakenly send your mortgage payment to the old servicer. In addition, the fact that your new servicer may have received your payment late as a result cannot be reported to a credit bureau.

Posting Payments

Some consumers have complained that they've been charged late fees, even when they know they made their payments on time. To help protect yourself, keep good records of what you've paid, including any billing statements, canceled checks, or bank account statements. You also may check your account history online if your servicer's website has this feature. If you have a dispute, continue to make your mortgage payments, but challenge the servicing in writing and keep a copy of the letter and any enclosures for your records. Send your correspondence by certified mail, and request a return receipt. Or send it by fax, and keep a copy of the transmittal confirmation.

Force Placed Insurance

It's important to maintain the required property insurance on your home. If you don't, your servicer can buy insurance on your behalf. This type of policy is known as force placed insurance; it usually is more expensive than typical insurance; and it provides less coverage. The primary purpose of a force placed policy is to protect the mortgage holder, not the property owner.

Review all correspondence you receive from your mortgage servicer. Your mortgage servicer may request that you provide a copy of your property insurance policy. Respond promptly to requests regarding property insurance, and keep copies of all documents you send to your mortgage servicer.

If you believe there's a paperwork error and that your coverage is adequate, provide a copy of your insurance policy to your servicer. Once the servicer corrects the error, removes the force placed coverage, and refunds the cost of the force placed policy, make sure that any late fees or interest you were charged as a result of the coverage also are removed.

Fees

Review your billing statements carefully to make sure that any fees the servicer charges are legitimate. For example, the fees may have been authorized by the mortgage contract or by you to pay for a service. If you do not understand what the fees are for, send a written inquiry and ask for an itemization and explanation of the fees. Also, if you call your mortgage servicer to request a service, such as faxing copies of loan documents, make sure you ask whether there is a fee for the service and what it is.

Inquiries and Disputes

Under RESPA, your mortgage servicer must respond promptly to written inquiries, known as qualified written requests. If you believe you've been charged a penalty or late fee that you don't owe, or if you have other problems with the servicing of your loan, contact your servicer in writing. Be sure to include your account number and clearly explain why you believe your account is incorrect. Your inquiry should not be just a note on the payment coupon supplied by your servicer, but should be sent separately to the customer service address.

Within 20 business days of receiving your inquiry, the servicer must send you a written response acknowledging it. Within 60 business days, the servicer either must correct your account or determine that it is accurate. The servicer must send you a written notice of the action it took and why, along with the name and telephone number of someone you can contact for additional assistance.

Do not subtract any disputed amount from your mortgage payment. Some mortgage servicers might refuse to accept what they consider to be partial payments. They might return your check and charge you a late fee, or claim that your mortgage is in default and start foreclosure proceedings.

If You Have a Complaint

If you believe your mortgage servicer has not responded appropriately to your written inquiry, contact your local or state consumer protection office. You also should contact the Department of Housing and Urban Development (HUD) to file a complaint under the RESPA regulations. Write to:

Office of RESPA and Interstate Land Sales
Department of Housing and Urban Development
451 Seventh Street, S.W., Room 9154
Washington, DC 20410

In addition, you may want to contact an attorney to advise you of your legal rights. Under certain sections of the RESPA, consumers can initiate lawsuits and obtain actual damages, plus additional damages, for a pattern or practice of noncompliance. In successful actions, consumers also may obtain court costs and attorney's fees.

You may want to contact a housing counselor to discuss your situation. You can call HUD's hotline at 800-217-6970 for a referral to a local HUD-approved housing counselor.

You also may wish to contact the FTC.

The FTC works for the consumer to prevent fraudulent, deceptive and unfair business practices in the marketplace and to provide information to help consumers spot, stop and avoid them. To file a complaint or to get free information on consumer issues, visit http://www.ftc.gov or call toll-free, 877-FTC-HELP (877-382-4357); TTY: 866-653-4261. The FTC enters internet, telemarketing, identity theft, and other fraud-related complaints into Consumer Sentinel, a secure, online database available to hundreds of civil and criminal law enforcement agencies in the U.S. and abroad.

Section 34.8

Cancellation of Private Mortgage Insurance May Save You Money

"Cancellation of Private Mortgage Insurance: Federal Law May Save You Hundreds of Dollars Each Year," U.S. Federal Trade Commission (www.ftc.gov), July 2000; available online at http://www.ftc.gov/bcp/conline/pubs/alerts/pmialrt.htm, accessed July 17, 2006.

If you put less than 20 percent down on a home mortgage, lenders often require you to have private mortgage insurance (PMI). PMI protects the lender if you default on the loan. The Homeowners Protection Act of 1998—which became effective in 1999—establishes rules for automatic termination and borrower cancellation of PMI on home mortgages. These protections apply to certain home mortgages signed on or after July 29, 1999 for the purchase, initial construction, or refinance of a single-family home. These protections do not apply to government-insured FHA or VA loans or to loans with lender-paid PMI.

For home mortgages signed on or after July 29, 1999, your PMI must—with certain exceptions—be terminated automatically when you reach 22 percent equity in your home based on the original property value, if your mortgage payments are current. Your PMI also can be canceled, when you request—with certain exceptions—when you reach 20 percent equity in your home based on the original property value, if your mortgage payments are current.

One exception is if your loan is "high-risk." Another is if you have not been current on your payments within the year prior to the time for termination or cancellation. A third is if you have other liens on your property. For these loans, your PMI may continue. Ask your lender or mortgage servicer (a company that collects your payments) for more information about these requirements.

If you signed your mortgage before July 29, 1999, you can ask to have the PMI canceled once you exceed 20 percent equity in your home. But federal law does not require your lender or mortgage servicer to cancel the insurance.

On a $100,000 loan with 10 percent down ($10,000), PMI might cost you $40 a month. If you can cancel the PMI, you can save $480 a year and many thousands of dollars over the loan. Check your annual escrow account statement or call your lender to find out exactly how much PMI is costing you each year.

Additional Provisions in the Law

- New borrowers covered by the law must be told—at closing and once a year—about PMI termination and cancellation.

- Mortgage servicers must provide a telephone number for all their mortgage borrowers to call for information about termination and cancellation of PMI.

- Even though the law's termination and cancellation rights do not cover loans that were signed before July 29, 1999, or loans with lender-paid PMI signed on any date, lenders or mortgage servicers must tell borrowers about the termination or cancellation rights they may otherwise have under those loans (such as rights established by the contract or state law).

Next Steps

Some states may have laws that apply to early termination or cancellation of PMI—even if you signed your mortgage before July 29, 1999. Call your state consumer protection agency for more information about your state's rules. Fannie Mae and Freddie Mac, which buy home mortgages from lenders, also may have guidelines affecting termination or cancellation of PMI on home mortgages signed before July 29, 1999. Check with your lender or mortgage servicer, or call Fannie Mae or Freddie Mac, for more information.

Contact your lender or mortgage servicer to learn whether you're paying PMI. If you are, ask how and when it can be terminated or canceled.

Chapter 35

Home Equity Loans

Putting Your Home on the Loan Line Is Risky Business

- Are you in need of cash?

- Do you want to consolidate your debts?

- Are you receiving home equity loan or refinancing offers that seem too good to be true?

- Does your home need repairs that contractors tell you can be easily financed?

If you are a homeowner who needs money to pay bills or for home repairs, you may think a home equity loan is the answer. But not all loans and lenders are the same—you should shop around. The cost of doing business with high-cost lenders can be excessive and, sometimes, downright abusive. For example, certain lenders—often called "predatory lenders"—target homeowners who have low incomes or credit problems or who are elderly by deceiving them about loan terms or giving them loans they cannot afford to repay.

This chapter begins with "Putting Your Home on the Loan Line Is Risky Business," Federal Trade Commission (FTC), October 2003. Text under the heading "Watch Out for These Abusive Loan Practices" is excerpted from "Home Equity Loans: Borrowers Beware," FTC, April 1998. Text under the heading "Your Rights under the Home Ownership and Equity Protection Act" is excerpted from "Need a Loan? Think Twice About Using Your Home as Collateral," FTC, January 2004.

Borrowing from an unscrupulous lender, especially one who offers you a high-cost loan using your home as security, is risky business. You could lose your home and your money. Before you sign on the line think about your options, do your homework, think twice before you sign, and know that you have rights under the law.

Think about Your Options

If you're having money problems, consider these options before you put your home on the loan line.

- Talk with your creditors or with representatives of non-profit or other reputable credit or budget counseling organizations to work out a plan that reduces your bill payments to a more manageable level.

- Contact your local social service agency, community or religious groups, and local or state housing agencies. They may have programs that help consumers, including the elderly and those with disabilities, with energy bills, home repairs, or other emergency needs.

- Contact a local housing counseling agency to discuss your needs. Call the U.S. Department of Housing and Urban Development toll-free at 800-569-4287 or visit www.hud.gov/offices/hsg/sfh/hcc/hccprof14.cfm to find a center near you.

- Talk with someone—other than the lender or broker offering the loan—who is knowledgeable and you trust before making any decisions. Remember, if you decide to get a home equity loan and can't make the payments, the lender could foreclose and you would lose your home.

If you decide a loan is right for you, talk with several lenders, including at least one bank, savings and loan, or credit union in your community. Their loans may cost less than loans from finance companies. And don't assume that if you're on a fixed income or have credit problems, you won't qualify for a loan from a bank, savings and loan, or credit union—they may have the loan you want.

Do Your Homework

Contact several lenders—and be very careful about dealing with a lender who just appears at your door, calls you, or sends you mail. Ask friends and family for recommendations of lenders. Talk with banks, savings and loans, credit unions, and other lenders. If you choose to use a mortgage broker, remember they arrange loans but most do not lend directly. Compare their offers with those of other direct lenders.

Be wary of home repair contractors that offer to arrange financing. You should still talk with other lenders to make sure you get the best deal. You may want to have the loan proceeds sent directly to you, not the contractor.

Comparison shop. Comparing loan plans can help you get a better deal. Whether you begin your shopping by reading ads in your local newspapers, searching on the internet, or looking in the phone book, ask lenders to explain the best loan plans they have for you. Beware of loan terms and conditions that may mean higher costs for you. Get answers to these questions and use a worksheet like the one shown in Figure 35.1 to compare loan plans:

Interest Rate and Payments

- What are the monthly payments? Ask yourself if you can afford them.

- What is the annual percentage rate (APR) on the loan? The APR is the cost of credit, expressed as a yearly rate. You can use the APR to compare one loan with another.

- Will the interest rate change during the life of the loan? If so, when, how often, and by how much?

Term of Loan

- How many years will you have to repay the loan?

- Is this a loan or a line of credit? A loan is for a fixed amount of money for a specific period of time; a line of credit is an amount of money you can draw as you need it.

- Is there a balloon payment—a large single payment at the end of the loan term after a series of low monthly payments? When the balloon payment is due, you must pay the entire amount.

Points and Fees

- What will you have to pay in points and fees? One point equals 1 percent of the loan amount (1 point on a $10,000 loan is $100). Generally, the higher the points, the lower the interest rate. If points and fees are more than 5 percent of the loan amount, ask why. Traditional financial institutions normally charge between 1 and 3 percent of the loan amount in points and fees.

- Are any of the application fees refundable if you don't get the loan?

- How and how much will the lender or broker be paid? Lenders and brokers may charge points or fees that you must pay at closing or add on to the cost of your loan, or both.

Penalties

- What is the penalty for late or missed payments?

- What is the penalty if you pay off or refinance the loan early (that is, is there a pre-payment penalty)?

Credit Insurance

- Does the loan package include optional credit insurance, such as credit life, disability, or unemployment insurance? Depending on the type of policy, credit insurance can cover some or all of your payments if you can't make them. Understand that you don't have to buy optional credit insurance—that's why it's called "optional." Don't buy insurance you don't need.

- Credit insurance may be a bad deal for you, especially if the premiums are collected up-front at the closing and financed as part of the loan. If you want optional credit insurance, ask if you can pay for it on a monthly basis after the loan is approved and closed. With monthly insurance premiums, you don't pay interest, and you can decide to cancel if the premiums are too high or if you believe you no longer want the insurance.

After you have answers to these questions, start negotiating with more than one lender. Don't be afraid to make lenders and brokers compete for your business by letting them know you are shopping for the best deal. Ask each lender to lower the points, fees, or interest rate. And ask each to meet—or beat—the terms of the other lenders.

Once You've Selected a Lender, Get the Following

- A "Good Faith Estimate" of all loan charges. The estimate must be sent within three days of applying.

- Blank copies of the forms you'll sign at closing, when the loan is final. Study them. If you don't understand something, ask for an explanation.

- Advance copies of the forms you'll sign at closing with the terms filled in. A week or two before closing, contact the lender to find out if there have been any changes in the Good Faith Estimate. By law, you can inspect the final settlement statement (also

Use this worksheet to help you shop for the best deal

Compare answers to these questions	Lender A	Lender B	Lender C	My Current Mortgage
What are the monthly payments?				
What is the Annual Percentage Rate (APR)? *the cost of credit expressed as a yearly rate; includes the interest rate, points, broker fees, and other credit charges*				
What is the interest rate? *the cost of borrowing money expressed as a percentage rate*				
Will the interest rate change?				
When?				
How often?				
By how much?				
What will you have to pay in points				
What will you have to pay in fees?				
Application or loan processing fee				
Origination or underwriting fee				
Lender or funding fee				
Appraisal fee				
Document preparation and recording fees				
Broker fees				
Other fees				
Are any of the application fees refundable if you don't get the loan?				
How many years will you have to repay the loan?				
Is this an installment loan or a line of credit?				
Is there a balloon payment?				
What are the total closing costs?				
If you use a broker, how and how much will he or she be paid?				
What is the penalty for late or missed payments?				
What is the penalty if you pay off or refinance the loan early?				
Does the loan include optional credit insurance? *You don't have to accept optional credit insurance to get your loan. If you want optional credit insurance, ask about paying for it monthly instead of financing the premiums as part of your loan.*				
Can you afford this loan?				

Figure 35.1. *Comparison Shopping for a Home Equity Loan*

called the HUD-1 or HUD-1A form) one day prior to closing. Study these forms. Write down any questions you want to ask.

Think Twice before You Sign

- Have a knowledgeable friend, relative, attorney, or housing counselor review the Good Faith Estimate and other loan papers before you sign the loan contract. Be sure the terms are the same ones you agreed to. For example, a lender should not promise one APR and then—without good reason—increase it at closing.

- Refer to the list of questions you've written down. Ask where these terms are covered in the loan contract. And ask for an explanation of any dollar amount or term you don't understand. Don't let anyone rush you into signing the loan contract.

- Make sure all promises, oral and otherwise, are put in writing. It's only what's in writing that counts.

- Get a copy of the documents you signed before you leave the closing.

When You Shouldn't Sign on the Dotted Line

- If the lender tells you to falsify information on the loan application (for example, suggests that you write down more income than you really have).

- If the lender pressures you into applying for a loan for more money than you need, or one that has monthly payments larger than you can afford.

- If the lender promises one set of terms but gives you another with no good reason for the change.

- If the lender tells you to sign blank forms or forms that aren't completely filled in. If an item is supposed to be blank, draw a line through the space and initial it.

- If a lender pressures you to sign today. A good deal today should be available tomorrow.

Know that You Have Rights under the Law

You have three business days to cancel the loan: If you're using your home as security for a home equity loan (or for a second mortgage loan or a line of credit), federal law gives you three business

408

days after signing the loan papers to cancel the deal—for any reason—without penalty. You must cancel in writing. The lender must return any money you have paid to date.

Do you think you've made a mistake? Has the three-day period during which you may cancel passed and you're worried that you've gotten in over your head? Do you think your loan fees were too high? Do you believe you were steered into monthly payments you can't afford? Has your lender repeatedly pressured you to refinance? Is your loan covered by insurance you don't need or want?

If you think you've been taken advantage of, state and federal laws may protect you. Also, the following organizations may be able to help:

- Your local or state bar association—sometimes listed under "Lawyers Referral Service" in the Yellow Pages of your phone book. The association may be able to refer you to low-cost or no-cost lawyers who can help.

- Your local consumer protection agency, state attorney general's office, or state office on aging, listed in the Blue Pages of your phone book.

- Your local fair housing group or affordable housing agency, housing counseling agency, or state housing agency.

Watch Out for These Abusive Loan Practices

Equity stripping: You need money. You don't have much income coming in each month. You have built up equity in your home. A lender tells you that you could get a loan, even though you know your income is just not enough to keep up with the monthly payments. The lender encourages you to "pad" your income on your application form to help get the loan approved.

This lender may be out to steal the equity you have built up in your home. The lender doesn't care if you can't keep up with the monthly payments. As soon as you don't, the lender will foreclose—taking your home and stripping you of the equity you have spent years building. If you take out a loan but don't have enough income to make the monthly payments, you are being set up. You probably will lose your home.

Hidden loan terms: The balloon payment: You've fallen behind in your mortgage payments and may face foreclosure. Another lender offers to save you from foreclosure by refinancing your mortgage and lowering your monthly payments. Look carefully at the loan terms. The payments may be lower because the lender is offering a loan on which you repay only the interest each month. At the end of the loan term, the principal—that is, the entire amount that you borrowed—is due in one lump sum called a balloon payment. If you can't make the balloon payment or refinance, you face foreclosure and the loss of your home.

Loan flipping: Suppose you've had your mortgage for years. The interest rate is low and the monthly payments fit nicely into your budget, but you could use some extra money. A lender calls to talk about refinancing, and using the availability of extra cash as bait, claims it's time the equity in your home started "working" for you. You agree to refinance your loan. After you've made a few payments on the loan, the lender calls to offer you a bigger loan for, say, a vacation. If you accept the offer, the lender refinances your original loan and then lends you additional money. In this practice—often called "flipping"—the lender charges you high points and fees each time you refinance, and may increase your interest rate as well. If the loan has a prepayment penalty, you will have to pay that penalty each time you take out a new loan.

You now have some extra money and a lot more debt, stretched out over a longer time. The extra cash you receive may be less than the additional costs and fees you were charged for the refinancing. And what's worse, you are now paying interest on those extra fees charged in each refinancing. Long story short? With each refinancing, you've increased your debt and probably are paying a very high price for some extra cash. After a while, if you get in over your head and can't pay, you could lose your home.

The "home improvement" loan: A contractor calls or knocks on your door and offers to install a new roof or remodel your kitchen at a price that sounds reasonable. You tell him you're interested, but can't afford it. He tells you it's no problem—he can arrange financing through a lender he knows. You agree to the project, and the contractor begins work. At some point after the contractor begins, you are asked to sign a lot of papers. The papers may be blank or the lender may rush you to sign before you have time to read what you've been given. The contractor threatens to leave the work on your house unfinished if you don't sign. You sign the papers. Only later, you realize that the papers you signed are a home equity loan. The interest rate, points and fees seem very high. To make matters worse, the work on your home isn't done right or hasn't been completed, and the contractor, who may have been paid by the lender, has little interest in completing the work to your satisfaction.

Credit insurance packing: You've just agreed to a mortgage on terms you think you can afford. At closing, the lender gives you papers to sign that include charges for credit insurance or other "benefits" that you did not ask for and do not want. The lender hopes you don't notice this, and that you just sign the loan papers where you are asked to sign. The lender doesn't explain exactly how much extra money this will cost you each month on your loan. If you do notice, you're afraid that if you ask questions or object, you might not get the loan. The lender may tell you that this insurance comes with the loan, making you think that it comes at no additional cost. Or, if you object, the lender may even tell you that if you want the loan without the insurance, the loan papers will have to be rewritten, that it could take several days, and that the manager may reconsider the loan altogether. If you agree to buy the insurance, you really are paying extra for the loan by buying a product you may not want or need.

Mortgage servicing abuses: After you get a mortgage, you receive a letter from your lender saying that your monthly payments will be higher than you expected. The lender says that your payments include escrow for taxes and insurance even though you arranged to pay those items yourself with the lender's okay. Later, a message from the lender says you are being charged late fees. But you know your payments were on time. Or, you may receive a message saying that you failed to maintain required property insurance, and the lender is buying more costly insurance at your expense. Other charges that you don't understand—like legal fees—are added to the amount you owe, increasing your monthly payments or the amount you owe at the end of the loan term. The lender doesn't provide you with an accurate or complete account of these charges. You ask for a payoff statement to refinance with another lender and receive a statement that's inaccurate or incomplete. The lender's actions make it almost impossible to determine how much you've paid or how much you owe. You may pay more than you owe.

Signing over your deed: If you are having trouble paying your mortgage and the lender has threatened to foreclose and take your home, you may feel desperate. Another "lender" may contact you with an offer to help you find new financing. Before he can help you, he asks you to deed your property to him, claiming that it's a temporary measure to prevent foreclosure. The promised refinancing that would let you save your home never comes through.

411

Once the "lender" has the deed to your property, he starts to treat it as his own. He may borrow against it (for his benefit, not yours) or even sell it to someone else. Because you don't own the home any more, you won't get any money when the property is sold. The lender will treat you as a tenant and your mortgage payments as rent. If your "rent" payments are late, you can be evicted from your home.

Protecting Yourself

You can protect yourself against losing your home to inappropriate lending practices. Here's how:

- Ask specifically if credit insurance is required as a condition of the loan. If it isn't, and a charge is included in your loan and you don't want the insurance, ask that the charge be removed from the loan documents. If you want the added security of credit insurance, shop around for the best rates.

- Keep careful records of what you've paid, including billing statements and canceled checks. Challenge any charge you think is inaccurate.

- Check contractors' references when it is time to have work done in your home. Get more than one estimate.

- Read all items carefully. If you need an explanation of any terms or conditions, talk to someone you can trust, such as a knowledgeable family member or an attorney. Consider all the costs of financing before you agree to a loan.

Your Rights under the Home Ownership and Equity Protection Act

The Home Ownership and Equity Protection Act (HOEPA) may give you additional rights if your loan is a home equity loan, second mortgage, or refinance secured by your principal residence and if:

- the loan's APR exceeds by more than 8 percent the rate on a Treasury note of comparable maturity on a first mortgage, or the loan's APR exceeds by more than 10 percent the rate on a Treasury note of comparable maturity on a second mortgage.

- the total fees and points at or before closing exceed $499 or 8 percent of the total loan amount, whichever is larger. (The $499 figure is for 2004 and is adjusted annually.) Credit insurance premiums written in connection with the loan count as fees for this purpose.

If HOEPA applies:

- A lender may not engage in a pattern or practice of lending based on home equity without regard to the borrower's ability to repay the loan.

- You must get certain disclosures from the lender at least three business days before closing.

- Your lender cannot make a direct payment to a home improvement contractor.

- Certain loan terms are illegal—such as most prepayment penalties and increased interest rates at default.

- In most situations, your loan cannot have a balloon payment due in less than five years.

- Due-on-demand clauses may not be used unless the consumer defaults.

- A lender that has made a HOEPA loan to a borrower generally may not refinance that loan into another HOEPA loan within the first year.

- Your lender may not call a one-time loan a line of credit.

A high-rate or high-fee loan might be right for you, but be aware that it has risks. It is an extremely expensive way to borrow money. You could lose your home if you can't make the payments.

Where to Complain

If you think your lender has violated the law, you may wish to contact the lender or loan servicer to register your concerns. At the same time, you may want to contact an attorney, your state Attorney General's office or banking regulatory agency, or the Federal Trade Commission (http://www.ftc.gov).

You can learn more about credit and home equity loans by visiting the federal government's website for consumers, http://www.consumer.gov (see the Home and Community section). If you don't have access to the internet, ask a friend or relative to get the information for you. Or visit your local library or senior center, which may offer you free access to the internet on their computers.

Chapter 36

Home Equity Lines of Credit

More and more lenders are offering home equity lines of credit. By using the equity in your home, you may qualify for a sizable amount of credit, available for use when and how you please, at an interest rate that is relatively low.

Furthermore, under the tax law—depending on your specific situation—you may be allowed to deduct the interest because the debt is secured by your home.

If you are in the market for credit, a home equity plan may be right for you. Or perhaps another form of credit would be better. Before making a decision, you should weigh carefully the costs of a home equity line against the benefits. Shop for the credit terms that best meet your borrowing needs without posing undue financial risk. And remember, failure to repay the amounts you've borrowed, plus interest, could mean the loss of your home.

What is a home equity line of credit?

A home equity line of credit is a form of revolving credit in which your home serves as collateral. Because the home is likely to be a consumer's largest asset, many homeowners use their credit lines only for major items such as education, home improvements, or medical bills and not for day-to-day expenses.

"What You Should Know about Home Equity Lines of Credit," Federal Reserve Board of Governors (www.federalreserve.gov), March 2004.

With a home equity line, you will be approved for a specific amount of credit—your credit limit, the maximum amount you may borrow at any one time under the plan. Many lenders set the credit limit on a home equity line by taking a percentage (say, 75 percent) of the home's appraised value and subtracting from that the balance owed on the existing mortgage. Here's an example:

Appraised value of home	$100,000
Percentage	x 75%
Percentage of appraised value	= $ 75,000
Less balance owed on mortgage	- $ 40,000
Potential credit	$ 35,000

In determining your actual credit limit, the lender will also consider your ability to repay, by looking at your income, debts, and other financial obligations as well as your credit history.

Many home equity plans set a fixed period during which you can borrow money, such as 10 years. At the end of this "draw period," you may be allowed to renew the credit line. If your plan does not allow renewals, you will not be able to borrow additional money once the period has ended. Some plans may call for payment in full of any outstanding balance at the end of the period. Others may allow repayment over a fixed period (the "repayment period"), for example, 10 years.

Once approved for a home equity line of credit, you will most likely be able to borrow up to your credit limit whenever you want. Typically, you will use special checks to draw on your line. Under some plans, borrowers can use a credit card or other means to draw on the line.

There may be limitations on how you use the line. Some plans may require you to borrow a minimum amount each time you draw on the line (for example, $300) and to keep a minimum amount outstanding. Some plans may also require that you take an initial advance when the line is set up.

What should you look for when shopping for a plan?

If you decide to apply for a home equity line of credit, look for the plan that best meets your particular needs. Read the credit agreement carefully, and examine the terms and conditions of various plans, including the annual percentage rate (APR) and the costs of establishing the plan. The APR for a home equity line is based on the interest rate alone and will not reflect the closing costs and other fees and charges, so you'll need to compare these costs, as well as the APRs, among lenders.

Interest rate charges and related plan features: Home equity lines of credit typically involve variable rather than fixed interest rates. The variable rate must be based on a publicly available index (such as the prime rate published in some major daily newspapers or a U.S. Treasury bill rate); the interest rate for borrowing under the home equity line changes, mirroring fluctuations in the value of the index. Most lenders cite the interest rate you will pay as the value of the index at a particular time plus a "margin," such as two percentage points. Because the cost of borrowing is tied directly to the value of the index, it is important to find out which index is used, how often the value of the index changes, and how high it has risen in the past as well as the amount of the margin.

Lenders sometimes offer a temporarily discounted interest rate for home equity lines—a rate that is unusually low and may last for only an introductory period, such as six months.

Variable-rate plans secured by a dwelling must, by law, have a ceiling (or cap) on how much your interest rate may increase over the life of the plan. Some variable-rate plans limit how much your payment may increase and how low your interest rate may fall if interest rates drop.

Some lenders allow you to convert from a variable interest rate to a fixed rate during the life of the plan, or to convert all or a portion of your line to a fixed-term installment loan.

Plans generally permit the lender to freeze or reduce your credit line under certain circumstances. For example, some variable-rate plans may not allow you to draw additional funds during a period in which the interest rate reaches the cap.

What are the costs of establishing and maintaining a home equity line?

Many of the costs of setting up a home equity line of credit are similar to those you pay when you buy a home. Examples of typical costs include the following:

- A fee for a property appraisal to estimate the value of your home

- An application fee, which may not be refunded if you are turned down for credit

- Up-front charges, such as one or more points (one point equals 1 percent of the credit limit)

- Closing costs, including fees for attorneys, title search, and mortgage preparation and filing; property and title insurance; and taxes.

In addition, you may be subject to certain fees during the plan period, such as annual membership or maintenance fees and a transaction fee every time you draw on the credit line.

You could find yourself paying hundreds of dollars to establish the plan. If you were to draw only a small amount against your credit line, those initial charges would substantially increase the cost of the funds borrowed. On the other hand, because the lender's risk is lower than for other forms of credit, as your home serves as collateral, annual percentage rates for home equity lines are generally lower than rates for other types of credit. The interest you save could offset the costs of establishing and maintaining the line. Moreover, some lenders waive some or all of the closing costs.

How will you repay your home equity plan?

Before entering into a plan, consider how you will pay back the money you borrow. Some plans set minimum payments that cover a portion of the principal (the amount you borrow) plus accrued interest. But (unlike with the typical installment loan) the portion that goes toward principal may not be enough to repay the principal by the end of the term. Other plans may allow payment of interest alone during the life of the plan, which means that you pay nothing toward the principal. If you borrow $10,000, you will owe that amount when the plan ends.

Regardless of the minimum required payment, you may choose to pay more, and many lenders offer a choice of payment options. Many consumers choose to pay down the principal regularly as they do with other loans. For example, if you use your line to buy a boat, you may want to pay it off as you would a typical boat loan.

Whatever your payment arrangements during the life of the plan—whether you pay some, a little, or none of the principal amount of the loan—when the plan ends you may have to pay the entire balance owed, all at once. You must be prepared to make this "balloon payment" by refinancing it with the lender, by obtaining a loan from another lender, or by some other means. If you are unable to make the balloon payment, you could lose your home.

If your plan has a variable interest rate, your monthly payments may change. Assume, for example, that you borrow $10,000 under a plan that calls for interest-only payments. At a 10 percent interest rate, your monthly payments would be $83. If the rate rises over time to 15 percent, your monthly payments will increase to $125. Similarly, if you are making payments that cover interest plus some portion of the principal, your monthly payments may increase, unless your agreement calls for keeping payments the same throughout the plan period.

If you sell your home, you will probably be required to pay off your home equity line in full immediately. If you are likely to sell your home in the near future, consider whether it makes sense to pay the up-front costs of setting up a line of credit. Also keep in mind that renting your home may be prohibited under the terms of your agreement.

Lines of Credit vs. Traditional Second Mortgage Loans

If you are thinking about a home equity line of credit, you might also want to consider a traditional second mortgage loan. A second mortgage provides you with a fixed amount of money repayable over a fixed period. In most cases the payment schedule calls for equal payments that will pay off the entire loan within the loan period. You might consider a second mortgage instead of a home equity line if, for example, you need a set amount for a specific purpose, such as an addition to your home.

In deciding which type of loan best suits your needs, consider the costs under the two alternatives. Look at both the APR and other charges. Do not, however, simply compare the APRs, because the APRs on the two types of loans are figured differently:

- The APR for a traditional second mortgage loan takes into account the interest rate charged plus points and other finance charges.

- The APR for a home equity line of credit is based on the periodic interest rate alone. It does not include points or other charges.

Disclosures from lenders: The federal Truth in Lending Act requires lenders to disclose the important terms and costs of their home equity plans, including the APR, miscellaneous charges, the payment terms, and information about any variable-rate feature. And in general, neither the lender nor anyone else may charge a fee until after you have received this information. You usually get these disclosures when you receive an application form, and you will get additional disclosures before the plan is opened. If any term (other than a variable-rate feature) changes before the plan is opened, the lender must return all fees if you decide not to enter into the plan because of the change.

When you open a home equity line, the transaction puts your home at risk. If the home involved is your principal dwelling, the Truth in Lending Act gives you three days from the day the account was opened to cancel the credit line. This right allows you to change your mind for any reason. You simply inform the lender in writing within the three-day period. The lender must then cancel its security interest in your home and return all fees—including any application and appraisal fees—paid to open the account.

Chapter 37

Reverse Mortgages: Facts You Should Know

Whether seeking money to finance a home improvement, pay off a current mortgage, supplement their retirement income, or pay for healthcare expenses, many older Americans are turning to "reverse" mortgages. They allow older homeowners to convert part of the equity in their homes into cash without having to sell their homes or take on additional monthly bills.

In a "regular" mortgage, you make monthly payments to the lender. But in a "reverse" mortgage, you receive money from the lender and generally don't have to pay it back for as long as you live in your home. Instead, the loan must be repaid when you die, sell your home, or no longer live there as your principal residence. Reverse mortgages can help homeowners who are house-rich but cash-poor stay in their homes and still meet their financial obligations.

To qualify for most reverse mortgages, you must be at least 62 and live in your home. The proceeds of a reverse mortgage (without other features, like an annuity) are generally tax-free, and many reverse mortgages have no income restrictions.

Three Types of Reverse Mortgages

The three basic types of reverse mortgage are: single-purpose reverse mortgages, which are offered by some state and local government agencies and nonprofit organizations; federally insured reverse

"Reverse Mortgages: Get the Facts Before Cashing In On Your Home's Equity," Federal Trade Commission, June 2005.

mortgages, which are known as Home Equity Conversion Mortgages (HECMs), and are backed by the U.S. Department of Housing and Urban Development (HUD); and proprietary reverse mortgages, which are private loans that are backed by the companies that develop them.

Single-purpose reverse mortgages generally have very low costs. But they are not available everywhere, and they only can be used for one purpose specified by the government or nonprofit lender, for example, to pay for home repairs, improvements, or property taxes. In most cases, you can qualify for these loans only if your income is low or moderate.

HECMs and proprietary reverse mortgages tend to be more costly than other home loans. The up-front costs can be high, so they are generally most expensive if you stay in your home for just a short time. They are widely available, have no income or medical requirements, and can be used for any purpose.

Before applying for a HECM, you must meet with a counselor from an independent government-approved housing counseling agency. The counselor must explain the loan's costs, financial implications, and alternatives. For example, counselors should tell you about government or nonprofit programs for which you may qualify, and any single-purpose or proprietary reverse mortgages available in your area.

The amount of money you can borrow with a HECM or proprietary reverse mortgage depends on several factors, including your age, the type of reverse mortgage you select, the appraised value of your home, current interest rates, and where you live. In general, the older you are, the more valuable your home, and the less you owe on it, the more money you can get.

The HECM gives you choices in how the loan is paid to you. You can select fixed monthly cash advances for a specific period or for as long as you live in your home. Or you can opt for a line of credit, which allows you to draw on the loan proceeds at any time in amounts that you choose. You also can get a combination of monthly payments plus a line of credit.

HECMs generally provide larger loan advances at a lower total cost compared with proprietary loans. But owners of higher-valued homes may get bigger loan advances from a proprietary reverse mortgage. That is, if you have a higher appraised value without a large mortgage, then you may likely qualify for greater funds. Location (for example, your neighborhood) is only one part of the determination of appraised value.

Loan Features

Reverse mortgage loan advances are not taxable, and generally do not affect Social Security or Medicare benefits. You retain the title to your home and do not have to make monthly repayments. The loan must be repaid when the last surviving borrower dies, sells the home, or no longer lives in the home as a principal residence. In the HECM program, a borrower can live in a nursing home or other medical facility for up to 12 months before the loan becomes due and payable.

As you consider a reverse mortgage, be aware of these concerns:

- Lenders generally charge origination fees and other closing costs for a reverse mortgage. Lenders also may charge servicing fees during the term of the mortgage. The lender generally sets these fees and costs.

- The amount you owe on a reverse mortgage generally grows over time. Interest is charged on the outstanding balance and added to the amount you owe each month. That means your total debt increases over time as loan funds are advanced to you and interest accrues on the loan.

- Reverse mortgages may have fixed or variable rates. Most have variable rates that are tied to a financial index and will likely change according to market conditions.

- Reverse mortgages can use up all or some of the equity in your home, leaving fewer assets for you and your heirs. A "nonrecourse" clause, found in most reverse mortgages, prevents either you or your estate from owing more than the value of your home when the loan is repaid.

- Because you retain title to your home, you remain responsible for property taxes, insurance, utilities, fuel, maintenance, and other expenses. So, for example, if you don't pay property taxes or maintain homeowner's insurance, you risk the loan becoming due and payable.

- Interest on reverse mortgages is not deductible on income tax returns until the loan is paid off in part or whole.

Getting a Good Deal

If you are considering a reverse mortgage, shop around to compare your options and the offered terms. Learn as much as you can about reverse mortgages before you talk to a counselor or lender. It will help you ask more informed questions, which could lead to a better deal.

- If you want to make a home repair or improvement or need help paying your property taxes, you may want to find out if you qualify for any low-cost single-purpose loans that may be available in your area. Area Agencies on Aging (AAAs) generally know about these programs. To find the nearest agency, visit www.eldercare.gov or call toll-free, 800-677-1116. Ask the AAA for information about available "loan programs for home repairs or improvements," or "property tax deferral" or "property tax postponement" programs.

- If you are interested in a federally-insured HECM, know that all HECM lenders must follow HUD rules, and that many of the loan costs including the interest rate will be the same no matter which lender you select. Still, some costs including the origination fee, other closing costs, and servicing fees may vary among lenders.

- If you live in a higher-valued home, you may be able to borrow more from a proprietary reverse mortgage. But it generally will cost more. The best way to see key differences between a HECM and a proprietary loan is with a detailed side-by-side comparison of future costs and benefits. Many HECM counselors and lenders can provide you with this important information.

- No matter which type of reverse mortgage you are considering, be certain you understand all the conditions that could make the loan due and payable. Ask a counselor or lender to explain the Total Annual Loan Cost (TALC) rates, which show the projected annual average cost of a reverse mortgage, including all itemized costs.

Be a Savvy Consumer

Be cautious if anyone tries to sell you something, like an annuity, and suggests that a reverse mortgage would be an easy way to pay for it. If you don't fully understand what they're selling, or you're not sure you need what they're selling, be even more skeptical.

Keep in mind that your total cost would be the cost of what they're selling plus the cost of the reverse mortgage. If you think you need what they're selling, shop around before you buy.

No matter why you decide to take a reverse mortgage, you generally have at least three business days after signing the loan documents to cancel it for any reason without penalty. Remember that you must cancel in writing. The lender must return any money you have paid so far for the financing.

Reporting Possible Fraud

If you suspect that anyone is violating the law, let the counselor, lender, or loan servicer know. Then, file a complaint with these agencies:

- Your state Attorney General's office or state banking regulatory agency, and

- The Federal Trade Commission (FTC). You can do that online at ftc.gov or by phone, toll-free, at 877-FTC-HELP (877-382-4357).

Whether a reverse mortgage is right for you is a big question. Consider all your options. You may qualify for less costly alternatives.

Chapter 38

Beware of High-Cost Loans and Predatory Practices

Chapter Contents

Section 38.1

Refund Anticipation Loans: A Costly Way to Borrow Your Own Money

This section begins with information excerpted from "Refund Anticipation Loans: Updated Facts and Figures" © 2006 Consumer Federation of America. All rights reserved. Reprinted with permission. For additional information, visit www.consumerfed.org. Additional text under the heading "Better Alternatives" is from "Don't Pay to Borrow Your Own Money," Copyright © National Consumer Law Center, reprinted with permission from www.consumerlaw.org.

Based on an analysis of Internal Revenue Service (IRS) data, the National Consumer Law Center, Inc. (NCLC) and Consumer Federation of America (CFA) estimate that approximately 12.38 million American taxpayers spent an unnecessary $1.6 billion in 2004 (the latest year for which data is available) to obtain their refund moneys faster by two weeks or less than if they used electronic filing and direct deposit.

RALs Examined

Refund anticipation loans (RALs) are extremely high-cost bank loans secured by the taxpayer's expected tax refund—loans that last about 7–14 days until the actual Internal Revenue Service (IRS) refund repays the loan. RALs cost from $29 to $120 in loan fees. Some tax preparers also charge a separate fee, often called an "administrative" or "application" fee; however, this fee will become less common now that the largest commercial tax preparation chains have eliminated it to a great extent. Tax preparers and their bank partners also offer an "instant" same day RAL for an extra $20 to $39.

The effective annual interest rate (APR) for a RAL can range from about 40% (for a loan of $9,999) to over 700% (for a loan of $200). If administrative fees are charged and included in the calculation, RALs cost about 70% to over 1,800% APR.

Using the most recent data available from the IRS, NCLC and CFA calculate that approximately 12.38 million taxpayers received RALs in the 2004 tax filing season (for tax year 2003). For that year alone, about one in ten tax returns involved a RAL. These 12.38 million RALs represent a slight increase from the 12.15 million RALs taken in 2003. These consumers paid a total of $1.24 billion in loan fees, plus $360 million in administrative fees (since they were still being charged in 2004), for these loans.

This year, a RAL for the average refund of around $2,150 will cost about $100. A loan under those terms bears an effective APR of about 178%. If the taxpayer goes to a preparer who charges an additional $30 administrative fee, the effective APR including the administrative fee would be 235%. These loan charges are in addition to tax preparation fees averaging $146, so the grand total could be as high as $276.

RALs Target Working Families

RALs particularly target low-income working families claiming the Earned Income Tax Credit (EITC), draining hundreds of millions of dollars from EITC anti-poverty benefits. Over 56% of all RAL borrowers are EITC recipients according to IRS data, despite the fact that EITC recipients only make up 17% of taxpayers. One out of every three EITC recipients gets a RAL.

Table 38.1. RAL Fees

Type of Fee	Cost to Taxpayer	Drain on EITC Program
RAL loan fee (inc. dummy account fee)	$100	$700 million
Application/Admin. Fee (for 91%)	$32	$204 million
Total	**$132**	**$904 million**
Tax preparation fee	$146	$1 billion
Check cashing fee (for 45% of EITC recipients)	$65	$205 million
Total with tax preparation and check cashing	**$343**	**$2.1 billion**

Based on IRS data for 2004, NCLC and CFA estimate that 7 million working poor families spent over $900 million in RAL fees in order to get their tax refund moneys less than two weeks sooner than they otherwise could. These families paid about $700 million in RAL loan fees and $204 million in administrative fees. In terms of others fees, these families also paid $1 billion in tax preparation fees, and about 45% of them spent approximately $205 million to cash their RAL checks with check cashers.

Data on RAL Users

A telephone polling survey commissioned by the Consumer Federation of America provides new information about RAL users. The national survey found that RAL users are vulnerable to quick cash loan offers. RAL users are more likely than non-RAL users to be less well educated, work in service or semi-skilled/unskilled jobs, rent instead of own their homes, and be female and African American. RAL users are also heavier users than non-RAL users of other high cost fringe financial services, such as rent-to-own, payday loans, and pawnshop loans. These consumers are more likely to be unbanked than non-RAL users and those who do have bank accounts are more likely to have overdrawn in the past year.

The survey was conducted by Opinion Research Corporation in early November 2005 and interviewed 2,038 representative adult Americans. The margin of error for the sample is plus or minus two percentage points.

Free File

A significant development in 2005 occurred when the IRS renewed its agreement with the Free File Alliance to provide for free web-based electronic filing for taxpayers who make less than $50,000 annually. Unfortunately, this new agreement does not ban Free File commercial preparers from marketing RALs to taxpayers. Since taxpayers reach Free File preparers by going through www.irs.gov, the IRS agreement continues to permit the appearance of an implicit government endorsement of the marketing of RALs and other ancillary products, such as audit "insurance" or preparing state tax returns. This new agreement also will not benefit the millions of lower income consumers who are on the other side of the "digital divide" without computer and internet access at home.

Advice to Consumers

Taxpayers can save themselves expensive fees by saying "no" to RALs. If they want quick refunds, they can get them in two weeks or less by filing their tax returns electronically and having refunds directly deposited into their own bank accounts. That's a free quick refund. In addition to their high costs, RALs can be a risky proposition. A RAL must be repaid even if the taxpayer's refund is denied, is smaller than expected, or frozen (something that the National Taxpayer Advocate has noted happens to hundreds of thousands of taxpayers, particularly EITC recipients). If the taxpayer cannot pay back the RAL, the lender may send the account to a debt collector. The unpaid RAL will also show up as a black mark on the taxpayer's credit record. If the taxpayer applies for a RAL or other refund financial product from a commercial preparer next year, she may find that her next year's refund gets grabbed to repay this year's unpaid RAL debt.

Better Alternatives

Here are ways to take a pass on that RAL—most folks don't need one—and save money at tax time:

E-file with direct deposit: File your tax return electronically (E-file) to speed up your refund. Tell the IRS to deposit the refund directly into your bank account—you provide your account number right on your tax return. You can get a refund in about ten days this way—without paying one cent extra for a loan. Some of the free tax preparation programs (called "VITA" sites, which stands for volunteer income tax assistance) can file taxes electronically. If you have internet access, you may be able to get free tax preparation and electronic filing at http://www.icanefile.org.

Get a bank account: If you don't have a bank account, open one up to take advantage of direct deposit. You can use a savings account to receive your tax refund, and maybe save some of it for a down payment on a house or a car or to build a nest egg.

Wait just a bit longer: Do you really have to get cash from your tax refund today? Can you wait a few weeks to save almost $100? If you have an urgent bill to pay, ask for more time until the tax refund check comes from the IRS. Don't take on a new expensive debt to pay an old bill.

Avoid check cashers: Check cashers charge an extra fee to cash RAL and tax refund checks. Some check cashers charge up to 7% to cash a RAL check—the average is about 3%. So if you receive a $2,000 refund, it would cost you an average of $60 to cash the RAL check—on top of the RAL and tax preparation fees. A smarter move is to use a bank account.

Use a VITA site: A great way to save money at tax time is to go to a volunteer income tax assistance (VITA) site. VITA sites provide free tax preparation to low- and moderate-income taxpayers. VITA sites are sponsored by the IRS and can be found in libraries, community centers, and other locations during tax time.

For the nearest VITA site, call the IRS general help line at 800-TAX-1040 or go to http://www.tax-coalition.org.

Section 38.2

Payday Loans Equal Costly Cash

"Payday Loans = Costly Cash," Federal Trade Commission
(www.ftc.gov), February 2000; reviewed for currency in February 2006.

- "I just need enough cash to tide me over until payday."
- "GET CASH UNTIL PAYDAY! . . . $100 OR MORE . . . FAST."

The ads are on the radio, television, the internet, even in the mail. They refer to payday loans—which come at a very high price.

Check cashers, finance companies and others are making small, short-term, high-rate loans that go by a variety of names: payday loans, cash advance loans, check advance loans, post-dated check loans or deferred deposit check loans.

Usually, a borrower writes a personal check payable to the lender for the amount he or she wishes to borrow plus a fee. The company gives the borrower the amount of the check minus the fee. Fees charged for payday loans are usually a percentage of the face value of the check or a fee charged per amount borrowed—say, for every $50 or $100 loaned. And, if you extend or "roll-over" the loan—say for another two weeks—you will pay the fees for each extension.

Under the Truth in Lending Act, the cost of payday loans—like other types of credit—must be disclosed. Among other information, you must receive, in writing, the finance charge (a dollar amount) and the annual percentage rate or APR (the cost of credit on a yearly basis).

A cash advance loan secured by a personal check—such as a payday loan—is very expensive credit. Let's say you write a personal check for $115 to borrow $100 for up to 14 days. The check casher or payday lender agrees to hold the check until your next payday. At that time, depending on the particular plan, the lender deposits the check, you redeem the check by paying the $115 in cash, or you roll-over the check by paying a fee to extend the loan for another two weeks. In this example, the cost of the initial loan is a $15 finance charge and 391 percent APR. If you roll-over the loan three times, the finance charge would climb to $60 to borrow $100.

Alternatives to Payday Loans

There are other options. Consider the possibilities before choosing a payday loan:

- When you need credit, shop carefully. Compare offers. Look for the credit offer with the lowest APR—consider a small loan from your credit union or small loan company, an advance on pay from your employer, or a loan from family or friends. A cash advance on a credit card also may be a possibility, but it may have a higher interest rate than your other sources of funds: find out the terms before you decide. Also, a local community-based organization may make small business loans to individuals.

- Compare the APR and the finance charge (which includes loan fees, interest and other types of credit costs) of credit offers to get the lowest cost.

- Ask your creditors for more time to pay your bills. Find out what they will charge for that service—as a late charge, an additional finance charge or a higher interest rate.

- Make a realistic budget, and figure your monthly and daily expenditures. Avoid unnecessary purchases—even small daily items. Their costs add up. Also, build some savings—even small deposits can help—to avoid borrowing for emergencies, unexpected expenses or other items. For example, by putting the amount of the fee that would be paid on a typical $300 payday loan in a savings account for six months, you would have extra dollars available. This can give you a buffer against financial emergencies.

- Find out if you have, or can get, overdraft protection on your checking account. If you are regularly using most or all of the funds in your account and if you make a mistake in your checking (or savings) account ledger or records, overdraft protection can help protect you from further credit problems. Find out the terms of overdraft protection.

- If you need help working out a debt repayment plan with creditors or developing a budget, contact your local consumer credit counseling service. There are non-profit groups in every state that offer credit guidance to consumers. These services are available at little or no cost. Also, check with your employer, credit union or housing authority for no- or low-cost credit counseling programs.

- If you decide you must use a payday loan, borrow only as much as you can afford to pay with your next paycheck and still have enough to make it to the next payday.

To Complain or Receive More Information

If you believe a lender has violated the Truth in Lending Act, file a complaint with the Federal Trade Commission (FTC).

The FTC works for the consumer to prevent fraudulent, deceptive and unfair business practices in the marketplace and to provide information to help consumers spot, stop, and avoid them. To file a complaint or to get free information on consumer issues, visit http://www.ftc.gov/ or call toll-free, 877-FTC-HELP (877-382-4357); TTY: 866-653-4261. The FTC enters internet, telemarketing, identity theft, and other fraud-related complaints into Consumer Sentinel, a secure, online database available to hundreds of civil and criminal law enforcement agencies in the U.S. and abroad.

Section 38.3

The High Cost of Small Loans, Pawnbrokers, and Rent-to-Own Stores

"Borrower Beware: The High Cost of Small Loans, Pawnbrokers and Rent-To-Own Stores," February 2002, Copyright © National Consumer Law Center, reprinted with permission from www.consumerlaw.org.

What Are Loans?

A loan is borrowed money which must be repaid in one or more payments. Lenders charge interest on the amount you borrow. This means that you pay back more than you receive. This is how a lender covers the cost of doing business and makes profit. The higher the interest rate, the more you must repay. You should know that the lower the monthly payment, the longer it will take you to repay the loan and the more you will pay to borrow the same amount at the same interest rate.

Compare:

- You borrow $500 at 18% interest for 12 months
  - You pay $45.84/month x 12 months

    $500.00 principal (you get)
    + $50.08 interest you pay
    = $550.08 total to repay

- You borrow $500 at 18% interest for 24 months:
  - You pay $24.96/month x 24 months

    $500.00 principal (you get)
    + $99.04 interest (you pay)
    = $599.04 total to repay

Sometimes you may need to borrow a few hundred dollars because of an unexpected medical bill, broken appliance, or to buy a used car to obtain keep a job. While the amount of cash you may need is small, the amount of interest you will repay may be large.

Payday Lenders

Some check cashers will offer to take a personal check from you or from someone else you know. The lender will hold that check and not cash it for one or two weeks. In return they will give you an amount of cash that is less than the written amount of your check. Sometimes, the lender will charge another fee on top of the interest.

At the end of the two weeks, you must either pay back the full amount of the check (more than what the lender gave you), or the lender will cash the check. Often, the lender will try to get you to write another check in a larger amount and give you little or no cash back. In this way, the lender gets more money from you and you get further in debt.

The difference between the amount of your check and the amount of cash you get in return is interest that the lender is charging you.

For example:

- You write a

    $256.00 check
    - $200.00 loan you get back

    = $56.00 interest you pay (730% on an annual basis)

Compare this to annual interest rates as low as 10–15% that banks and finance companies charge.

Pawnbrokers

Pawnbrokers are companies that allow you to trade something of value such as jewelry, a stereo, or even your car, in exchange for cash. Usually, a pawnbroker will lend less than one-half of the value of your property. You must pay back the loan within a certain period of time or the pawnbroker can sell your property and keep the money. Since you are charged fees, and only receive at most half of the value of your property in cash, you may be paying up to 200% interest per year.

Pawning Your Car Title

Some pawnbrokers will allow you to keep the use of your car but take the paper that is your title to the car. In exchange you will get cash; but, again, no more than one half of the car's value. If you do not repay the loan, the pawnbroker will find your car, take it, and sell it. If you can make all the installment repayments, the pawnbroker still makes quite a profit off you.

For example:

- You give your car title ($1,000 value) - $500 loan you get back

- You pay weekly installments of $103.30 for 10 weeks

- $103.30 x 10 weeks = $1,033

> $1,033.00 you pay
> - $500.00 you get
> _____
> = $533.00 interest you pay (830% on an annual basis)

Renting a TV, Stereo, Furniture, or Appliances

When you go to a store and rent these items instead of buying them, you will often pay at least three or four times what it would cost to buy them.

For example:

- You rent a 19-inch color TV ($300 value)

- You pay $16/week x 52 weeks = $832

> $832.00 you pay
> - $300.00 value of the TV you get
> _____
> = $532.00 interest you pay (254% an on annual basis)

Sometimes the rent-to-own company will rent you a used TV and tell you it was new. Then, they make even more money from you. And if you miss a payment, the company may repossess the TV, leaving you nothing to show for all the payments you made.

Abuses by Some Small Loan Lenders

- Some lenders charge very high interest rates.

- Most lenders will also add fees to the cost of the loan and try to sell you insurance. These extras make the loan even more profitable for the lender and more costly for you.

- Some lenders make it hard for you to figure out how much the loan is really going to cost.

- Some will encourage you to borrow from them over and over again so that they can make more money at your expense.

What You Can Do To Avoid Problems

- **Save now for unexpected expenses:** Even putting aside a small amount each week will help: Try to save your money before there is an unexpected expense so that you can avoid borrowing. You can talk with budget counselors who can help you understand how you spend your money each month and how you might save.

- **Shop around:** Do not look just at the monthly payment. Compare the interest rate (also called the "annual percentage rate"), the total amount you will repay, the number of payments, and the amount of fees added on to the loan.

- **Read before you sign:** Make sure you or someone you trust reads the loan papers before you sign them. If the lender will not let you take them home to study them and tries to rush you, walk away. That is a sign of trouble.

- **Consider alternative credit:** If you open an account at a credit union (which is like a bank and is backed by the federal government), you can get a small loan at interest rates of 10–20% instead of the 254–830% (for pawnbrokers and rent-to-own stores) or 730% (for the payday loan).

If you need a loan to start up a small business, there may be a non-profit organization in your area that can help.

Where Else to Go for Help?

If you borrowed money from a high-cost lenders and want to know your rights, you may be able to get free assistance from your local legal aid office.

Section 38.4

The Truth about Advance-Fee Loan Scams

Federal Trade Commission (www.ftc.gov), May 2005.

Advance-fee loan sharks are preying on unwary consumers, taking their money for the promise of a loan or credit, and leaving them in hot water. The scam artists often impersonate legitimate lenders to entice consumers into falling for their bogus offer.

According to law enforcement agencies in the U.S. and Canada, ads and promotions for advance-fee loans suggest—or even "guarantee"—that there's a high likelihood that a loan will be approved, regardless of the applicant's credit history. But to take advantage of the offer, the consumer has to pay a fee. The catch? The scam artist takes off with your fee, and the loan never materializes.

Many advance-fee loans are promoted in the classified sections of daily and weekly newspapers and magazines. Often, the ads feature toll-free 800, 866, or 877 numbers, or area codes from Canada, such as 416, 647, 905, or 705. The loans also are promoted through direct mail, radio, and cable TV spots. The fact that an ad is in a legitimate media outlet—like the local newspaper or radio station—doesn't guarantee that the company placing it is trustworthy.

Legitimate offers of credit do not require an up-front payment. Although legitimate lenders may charge application, appraisal, or credit report fees, the fees generally are taken from the amount borrowed. And the fees usually are paid to the lender or broker after the loan is approved. Legitimate lenders may guarantee firm offers of credit to "credit-worthy" consumers, but first, they evaluate the consumer's creditworthiness and confirm the information in the application. Canadian law enforcers caution that it is highly unlikely that legitimate Canadian lenders would take a risk on U.S. citizens whose credit problems preclude them from getting a loan in the U.S.

Often, advance-fee loan sharks claim that their fees will go to a third party for credit insurance or a related service. Sometimes, they even fax materials using stolen or forged logos and letterheads from legitimate companies. The materials are fakes, according to enforcement officials, and the contracts the scam artists ask consumers to sign are worthless. Adding insult to injury, some scammers have used the information they collect from consumers to commit identity theft.

Often, advance-fee loan scammers direct applicants to send the fees via Western Union money transfers payable to an individual, rather than a business. They ask applicants to use a "password code" with their Western Union payment, which allows the scammers to hide their identity.

U.S. and Canadian law enforcers say consumers can avoid being taken by advance-fee loan sharks. Here's how:

- Don't pay for the promise of a loan. It's illegal for companies doing business by phone in the U.S. to promise you a loan and ask you to pay for it before they deliver. Requiring advance fees for loans also is illegal in Canada.

- Ignore any ad—or hang up on any caller—that guarantees a loan in exchange for a fee in advance.

- Remember that legitimate lenders never guarantee or say that you will receive a loan before you apply, or before they have checked out your credit status or contacted your references, especially if you have bad credit or no credit record.

- Don't give your credit card, bank account, or Social Security number on the telephone, by fax, or via the internet unless you are familiar with the company and know why the information is necessary.

- Don't make a payment to an individual for a loan; no legitimate lending organization would make such a request.

- Don't wire money or send money orders for a loan through Western Union or similar companies. You have little recourse if there's a problem with a wire transaction. Legitimate lenders don't pressure you to wire funds.

- If you are not absolutely sure who you are dealing with, get the company's number in the phone book or from directory assistance, and call it to make sure you're dealing with the company you think you are. Some scam artists have pretended to be the Better Business Bureau or another legitimate organization.

- Check out questionable ads by calling Project Phonebusters in Canada toll-free at 888-495-8501. If you live in the U.S. and think you've been a victim of an advance-fee loan scam, report it to the FTC online at www.ftc.gov or by phone, toll-free, at 877-FTC-HELP (877-382-4357).

Finding Low-Cost Help for Credit Problems

It's a good idea to try to solve your debt problems with your creditors as soon as you realize you won't be able to make your payments. If you can't resolve your credit problems yourself or need additional help, you may want to contact a credit counseling service. There are nonprofit organizations in every state that counsel and educate individuals and families on debt problems, budgeting and using credit wisely. There is little or no cost for these services. Universities, military bases, credit unions, and housing authorities also may offer low- or no-cost credit counseling programs. Check the white pages of your telephone directory for a service near you.

The Toronto Strategic Partnership is a group of law enforcement agencies in the U.S. and Canada that works together to prosecute cross border fraud. Formal members include the Toronto Police Service, the Competition Bureau Canada, the Ontario Ministry of Consumer and Business Services, the Ontario Provincial Police, the U.S. Federal Trade Commission and the U.S. Postal Inspection Service. Other partners include the Ohio Attorney General's Office, the Royal Canadian Mounted Police, and the Police Services of York, Durham and Peel in Ontario.

The FTC works for the consumer to prevent fraudulent, deceptive and unfair business practices in the marketplace and to provide information to help consumers spot, stop, and avoid them. To file a complaint or to get free information on consumer issues, visit http://www.ftc.gov/ or call toll-free, 877-FTC-HELP (877-382-4357); TTY: 866-653-4261. The FTC enters internet, telemarketing, identity theft, and other fraud-related complaints into Consumer Sentinel, a secure, online database available to hundreds of civil and criminal law enforcement agencies in the U.S. and abroad.

Chapter 39

What to Consider before You Buy Credit Insurance

Credit Protection: What to Consider Before You Buy

Lenders offer insurance or similar products that would make your loan payments if you die or become ill or unemployed, but there are costs and limitations. Here's a guide for evaluating this coverage.

Think about the last time you applied for a new loan or a credit card. Did the lender ask if you'd like to buy something called "credit insurance" or a similar credit protection product that would make your loan payments if you die, become ill, or unemployed? And after you got the loan or credit card, did your lender continue to offer credit protection programs in mail solicitations or telemarketing calls? Chances are you answered "yes" to these questions. But it's also likely that you have your own questions, such as: Do I really need this insurance? And, how can I tell if this coverage is a good deal?

The Federal Deposit Insurance Corporation (FDIC) wants to help you answer these questions. Why? Because applying for a loan, particularly on a major purchase such as a home or a car, can be confusing for many consumers. And it's possible that many consumers may buy optional credit protection without evaluating whether they need it, how much it will cost, or if they can get a better deal elsewhere. FDIC also reports hearing about instances in which some consumers

This chapter includes "Credit Protection: What to Consider before You Buy," *FDIC Consumer News*, Federal Deposit Insurance Corporation (FDIC), Summer 2003, and excerpts from "Credit Insurance: Is It for You?" Federal Trade Commission (www.ftc.gov), November 2002.

have fallen prey to high-pressure sales pitches or purchased high-cost credit protection that they really didn't need or understand.

"We're all prone to focus on the benefits of an offer, written in bold, without evaluating the conditions and exclusions," says Deirdre Foley, an FDIC senior policy analyst. "You should review your financial situation and weigh the costs and benefits before deciding if this type of coverage makes sense for you."

Here's an overview of what credit protection is and what you need to know to protect yourself from high-cost or unnecessary coverage.

Credit Insurance, Debt Cancellation, and Debt Suspension Programs

Credit insurance is offered with certain kinds of financing, such as some home loans, credit cards, and loans offered by department stores or auto dealers. In general, credit insurance is a type of life, accident, health, disability, or unemployment insurance that will pay off a debt if the borrower dies or make monthly payments if the borrower becomes ill, injured, or unemployed.

For the most part, each state government regulates credit insurance sales in that state, and the insurance department enforces the state laws and regulations governing pricing, disclosures to buyers, minimum insurance benefits, and other consumer protections.

Moreover, most types of credit insurance are voluntary. An important exception is property or hazard insurance. A creditor may require that you maintain this kind of insurance to cover the costs of repairing or replacing property (such as your home or auto) that serves as collateral for a loan. And in those instances in which insurance is required, a bank cannot condition approval of the loan on the purchase of insurance from the bank or an affiliate.

In addition, some depository institutions (such as banks and credit unions) sell "debt cancellation" and "debt suspension" programs under various names. In general, debt cancellation eliminates the debt if the borrower dies or cancels the monthly payment if the borrower becomes disabled, unemployed, or suffers some other specified hardship. Debt suspension is different. It temporarily postpones all or part of the monthly payment while the borrower is facing a specified hardship—the borrower is still expected to make the suspended payments in the future. These programs are similar to credit insurance products in terms of their function, but fees and other features may be significantly different. Debt protection programs are offered by depository institutions directly, not by insurance companies. These programs are subject to regulation by the appropriate federal or state depository institutions supervisor.

The Pros and Cons

Credit protection products may provide borrowers peace of mind and security and can be a good deal for certain consumers. Providers of credit protection also advertise the product as "easy to buy" because, unlike traditional life or disability insurance, it often does not require a physical examination, premiums are the same regardless of your age or health, and coverage can be purchased in small dollar amounts. Credit protection programs may be the best or only coverage for some older consumers, people who smoke or are ill, or workers concerned about making loan payments if they lose their job.

Also, other types of life and disability insurance may carry higher minimum-coverage amounts than those for credit insurance, which is based on the size of the consumer's debt. This means, for example, that instead of buying a traditional life insurance policy for $50,000, a consumer would obtain credit insurance based on the loan balance, which may be much less.

However, despite these benefits, credit insurance and debt cancellation, or debt suspension programs typically cost far more than a comparable term life insurance policy (which provides protection for a specified period) and perhaps other insurance not sold with a loan. These credit protection programs also can only be used for one purpose—to repay a specific debt.

Let's say you buy credit insurance or debt cancellation/suspension coverage to pay off a credit card debt if you become sick or die, and you consistently carry a card balance of $4,000. Various sources indicate that you'd likely pay between $150 and $350 a year for credit protection. For that money, you might be able to buy a much larger term life insurance policy or add to your emergency savings, both of which could be used to pay off any obligations, not just the credit card debt.

Other restrictions, limitations, or costs may apply to the various credit protection programs. Here are some examples:

- Some debt cancellation programs limit death benefits only to accidental death—a relatively infrequent occurrence compared to death because of illness, disease, or natural causes. In contrast, credit insurance providing a death benefit is rarely limited to accidental death.

- The typical credit insurance policy covering disability or unemployment will make the borrower's monthly payment on a loan during the benefit period. In contrast, a debt suspension program only puts loan payments on hold.

- If you become ill or unemployed and you apply for benefits under a debt suspension program for a credit card or a home equity
  loan, the contract probably will indicate that you cannot continue
  using the card or equity loan. "If you're unaware of this restriction,
  you may be cutting off an important source of emergency cash
  just when you need it the most," according to April Breslaw,
  Chief of the FDIC's Compliance Examination Support Section.

- Some creditors offer single-premium credit insurance, which
  means that the premium is paid in a lump sum up front instead
  of monthly or annually. The one-time payment typically is so
  large that consumers add the fee to their loan amount and then
  must pay interest on it each month. This adds significantly to
  the monthly loan payment and the overall cost of the loan. Moreover, even though the premium may be added to the loan balance and paid for 15 to 30 years, it's possible that the insurance
  may only cover the first five to ten years of the loan.

How to Protect Yourself

Here are a few steps you can take to evaluate credit protection
plans and decide what's best for you.

Remember that most credit protection is optional: If you are
asked to purchase credit protection before your loan closes, find out
whether your lender requires that you purchase it, and why. Don't assume that credit protection is required. When in doubt, contact the
appropriate state or federal regulator for more information. If you obtain optional credit protection and later decide you don't want it, you
may have a right to cancel the coverage and obtain a refund for up-
front payments.

**Evaluate your family's insurance costs, coverage, and needs
annually:** You could be under-insured in certain areas or over-insured
in others. Talk with your insurance agent or financial adviser about
your situation, including any questions about credit protection. You
may, for example, have enough savings to cover your minimum loan
payments due, the amount generally covered by these programs, if you
become sick or unemployed.

Consider traditional insurance: Before purchasing a credit protection product, consider if you already have, or would be better off with,
traditional insurance. For many people, especially those in good health,

they probably can get traditional insurance that can meet their needs at a more reasonable price than a credit protection plan. But for some people, especially those who are elderly, have a serious health problem, or are concerned about making loan payments if they lose their job, credit protection may be the best or only coverage they can obtain.

If you're considering a credit protection program, understand what is covered, what isn't, and whether the costs and restrictions outweigh the benefits. For example, remember that credit insurance and debt cancellation programs only apply to a specific debt. In many situations, you and your family might be better served with the proceeds from a traditional insurance policy that can be used to pay off any debts and expenses as you see fit, not just that one loan.

"Consumers who do not read the terms and conditions of these programs may be unaware of the limitations and as a result, they might pay more for less coverage than they expect," cautions Tim Burniston, FDIC Associate Director for Compliance Policy and Examination Support.

Keep an eye on fees: Pay attention to loan documents and monthly statements from your lender and question any unusual charges or fees. For example, if you fail to maintain the required property or hazard insurance coverage or you forget to give the lender evidence of your coverage, the creditor typically reserves the right to purchase the insurance and charge you for it, perhaps as part of your loan payment. If you're not monitoring your payments, you could be paying for a property insurance policy purchased by the lender that is more expensive and more limited than what you could obtain by shopping around.

Try to resolve problems as soon as possible: First contact the creditor or insurance company. If you're not satisfied with the outcome, contact your state insurance commissioner or, in the case of a debt cancellation/suspension contract, the appropriate federal or state regulator. Also, retain copies of your loan documents and related credit protection policies, terms and conditions. You may need to refer to this information if you have a question, a concern, or an insurance claim.

If You Decide to Buy Credit Insurance

Before deciding to buy credit insurance from a lender, think about your needs, your options, and the rates you're going to pay. You may decide you don't need credit insurance. If you do, credit insurance can be an expensive form of insurance. For example, it may be less expensive and more practical for you to get life insurance than credit insurance. Before deciding to buy credit insurance, you should ask these questions:

- How much is the premium?
- Will the premium be financed as part of the loan? If so, it will increase your loan amount and you'll pay additional interest and more for points (if points are on your loan).
- Can you pay monthly instead of financing the entire premium as part of your loan?
- How much lower would your monthly loan payment be without the credit insurance?
- Will the insurance cover the full length of your loan and the full loan amount?
- What are the limits and exclusions on payment of benefits? Spell out exactly what's covered and what's not.
- Is there a waiting period before the coverage becomes effective?
- If you have a co-borrower, what coverage does he or she have and at what cost?
- Can you cancel the insurance? If so, what kind of refund is available?

Before you sign any loan papers, ask the lender whether the loan includes any charges for voluntary credit insurance. If you don't want credit insurance, tell the lender. If the lender still pressures you to buy insurance, find another lender. And review your loan papers carefully to be sure they have been drawn up correctly. Lenders can't deny you credit if you don't buy optional credit insurance—and if you don't buy it directly from them. If a lender tells you that you'll only get the loan if you buy the optional credit insurance, report the lender to your state attorney general, your state insurance commissioner or the Federal Trade Commission (FTC). Consumers should ask these same questions about other extra products offered with their loan, such as auto or shopping clubs, home or auto security plans, and debt cancellation products.

Chapter 40

Laws that Protect Loan Recipients

The Credit Practices Rule

If you are one of the millions of Americans who borrows money, buys items on installment credit, or cosigns for another person's debt, you may want to know about the Federal Trade Commission's Credit Practices Rule. The Rule, which became effective March 1, 1985, prohibits many creditors from including certain provisions in consumer credit contracts. It also requires creditors to provide a written notice to consumers before they cosign obligations for others about their potential liability if the other person fails to pay. Finally, it prohibits one method of assessing late charges.

What contracts are covered?

The Rule applies to consumer credit contracts offered by finance companies, retailers (such as auto dealers and furniture and department stores), and credit unions for any personal purpose except to buy real estate. It does not apply to banks or bank credit cards; to savings and loan associations; or to some non-profit organizations.

This chapter includes text from "The Credit Practices Rule," Federal Trade Commission (www.ftc.gov), November 1992; reviewed for currency in February 2006. "Credit Protection Laws," is from "Credit Protection and the Laws Protecting You," *FDIC Consumer News*, Federal Deposit Insurance Corporation (FDIC), Summer 2003.

(However, similar rules for banks—under the Federal Reserve Board—and for savings and loans—under the Office of Thrift Supervision—went into effect January 1, 1986.) The Rule does not apply to business credit.

What contract provisions are prohibited?

The Rule prohibits creditors from including certain provisions in their consumer credit contracts. Specifically, credit contracts no longer can include these provisions:

- Require you to agree in advance, should the creditor sue you for non-payment of a debt, to give up your right to be notified of a court hearing to present your side of the case or to hire an attorney to represent you. (These clauses were often called "confessions of judgment" or "cognovits.")

- Require you to give up your state-law protections that allow you to keep certain personal belongings even if you do not pay your debt as agreed. (These clauses were called "waivers of exemption.") State law generally allows you to keep your home, clothing, dishes, and other belongings of a fixed minimum value. However, when the debt incurred is to purchase an item and that item is used as security for the debt, it is permissible under the Rule for a creditor to repossess that item.

- Permit you to agree in advance to wage deductions that would pay the creditor directly if you default on the debt, unless you can cancel that permission at any time. (These clauses were called "wage assignments.") However, a wage or payroll deduction plan, through which you arrange to repay a loan, is a common payment method and is permissible under the Rule.

- Require you to use as collateral certain household and uniquely personal items that are of significant value to you but are of little economic value to a creditor. Such items include appliances, linens, china, crockery, kitchenware, wedding rings, family photographs, personal papers, the family Bible, and household pets. (These were called "household goods security" clauses.) However, if you borrowed money to buy any of these household or personal items, and use the items as collateral, the creditor can repossess the purchased item if you do not repay the loan.

450

What notices must be given to cosigners?

When you agree to be a cosigner for someone else's debt, you are guaranteeing to pay if that person fails to pay the debt. The Rule requires that you be given a notice that explains the responsibility you are undertaking. Under the Rule, the cosigner notice must say:

- You are being asked to guarantee this debt. Think carefully before you do. If the borrower doesn't pay the debt, you will have to. Be sure you can afford to pay if you have to, and that you want to accept this responsibility.

- You may have to pay up to the full amount of the debt if the borrower does not pay. You may also have to pay late fees or collection costs, which increase this amount.

- The creditor can collect this debt from you without first trying to collect from the borrower. Depending on your state, this may not apply. If state law forbids a creditor from collecting from a cosigner without first trying to collect from the primary debtor, this sentence may be crossed out or omitted on your cosigner notice. The creditor can use the same collection methods against you that can be used against the borrower, such as suing you, or garnishing your wages. If this debt is ever in default, that fact may become a part of your credit record.

- This notice is not the contract that makes you liable for the debt.

This notice is not required when you receive benefits from the contract, such as when you buy goods, take out a loan, or open a joint credit-card account with another person. In these cases, you would be a co-buyer, co-borrower, or co-applicant (co-cardholder) rather than a cosigner. Therefore, the creditor would not be required to provide the notice.

How can late charges be assessed?

A creditor can charge a late fee if you do not make your loan payment on time. However, it is illegal under the Rule for a creditor to charge you late fees or payments simply because you have not yet paid a late fee you owe. This practice is called "pyramiding late fees." Under the Rule, this means that if you do not include the late fee you owe with your next regular payment, it is illegal for a creditor to subtract the late fee from your payment and then charge you a second

451

late fee because the current payment is insufficient. For example, your loan contract may state that your monthly payments are $100 and that you will be assessed a $10 late fee if you pay after the grace period. If you make your $100 loan payment after that time and you do not include the $10 late fee with your next $100 payment, a creditor cannot first deduct the missing $10 late fee from the $100 payment, claim you have now paid $90, and then charge you an additional late fee. But, if you skip one month's payment entirely, the creditor can charge late fees on all subsequent payments until you bring your account up to date.

Credit Protection Laws

Your state is likely to have laws governing credit insurance and debt protection coverage. These laws may cover premiums, rates, and the insurance claims process.

The federal Bank Holding Company Act prohibits a banking institution from tying the approval of a loan to the purchase of credit insurance from the bank or an affiliate. Federal regulations governing debt cancellation/suspension programs contain similar prohibitions.

The federal Truth in Lending Act (TILA) requires that lenders disclose the terms and costs of a loan. Depending on the specific circumstances, the TILA says that the terms and costs of voluntary credit insurance (such as credit life or disability insurance) and property or hazard insurance (often required) must be disclosed by the creditor before a loan is consummated.

The Gramm-Leach-Bliley Act prohibits depository institutions and their insurance sales representatives from engaging in coercive or misleading practices. The law also requires certain advertising and disclosure requirements. For example, a bank or a company selling insurance for the bank must disclose that its insurance products are not insured by the FDIC against loss.

The Real Estate Settlement Procedures Act helps consumers understand the costs of a mortgage transaction and be "smarter" shoppers for services. For example, when someone applies for a mortgage, the lender or loan broker must provide a "good faith estimate" of the individual costs to be paid at the loan settlement, in part so that the borrower can compare the estimate to the actual charges imposed. The law also ensures that certain payments are properly handled from escrow accounts, such as those for homeowner's insurance.

Part Five

When Debt Is a Problem

Chapter 41

When You're Knee Deep in Debt

Having trouble paying your bills? Getting dunning notices from creditors? Are your accounts being turned over to debt collectors? Are you worried about losing your home or your car?

You're not alone. Many people face a financial crisis some time in their lives. Whether the crisis is caused by personal or family illness, the loss of a job, or overspending, it can seem overwhelming. But often, it can be overcome. Your financial situation doesn't have to go from bad to worse.

If you or someone you know is in financial hot water, consider these options: realistic budgeting, credit counseling from a reputable organization, debt consolidation, or bankruptcy. Debt negotiation is yet another option. How do you know which will work best for you? It depends on your level of debt, your level of discipline, and your prospects for the future.

Self-Help

Developing a budget: The first step toward taking control of your financial situation is to do a realistic assessment of how much money you take in and how much money you spend. Start by listing your income from all sources. Then, list your "fixed" expenses—those that are the same each month—like mortgage payments or rent, car payments, and insurance premiums. Next, list the expenses

"Knee Deep in Debt," Federal Trade Commission (www.ftc.gov), December 2005.

that vary—like entertainment, recreation, and clothing. Writing down all your expenses, even those that seem insignificant, is a helpful way to track your spending patterns, identify necessary expenses, and prioritize the rest. The goal is to make sure you can make ends meet on the basics: housing, food, health care, insurance, and education.

Your public library and bookstores have information about budgeting and money management techniques. In addition, computer software programs can be useful tools for developing and maintaining a budget, balancing your checkbook, and creating plans to save money and pay down your debt.

Contacting your creditors: Contact your creditors immediately if you're having trouble making ends meet. Tell them why it's difficult for you, and try to work out a modified payment plan that reduces your payments to a more manageable level. Don't wait until your accounts have been turned over to a debt collector. At that point, your creditors have given up on you.

Dealing with debt collectors: The Fair Debt Collection Practices Act is the federal law that dictates how and when a debt collector may contact you. A debt collector may not call you before 8 a.m., after 9 p.m., or while you're at work if the collector knows that your employer doesn't approve of the calls. Collectors may not harass you, lie, or use unfair practices when they try to collect a debt. And they must honor a written request from you to stop further contact.

Managing your auto and home loans: Your debts can be unsecured or secured. Secured debts usually are tied to an asset, like your car for a car loan, or your house for a mortgage. If you stop making payments, lenders can repossess your car or foreclose on your house. Unsecured debts are not tied to any asset, and include most credit card debt, bills for medical care, signature loans, and debts for other types of services.

Most automobile financing agreements allow a creditor to repossess your car any time you're in default. No notice is required. If your car is repossessed, you may have to pay the balance due on the loan, as well as towing and storage costs, to get it back. If you can't do this, the creditor may sell the car. If you see default approaching, you may be better off selling the car yourself and paying off the debt: you'll avoid the added costs of repossession and a negative entry on your credit report.

If you fall behind on your mortgage, contact your lender immediately to avoid foreclosure. Most lenders are willing to work with you if they believe you're acting in good faith and the situation is temporary. Some lenders may reduce or suspend your payments for a short time. When you resume regular payments, though, you may have to pay an additional amount toward the past due total. Other lenders may agree to change the terms of the mortgage by extending the repayment period to reduce the monthly debt. Ask whether additional fees would be assessed for these changes, and calculate how much they total in the long term.

If you and your lender cannot work out a plan, contact a housing counseling agency. Some agencies limit their counseling services to homeowners with FHA (Federal Housing Administration) mortgages, but many offer free help to any homeowner who's having trouble making mortgage payments. Call the local office of the Department of Housing and Urban Development or the housing authority in your state, city, or county for help in finding a legitimate housing counseling agency near you.

Credit Counseling and Debt Management Plans

Credit counseling: If you're not disciplined enough to create a workable budget and stick to it, can't work out a repayment plan with your creditors, or can't keep track of mounting bills, consider contacting a credit counseling organization. Many credit counseling organizations are nonprofit and work with you to solve your financial problems. But be aware that, just because an organization says it's "nonprofit," there's no guarantee that its services are free, affordable, or even legitimate. In fact, some credit counseling organizations charge high fees, which may be hidden, or urge consumers to make "voluntary" contributions that can cause more debt.

Most credit counselors offer services through local offices, the internet, or on the telephone. If possible, find an organization that offers in-person counseling. Many universities, military bases, credit unions, housing authorities, and branches of the U.S. Cooperative Extension Service operate nonprofit credit counseling programs. Your financial institution, local consumer protection agency, and friends and family also may be good sources of information and referrals.

Reputable credit counseling organizations can advise you on managing your money and debts, help you develop a budget, and offer free educational materials and workshops. Their counselors are certified and trained in the areas of consumer credit, money and debt management,

457

and budgeting. Counselors discuss your entire financial situation with you, and help you develop a personalized plan to solve your money problems. An initial counseling session typically lasts an hour, with an offer of follow-up sessions.

Debt management plans: If your financial problems stem from too much debt or your inability to repay your debts, a credit counseling agency may recommend that you enroll in a debt management plan (DMP). A DMP alone is not credit counseling, and DMPs are not for everyone. You should sign up for one of these plans only after a certified credit counselor has spent time thoroughly reviewing your financial situation, and has offered you customized advice on managing your money. Even if a DMP is appropriate for you, a reputable credit counseling organization still can help you create a budget and teach you money management skills.

In a DMP, you deposit money each month with the credit counseling organization, which uses your deposits to pay your unsecured debts, like your credit card bills, student loans, and medical bills, according to a payment schedule the counselor develops with you and your creditors. Your creditors may agree to lower your interest rates or waive certain fees, but check with all your creditors to be sure they offer the concessions that a credit counseling organization describes to you. A successful DMP requires you to make regular, timely payments, and could take 48 months or more to complete. Ask the credit counselor to estimate how long it will take for you to complete the plan. You may have to agree not to apply for—or use—any additional credit while you're participating in the plan.

Protect Yourself

Be wary of credit counseling organizations that exhibit the following warning signs:

- Charge high up-front or monthly fees for enrolling in credit counseling or a DMP

- Pressure you to make "voluntary contributions," another name for fees

- Won't send you free information about the services they provide without requiring you to provide personal financial information, such as credit card account numbers, and balances

- Try to enroll you in a DMP without spending time reviewing your financial situation

- Offer to enroll you in a DMP without teaching you budgeting and money management skills

- Demand that you make payments into a DMP before your creditors have accepted you into the program

Debt Consolidation

You may be able to lower your cost of credit by consolidating your debt through a second mortgage or a home equity line of credit. Remember that these loans require you to put up your home as collateral. If you can't make the payments—or if your payments are late—you could lose your home.

What's more, the costs of consolidation loans can add up. In addition to interest on the loans, you may have to pay "points," with one point equal to one percent of the amount you borrow. Still, these loans may provide certain tax advantages that are not available with other kinds of credit.

Bankruptcy

Personal bankruptcy generally is considered the debt management option of last resort because the results are long-lasting and far reaching. People who follow the bankruptcy rules receive a discharge—a court order that says they don't have to repay certain debts. However, bankruptcy information (both the date of your filing and the later date of discharge) stay on your credit report for 10 years, and can make it difficult to obtain credit, buy a home, get life insurance, or sometimes get a job. Still, bankruptcy is a legal procedure that offers a fresh start for people who have gotten into financial difficulty and can't satisfy their debts.

There are two primary types of personal bankruptcy: Chapter 13 and Chapter 7. Each must be filed in federal bankruptcy court. As of April 2006, the filing fees run about $274 for Chapter 13 and $299 for Chapter 7. Attorney fees are additional and can vary.

Effective October 2005, Congress made sweeping changes to the bankruptcy laws. The net effect of these changes is to give consumers more incentive to seek bankruptcy relief under Chapter 13 rather than Chapter 7. Chapter 13 allows people with a steady income to keep property, like a mortgaged house or a car, that they might otherwise lose through the bankruptcy process. In Chapter 13, the court approves a repayment plan that allows you to use your future income to pay off your debts during a three-to-five-year period, rather than surrender any property. After you have made all the payments under the plan, you receive a discharge of your debts.

Chapter 7 is known as straight bankruptcy, and involves liquidation of all assets that are not exempt. Exempt property may include automobiles, work-related tools, and basic household furnishings. Some of your property may be sold by a court-appointed official—a trustee—or turned over to your creditors. The new bankruptcy laws have changed the time period during which you can receive a discharge through Chapter 7. You now must wait eight years after receiving a discharge in Chapter 7 before you can file again under that chapter. The Chapter 13 waiting period is much shorter and can be as little as two years between filings.

Both types of bankruptcy may get rid of unsecured debts and stop foreclosures, repossessions, garnishments and utility shut-offs, and debt collection activities. Both also provide exemptions that allow people to keep certain assets, although exemption amounts vary by state. Note that personal bankruptcy usually does not erase child support, alimony, fines, taxes, and some student loan obligations. And, unless you have an acceptable plan to catch up on your debt under Chapter 13, bankruptcy usually does not allow you to keep property when your creditor has an unpaid mortgage or security lien on it.

Another major change to the bankruptcy laws involves certain hurdles that a consumer must clear before even filing for bankruptcy, no matter what the chapter. You must get credit counseling from a government-approved organization within six months before you file for any bankruptcy relief. You can find a state-by-state list of government-approved organizations at www.usdoj.gov/ust. That is the website of the U.S. Trustee Program, the organization within the U.S. Department of Justice that supervises bankruptcy cases and trustees. Also, before you file a Chapter 7 bankruptcy case, you must satisfy a "means test." This test requires you to confirm that your income does not exceed a certain amount. The amount varies by state and is publicized by the U.S. Trustee Program at www.usdoj.gov/ust.

Debt Negotiation Programs

Debt negotiation differs greatly from credit counseling and DMPs. It can be very risky, and have a long term negative impact on your credit report and, in turn, your ability to get credit. See Chapter 44— Choosing a Credit Counselor or Debt Management Plan for more information about the potential pitfalls of these types of programs or contact your state Attorney General.

Damage Control

Turning to a business that offers help in solving debt problems may seem like a reasonable solution when your bills become unmanageable. But before you do business with any company, check it out with your state Attorney General, local consumer protection agency, and the Better Business Bureau. They can tell you if any consumer complaints are on file about the firm you're considering doing business with. Ask your state Attorney General if the company is required to be licensed to work in your state and, if so, whether it is.

Some businesses that offer to help you with your debt problems may charge high fees and fail to follow through on the services they sell. Others may misrepresent the terms of a debt consolidation loan, failing to explain certain costs or mention that you're signing over your home as collateral. Businesses advertising voluntary debt reorganization plans may not explain that the plan is a bankruptcy filing, tell you everything that's involved, or help you through what can be a long and complex process.

In addition, some companies guarantee you a loan if you pay a fee in advance. The fee may range from $100 to several hundred dollars. Resist the temptation to follow up on these advance-fee loan guarantees. They may be illegal. It is true that many legitimate creditors offer extensions of credit through telemarketing and require an application or appraisal fee in advance. But legitimate creditors never guarantee that the consumer will get the loan—or even represent that a loan is likely. Under the federal Telemarketing Sales Rule, a seller or telemarketer who guarantees or represents a high likelihood of your getting a loan or some other extension of credit may not ask for or accept payment until you've received the loan.

You should be cautious of claims from so-called credit repair clinics. Many companies appeal to consumers with poor credit histories, promising to clean up credit reports for a fee. But you already have the right to have any inaccurate information in your file corrected. And a credit repair clinic cannot have accurate information removed from your credit report, despite their promises. You also should know that federal and some state laws prohibit these companies from charging you for their services until the services are fully performed. Only time and a conscientious effort to repay your debts will improve your credit report.

If you're thinking about getting help to stabilize your financial situation, do some homework first. Find out what services a business provides and what it costs, and don't rely on verbal promises. Get everything in writing, and read your contracts carefully.

461

Chapter 42

Adjusting to Suddenly Reduced Income

Adjusting to a sudden income loss in your family involves thinking about more than just dollars and cents. You have many attitudes, values, and feelings about money from your childhood and family upbringing. Many of these are so deeply a part of your everyday life that you don't even realize how those feelings affect your money decisions or your reactions to money decisions of other family members.

Everyone experiences changes in life. Sometimes you plan for it and sometimes things happen over which you have little control. When the latter happens, you are facing an unplanned change. Unplanned income changes can result from unexpected job loss or loss to your home or business by forces of nature such as tornadoes, floods, and drought. Market changes in commodities or stocks, or major expenses resulting from an illness, equipment breakdown, burglary, or accident can also cause such changes. Unlike a planned change, it is much more difficult to make adjustments for unplanned income changes because the choice to change has been taken away from you.

This chapter will help you understand what happens in the first few months after an unplanned income loss as you deal with the overlapping emotional, economic, and social effect. A major decrease in income requires that all family members recognize the grief they feel over the loss (emotional effect), reassess how money will be used

"Adjusting to Suddenly Reduced Income," by Sharon M. Danes Ph.D. and Patricia Stumme M.S., University of Minnesota Extension Service. © 2002 Regents of the University of Minnesota. All rights reserved. Reprinted with permission.

within the family (economic effect), and make a conscious effort to manage the inevitable disagreement and potential conflict that might arise (social effect). Doing so will help you live with the consequences of the unplanned income change, develop new options, and move on.

The Importance of How You View the Situation

How you perceive or see a problem or situation affects how you deal with it. Two people can experience the same set of circumstances, but view them differently. For one person, a forced reduction in the number of hours he or she can work might seem devastating, but to the person who no longer has any job, the loss of hours does not seem so bad. How you view or perceive a situation will influence how you communicate, make decisions, and solve problems as you deal with it.

How much stress you experience in a situation depends on the intensity of meaning you have attached to it. You can change your interpretation of an event by reassessing your priorities. Studies on families who suffered major income loss show how they were able to adjust their perception of the situation. These families changed their priorities from "What we are losing is the most important part of our lives, to "Our family and our health are the most important parts of our lives." Sometimes you can limit your options or fail to consider possible solutions because of the way you see, define, or describe the problem.

Recognizing Grief Over the Loss of Income

When people experience a major income loss they go through certain stages of grief. People often move back and forth between the stages and sometimes get stuck at a particular stage for a while.

Stage 1—Shock and Denial

Shock and denial are the first reactions of people experiencing unplanned changes. At this stage in the loss cycle, it is normal for people to feel confused and afraid, and to want to place blame. However, many people are just numb when facing an unplanned change as if they were on automatic pilot. It is very common for people to avoid making decisions or taking action at this point. People are often unable to function or perform simple, routine tasks during this stage.

Denial can occasionally be healthy for a short time, but prolonged denial can have devastating consequences for the person and for the situation. Denial of something that has happened or of the pain and fear being experienced is a way in which people protect themselves when faced with a painful situation. Continued denial of the pain and fear, however, will block them from doing something about it.

Stage 2—Anger

Anger is a feeling that is often intensely felt during this time. Anger is identified by feelings of second-guessing, hate, self-doubt, embarrassment, irritation, shame, hurt, frustration, and anxiety. People usually understand more clearly what is happening, but they may look for someone to blame at this stage. If there is no one on whom to focus the anger or blame, a feeling of helplessness may take over and the anger may be turned inside. Some people take it out on themselves by taking responsibility for a situation over which they have had little control.

People are often afraid that if they let themselves acknowledge the anger they feel, they will immediately need to express it and act on it in a way that they will regret later. However, by not admitting to themselves and others close to them the loss and pain they feel, they will be blocked from doing something about the situation. It will also prevent them from moving on. Some people get stuck at this stage.

To express anger in a positive way, people need to change how they view the situation. It is also helpful to talk to others about it or write down their feelings in order to figure out what they need to do to make the feelings less intense. Another option is to turn the anger into energy through an active sport or brisk physical activity or to express it through playing a musical instrument.

Stage 3—Depression and Detachment

The third stage of the loss cycle, depression and detachment, is characterized by feelings of helplessness, hopelessness, and being overwhelmed. People often feel down, lack energy, and have no desire to do anything. Withdrawal from activities and other people is common. Because it is also hard to make decisions at this stage, ask a family member, friend, or professional to help you if important decisions need to be made.

Stage 4—Dialogue and Bargaining

The fourth stage, dialogue and bargaining, is a time when people struggle to find meaning in what has happened. They begin to reach out to others and want to tell their story. People become more willing to explore alternatives after expressing their feelings. They may, however, still be angry or depressed. People do not move neatly from one stage to another. Rather, the stages overlap and people often slip back to earlier stages.

Stage 5—Acceptance

At this stage, people are ready to explore and consider options. As the acceptance stage progresses, a new plan begins to take shape or, at the very least, people are open to new options.

Getting Back to "Normal"

A person's "normal" state of functioning becomes disrupted by a sudden income loss. It is possible to return to a purposeful state of functioning after going through the stages described above and after exploring options and setting a plan. People then begin to feel secure and in control and have a more positive self-esteem. People get renewed energy to tackle life again but in different ways than before the sudden income change. It is perhaps better to think of the end of the grief cycle as returning to a meaningful life rather than returning to a "normal" life. "Normal" at this stage will not be the same as "normal" before the loss.

Dealing with Your Feelings

People often deny the intense feelings associated with unplanned income changes. However, when feelings become overwhelming, it sometimes helps to understand how a feeling happens. A feeling can be experienced, expressed, or acted on.

When people experience feelings, they allow the feelings to surface, they own the feelings, and can begin to deal with them. For example, they begin to realize that they feel afraid, confused, silly, etc. Identifying the feeling is a key step in dealing with it constructively.

Expressing feelings involves getting them out, talking about them with someone else or writing them down. This relieves the person's mind almost as if a weight has been lifted. Now energy can go toward seeking options for resolving the circumstances of that feeling.

When people act on their feelings, they do so with others around them. People often assume that if they experience a feeling, it is necessary to either express it or act on it at the same time that they experience it. This way of approaching a feeling may not have a successful result and may hurt others in the process. Rather, there may be times when you only experience and express a feeling but wait until a more appropriate time to act on it. Feelings are neither good nor bad. It is what a person does with them that makes the difference.

Reassessing How the Money Will Be Used

Expectations about Change

Willingness to change occurs gradually and does not come at the same time for everyone. People tend to want to keep everything the same as it has always been. For some people change is so scary that they pretend that they don't need to make any changes and can continue to live as they always have.

Most people do not make immediate spending changes to compensate for an income loss. These changes usually take several months and often occur at crisis points. People who more quickly change their spending or consider different options are usually more satisfied with the adjustments they need to make. Some people take longer to get through the spending reduction steps because they get temporarily stuck in different stages of the grief cycle.

Examining Your Spending Patterns

The whole family needs to talk about the necessary spending changes, because these decisions affect all members.

It is important to take action quickly to adjust excess spending. The whole family, including children, needs to talk about the necessary spending changes, because these decisions affect all members. When children are not included in this planning and discussion, they may develop unrealistic fears. They may think that they are somehow bad or the cause of a problem that they sense, but that has been kept a secret from them. If family members understand and have a voice in the tough choices that must be made, they will be more willing to follow through on them. Family members can help each other stick to these decisions.

Management of money can be relaxed when money is plentiful. When money is scarce, however, careful management is necessary to get the most from the money you have. Members of the household need to develop or readjust a spending plan to make it easier to pay bills. If your family has not kept close tabs on its spending patterns, they will have to figure out how much they have been spending on various categories of expenses before completing Worksheet 1 (see Figure 42.1).

If your family has been keeping track, then you can go directly to Worksheet 1 to discuss how family expenses can be changed.

If you do not know where the money has been going, draw a calendar of the month on a piece of paper. Mark the due dates of fixed bills on the calendar. These bills are the same amount each month such as rent, mortgage, and loan payments. Then place the calendar in a

Worksheet 1. Monthly Spending Plan

Month_____ 20_____

	Before Income Was Reduced	Current Income
Step 1 -- Your Monthly Income (Take-home)*	$ _____	$ _____
Salary, wages	$ _____	$ _____
Unemployment compensation	$ _____	$ _____
Other	$ _____	$ _____
A. Total monthly income	$ _____	$ _____ (A)
Step 2 -- Monthly Expenses	$ _____	$ _____
Housing (mortgage or rent)	$ _____	$ _____
Utilities (electric, gas, phone, etc.)	$ _____	$ _____
Food (at home and away)	$ _____	$ _____
Transportation (gas, car repairs)	$ _____	$ _____
Medical care (doctor, dentist, hospital, prescriptions)	$ _____	$ _____
Credit payments (loans, credit cards)	$ _____	$ _____
Insurance (life, health, disability, car, property, house)	$ _____	$ _____
Household operations and maintenance (repairs, cleaning, laundry supplies, etc.)	$ _____	$ _____
Clothing and personal care (clothes, laundry, toiletries, etc.)	$ _____	$ _____
Education and recreation	$ _____	$ _____
Miscellaneous (childcare, gifts, allowances)	$ _____	$ _____
Funds set aside for seasonal and occasional expenses	$ _____	$ _____
B. Total monthly expenses	$ _____	$ _____ (B)

Step 3 -- Balance Income and Expenses

Total monthly income (A) $ _____ = $ _____ Total monthly expenses (B)

*Because most bills are monthly, it's easiest to look at income and expenses on a monthly basis. Multiply weekly income by 4.33 and bi-weekly income by 2.17 to convert them to monthly amounts.

***Figure 42.1.** Worksheet 1: Monthly spending plan.*

prominent place such as the refrigerator door. Each day write down the flexible expenses, those that vary from time to time, for things such as food or transportation. After a month, your family will have a feel for the flow of cash and can discuss how the expenses can be changed to adjust to the income loss.

You also need to take into account your credit card and other installment debts including the interest rate, balance due, and the payment due date. When your bills exceed the money to pay them, you will need to contact the people to whom you owe money, your creditors, and explain your situation. Creditors are more understanding if you do this early rather than waiting for them to send you late notices. Knowing your spending patterns is the first step in getting ready to talk to creditors. You will also need to take a hard look at your situation and make some decisions about how much and when you can pay them. Creditors are much more open to adjustments when you talk to them soon after an income loss and when you come well-prepared to discuss a readjustment plan.

Together, the family should go through the flexible expenses from Worksheet 1 or from the calendar. Talk about ways in which each family member can reduce spending. Get everyone to commit to the spending reduction plan. Ask these questions during this discussion:

- Can we substitute a less costly item?

- How can we conserve what we have and avoid waste?

- Are there opportunities to cooperate with others by trading or sharing what we can do or learn to do?

- Can we save if we do it ourselves?

- Can we do without or do it less often?

As the family talks about what is most important, be sure you are all listening to each other. True listening is not letting someone's words go in one ear and out the other as your mind is off thinking about something else. It is devoting your energies to what the person is saying. You may need to ask each person a question about what he or she said to clarify what you heard.

Setting Goals to Target Limited Money

When an income loss occurs, it is not only a time to reassess daily spending patterns, but a crucial time to rethink goals. People often create goals unconsciously, but at times of income loss it is important to discuss them with others who are affected. Doing so will focus the use of the reduced amount of money available during the next several months.

Goals reflect what is important to you and help you get what you need and want. They give direction and meaning to how you spend your money. They need to be specific. For example, rather than, "We are going to reduce our spending," a more specific goal would be, "Each of us will identify two ways we can reduce or stop spending for the next two to four months."

Discussions about goals need to involve all who will be affected. Reducing spending patterns is most effective if decisions are made together. Unplanned income changes often affect the goals of individual family members, the mutual or combined family goals, and the goals of the family business or enterprise if there is one.

Identifying Goals

You will need to identify goals at the personal level and the family level. If you are part of family business or a farm enterprise, you will also need to identify goals at that level. Discussion and agreement of

Worksheet 2. Reassessing Targets for your Money, Time and Energy as a Result of Income Loss

DIRECTIONS: Write down the individual high priority goals that you had before the income loss in the appropriate Prior Goal section. Do not consult with others. Under the Reassessment column indicate whether you will need to postpone it, continue it, or adjust it. Then, under the Evaluation column, ask yourself, "What will happen if I can't achieve the goal in the next six months?" Write one of the following answers or one that expresses your situation more accurately: a) nothing, b) it's highly important and the world will fall apart, or c) I need to keep working on it, but it needs to be adjusted for now. Finally, in the Current Goal column, identify and write down a new or adjusted goal that you can achieve in the next several months.

	Prior Goal	Reassessment	Evaluation	Current Goal
Personal				
Couple/Family				
Business/Enterprise				

Figure 42.2. Worksheet 2: Reassessing Targets for Your Money, Time, and Energy as a Result of Income Loss.

mutual goals is needed at both the family level and the business/ enterprise level. It is harder to decide on mutual family and business/ enterprise goals than personal goals because the whole group needs to agree on them. However, setting these goals together will allow you to use money more effectively and reduce the possibility of conflict in the group. Worksheet 2 (see Figure 42.2) can help you target where your limited money resources need to go in the next few months. This worksheet is best completed alone so other people cannot influence your goals.

How Men and Women Set Goals

Research has indicated that men and women tend to look at things differently and, thus, they may have different types of goals. Women have been socialized to take care of others' desires ahead of their own. It is often very hard for them to know clearly what they would like for themselves. They often go along with their spouse's expectations only to experience considerable resentment later. Therefore, it is critical that the woman figure out for herself what her goals are in light of the income loss and how they can best be met.

Men, on the other hand, are mainly task-oriented when communicating and making decisions. Doing what needs to be done to put the finances in order seems the most logical thing for them to do. They take a business-like approach to most family situations. It is important for men to consider the expectations of other family members and share ideas about adjusting to the family's income loss.

Family Discussion of Goals

Personal and family goals need to be shared. The family discussion lets all family members know which personal goals of individual family members and which agreed-upon family goals will need money resources in the near future. Children need to be involved, too. Their goals may be more simple and less expensive, depending on their ages and needs. Not being able to buy the special shoes may be important to them. When children are included in discussions, they will see what the adults are giving up and understand why they must give up something, too. Once family goals have been talked over, those involved in the family business should meet to discuss their agreed-upon business goals and how they are affected by the income reduction.

Setting personal, family, and business goals in this manner makes it easier to identify each person's goals, whose need has not been met, or who must be involved to meet a given goal. Many times families or family businesses discuss goals together without having considered their goals at either the personal or family level. This becomes very confusing because individuals are not clear about which goals are personal, which are family goals, and which are business goals.

Without clarifying this first, agreeing on mutual goals for the family or family business is very difficult and often cannot be accomplished. When this happens, one person may dictate the family goals or the family business goals. Instead of having resources of time, money, energy, and skills focused toward agreed-upon goals, family members compete for these resources to meet conflicting goals.

Having mutually agreed-upon goals does not mean everyone works on each goal all the time or in the same location. It may even be that you agree to live with some disagreement. Concretely, it may mean that someone who is good at numbers does the financial record-keeping for the family and others agree not to spend more than a specified amount before consulting the rest. In a family business it may mean that each person will contribute to the family business according to his or her skills or interests. For example, someone may work primarily with the machinery and another deals with the customers.

After goals are identified, you can begin to allocate the money and other resources to meet these goals. Worksheet 3 (see Figure 43.3) guides you through this process. The more concrete you can be about the goal and the steps needed to achieve it, the quicker you will begin to take action to reach it.

Worksheet 3. Goals

DIRECTIONS: Write down your current goal from **Worksheet 2** in the section below and answer each question across

Current Goal	Activity to Achieve Goal	When to Do It?	Cost?	Who Will Do It?

Figure 42.3. Worksheet 3: Goals.

Managing Disagreement and Conflict Over Money

As families or family business members negotiate mutual goals, disagreement or conflict may surface. Disagreement and conflict are not the same. Disagreement is a difference of opinion while conflict is more threatening. Disagreement is usually restrained and fairly calm; conflict is a clash of feelings and interests that can be unreasonable and angry. Anger results from underlying feelings, intentions, beliefs, and values that have not been "owned" and are often unclear.

Because many people are extremely uncomfortable with conflict, they seek an immediate solution to it. Doing so, however, results in poor decisions that people can't or won't support over time. To use conflict constructively requires that things are worked out so more people in the group feel they have won than lost. This takes time, energy, and patience on everyone's part. It is worth the effort because it brings people closer together, achieves a workable solution that people will support, and improves future communication. Don't expect to work out a solution to a conflict in one sitting. You need time out to allow tensions to ease, to reflect on what's been discussed, and to let creative solutions evolve.

Five Steps to Manage Conflict

In order to make any progress on managing a conflict situation, all parties involved must agree to work on the problem. As you begin to address the conflict, the people involved must agree on the problem, identify the feelings of each person tangled up in the problem, and then identify and agree on ways to tackle the problem.

The five steps that follow can help you manage a conflict about money. Each person involved in the conflict needs to complete the exercise separately and then discuss and compare answers with others involved.

Step 1: State the problem to be solved in one sentence. Take time to think about this, because often what people argue about is not the real root of the problem.

Step 2: Have you written the problem in an "I" statement rather than a "you" statement? This means that you have stated the problem in terms of how you feel, not just in terms of what the other person or persons have done. For example, "I feel anxious and frustrated when bills come that are bigger than we can pay in a month." rather

473

than "You always spend too much money." If you cannot write it in an "I" statement, go to Step 3 and try to identify your feelings. Then rewrite the statement in an "I" form. If you have written the problem statement in an "I" form indicated what will reduce the intensity of those feelings, go on to Step 3 to identify the feelings involved.

Step 3: Identify the feelings you have about the problem. Several feelings have been identified in Table 42.1. Be sure that you add others you may be experiencing. Circle the number that best describes the intensity you feel on a scale from 0 to 5.

Table 42.1. Identifying Feelings about a Problem

a.	Not at all Angry	0	1	2	3	4	5	Very Angry
b.	Not at all Frustrated	0	1	2	3	4	5	Very Frustrated
c.	Not at all Excited	0	1	2	3	4	5	Very Excited
d.	Not at all Anxious	0	1	2	3	4	5	Very Anxious
e.	Not at all Confused	0	1	2	3	4	5	Very Confused
f.	Not at all Resentful	0	1	2	3	4	5	Very Resentful
g.	Not at all Hopeful	0	1	2	3	4	5	Very Hopeful
h.	Not at all (other)	0	1	2	3	4	5	Very (other)

Ask yourself, "What do I need to do to reduce these feelings?" Identifying this need will more clearly target the underlying problem causing the conflict.

Step 4: Now get together with the others involved with the disagreement or conflict. Do you all view the problem in a similar manner? If you don't, everyone involved should complete Worksheet 4 (see Figure 42.4). Be sure to complete the "Points of Agreement" first and then the "Points of Disagreement." Doing so places the level of disagreement in perspective because the focus has been the tension rather than the whole picture.

Step 5: Once there is agreement about the problem to be solved, the feelings and their intensity have been recognized, and the needs of each person have been identified regarding the conflict, alternative solutions to the problem can be identified and investigated.

List the alternative solution(s) to the problem.

Once you decide on a solution, set a time to review your progress. This gives you a chance to try another solution if the first one doesn't work, or it gives you a chance to celebrate if the first solution worked.

This process is about managing conflict rather than resolving conflict. Resolving conflict implies that there is an end to both the problem and the feelings surrounding it. Managing conflict involves redefining or restructuring the part of the situation that is causing the tension. There may be some remaining tension and disagreement as new approaches are tried.

Managing conflict is a more realistic way of thinking about challenges that develop in families and family businesses. When people spend as much time together as they do in these two cases, disagreements and conflict are normal. That's especially true when the money available is suddenly reduced.

The ideas presented here assume that there is agreement about what the problem is and agreement to work on the problem. When you are the only one willing to recognize and try to solve the problem, then you can only address the situation in ways that you can

Worksheet 4. Conflict Management

Statement of the problem: _____

Points of Agreement	What are the hopes and positive ideas?	What is most important?	Who should do what?	What are some possible options?	Who is helping in positive ways?

Points of Disagreement	What do you need to reduce emotional intensity related to the problem?	What do you want the other person to understand about your position?	Which parts of the problem are your responsibility?	Which parts of the problem do you have control over?	Who is interfering with whom?
Person 1 Viewpoint					
Person 2 Viewpoint					

Figure 42.4. Worksheet 4: Conflict Management.

475

control. You can adjust your view of the situation, your involvement in the situation, and your reaction to the situation.

Summary

Reactions to an unplanned, sudden decrease in income are not simple. The situation probably involves circumstances over which you have had little control. Many people tend to blame themselves and end up "beating themselves up" or hurting others. What happens in such situations involves a complex web of emotional, economic, and social interactions. It is important to recognize that there are various stages of grief that you will experience as you adjust to the income loss. Reach out to others rather than blaming yourself or others. Involve the whole family including children in reassessing how money will be used. Take stock of current expenses, discuss how spending can be adjusted, communicate with creditors, and look again at your financial goals for the next few months. Personal goals can be assessed individually. However, when you spend the time and effort to set mutual, agreed-upon family or family business goals, the decreased amount of money available will be used more effectively and efficiently. Recognize and be ready to manage the inevitable disagreement or conflict over how the reduced amount of money will be used. Doing so will help you and your family live with the consequences of the unplanned income change, develop new options, and begin to move on.

Chapter 43

How to Regain Financial Health

Can't pay your bills? You're not alone. Today, millions of Americans are having difficulty paying their debts. Most of those in financial distress are middle-income families with jobs who want to pay off what they own.

But it is important for you to act. Doing nothing can lead to much larger problems in the future—even bigger debts, the loss of assets such as your house, and a bad credit record.

The good news is that there are solutions. The remedies provided in this chapter can help improve your relationships with creditors, reduce your debts, and help you manage your money. In brief, these solutions can help give you a new, fresh start.

Are you in financial trouble?

If bill collectors are calling you, you know you're in financial trouble. But what if you're just having difficulty stretching your paycheck to pay monthly bills? If you answer yes to any one of the following questions, you should act:

- Do you routinely spend more than you earn?

- Are you forced to make day-to-day purchases on credit?

- Are you able to make only the minimum payments on monthly credit card debts?

- If you lost your job, would you have difficulty paying next month's bills?

What can you do for yourself?

Review your specific obligations that creditors claim you owe to make certain you really owe them. If you dispute a debt, first contact the creditor directly to resolve your questions. If you still have questions about the debt, contact your state or local consumer protection office or state Attorney General.

Contact your creditors to let them know you're having difficulty making your payments. Tell them why you're having trouble—perhaps it's because you recently lost your job or have unexpected medical bills. Try to work out an acceptable payment schedule with your creditors. Most are willing to work with you and will appreciate your honesty and forthrightness.

Budget your expenses. Create a spending plan that allows you to reduce your debts. Itemize your necessary expenses (such as housing and health care) and optional expenses (such as entertainment and vacation travel). Stick to the plan.

Try to reduce your expenses. Cut out any unnecessary spending such as eating out and purchasing expensive entertainment. Consider taking public transportation rather than owning a car. Clip coupons, purchase generic products at the supermarket, and avoid impulse purchases. Above all, stop incurring new debt. Consider substituting a debit card for your credit cards.

Use your savings and other assets to pay down debts. Withdrawing savings from low-interest accounts to settle high-rate loans usually makes sense. Selling off a second car not only provides cash but also reduces insurance and other maintenance expenses.

Look for additional resources from governmental and private sources for which you may be eligible. Government assistance includes unemployment compensation, Aid to Families with Dependent Children (AFDC), food stamps, low-income energy assistance, Medicaid, and Social Security, including disability. Other resources may be available from churches and community groups. Often these sources are listed in the Yellow Pages of your phone book.

What can others do for you?

Credit counseling. If you are unable to make satisfactory arrangements with your creditors, there are organizations that can help. An organization that you can call is a Consumer Credit Counseling Service (CCCS) agency. These local, non-profit organizations affiliated with the National Foundation for Credit Counseling (NFCC) provide education and counseling to families and individuals.

For consumers who want individual help, CCCS counselors with professional backgrounds in money management and counseling can provide support. To promote high standards, the NFCC has developed a certification program for these counselors. A counselor will work with you to develop a budget to maintain your basic living expenses and outline options for addressing your total financial situation.

If creditors are pressuring you, a CCCS counselor can also negotiate with these creditors to repay your debts through a financial management plan. Under this plan, creditors often agree to reduce payments, lower or drop interest and finance charges, and waive late fees and over-the-limit fees. After starting the plan, you will deposit money with the CCCS each month to cover these new negotiated payment amounts. The CCCS will distribute this money to your creditors to repay your debts.

With more than 1,100 locations nationwide, CCCS agencies are available to nearly all consumers. Supported mainly by contributions from community organizations, financial institutions, and merchants, CCCS provides services free or at low cost to individuals seeking help. To contact a CCCS office for confidential help, look in your telephone directory white pages, or call 800-388-2227, 24 hours a day, for an office near you.

Personal bankruptcy. Bankruptcy is a legal procedure which can give people who cannot pay their bills a fresh start. A decision to file for bankruptcy is a serious step. You should make it only if it is the best way to deal with financial problems.

There are two types of bankruptcy available to most individuals. Chapter 13—or "reorganization"—allows debtors to keep property which they might otherwise lose, such as a mortgaged house or car.

479

Reorganizations may allow debtors to pay off or cure a default over a period of three to five years, rather than surrender property.

Chapter 7—or "straight bankruptcy"—involves liquidation of all assets that are not exempt in your state. The exempt property may include items such as work-related tools and basic household furnishings, among others. Some of your property may be sold by a court-appointed official or turned over to your creditors. You can file for Chapter 7 only once every six years.

Both types of bankruptcy may get rid of unsecured debts (those where creditors have no rights to specific property), and stop foreclosures, repossessions, garnishments, utility shutoffs, and debt collection activities. Both types also provide exemptions that permit most individual debtors to keep most of their assets, though these "exemption" amounts vary greatly from state to state.

Bankruptcy cannot clean up a bad credit record and will be part of this record for up to ten years. It can, for example, make it more difficult to get a mortgage to buy a house. It usually does not wipe out child support, alimony, fines, taxes, and some student loan obligations. Also, unless under Chapter 13 you have an acceptable plan to catch up on your debt, bankruptcy usually does not permit you to keep property when the creditor has an unpaid mortgage or lien on it.

Bankruptcy cases must be filed in federal court. The filing fee is $160, which sometimes may be paid in installments. This fee does not include the fees of your bankruptcy lawyer.

Choosing a bankruptcy lawyer may be difficult. Some of the least reputable lawyers make easy money by handling hundreds of bankruptcy cases without adequately considering individual needs. Recommendations from those you know and trust, and from employee assistance programs, are most useful.

Some public-funded legal services programs handle bankruptcy cases without charging attorney fees. Or these programs may provide referrals to private bankruptcy lawyers. Keep in mind that the fees of these attorneys may vary widely.

Possible Pitfalls

Credit counselors who aren't helpful. Often for-profit or non-credentialed counseling organizations make promises that they cannot or do not keep. Be especially careful when asked for a large sum of money in advance. To check the organization's reputation, contact your state Attorney General, consumer protection agency, or Better Business Bureau.

"Credit repair" clinics and "credit doctors" have been frequently criticized for promising that they can remove negative information from your credit report. But accurate information cannot be changed. If information is old or inaccurate, you can contact a credit bureau yourself and ask that it be removed.

Risky refinancing options. When already in financial trouble, second mortgages greatly increase the risk that you may lose your home. Be wary of any loan consolidations or other refinancing that actually increase interest owed or require payments of points or large fees.

A Final Word

Don't lose hope, even if you despair of ever recovering financially. You can regain financial health if you act. Pursuing the options presented in this chapter can put you on the road to financial recovery.

Chapter 44

Choosing a
Credit Counselor or
Debt Management Plan

Living paycheck to paycheck? Worried about debt collectors? Can't seem to develop a workable budget, let alone save money for retirement? If this sounds familiar, you may want to consider the services of a credit counselor. Many credit counseling organizations are nonprofit and work with you to solve your financial problems. But beware—just because an organization says it is "nonprofit" doesn't guarantee that its services are free or affordable, or that its services are legitimate. In fact, some credit counseling organizations charge high fees, some of which may be hidden, or urge consumers to make "voluntary" contributions that cause them to fall deeper into debt.

Most credit counselors offer services through local offices, the internet, or on the telephone. If possible, find an organization that offers in-person counseling. Many universities, military bases, credit unions, housing authorities, and branches of the U.S. Cooperative Extension Service operate nonprofit credit counseling programs. Your financial institution, local consumer protection agency, and friends and family also may be good sources of information and referrals.

Choosing a Credit Counseling Organization

Reputable credit counseling organizations advise you on managing your money and debts, help you develop a budget, and usually offer free educational materials and workshops. Their counselors are

"Fiscal Fitness: Choosing a Credit Counselor," Federal Trade Commission (www.ftc.gov), December 2005.

certified and trained in the areas of consumer credit, money and debt management, and budgeting. Counselors discuss your entire financial situation with you, and help you develop a personalized plan to solve your money problems. An initial counseling session typically lasts an hour, with an offer of follow-up sessions.

A reputable credit counseling agency should send you free information about itself and the services it provides without requiring you to provide any details about your situation. If a firm doesn't do that, consider it a red flag and go elsewhere for help.

Once you've developed a list of potential counseling agencies, check them out with your state Attorney General, local consumer protection agency, and Better Business Bureau. They can tell you if consumers have filed complaints about them (but even if there are no complaints about them, it's not a guarantee that they're legitimate). The United States Trustee Program also keeps a list of credit counseling agencies that have been approved to provide pre-bankruptcy counseling. After you've done your background investigation, it's time for the most important research—you should interview the final "candidates."

Questions to Ask

Here are some questions to ask to help you find the best counselor for you.

- What services do you offer? Look for an organization that offers a range of services, including budget counseling, and savings and debt management classes. Avoid organizations that push a debt management plan (DMP) as your only option before they spend a significant amount of time analyzing your financial situation.

- Do you offer information? Are educational materials available for free? Avoid organizations that charge for information.

- In addition to helping me solve my immediate problem, will you help me develop a plan for avoiding problems in the future?

- What are your fees? Are there set-up or monthly fees? Get a specific price quote in writing.

- What if I can't afford to pay your fees or make contributions? If an organization won't help you because you can't afford to pay, look elsewhere for help.

- Will I have a formal written agreement or contract with you? Don't sign anything without reading it first. Make sure all verbal promises are in writing.

- Are you licensed to offer your services in my state?

- What are the qualifications of your counselors? Are they accredited or certified by an outside organization? If so, by whom? If not, how are they trained? Try to use an organization whose counselors are trained by a non-affiliated party.

- What assurance do I have that information about me (including my address, phone number, and financial information) will be kept confidential and secure?

- How are your employees compensated? Are they paid more if I sign up for certain services, if I pay a fee, or if I make a contribution to your organization? If the answer is yes, consider it a red flag and go elsewhere for help.

Debt Management Plans

If your financial problems stem from too much debt or your inability to repay your debts, a credit counseling agency may recommend that you enroll in a debt management plan. A DMP alone is not credit counseling, and DMPs are not for everyone. Consider signing on for one of these plans only after a certified credit counselor has spent time thoroughly reviewing your financial situation, and has offered you customized advice on managing your money. Even if a DMP is appropriate for you, a reputable credit counseling organization still will help you create a budget and teach you money management skills.

How a DMP Works

You deposit money each month with the credit counseling organization. The organization uses your deposits to pay your unsecured debts, like credit card bills, student loans, and medical bills, according to a payment schedule the counselor develops with you and your creditors. Your creditors may agree to lower your interest rates and waive certain fees, but check with all your creditors to be sure that they offer the concessions that a credit counseling organization describes to you. A successful DMP requires you to make regular, timely payments, and could take 48 months or longer to complete. Ask the credit counselor to estimate how long it will take for you to complete the plan. You also may have to agree not to apply for—or use—any additional credit while you're participating in the plan.

Is a DMP Right for You?

In addition to the questions already listed, here are some other important ones to ask if you're considering enrolling in a DMP.

- Is a DMP the only option you can give me? Will you provide me with on-going budgeting advice, regardless of whether I enroll in a DMP? If an organization offers only DMPs, find another credit counseling organization that also will help you create a budget and teach you money management skills.

- How does your DMP work? How will you make sure that all my creditors will be paid by the applicable due dates and in the correct billing cycle? If a DMP is appropriate, sign up for one that allows all your creditors to be paid before your payment due dates and within the correct billing cycle.

- How is the amount of my payment determined? What if the amount is more than I can afford? Don't sign up for a DMP if you can't afford the monthly payment.

- How often can I get status reports on my accounts? Can I get access to my accounts online or by phone? Make sure that the organization you sign up with is willing to provide regular, detailed statements about your account.

- Can you get my creditors to lower or eliminate interest and finance charges, or waive late fees? If yes, contact your creditors to verify this, and ask them how long you have to be on the plan before the benefits kick in.

- What debts aren't included in the DMP? This is important because you'll have to pay those bills on your own.

- Do I have to make any payments to my creditors before they will accept the proposed payment plan? Some creditors require a payment to the credit counselor before accepting you into a DMP. If a credit counselor tells you this is so, call your creditors to verify this information before you send money to the credit counseling agency.

- How will enrolling in a DMP affect my credit? Beware of any organization that tells you it can remove accurate negative information from your credit report. Legally, it can't be done. Accurate negative information may stay on your credit report for up to seven years.

- Can you get my creditors to "re-age" my accounts—that is, to make my accounts current? If so, how many payments will I have to make before my creditors will do so? Even if your accounts are "re-aged," negative information from past delinquencies or late payments will remain on your credit report.

How to Make a DMP Work for You

The following steps will help you benefit from a DMP and avoid falling further into debt.

- Continue to pay your bills until the plan has been approved by your creditors. If you stop making payments before your creditors have accepted you into a plan, you'll face late fees, penalties, and negative entries on your credit report.

- Contact your creditors and confirm that they have accepted the proposed plan before you send any payments to the credit counseling organization for your DMP.

- Make sure the organization's payment schedule allows your debts to be paid before they are due each month. Paying on time will help you avoid late fees and penalties. Call each of your creditors on the first of every month to make sure the agency has paid them on time.

- Review monthly statements from your creditors to make sure they have received your payments.

- If your debt management plan depends on your creditors agreeing to lower or eliminate interest and finance charges, or waive late fees, make sure these concessions are reflected on your statements.

Debt Negotiation Programs

Debt negotiation is not the same thing as credit counseling or a DMP. It can be very risky and have a long term negative impact on your credit report and, in turn, your ability to get credit. That's why many states have laws regulating debt negotiation companies and the services they offer.

The Claims

Debt negotiation firms may claim they're nonprofit. They also may claim that they can arrange for your unsecured debt—typically, credit card debt—to be paid off for anywhere from 10 to 50 percent of the balance owed. For example, if you owe $10,000 on a credit card, a debt negotiation firm may claim it can arrange for you to pay off the debt with a lesser amount, say $4,000.

The firms often pitch their services as an alternative to bankruptcy. They may claim that using their services will have little or no negative impact on your ability to get credit in the future, or that any negative information can be removed from your credit report when you complete the debt negotiation program. The firms usually tell you to stop making payments to your creditors and instead, send your payments to the debt negotiation company. The firms may promise to hold your funds in a special account and pay the creditors on your behalf.

The Truth

Just because a debt negotiation company describes itself as a "nonprofit" organization, there's no guarantee that the services they offer are legitimate. There also is no guarantee that a creditor will accept partial payment of a legitimate debt. In fact, if you stop making payments on a credit card, late fees and interest usually are added to the debt each month. If you exceed your credit limit, additional fees and charges also can be added. All this can quickly cause a consumer's original debt to double or triple. What's more, most debt negotiation companies charge consumers substantial fees for their services, including a fee to establish the account with the debt negotiator, a monthly service fee, and a final fee of a percentage of the money you've supposedly saved.

While creditors have no obligation to agree to negotiate the amount a consumer owes, they have a legal obligation to provide accurate information to the credit reporting agencies, including your failure to make monthly payments. That can result in a negative entry on your credit report. And in certain situations, creditors may have the right to sue you to recover the money you owe. In some instances, when creditors win a lawsuit, they have the right to garnish your wages or put a lien on your home. Finally, the Internal Revenue Service may consider any amount of forgiven debt to be taxable income.

Tip-offs to Rip-offs

Steer clear of debt negotiation companies that exhibit these warning signs:

- Guarantee they can remove your unsecured debt

- Promise that unsecured debts can be paid off with pennies on the dollar

- Require substantial monthly service fees

- Demand payment of a percentage of savings

- Tell you to stop making payments to or communicating with your creditors

- Require you to make monthly payments to them, rather than with your creditor

- Claim that creditors never sue consumers for non-payment of unsecured debt

- Promise that using their system will have no negative impact on your credit report

- Claim that they can remove accurate negative information from your credit report

If you decide to work with a debt negotiation company, be sure to check it out with your state Attorney General, local consumer protection agency, and the Better Business Bureau. They can tell you if any consumer complaints are on file about the firm you're considering doing business with. Also, ask your state Attorney General if the company is required to be licensed to work in your state and, if so, whether it is.

Chapter 45

Fair Debt Collection

If you use credit cards, owe money on a personal loan, or are paying on a home mortgage, you are a "debtor." If you fall behind in repaying your creditors, or an error is made on your accounts, you may be contacted by a "debt collector."

You should know that in either situation, the Fair Debt Collection Practices Act requires that debt collectors treat you fairly and prohibits certain methods of debt collection. Of course, the law does not erase any legitimate debt you owe.

This chapter answers commonly asked questions about your rights under the Fair Debt Collection Practices Act.

What debts are covered?

Personal, family, and household debts are covered under the Act. This includes money owed for the purchase of an automobile, for medical care, or for charge accounts.

Who is a debt collector?

A debt collector is any person who regularly collects debts owed to others. This includes attorneys who collect debts on a regular basis.

Federal Trade Commission (www.ftc.gov), March 1999; reviewed for currency in February 2006.

How may a debt collector contact you?

A collector may contact you in person, by mail, telephone, telegram, or fax. However, a debt collector may not contact you at inconvenient times or places, such as before 8 a.m. or after 9 p.m., unless you agree. A debt collector also may not contact you at work if the collector knows that your employer disapproves of such contacts.

Can you stop a debt collector from contacting you?

You can stop a debt collector from contacting you by writing a letter to the collector telling them to stop. Once the collector receives your letter, they may not contact you again except to say there will be no further contact or to notify you that the debt collector or the creditor intends to take some specific action. Please note, however, that sending such a letter to a collector does not make the debt go away if you actually owe it. You could still be sued by the debt collector or your original creditor.

May a debt collector contact anyone else about your debt?

If you have an attorney, the debt collector must contact the attorney, rather than you. If you do not have an attorney, a collector may contact other people, but only to find out where you live, what your phone number is, and where you work. Collectors usually are prohibited from contacting such third parties more than once. In most cases, the collector may not tell anyone other than you and your attorney that you owe money.

What must the debt collector tell you about the debt?

Within five days after you are first contacted, the collector must send you a written notice telling you the amount of money you owe; the name of the creditor to whom you owe the money; and what action to take if you believe you do not owe the money.

May a debt collector continue to contact you if you believe you do not owe money?

A collector may not contact you if, within 30 days after you receive the written notice, you send the collection agency a letter stating you do not owe money. However, a collector can renew collection activities if you are sent proof of the debt, such as a copy of a bill for the amount owed.

What types of debt collection practices are prohibited?

Harassment: Debt collectors may not harass, oppress, or abuse you or any third parties they contact. For example, debt collectors may not employ the following practices:

- Use threats of violence or harm
- Publish a list of consumers who refuse to pay their debts (except to a credit bureau)
- Use obscene or profane language
- Repeatedly use the telephone to annoy someone

False statements: Debt collectors may not use any false or misleading statements when collecting a debt. Here are some examples of things a debt collector may not do:

- Falsely imply that they are attorneys or government representatives
- Falsely imply that you have committed a crime
- Falsely represent that they operate or work for a credit bureau
- Misrepresent the amount of your debt
- Indicate that papers being sent to you are legal forms when they are not
- Indicate that papers being sent to you are not legal forms when they are

Debt collectors also may not make the following statements:

- You will be arrested if you do not pay your debt.
- They will seize, garnish, attach, or sell your property or wages, unless the collection agency or creditor intends to do so, and it is legal to do so.
- Actions, such as a lawsuit, will be taken against you, when such action legally may not be taken, or when they do not intend to take such action.

Debt collectors may not use these tactics:

- Give false credit information about you to anyone, including a credit bureau

- Send you anything that looks like an official document from a court or government agency when it is not

- Use a false name

Unfair practices: Debt collectors may not engage in unfair practices when they try to collect a debt. For example, collectors are not permitted to take these actions:

- Collect any amount greater than your debt, unless your state law permits such a charge

- Deposit a post-dated check prematurely

- Use deception to make you accept collect calls or pay for telegrams

- Take or threaten to take your property unless this can be done legally

- Contact you by postcard

What control do you have over payment of debts?

If you owe more than one debt, any payment you make must be applied to the debt you indicate. A debt collector may not apply a payment to any debt you believe you do not owe.

What can you do if you believe a debt collector violated the law?

You have the right to sue a collector in a state or federal court within one year from the date the law was violated. If you win, you may recover money for the damages you suffered plus an additional amount up to $1,000. Court costs and attorney's fees also can be recovered. A group of people also may sue a debt collector and recover money for damages up to $500,000, or one percent of the collector's net worth, whichever is less.

Where can you report a debt collector for an alleged violation?

Report any problems you have with a debt collector to your state Attorney General's office and the Federal Trade Commission. Many states have their own debt collection laws, and your Attorney General's office can help you determine your rights.

Chapter 46

Avoiding Foreclosure

Falling behind on your bills can be very stressful, but falling behind on your mortgage can be downright frightening. The thought of losing your home may be so overwhelming that you try to avoid even thinking about it, but that's never the best approach.

If you're having trouble keeping up with your mortgage, this chapter will give you strategies for getting back on track.

How Does It Work?

How long it takes a lender to foreclose on your home, and the steps they must take to do so, varies by state. Foreclosure laws are specific to the state in which the property is located. States usually have either judicial foreclosure proceedings or non-judicial or statutory foreclosure proceedings. In judicial foreclosure states, the mortgage holder must take you to court and get the court's order to foreclose. If you're working with an attorney, this may give you an opportunity to stay in your home longer, or even stop the proceedings.

In non-judicial or statutory foreclosure states, lenders may be able to foreclose without going to court, which can be faster and easier for the lender. Some states allow a combination of both, depending on how the contract is written.

This text is from the undated factsheet "Avoiding Foreclosure," © Consolidated Credit Counseling Services, Inc. Reprinted with permission. Available online at http://www.consolidatedcredit.org/pdfs/foreclosure.pdf; accessed July 16, 2006.

For information on state foreclosure laws, visit: www.foreclosures.com or talk with a consumer law attorney in your area.

While the rules regarding foreclosure proceedings vary by state, here's what you can generally expect if you fall behind on your mortgage payments.

If you haven't made your payment by the 15th day after the due date, you'll be assessed a late fee, which is usually 4% of the loan amount. If you have still not paid by the second month, you'll likely get a phone call and/or letter to find out what's going on.

Lenders can usually begin the foreclosure process after you have missed a few payments. If you can't work out an arrangement with the lender to catch up, they may then send a Notice of Acceleration, which basically tells you that you now must pay the loan in full if you want to keep your home. Getting one of these letters is serious, because lenders may not be willing—or obligated—to work out a payment arrangement with you.

In some states, borrowers still have an opportunity to "redeem" the property by paying the amount due plus costs for a certain period after foreclosure.

Important: Many states allow lenders to collect a "deficiency judgment" if the home is sold for less than the full balance due, or for less than market value. This may leave the former homeowner with a debt that must be paid even after the home has been sold.

Credit history: A foreclosure remains on your credit report for seven years from the date of the foreclosure and is considered a very serious negative mark.

Your Options If You Are behind on Your Mortgage

Negotiate with Your Lender

Lenders don't want to foreclose on homes. It's expensive for them, and can drag out for months in many states. At the same time, they don't want to waste time and money on risky borrowers who are chronically late with payments—and who may not be taking good care of the home they may have to later take back and sell.

Negotiating with the lender, therefore, can be difficult if you either have a history of late payments or if you can't show the lender why this is an isolated incident and is not likely to happen again. If your financial problems are truly temporary—you were laid off but have now returned to work, or you had unexpected medical bills, for example—you may be able to work something out.

If your lender is open to negotiation, they may agree to take smaller payments for a short period of time, and then add the rest to the balance of the loan. Or they may agree to interest-only payments for a time. In some cases, they may even agree to add a couple of missed payments to the end of the loan.

If you are going to try to work out a modified payment arrangement with your lender, it's important to present them with factual—not emotional—information about your situation, and be willing to back it up with documentation.

If you find it difficult to negotiate on your own, and many people do, get help from a professional organization like www.HomesaversUSA.com. Whatever you do, don't keep falling further and further behind without contacting your lender or getting outside help.

Pre-Foreclosure Sale

If your problems aren't temporary, you may need to sell your home. If you have built up equity in your home that you would lose in a foreclosure, then this may be your best bet.

If you do have enough equity in your home to be able to afford to pay a real estate professional's fee (usually 6% of the sales price, sometimes lower), it's a good idea to interview three real estate professionals and let them handle the sale for you. Statistics show that homes sold by professionals sell faster than ones where the owner is making the sale.

Make sure you get any agreements in writing from them as to what they will do to market your home. Don't necessarily go with the agent who tells you she can sell your home for top dollar. Choose the one who you believe will do the most to help your home sell quickly at a fair price.

If you're going to go this route, talk with your lender and let them know that you have put the home up for sale. Ask if they will hold off on their foreclosure proceedings longer since you have the house listed.

If you don't have much equity in your home, you may need to list your home for sale by owner—also known a "FSBO."

Beware: This can be a lot of work. Visit your local library for books on selling your own home and implement as many strategies as you can. You don't want to add to your stress by having no buyers show up to take a look at your home.

You may also be able to save the real estate commission by working with a real estate investor who will offer you a quick but fair sale on your home. Keep in mind that even while you're trying to sell, the lender may continue foreclosure proceedings so again, it's important to try to maintain an open dialogue with the lender.

Short Sales

You've probably seen the signs or ads in the newspaper: "We buy homes for cash, any condition!" These ads are usually placed by real estate investors looking for bargain homes. If you've borrowed on your home recently, you may not have a lot of equity. But an experienced real estate investor may still be able to buy your home and give you enough cash to cover your moving expenses. They do this through a "short sale."

In a short sale, the buyer will prepare documentation showing the lender that you are in financial hardship and will end up in foreclosure anyway. They will then offer to buy the home for less than you owe on it.

Let's say, for example, your home is worth $75,000 and you owe $60,000 on your first mortgage and $10,000 on the second for a total of $70,000. The buyer may convince the first mortgage lender to settle for $65,000 and the second lender (who may get nothing in a foreclosure or bankruptcy) to settle for $3,000. They may even pay you $500 or so to cover your moving expenses.

A short sale will help you avoid foreclosure, but it will still appear on your credit report as paid for less than the total amount and that will be a negative remark. On the other hand, if the documents are properly drawn up, you won't risk a deficiency judgment if the home was sold and didn't bring in enough to pay the lenders.

To make sure you are protected, ask the seller if they will pay to have your documents reviewed by an attorney of your choice.

Equity Skimming or Leasebacks

One of the less scrupulous methods for "helping" homeowners stay in their homes is equity skimming or leaseback programs. The individual offering to help you out will offer to catch you up on your payments and take them over for a period of time while you continue to "rent" the home. The contract, however, usually contains strict provisions so that if you are one day late with your monthly payment, for example, the home is no longer yours. Or you may have actually signed over your home to that buyer with the opportunity to buy it back at terms you'll never be able to afford. Either way, you lose.

Be very careful if someone offers you an easy way out of your foreclosure situation. When you are in foreclosure, you're a high-risk borrower. Your lender won't let you off the hook easily, why would someone else?

A note about quitclaims: You can quitclaim your ownership in a property by signing a legal document turning your rights over to someone else. This does not get you off the hook with the lender. It just leaves you with no rights to the property. Do not quitclaim your property if you cannot get an attorney to look over the documents for you.

Deed in Lieu of Foreclosure

With a deed-in-lieu, you basically give the lender back the home. By doing so, you may minimize the foreclosure expenses. But your credit report will likely say "deed in lieu of foreclosure" which is pretty much as negative as a foreclosure.

Bankruptcy

In some states and in some situations, filing for bankruptcy can delay or stop the foreclosure process. Since bankruptcy laws vary from state to state, it's a good idea to talk with an attorney as soon as possible if you think you may need to go this route.

Chapter 47

Vehicle Repossession

When you finance or lease a car, truck or other vehicle, your creditor or lessor holds important rights on the vehicle until you've made the last loan payment or fully paid off your leasing obligation. These rights are established by the signed contract and by state law. For example, if your payments are late or you default on your contract in any way, your creditor or lessor may have the right to repossess your car. In many states, creditors or lessors can do this legally without going to court or warning you in advance, as long as they do not breach the peace. In addition, your creditor or lessor may be able to sell your contract to a third party, called an assignee, who may have the same rights and responsibilities as the original creditor or lessor.

However, some state laws limit the ways a creditor or lessor can repossess and sell a vehicle to reduce or eliminate your debt. If any rules are violated, the creditor or lessor may be required to pay you damages.

Seizing the Car

In many states, your creditor or lessor has legal authority to seize your vehicle as soon as you default on your loan or lease. Because state laws differ, read your contract to find out what constitutes a default. In some states, failure to make a payment on time or to meet your other contractual responsibilities is considered defaults.

Federal Trade Commission (www.ftc.gov), February 1998; reviewed for currency in February 2006.

If your creditor or lessor has agreed to change your payment date or any other contractual obligations, it's possible that the terms of your original contract may no longer apply. Such a change may be made orally or in writing. It's best to get any changes in writing because oral agreements are difficult to prove.

If you default on your loan, the law in most states allows the creditor or lessor to repossess your car. In some states, creditors or lessors are allowed on your property to seize your car without letting you know in advance.

At the same time, the law usually doesn't allow your creditor or lessor to commit a breach of the peace in connection with repossession. In some states, removing your car from a closed garage without your permission may constitute a breach of the peace. Creditors or lessors who breach the peace in seizing your car may be required to compensate you if they harm you or your property.

Selling the Car

Once your car has been repossessed, your creditor or lessor may decide to keep the car as compensation for your debt or sell it in either a public or private sale. In some states, your creditor or lessor must let you know what will happen to the car. For example, if a creditor or lessor chooses to sell the car at public auction, state law may require that the creditor or lessor tells you the date of the sale so that you can attend and participate in the bidding. If the vehicle is to be sold privately, you may have a right to know the date it will be sold.

In either of these circumstances, you may be entitled to buy back the vehicle by paying the full amount you owe, plus any expenses connected with its repossession, such as storage and preparation for sale. In some states, the law allows you to reinstate your contract—reclaim your car by paying the amount you owe, as well as repossession and related expenses (such as attorney fees). If you reclaim your car, you must make your payments on time and meet the terms of your reinstated or renegotiated contract to avoid another repossession.

The sale of a repossessed car must be conducted in a commercially reasonable manner—according to standard custom in a particular business or an established market. For example, the sale price might not be the highest possible price—or even what you may consider a good price—but a sale price far below fair market value may indicate that the sale was not commercially reasonable. Depending on state law, failure to sell the car in a commercially reasonable manner may give you either a claim against your creditor or lessor for damages or a defense against a deficiency judgment—a court order mandating you to pay the debt you owe.

Regardless of the method used to dispose of a repossessed car, a creditor or lessor usually may not keep or sell any personal property found inside. Since state laws vary, check to see if this applies in your state. State laws also may require your creditor or lessor to use reasonable care to prevent others from removing your property from the repossessed car. If you find that your creditor or lessor cannot account for articles left in your car, talk to an attorney about whether your state offers a right to compensation.

Paying the Deficiency

A deficiency is any amount you still owe on your contract after your creditor or lessor sells the vehicle and applies the amount received to your unpaid obligation. For example, if you owe $2,500 on the car and your creditor or lessor sells the car for $1,500, the deficiency is $1,000 plus any other fees you owe under the contract, such as those related to the repossession and early termination of your lease or early payoff of your financing. In most states, a creditor or lessor who has followed the proper procedures for repossession and sale is allowed to sue you for a deficiency judgment to collect the remaining amount owed on your credit or lease contract.

Depending on your state's law and other factors, if you are sued for a deficiency judgment, you should be notified of the date of the court hearing. This may be your only opportunity to present any legal defense. If your creditor or lessor breached the peace when seizing the vehicle or failed to sell the car in a commercially reasonable manner, you may have a legal defense against a deficiency judgment. An attorney will be able to tell you whether you have grounds to contest a deficiency judgment.

Talking with Your Creditor or Lessor

It's easier to try to prevent a vehicle repossession from taking place than to dispute it afterward. Contact your creditor or lessor when you realize you will be late with a payment. Many creditors or lessors will work with you if they believe you will be able to pay soon, even if slightly late.

Sometimes you may be able to negotiate a delay in your payment or a revised schedule of payments. If you reach an agreement to modify your original contract, get it in writing to avoid questions later.

Still, your creditor or lessor may refuse to accept late payments or make other changes in your contract and may demand that you return the car. By voluntarily agreeing to a repossession, you may reduce your creditor or lessor's expenses, which you would be responsible for paying. Remember that even if you return the car voluntarily, you are responsible for paying any deficiency on your credit or lease contract, and your creditor or lessor still may enter the late payments and/or repossession on your credit report.

If you need help in dealing with your credit or lease contract, consider using a credit counseling service. There are nonprofit organizations in every state that advise consumers on debt management. Counselors often try to arrange a repayment plan that is acceptable to you and your creditors. They also can help you set up a realistic budget and plan expenditures. These counseling services are offered at little or no cost to consumers. Check your telephone directory for the office nearest you.

In addition, universities, military bases, credit unions, and housing authorities often operate nonprofit counseling programs. They also are likely to charge little or nothing for their assistance. Or check with your local bank or consumer protection office to see if it has a list of reputable, low-cost financial counseling services.

Chapter 48

Time-Barred Debts

There's no doubt about it: you are responsible for your debts. If you fall behind in paying your creditors—or if you dispute the legitimacy of a debt—a debt collector may contact you.

"Time-barred" debts are debts so old they are beyond the point at which a creditor or debt collector may sue you to collect. State law varies as to when a creditor or debt collector may no longer sue to collect: in most states, the statute of limitations period on debts is between three and ten years; in some states, the period is longer. Check with your State Attorney General's Office at http://www.naag.org to determine when a debt is considered time-barred in your state.

Federal law imposes limitations on how debt collectors can collect debts, including time-barred debts. Under the Fair Debt Collection Practices Act (FDCPA), a "debt collector" generally is any person or organization that regularly collects debts owed to others. The term includes lawyers who collect debts for others on a regular basis, but it does not include creditors collecting their own debts.

The FDCPA prohibits debt collectors from engaging in any unfair, deceptive, or abusive practices while collecting debts. It does not erase any legitimate debt that you owe. To learn more about your rights under the FDCPA, click on www.ftc.gov/bcp/conline/pubs/credit/fdc.htm.

Federal Trade Commission, October 2004.

Collecting Time-Barred Debts

Most courts that have addressed the issue have ruled that the FDCPA does not prohibit debt collectors from trying to collect time-barred debts, as long as they do not sue or threaten to sue you for the debt. If a debt collector sues you to collect a time-barred debt, you can have the suit dismissed by letting the court or judge know the debt is, indeed, time-barred.

Whether a time-barred debt—or any debt for that matter—can appear on your credit report depends on how long the debt has been delinquent: debts that have been delinquent more than seven years cannot appear on your credit report, with certain exceptions. In addition, a debt collector may not try to collect a debt that has been discharged in bankruptcy, no matter when it was incurred. To learn more about credit reporting, click on www.ftc.gov/bcp/conline/pubs/credit/fcra.htm.

Contact with Collectors

Can a debt collector continue to contact you about a time-barred debt you don't think you owe? According to the law, if you send the debt collector a letter stating that you do not owe some or all of the money within 30 days after you receive written notice of a debt, the collector must stop trying to collect until you've been given written verification of the debt, like a copy of the bill for the amount you supposedly owe. The collector can renew collection activities once you've gotten proof of the debt.

You can stop debt collectors from contacting you about any debt, regardless of whether you owe it, by writing a letter telling them to stop contacting you. Once the collector gets your letter, it may not contact you again—except to say there will be no further contact or to let you know that the collector or creditor intends to take some specific action. Sending a letter doesn't absolve you of the debt if you actually owe it; the debt collector or creditor still could sue you for the debt.

Future Collection Efforts

The best way to protect yourself from future collection on any disputed or partially settled debt is to get a form or letter from the creditor or collector that releases you from further obligation. To make sure the release is valid, you may want to consult an attorney. If you believe that a debt collector violated the law, you have the right to sue in a state or federal court within a year from the date the law was violated. If you win, you may recover money for the damages you suffered, plus an additional amount up to $1,000. You also may recover court costs and attorney's fees. You also may want to report any problems you have with a debt collector to your State Attorney General and to the Federal Trade Commission.

Chapter 49

Personal Bankruptcy

Chapter Contents

Section 49.1

Before You File for Personal Bankruptcy

Federal Trade Commission (FTC), produced in
cooperation with the Department of Justice's U.S. Trustee
Program, May 2006.

The Bankruptcy Abuse Prevention and Consumer Protection Act
of 2005 launched a new era: With limited exceptions, people who plan
to file for bankruptcy protection must get credit counseling from a
government-approved organization within six months before they file.
They also must complete a debtor education course to have their debts
discharged.

The Department of Justice's U.S. Trustee Program approves organizations to provide the mandatory credit counseling and debtor education. Only the counselors and educators that appear on the U.S.
Trustee Program's lists can advertise that they are, indeed, approved
to provide the required counseling and debtor education. By law, the
U.S. Trustee Program does not operate in Alabama and North Carolina; in these states, court officials called Bankruptcy Administra-
tors approve pre-bankruptcy credit counseling organizations and
pre-discharge debtor education course providers.

Counseling and Education Requirements

As a rule, pre-bankruptcy credit counseling and pre-discharge
debtor education may not be provided at the same time. Credit counseling must take place before you file for bankruptcy; debtor education must take place after you file.

In general, you must file a certificate of credit counseling completion when you file for bankruptcy, and evidence of completion of debtor
education after you file for bankruptcy—but before your debts are
discharged. Only credit counseling organizations and debtor education course providers that have been approved by the U.S. Trustee
Program may issue these certificates. To protect against fraud, the
certificates are produced through a central automated system and are
numbered.

Pre-Bankruptcy Counseling

A pre-bankruptcy counseling session with an approved credit counseling organization should include an evaluation of your personal financial situation, a discussion of alternatives to bankruptcy, and a personal budget plan. A typical counseling session should last about an hour or so, and can take place in person, on the phone, or online. The counseling organization is required to provide the counseling free of charge for those consumers who cannot afford to pay. If you cannot afford to pay a fee for credit counseling, you should request a fee waiver from the counseling organization before the session begins. Otherwise, you may be charged a fee for the counseling, which will generally be about $50, depending on where you live, the types of services you receive, and other factors. The counseling organization is required to discuss any fees with you before starting the counseling session.

Once you have completed the required counseling, you must get a certificate as proof. Check the U.S. Trustee's website, www.usdoj.gov, to be sure that you receive the certificate from a counseling organization that is approved in the judicial district where you are filing bankruptcy. Credit counseling organizations may not charge an extra fee for the certificate.

Post-Filing Debtor Education

A debtor education course by an approved provider should include information on developing a budget, managing money, using credit wisely, and other resources. Like pre-filing counseling, debtor education may be provided in person, on the phone, or online. The debtor education session might last longer than the pre-filing counseling—about two hours—and the typical fee is between $50 and $100. As with pre-filing counseling, if you are unable to pay the session fee, you should seek a fee waiver from the debtor education provider. Check the list of approved debtor education providers through www.usdoj.gov or at the bankruptcy clerk's office in your district.

Once you have completed the required debtor education course, you should receive a certificate as proof. This certificate is separate from the certificate you received after completing your pre-filing credit counseling. Check the U.S. Trustee's website to be sure that you receive the certificate from a debtor education provider that is approved in the judicial district where you filed bankruptcy. Debtor education providers may not charge an extra fee for the certificate.

Important Questions to Ask when Choosing a Credit Counselor

It's wise to do some research when choosing a credit counseling organization. If you are in search of credit counseling to fulfill the bankruptcy law requirements, make sure you receive services only from approved providers for your judicial district. Check the list of approved credit counseling agencies through www.usdoj.gov or at the bankruptcy clerk's office for the district where you will file. Once you have the list of approved organizations in your judicial district, call several to gather information before you make your choice. Some key questions to ask are:

- What services do you offer?

- Will you help me develop a plan for avoiding problems in the future?

- What are your fees?

- What if I can't afford to pay your fees?

- What qualifications do your counselors have? Are they accredited or certified by an outside organization? What training do they receive?

- What do you do to keep information about me (including my address, phone number, and financial information) confidential and secure?

- How are your employees paid? Are they paid more if I sign up for certain services, if I pay a fee, or if I make a contribution to your organization?

For More Information and Assistance

The U.S. Trustee Program promotes integrity and efficiency in the nation's bankruptcy system by enforcing bankruptcy laws, providing oversight of private trustees, and maintaining operational excellence. The Program has 21 regions and 95 field offices, and oversees the administration of bankruptcy in all states except Alabama and North Carolina. For more information, visit www.usdoj.gov/ust.

If you have concerns about approved credit counseling agencies or debtor education course providers, such as the failure to provide adequate service, please contact the U.S. Trustee Program by e-mail at

USTCCDEComplaintHelp@usdoj.gov, or in writing at Executive Office for U.S. Trustees, Credit Counseling and Debtor Education Unit, 20 Massachusetts Avenue, NW, Suite 8000, Washington, DC, 20530. Provide as much detail as you can, including the name of the credit counseling organization or debtor education course provider, the date of contact, and whom you spoke with.

Section 49.2

Filing for Bankruptcy

"Filing for Bankruptcy," revised 2004. © North Carolina Bar Association. All rights reserved. Reprinted with permission. This text was prepared as a public service by the Communications Committee and is not intended to be a comprehensive statement of the law. Laws may differ in other states, and laws change frequently. If you have specific questions with regard to any matters contained in this chapter, you are encouraged to consult an attorney.

Bankruptcy is a federal court procedure. When individuals cannot pay their creditors, they may seek a fresh start through complete debt relief or repay creditors through a payment plan which is approved by the bankruptcy court and monitored by a trustee. A company can also file a bankruptcy and seek either to restructure its debts or to liquidate its assets and have those proceeds used to pay its creditors.

Careful consideration should be given before filing a bankruptcy petition. Filing a bankruptcy petition normally has an adverse effect on your credit rating. Generally, the filing of a bankruptcy petition can be reported on your credit record for up to 10 years.

You should file for bankruptcy in a district where you live. In all bankruptcy cases, the person filing the bankruptcy petition is called a debtor and the person to whom the debtor owes money is called a creditor.

There are several kinds of bankruptcy. One is a Chapter 7, or straight bankruptcy. Most, but not all debts may be canceled in a Chapter 7 bankruptcy. Another kind of bankruptcy is a Chapter 13.

Under Chapter 13, debts or a percentage of debts are repaid over a three to five-year period. The court must approve the repayment plan which is administered by a trustee. Another kind of bankruptcy is Chapter 12. It is similar to Chapter 13 but is restricted to family farmers.

Bankruptcy cases begin when a petition is filed in Bankruptcy Court. The schedules filed with the petition list the debtor's assets as well as debts and to whom these debts are owed. The petition, schedules and statement of financial affairs are court-authorized forms which must be completed, signed and filed with the Bankruptcy Court along with the payment of the filing fee.

During the bankruptcy proceeding, the creditors cannot attempt to collect their debts or recover their collateral unless they have the permission of the Bankruptcy Court.

There is another form of bankruptcy known as Chapter 11, or "Reorganization." The debtor (which is usually a company) continues to operate under the supervision of the Bankruptcy Court. Chapter 11 might be helpful where the amount of the debt is extremely large. Because Chapter 11 bankruptcy cases are so complex, and because consumers rarely use it, Chapter 11 bankruptcy will not be discussed in this chapter.

Chapter 7—Straight Bankruptcy

In Chapter 7, or straight bankruptcy, the debtor is unable to repay debts and most, if not all, debts are canceled. To pay creditors, the debtor's nonexempt property is sold by a court-appointed trustee who pays creditors with the money from the sale of these nonexempt assets. The debts remaining are discharged or canceled at the conclusion of the case.

For individuals, much or all of their property may be exempt from sale by the trustee. Exempt property, therefore, is protected from your creditors. A certain dollar value of a car, a home, household furnishings, clothing, and tools of trade is exempt and cannot be sold to pay creditors.

When the bankruptcy case is over (often in a few months), the debtor receives a discharge canceling most debts listed in the schedules.

The debtor has several responsibilities in addition to completing the documents to be filed with the court. The debtor must attend required hearings and cooperate with the trustee in administering the estate.

The trustee's main job is to gather all nonexempt property and sell it to pay creditors. Not only do trustees have the power to take possession of nonexempt property, they may also, in certain situations, recover money or property transferred to creditors, relatives, or friends before the debtor filed the bankruptcy petition.

Most straight bankruptcy petitions are called "no-asset" cases because there is no non-exempt property to sell to generate funds for creditors. Generally, once the trustee determines that the case is a no-asset case, the proceeding will be closed shortly after the debtor is granted a discharge.

A creditor is designated a secured creditor if the debtor has pledged property as collateral. For example, if a debtor purchases furniture or a home through monthly installments, the item being purchased is security or collateral for the installments yet to be paid.

The lien held by the secured creditor on the property usually remains intact throughout the proceeding even though the money obligation is eventually canceled. If a valid secured claim is not paid or arrangements are not made to pay the debt, the secured creditor may bring an action to repossess the collateral. In certain limited situations, the lien of a secured creditor may be avoided in its entirety.

An unsecured creditor is one whose claim is not secured by any property. Examples include an open account with a store, a bank card account or medical bills. In the Chapter 7 bankruptcy proceeding not all claims are discharged. Exceptions include money owed for certain taxes and student loans, fraudulent debts, child support, alimony, and governmental fines. A debtor's obligations arising out of the equitable distribution of marital property may also be excepted from discharge.

A U.S. bankruptcy judge presides throughout the bankruptcy proceeding. The judge makes rulings on disputed issues. For example, the judge determines whether a claim is secured or unsecured, or whether a creditor is entitled to repossess its collateral. However, most straight bankruptcy cases are handled routinely, and such questions rarely arise.

When someone files for bankruptcy, the clerk of court schedules a meeting of creditors. The debtor and all creditors are notified of the meeting of creditors. The trustee is appointed to administer the case and conduct the meeting.

The meeting of creditors is usually held at a nearby federal courthouse. The trustee reviews the petition, schedules and statement of financial affairs and asks questions about the debtor's assets. The creditors are also allowed to ask the debtor questions.

After the meeting of creditors, the trustee arranges the sale of any nonexempt property. After the sales and completion of other administrative duties, the trustee prepares a report to the court, and with the court's approval, distributes funds to the creditors.

Debtors cannot receive a discharge if they have received a discharge within the preceding six years.

Chapter 13—'Wage Earners' Plan

Rather than seeking an immediate discharge of debts, a Chapter 13 debtor pays part of his or her future income to a Chapter 13 trustee. The trustee distributes these funds to the creditors over a period of time until the debts are satisfied according to the Chapter 13 plan or until the plan is dismissed. The plan may provide for repayment of all or a portion of debts, depending on the circumstances, through a series of monthly payments which typically run for a period of 36 to 60 months.

During the Chapter 13 proceeding, the creditors cannot attempt to collect their debts unless permission is given by the Bankruptcy Court. Chapter 13 provides a more comprehensive discharge than under Chapter 7. A Chapter 13 filing can also be used to stay foreclosure proceedings and allow a debtor time to cure a default on a residential mortgage.

Filed with the Chapter 13 petition, schedules and statement of financial affairs are a statement of the debtor's income and a plan to pay the creditors from the money sent every month to the Chapter 13 trustee. The plan must meet certain legal guidelines to be approved by the Bankruptcy Court.

If you file a Chapter 13 bankruptcy, a trustee will be appointed by the court to administer your case.

The creditors listed on the schedules are notified that you have filed for a Chapter 13 bankruptcy. They are also instructed to file a claim. A secured creditor should file a claim before the first meeting of creditors in order to ensure the classification as "secured."

An unsecured creditor must file a claim within approximately three months after the first meeting of creditors. A "proof of claim" is a form provided by the court and mailed to creditors with the notice of the meeting of creditors. The proof claim may be filed with the court or the Chapter 13 trustee.

The bankruptcy judge resolves any issues which may arise while the case is pending. For example, a creditor may ask for permission to foreclose the property pledged on a debt which is not being paid through the Chapter 13 plan.

When a petition is filed, the clerk of court schedules a meeting of creditors and a debtor education class which the debtor must attend. At that meeting, the trustee reviews the petition, schedules, statement of financial affairs, and plan and explains the plan to the creditors attending. The creditors may inquire about the location of their collateral or how their claim is to be paid within the Chapter 13 plan.

The plan is sent to the judge to review and confirm. The trustee then disburses funds each month to the debtor's creditors as set out in the plan. For a plan to be confirmed, the plan must provide for paying back child support and certain taxes in full.

If the debtor fails to make his monthly payments to the Chapter 13 trustee, the bankruptcy case may be dismissed by the court upon the request of the trustee or any creditor. Also, while the Chapter 13 plan is pending, the debtor may convert to a Chapter 7 straight bankruptcy or voluntarily dismiss the case.

When the Chapter 13 plan is successfully completed, the debts listed on the original petition are discharged. As in the Chapter 7 bankruptcy, certain long-term debts, child support, maintenance, alimony and student loans are not dischargeable in Chapter 13, but some other debts which are not dischargeable in Chapter 7 may be discharged in Chapter 13.

Chapters 11 and 12

Business bankruptcies and reorganizations under Chapter 11, and farm reorganizations under Chapter 12, are beyond the scope of this book. Please consult with your legal counsel should you have any questions regarding corporate and farm reorganizations.

Section 49.3

Advertisements Promising Debt Relief May Be Disguised Offers for Bankruptcy

"Advertisements Promising Debt Relief May Be Offering Bankruptcy," Federal Trade Commission, December 2005.

Debt got you down? You're not alone. Consumer debt is at an all time high. What's more, record numbers of consumers—more than 1.5 million in 2004—are filing for bankruptcy. Whether your debt dilemma is the result of an illness, unemployment, or simply overspending, it can seem overwhelming. In your effort to get solvent, be on the alert for advertisements that offer seemingly quick fixes. While the ads pitch the promise of debt relief, they rarely say relief may be spelled b-a-n-k-r-u-p-t-c-y. Although bankruptcy is one option to deal with financial problems, it's generally considered the option of last resort. The reason: its long-term negative impact on your creditworthiness. Bankruptcy information (both the date of your filing and the later date of discharge) stays on your credit report for 10 years, and can hinder your ability to get credit, a job, insurance, or even a place to live.

The Federal Trade Commission (FTC) cautions consumers to read between the lines when faced with ads in newspapers, magazines or even telephone directories that say:

- "Consolidate your bills into one monthly payment without borrowing."

- "STOP credit harassment, foreclosures, repossessions, tax levies and garnishments."

- "Keep Your Property."

- "Wipe out your debts! Consolidate your bills! How? By using the protection and assistance provided by federal law. For once, let the law work for you!"

You'll find out later that such phrases often involve filing for bankruptcy relief, which can hurt your credit and cost you attorneys' fees.

518

Personal Bankruptcy

If you're having trouble paying your bills, consider these possibilities before considering filing for bankruptcy:

- **Talk with your creditors:** They may be willing to work out a modified payment plan.

- **Contact a credit counseling service:** These organizations work with you and your creditors to develop debt repayment plans. Such plans require you to deposit money each month with the counseling service. The service then pays your creditors. Some nonprofit organizations charge little or nothing for their services.

- **Carefully consider a second mortgage or home equity line of credit:** While these loans may allow you to consolidate your debt, they also require your home as collateral.

If none of these options is possible, bankruptcy may be the likely alternative. There are two primary types of personal bankruptcy: Chapter 13 and Chapter 7. Each must be filed in federal bankruptcy court. As of April 2006, the filing fees are $274 for Chapter 13 and $299 for Chapter 7. Attorney fees are additional and can vary.

The consequences of bankruptcy are significant and require careful consideration.

Effective October 2005, Congress made sweeping changes to the bankruptcy laws. The net effect of these changes is to give consumers more incentive to seek bankruptcy relief under Chapter 13 rather than Chapter 7.

Chapter 13 allows you, if you have a steady income, to keep property, such as a mortgaged house or car, that you might otherwise lose. In Chapter 13, the court approves a repayment plan that allows you to use your future income to pay off your debts during a three-to-five-year period, rather than surrender any property. After you have made all the payments under the plan, you receive a discharge of your debts.

Chapter 7, known as straight bankruptcy, involves the sale of all assets that are not exempt. Exempt property may include cars, work-related tools, and basic household furnishings. Some of your property may be sold by a court-appointed official—a trustee—or turned over to your creditors. The new bankruptcy laws have changed the time period during which you can receive a discharge through Chapter 7. You now must wait eight years after receiving a discharge in Chapter 7 before you can file again under that chapter. The Chapter 13 waiting period is much shorter and can be as little as two years between filings.

519

Both types of bankruptcy may get rid of unsecured debts and stop foreclosures, repossessions, garnishments and utility shut-offs, and debt collection activities. Both also provide exemptions that allow you to keep certain assets, although exemption amounts vary by state. Personal bankruptcy usually does not erase child support, alimony, fines, taxes, and some student loan obligations. Also, unless you have an acceptable plan to catch up on your debt under Chapter 13, bankruptcy usually does not allow you to keep property when your creditor has an unpaid mortgage or security lien on it.

Another major change to the bankruptcy laws involves certain hurdles that you must clear before even filing for bankruptcy, no matter what the chapter. You must get credit counseling from a government-approved organization within six months before you file for any bankruptcy relief. You can find a state-by-state list of government-approved organizations at www.usdoj.gov. That is the website of the U.S. Trustee Program, the organization within the U.S. Department of Justice that supervises bankruptcy cases and trustees. Also, before you file a Chapter 7 bankruptcy case, you must satisfy a "means test." This test requires you to confirm that your income does not exceed a certain amount. The amount varies by state and is publicized by the U.S. Trustee Program at www.usdoj.gov/ust.

For More Information

Visit the Federal Trade Commission website (www.ftc.gov), or contact the American Financial Services Association's Education Foundation at 888-400-2233 for more credit/money management information.

Chapter 50

File Segregation Is Illegal

If you have filed for bankruptcy, you may be the target of a credit repair scheme called "file segregation." In this scheme, you are promised a chance to hide unfavorable credit information by establishing a new credit identity. That may sound perfect, especially if you're afraid that you won't get any credit as long as bankruptcy appears on your credit record. The problem: "File segregation" is illegal. If you use it, you could face fines or even a prison sentence.

The Pitch: A New Credit Identity

If you have filed for bankruptcy, you may receive a letter from a credit repair company that warns you about your inability to get credit cards, personal loans, or any other types of credit for ten years. For a fee, the company promises to help you hide your bankruptcy and establish a new credit identity to use when you apply for credit. These companies also make pitches in classified ads, on radio and TV, and even over the internet.

If you pay the fee and sign up for the service, you may be directed to apply for an Employer Identification Number (EIN) from the Internal Revenue Service (IRS). Typically, EINs—which resemble Social Security numbers—are used by businesses to report financial information to the IRS and the Social Security Administration.

"File Segregation: New ID Is a Bad Idea," Federal Trade Commission (www.ftc.gov), December 2005.

After you receive your EIN, the credit repair service will tell you to use it in place of your Social Security number when you apply for credit. They'll also tell you to use a new mailing address and some credit references.

The Catch: False Claims

To convince you to establish a new credit identity, the credit repair service is likely to make a variety of false claims. Listen carefully; these false claims, along with the pitch for getting a new credit identity, should alert you to the possibility of fraud. You'll probably hear inaccurate claims such as the following:

False Claim—You will not be able to get credit for 10 years (the period of time bankruptcy information may stay on your credit record): The truth—Each creditor has its own criteria for granting credit. While one may reject your application because of a bankruptcy, another may grant you credit shortly after you filed for bankruptcy or successfully completed a bankruptcy repayment plan. And, given a new reliable payment record, your chances of getting credit will probably increase as time passes.

False Claim—The company or "file segregation" program is affiliated with the federal government: The truth—The federal government does not support or work with companies that offer such programs.

False Claim—The "file segregation" program is legal: The truth—It is a federal crime to make any false statements on a loan or credit application. The credit repair company may advise you to do just that. It is a federal crime to misrepresent your Social Security number. It also is a federal crime to obtain an EIN from the IRS under false pretenses. Further, you could be charged with mail or wire fraud if you use the mail or the telephone to apply for credit and provide false information. Worse yet, file segregation likely would constitute civil fraud under many state laws.

Rights Under The Credit Repair Organizations Act

This law prohibits false claims about credit repair and makes it illegal for these operations to charge you until they have performed their services. It requires these companies to tell you about your legal rights. Credit repair companies must provide this in a written contract that also spells out just what services are to be performed, how long it will take to achieve results, the total cost, and any guarantees that are offered. Under the law, these contracts also must explain that consumers have three days to cancel at no charge.

Under the law, you also have the right to sue in federal court. The law allows you to seek either your actual losses or the amount you paid the company—whichever is more. You also can seek "punitive" damages: sums of money to punish the company for violating the law. The law also allows class actions in federal court: cases where groups of consumers join together in one lawsuit. If you win, the other side has to pay your attorney's fees.

Many states have laws regulating credit repair companies, and may be helpful if you've lost money to credit repair scams.

If you've had a problem with a credit repair company, report the company. Contact your local consumer affairs office or your state attorney general (AG). Many AGs have toll-free consumer hotlines. Check with your local directory assistance.

You also may wish to contact the FTC. Although the Commission cannot resolve individual credit problems for consumers, it can act against a company if it sees a pattern of possible law violations. If you believe a company has engaged in credit fraud, you can file a complaint online at http://www.ftc.gov, or send your complaint to: Consumer Response Center, Federal Trade Commission, Washington, DC 20580.

Part Six

Additional
Help and Information

Chapter 51

Money Talks: A Glossary

adjustable-rate loans: Usually offer a lower initial interest rate than fixed-rate loans. The interest rate fluctuates over the life of the loan based on market conditions, but the loan agreement generally sets maximum and minimum rates. When interest rates rise, generally so do your loan payments; and when interest rates fall, your monthly payments may be lowered (also known as variable-rate loans).[2]

annual percentage rate (APR): The cost of credit expressed as a yearly rate. The APR includes the interest rate, points, broker fees, and certain other credit charges that the borrower is required to pay.[2]

appraisal fee: The charge for estimating the value of property offered as security.[1]

automated teller machines (ATMs): Electronic terminals located on bank premises or elsewhere, through which customers of financial institutions may make deposits, withdrawals, or other transactions as they would through a bank teller.[1]

balloon payment: A large extra payment that may be charged at the end of a loan or lease.[1]

billing error: Any mistake in your monthly statement as defined by the Fair Credit Billing Act.[1]

Terms in this chapter marked [1] are excerpted from "Consumer Handbook to Credit Protection Laws," Federal Reserve Board of Governors, 2001; terms marked [2] are excerpted from "Looking for the Best Mortgage," Federal Trade Commission, 1999.

business days: Check with your institution to find out what days it counts as business days under the Truth in Lending and Electronic Fund Transfer Acts.[1]

closed-end lease: A lease in which you are not responsible for the difference if the actual value of the item at the scheduled end of the lease is less than the residual value, but you may be responsible for excess wear-and-use charges and for other lease requirements.[1]

closing costs: May include application fees; title examination, abstract of title, title insurance, and property survey fees; fees for preparing deeds, mortgages, and settlement documents; attorneys' fees; recording fees; and notary, appraisal, and credit report fees. Under the Real Estate Settlement Procedures Act, the borrower receives a good faith estimate of closing costs at the time of application or within three days of application. The good faith estimate lists each expected cost either as an amount or a range.[2]

collateral: Property, such as stocks, bonds, or a car, offered to support a loan and subject to seizure if you default.[1]

conventional loans: Mortgage loans other than those insured or guaranteed by a government agency such as the FHA (Federal Housing Administration), the VA (Veterans Administration), or the Rural Development Services (formerly know as Farmers Home Administration, or FmHA).[2]

co-signer: Another person who signs your loan and assumes equal responsibility for it.[1]

credit: The right granted by a creditor to pay in the future to buy or borrow in the present; a sum of money due a person or business.[1]

credit bureau: An agency that keeps your credit record; also called a credit-reporting agency.[1]

credit card: Any card, plate, or coupon book used periodically or repeatedly to borrow money or buy goods or services on credit.[1]

credit history: The record of how you've borrowed and repaid debts.[1]

credit insurance: Health, life, accident, or disruption of income insurance designed to pay the outstanding balance on a debt.[1]

creditor: A person or business from whom you borrow or to whom you owe money.[1]

credit-scoring system: A statistical system used to rate credit applicants according to various characteristics relevant to creditworthiness.[1]

creditworthiness: Past, present, and future ability to repay debts.[1]

debit card (EFT card): A plastic card, which looks similar to a credit card, that consumers may use at an ATM or to make purchases, withdrawals, or other types of electronic fund transfers.[1]

default: Failure to repay a loan or otherwise meet the terms of your credit agreement.[1]

disclosures: Information that must be given to consumers about their financial dealings.[1]

elderly applicant: As defined in the Equal Credit Opportunity Act, a person 62 years or older.[1]

electronic fund transfer (EFT) systems: A variety of systems and technologies for transferring funds electronically rather than by check.[1]

escrow: The holding of money or documents by a neutral third party (often prior to a real-estate closing). It can also be an account held by the lender (or servicer) into which a homeowner pays money for taxes and insurance.[2]

finance charge: The total dollar amount credit will cost.[1]

fixed-rate loans: Both the interest rate and the monthly payments (for principal and interest) stay the same during the life of the loan (for mortgages, generally have repayment terms of 15, 20, or 30 years).[2]

home equity line of credit: A form of open-end credit in which the home serves as collateral.[1]

interest rate: The cost of borrowing money expressed as a percentage rate. Interest rates can change because of market conditions.[2]

joint account: A credit account held by two or more people so that all can use the account and all assume legal responsibility to repay.[1]

late payment: A payment made later than agreed upon in a credit contract and on which additional charges may be imposed.[1]

lessee: The party to whom the item is leased. In a consumer lease, the lessee is you, the consumer. The lessee is required to make payments and to meet other obligations specified in the lease agreement.[1]

lessor: The person or organization who regularly leases, offers to lease, or arranges for the lease of the item.[1]

liability on an account: Legal responsibility to repay debt.[1]

lock-in: Refers to a written agreement guaranteeing a home buyer a specific interest rate on a home loan provided that the loan is closed within a certain period of time, such as 60 or 90 days. Often the agreement also specifies the number of points to be paid at closing.[2]

mortgage: A document signed by a borrower when a home loan is made that gives the lender a right to take possession of the property if the borrower fails to pay off on the loan.[2]

open-end credit: A line of credit that may be used repeatedly, including credit cards, overdraft credit accounts, and home equity lines.[1]

open-end lease: A lease agreement in which the amount you owe at the end of the lease term is based on the difference between the residual value of the leased property and its realized value. Your lease agreement may provide for a refund of any excess if the realized value is greater than the residual value. In an open-end consumer lease, assuming you have met the use and wear standards, the residual value is considered unreasonable if it exceeds the realized value by more than three times the base monthly payment (sometimes called the "three-payment rule").[1]

origination fees: Fees charged by the lender for processing the loan and are often expressed as a percentage of the loan amount.[2]

overages: The difference between the lowest available price and any higher price that the home buyer agrees to pay for the loan. Loan officers and brokers are often allowed to keep some or all of this difference as extra compensation.[2]

overdraft checking: A line of credit that allows you to write checks or draw funds with an EFT (debit) card for more than your actual balance, with an interest charge on the overdraft.[1]

point-of-sale (POS): A method by which consumers can pay for purchases by having their deposit accounts debited electronically without the use of checks.[1]

points: Fees paid to the lender for the loan. One point equals 1 percent of the loan amount. Points are usually paid in cash at closing. In some cases, the money needed to pay points can be borrowed, but doing so will increase the loan amount and the total costs.[2]

private mortgage insurance (PMI): Protects the lender against a loss if a borrower defaults on the loan. It is usually required for loans in which the down payment is less than 20 percent of the sales price or, in a refinancing, when the amount financed is greater than 80 percent of the appraised value.[2]

realized value: (1) The price the lessor or assignee receives for the leased item at disposition, (2) the highest offer for the leased item at disposition, or (3) the fair market value of the leased item at termination. The realized value may be either the wholesale or the retail value as specified in the lease agreement.[1]

rescission: The cancellation of a contract.[1]

residual value: The end-of-term value of the item established at the beginning of the lease and used in calculating your base monthly payment. The residual value is deducted from the adjusted capitalized cost to determine the depreciation and any amortized amounts. It is an estimate that may be determined in part by using residual value guidebooks. The residual value may be higher or lower than the realized value at the scheduled end of the lease.[1]

security: Property pledged to the creditor in case of a default on a loan; see collateral.[1]

security interest: The creditor's right to take property or a portion of property offered as security.[1]

service charge: A component of some finance charges, such as the fee for triggering an overdraft checking account into use.[1]

settlement costs: See closing costs.[2]

thrift institution: A general term for savings banks and savings and loan associations.[2]

transaction costs: See closing costs.[2]

variable-rate loans: See adjustable-rate loans.[2]

Chapter 52

How to File a Consumer Complaint about a Bank

If you have a complaint about a bank or other financial institution, the Federal Reserve System can help.

The Federal Reserve System is one of five federal banking agencies responsible for administering many of the federal laws that protect consumers in their dealings with financial institutions. The Federal Reserve investigates consumer complaints against banks that are members of the Federal Reserve System (state member banks). The Board of Governors, in Washington, DC, works with the twelve Federal Reserve Banks across the country to ensure that state member banks abide by the law.

The Federal Reserve Board help consumers as follows:

- Identifying the appropriate federal banking regulator and referring complaints to that agency

- Investigating complaints about state member banks

- Answering questions about banking practices

How to File a Consumer Complaint about a Bank

What complaints are investigated?

If you think a bank has been unfair or misleading, discriminated against you in lending, or violated a law or regulation, you have the

Federal Reserve Board of Governors (www.federalreserve.gov), June 2006.

right to file a complaint. Complaints about discrimination in housing are covered by the Fair Housing Act. These complaints are investigated by the Federal Reserve and referred to the U.S. Department of Housing and Urban Development.

How do you file a complaint?

First, please try to settle the problem directly with your bank. This may involve contacting senior bank management or the bank's customer service representative.

If you cannot resolve the problem with your bank, you may want to file a complaint with the appropriate federal regulator. If you cannot identify the federal regulator, contact the Federal Reserve Board, and they will forward your complaint to the appropriate agency.

For complaints about state member banks, you can file a written complaint with the Federal Reserve—either with the Board or with the appropriate Federal Reserve Bank. Please include the following:

- Your name, address, and daytime telephone number

- The complete legal name and address of the bank involved in your complaint

- Your bank or credit card account number, if applicable

- The names of the people you contacted at the bank, along with the dates

- A description of the complaint. Tell us what happened, the dates involved, and the names of those you dealt with at the bank. The more information they have about the problem, the quicker they will be able to help resolve it. Include copies of letters or other documents that may help us investigate your complaint. Please send only copies of documents—do not send originals.

Please remember to sign and date your letter, and send it to the following address:

Board of Governors of the Federal Reserve System
Division of Consumer and Community Affairs
20th and C Streets, NW, Stop 801
Washington, DC 20551

For more information, please call 202-452-3693.

What will the Federal Reserve do?

Consumer complaints filed against state member banks are investigated by one of the 12 regional Federal Reserve Banks, based upon the location of the bank involved in your complaint. If your complaint is received by the Board and involves a state member bank, Board staff will forward your complaint to the appropriate Reserve Bank for investigation.

The Reserve Bank may contact you to request additional information about your complaint. As the Reserve Bank investigates each issue raised in your letter, it will:

- Ask the state member bank involved for information and records regarding your complaint

- Determine if the bank's response addresses your concerns

- Send you a letter about its findings

The Reserve Bank will let you know if it finds an error or a violation of a federal law or regulation. Investigations usually last 30 to 60 days. If more than 60 days have passed, the Reserve Bank will contact you to let you know the status of the investigation. Please note that it may take several months to resolve complaints alleging illegal credit discrimination.

Although the Federal Reserve looks into every complaint that involves the banks they regulate, they do not have the authority to resolve every type of problem. For example, the Federal Reserve Board is unable to resolve contract disputes or undocumented factual disputes between a customer and a bank. In these cases, they suggest that you contact an attorney. Also, they cannot investigate matters that are the subject of a pending lawsuit.

Complaints about customer service or disagreements over specific bank policies and procedures—which are usually determined by the individual bank—are not addressed by federal law or regulation. However, if you file a complaint, a bank may voluntarily work with you to resolve the problem.

Chapter 53

Resources for Information about Budgeting and Personal Finances

American Bankers Association
1120 Connecticut Ave., NW
Washington, DC 20036
Toll-Free: 800-BANKERS
Phone: 202-663-5000
Fax: 202-663-7543
Website: http://www.aba.com

American College of Trust and Estate Counsel
3415 South Sepulveda
Boulevard, Suite 330
Los Angeles, CA 90034
Phone: 310-398-1888
Website: http://www.actec.org

American Financial Services Association Education Foundation
919 Eighteenth St., NW
Suite 300
Washington, DC 20006-5517
Phone: 202-466-8611
Fax: 202-223-0321
Website: http://www.afsaef.org

American Savings Education Council
2121 K Street NW
Suite 600
Washington, DC 20037-1896
Phone: 202-659-0670
Website: http://www.asec.org

This information was compiled from many sources deemed accurate; inclusion does not constitute endorsement and there is no implication associated with omission. All contact information was verified and updated in February 2007.

America's Community Bankers
900 19th St., NW, Suite 400
Washington, DC 20006
Phone: 202-857-3100
Fax: 202-296-8716
Website: http://
www.americascommunity
bankers.com

Asset Builders of America
Website: http://
www.assetbuilders.org

Center for the Study of Services
1625 K St., NW, 8th floor
Washington, DC 20006
Phone: 202-347-7283
Fax: 202-347-4000
Website: http://
www.checkbook.org

Choose to Save
2121 K Street NW
Suite 600
Washington, DC 20037-1896
Phone: 202-659-0670
Website: http://
www.choosetosave.org

Consumer Federation of America
1620 I Street, NW
Suite 200
Washington, DC 20006
Phone: 202-387-6121
Fax: 202-265-7989
Website: http://
www.consumerfed.org

Cooperative State Research, Education, and Extension Service
U.S. Department of Agriculture
Cooperative State Research,
Education, and Extension
Service
1400 Independence Avenue SW.,
Stop 2201
Washington, DC 20250-2201
Phone: 202-720-7441
Website: http://
www.csrees.usda.gov

Credit Union National Association
P.O. Box 431
Madison, WI 53701-0431
Phone: 800-356-9655
Fax: 608-231-4263
Website: http://www.cuna.org

Federal Citizen Information Center
Pueblo, CO 81009
Toll-Free: 800-FED-INFO
Website: http://
www.pueblo.gsa.gov

Federal Deposit Insurance Corporation (FDIC)
Division of Supervision and
Consumer Protection
550 17th St., NW
Washington, DC 20429
Toll-Free: 877-ASK-FDIC
(877-275-3342)
TDD Toll-Free: 800-925-4618
Website: http://www.fdic.gov

Federal Reserve System Board of Governors
Website: http://www.federalreserveeducation.org

Federal Trade Commission
Consumer Response Center
600 Pennsylvania Ave., NW
Mail to: CRC-240
Washington, DC 20580
Toll-Free: 877-382-4357
TDD/TTY: 866-653-4261
Website: http://www.ftc.gov

Financial Literacy Two Thousand and Ten
Website: http://www.fl2010.org

Freddie Mac
Credit Smart Program
Website: www.freddiemac.com/creditsmart

InCharge® Education Foundation, Inc.
2101 Park Center Dr., Suite 310
Orlando, FL 32835
Website: http://www.inchargefoundation.org

Institute for Financial Literacy
P.O. Box 1842
Portland, ME 04104
Toll-Free: 866-662-4932
TTY: 866-662-4937
Phone: 207-221-3600
Fax: 207-221-3691
Website: http://www.financiallit.org

Insurance Information Institute
Consumer Affairs
110 William St., 24th Floor
New York, NY 10038
Toll-Free: 800-331-9146
Phone: 212-346-5555
Website: http://www.iii.org

Internal Revenue Service (IRS)
General Information:
800-829-1040
Automated Refund Information:
800-829-4477
Taxpayer Advocate Service:
877-777-4778
TDD Toll-Free: 800-829-4059
Website: http://www.irs.gov

Iowa State University Cooperative Extension
Website: http://www.extension.iastate.edu/finances

Jump$tart Coalition for Personal Financial Literacy
919 18th Street, NW Suite 300
Washington, DC 20006
Toll-Free: 888-45-EDUCATE
Fax: 202-223-0321
Website: http://www.jumpstartcoalition.org
E-mail: info@jumpstartcoalition.org

MoneyWi$e
Website: http://www.money-wise.org

National Association of Personal Financial Advisors
3250 North Arlington Heights Road, Suite 109
Arlington Heights, IL 60004
Toll-Free: 800-366-2732
Website: http://www.napfa.org

National Association of Professional Insurance Agents
400 North Washington St.
Alexandria, VA 22314
Phone: 703-836-9340
Fax: 703-836-1279
Website: http://www.pianet.com
E-mail: piainfo@pianet.org

National Association of Realtors
430 North Michigan Ave.
Chicago, IL 60611
Toll-Free: 800-874-6500
Phone: 312-329-8200
Website: http://www.realtor.com

National Consumer Law Center, Inc.
Website: http://www.consumerlaw.org

National Consumers League
1701 K Street, NW, Suite 1200
Washington, DC 20006
Phone: 202-835-3323
Fax: 202-835-0747
Website: http://www.nclnet.org
E-mail: info@nclnet.org

National Council of LaRaza
Website: http://www.nclr.org

National Council on Economic Education
Website: http://www.ncee.net

National Council on Problem Gambling
Toll-Free: 800-522-4700

Native Financial Education Coalition
Website: http://www.nfec.info

NeighborWorks® Network
1325 G St., NW, Suite 800
Washington, DC 20005-3100
Phone: (202) 220-2300
Fax: (202) 376-2600
Website: http://www.nw.org

Office of Financial Education
U.S. Treasury Department
Website: http://www.treas.gov

Operation Hope: Banking on Our Future
Website: http://www.operationhope.org

Rutgers Cooperative Extension
Website: http://www.investing.rutgers.edu

Society of Financial Service Professionals
Toll-Free: 888-243-2258
Website: http://
www.financialpro.org

USAA Educational Foundation
Website: http://
www.usaaedfoundation.org

U.S. Department of Housing and Urban Development
Website: http://www.hud.gov

U.S. Financial Literacy and Education Commission
Website: http://
www.mymoney.gov

Volunteer Income Tax Assistance program
Toll-Free: 800-829-1040

Wi$eUp
Phone: 800-827-5335
Website: http://
wiseupwomen.tamu.edu

Women's Institute for a Secure Retirement
1725 K Street, NW, Suite 201
Washington, DC 200036
Phone: 202-393-5452
Fax: 202-393-5890
Website: http://
www.wiserwomen.org
Website: http://
www.wiser.heinz.org

Chapter 54

Resources for Information about Credit and Debt Management

Credit Reporting and Credit Scoring Agencies

***Annual Credit Report
Request Service***
P. O. Box 105281
Atlanta, GA 30348-5281
Toll-Free: 877-322-8228
Website: https://
www.annualcreditreport.com

Equifax
P.O. Box 740241
Atlanta, GA 30374-0241
Toll-Free: 800-685-1111
Website: http://www.equifax.com

Experian
P.O. Box 1017
Allen, TX 75013-0949
Toll-Free: 888-397-3742
Website: http://
www.experian.com

Fair Isaac Corporation
Website: http://
www.fairisaac.com
Website: http://www.myfico.com

TransUnion
P.O. 2000
Chester, PA 19022
Toll-Free: 800-916-8800
Website: http://
www.transunion.com

This information was compiled from many sources deemed accurate; inclusion does not constitute endorsement and there is no implication associated with omission. All contact information was verified and updated in February 2007.

Information about Debt Management, Collection Practices, and Bankruptcy

American Association of Credit and Collection Officials
Website: http://www.acainternational.org

American Bar Association
740 15th St., NW
Washington, DC 20005
Phone: 202-662-1000
Fax: 202-662-1683
Website: www.abanet.org

Borrower Services at the Direct Loan Servicing Center
Federal Student Aid
Toll-Free: 800-848-0979
TTY: 800-848-0983
Website: www.dl.ed.gov

Direct Loan Consolidation Center
Federal Student Aid
Toll-Free: 800-557-7392
TTY 800-557-7395
Website: http://www.loanconsolidation.ed.gov

"Don't Borrow Trouble" Campaign
Website: http://www.dontborrowtrouble.com

Federal Student Aid (FSA) Ombudsman
U.S. Department of Education
830 First Street, NE, Fourth Floor
Washington, DC 20202-5144
Toll-Free: 877-557-2575
Phone: 202-377-3800
Fax: 202-275-0549
www.studentaid.ed.gov
www.ombudsman.ed.gov
E-mail: fsaombudsmanoffice@ed.gov.

Federal Trade Commission
Consumer Response Center
600 Pennsylvania Ave., NW
Mail to: CRC-240
Washington, DC 20580
Toll-Free: 877-382-4357
TDD/TTY: 866-653-4261
Website: http://www.ftc.gov

National Foundation for Credit Counseling
801 Roeder Road, Suite 900
Silver Spring, MD 20910
Toll-Free: 800-388-2227
Phone: 301-589-5600
Website: http://www.nfcc.org

U.S. Trustee Program
Phone: 202-514-4100
Website: http://www.usdoj.gov/ust (for a state-by-state list of government-approved credit counseling organizations)

Index

Index

N

O

U

V

563